FOUR
VIEWS
ON
MOVING BEYOND
THE BIBLE TO THEOLOGY

Books in the Counterpoints Series

Church Life

Exploring Theology

FOUR VIEWS ON

MOVING BEYOND THE BIBLE TO THEOLOGY

A Principlizing Model: Walter C. Kaiser Jr.

A Redemptive-Historical Model: Daniel M. Doriani

A Drama-of-Redemption Model: Kevin J. Vanhoozer

A Redemptive-Movement Model: William J. Webb

Stanley N. Gundry, *series editor*
Gary T. Meadors, *general editor*

ZONDERVAN.com/
AUTHORTRACKER
follow your favorite authors

ZONDERVAN

Four Views on Moving beyond the Bible to Theology
Copyright © 2009 by Gary T. Meadors.

This title is also available as a Zondervan ebook.
Visit www.zondervan.com/ebooks.

Requests for information should be addressed to:

Zondervan, *Grand Rapids, Michigan* 49530

Library of Congress Cataloging-in-Publication Data

Four views on moving beyond the Bible to theology / Gary T. Meadors, general editor.
p. cm. – (Counterpoints)
Includes bibliographical references (p.   ) and indexes.
ISBN 978-0-310-27655-5 (softcover)
1. Bible – Use. 2. Theology – Methodology. 3. Bible – Hermeneutics. I. Meadors,
Gary T., 1945- II. Kaiser, Walter C. III. Doriani, Daniel M. IV. Vanhoozer, Kevin J. V.
Webb, William J.
BS538.3.F68 2009
220.601--dc22
2009021004

Cover and interior design by Matthew Van Zomeren

Printed in the United States of America

CONTENTS

INTRODUCTION

Gary T. Meadors

HOW IS A COLLECTION OF WRITINGS composed between 2,000 and 3,500 years ago relevant for current living? Informed Christians would immediately respond by affirming that the Jewish-Christian Scriptures contain truth that transcends time and space and therefore inform our decisions today. We are confronted with complicated modern questions concerning every aspect of life and death that call for biblical answers (e.g., abortion, euthanasia, genetic research, and gender and transgender patterns). We often struggle with what we are required to obey today (e.g., in regard to Sabbath patterns, household codes, male and female head coverings or the lack thereof, almsgiving, fasting, how to do church in the modern world, whether or not to go to court, and how to educate our children). At times we are confronted with issues for which there are no direct (e.g., a "proof text") or finalized biblical teachings (e.g., most Christians believe human slavery is wrong, but the Bible never directly finalizes this issue).

We wonder why the Bible seems silent in regard to serious social issues, issues that we believe violate a biblical worldview and demand to be addressed. We look for answers and often walk away feeling that the Bible is like a dummy in the hands of a ventriloquist—you can make it teach just about anything you desire. Your pastor or teacher may claim that their view represents "what the Bible teaches" and we should all accept their explanation. Then you have a pastoral change, and the same Bible is used to prove the opposite position! While sometimes the variations are the result of clearly delineated lines of interpretation, sometimes the

7

views are really just logical constructs the teacher brings to the table. This experience is also aggravated by the proliferation of English Bibles where translations differ and seem to slant toward one view or another. So what do you do as a Christian who desires to please God, to follow the leadership he has provided, and to obey his Word?

This book will assist you to progress in your understanding of how the Bible teaches. It will also force you to consider how you think about the Bible because you will hear several different views from authors, all of whom affirm an inspired Scripture, about how the Bible is relevant and authoritative for current issues. This experience will help you engage the fact that God has provided a special, inspired text for our benefit, but he has not provided inspired commentaries. The believing community glorifies God by engaging the debate about how the Bible informs contemporary questions it did not always originally envision.

WHAT DOES GOING "BEYOND THE BIBLE" MEAN?[1]

The use of the term *beyond* in relation to the Bible may seem contradictory. Some might react by saying, "Going beyond the Bible is surely a liberal idea or a compromise because of someone's agenda to make the Bible say what they desire to hear." This kind of a reaction misunderstands the role of theological analysis in relating the Bible to contemporary issues.

This use of "beyond" merely represents a theological construct that cannot claim a biblical context that directly teaches the point scored. The context may imply an interpreter's claim or legitimately be used to construct a larger premise to support a theological construct. Read-

---

1. The phrase "beyond the Bible" came to prominence with I. Howard Marshall, *Beyond the Bible: Moving from Scripture to Theology* (Grand Rapids: Baker Academic, 2004), although the issues the phrase represents are part of an ongoing debate. Marshall's ongoing project is to see "if there can be a *principled* way of moving from the ancient, authoritative text to its modern application" (ibid., 7).

ers have been going beyond the Bible since the inception of interpretation. When you shake someone's hand at church rather than greeting him or her with a holy kiss (1 Thess. 5:26), you have gone "beyond the Bible." You have decided that the holy kiss was a cultural expression and have chosen your own society's expression. The Bible never directed you or gave you permission to deviate from the command to greet one another in this manner; rather, you have merely assumed that times have changed and so has the manner of greeting (although in many countries outside the United States such greetings are still part of their culture).

At a more serious level, how do you account for the fact that the Bible did not demand that slaves be released but instead includes them as a typical part of the household structures of the society at that time? Furthermore, where is a proof text for God as a "trinity"? Yet, the church has almost universally declared that slavery is wrong and God is three in one. The church has reasoned theologically "beyond" the existing biblical statements to views it believes God holds to be true.

To be sure, there are texts that many believe hint at these conclusions, but there is more or less a going beyond the words on the page to achieve certain understandings. It is sort of like having your feet anchored in the canon while leaning over into the current world in order to achieve a full accounting of how biblical truth applies. This imagery seems somewhat supported by how the Wisdom literature of the Old Testament unpacks the implications of the law without quoting it directly. In the Old Testament, all of life seems "nested" in small bits of data that continue to frame life application. Theological paradigms are therefore required to make assertions about what is "biblical," that is, what God requires, in any given situation.

One might object to this and claim that good exegesis can answer all of our questions. But can it? What about resolving the multiple issues of 1 Timothy 2:11–15? What about Paul's statement in 2:12 that "I do not permit a woman to teach or to have authority over a man" (TNIV), or the more challenging items in 2:13–15 and how they inform 2:12. This text has been turned inside out in the gender debate without resolution, although the various gender views all claim it serves their position! When our interpretive methods require that we appeal to our theological assumptions (e.g., are gender statements a result of creation or the fall?) in order to explain a text, we have gone "beyond" the plain statements of the text in order to solve our theological issue. This is an inevitable and necessary part of doing theology. If we claim that exegesis has solved the problem while equally competent scholars disagree about the exegetical products, we have deceived ourselves and perhaps deified our own interpretive judgments. For whatever reasons, God has not made the process simple or final in the human interpretive arena.

Going beyond the immediate contexts and claiming that there are larger implications that teach us in those contexts, especially when a series of texts is evaluated, is a noble task. Let me illustrate this by a threefold model to account for how the Bible teaches. One can think of the Bible teaching us at three levels:

- *direct teaching* (teaching that best represents what the original author intended the original audience to understand from the text)
- *implied teaching* (teaching that seems reasonably clear by examining how texts speak; for example, Paul's speaking to Philemon about Onesimus, while never directly stating a view on manumission, implies a softer approach to an indentured servant)
- *creative constructs* (theologically constructed views that interpreters argue best represent the totality of the Bible)

One could think of *direct teaching* by noting how the New Testament abrogates the normative food laws of the Old Testament in Acts 10:9–16 and 1 Timothy 4:3–5. This is teaching that requires our acceptance. *Implied teaching* can be no less demanding although not backed by a non-debated proof text. The Trinity is a nonnegotiable belief for Christians, but it is an implied teaching. *Creative constructs*, however, represent more debatable categories that usually require certain interpretive grids for reading texts. Views on eschatological issues such as the millennium and the rapture of the church, and even forms for doing church, usually fall into systems that endeavor to make sense out of numerous connected texts by imposing certain grids by which these texts are read.

Think of this threefold model as the concentric rings of a bull's-eye target. All of the categories that the model surfaces reflect biblical teaching, but the farther we go from the inner circle (direct), the more we must present "lines of reason" to account for our assertions and how they best represent biblical teaching. The taxonomy becomes increasingly complicated as we move from "plain facts" to "constructed facts." This model is further complicated because we cannot just live in the assumed static safety of the inner circle of direct teaching; after all, we still have to account for what the Bible intends forever normative teaching to be. Sooner or later everyone must move outward from the inner circle.

As you read this book, you should reflect on each author's assertions and ask yourself, "Am I hearing direct, implied, or creative assertions?" How does each view connect itself to Scripture? At what point do the arguments of a view unpack biblical implications, and how do you view the "lines of reason" for that view's assertions? Or, if a view stretches you out beyond direct and perhaps implied statements (depends on whom you ask!) to what God would do in new settings or what Paul would say if he were alive today, how do you make decisions about such assertions? Your judgments in this regard will influence which view you believe best represents the teaching of the Bible for the modern world. If you can advance your understanding of why or how a writer holds a certain view, you will be well rewarded for the time you spend in the study of the issues this book addresses.

Consequently, "going beyond the Bible" is not only a legitimate task, it is a necessary one. Every time we make a judgment about how we relate to biblical patterns or commands and decide that "it doesn't apply to us now," we have made a "beyond" judgment to a greater or lesser extent. Or, if we fail to find a specific biblical context that addresses an issue of current concern, we do not assume the Bible has nothing to say, but we make a "beyond" judgment on the basis of our theological understandings. The question we need to face is, how do we justify our judgments? What model guides our process of applying ancient texts to modern questions?

ISSUES ATTENDANT TO MAKING "BEYOND" JUDGMENTS

Richard Longenecker's 1984 publication *New Testament Social Ethics for Today* stirred the pot in evangelical circles about how to maintain a relevant Bible in the modern world. Longenecker's burden was to address this issue: How "are the ideas and solutions of the writers of the New Testament [relevant] for contemporary social issues when society has changed so dramatically and situations are not at all the same?"[2] Longenecker labeled his model as a "developmental hermeneutic" and endeavored to show how the New Testament was pointing toward new ethical patterns (e.g., slaves and gender in relation to Gal. 3:28 were a major focus) and consequently how the modern church can apply ancient texts. Longenecker's work was a bit of a bombshell in some conservative circles because it challenged the use of the Bible as a static book of codes and called for an organic, dynamic method that engages each successive generation in the development of a Christian response to cultural challenges.

Longenecker's work is a wonderful primer for the current debate about how Scripture is relevant.[3] The issues he raised in 1984, and revisited in a 1999 publication,[4] are still at the center of current evangelicalism's search for a model

---

2. Richard N. Longenecker, *New Testament Social Ethics for Today* (Grand Rapids: Eerdmans, 1984), ix.

3. Professor Longenecker was invited to write a views chapter for this project but declined with regrets because of his writing commitments in retirement. The editor would encourage students interested in the issues debated in this book to study Longenecker's work as an introduction to the current debate. The suggestive thoughts of this introduction are fully unpacked by Longenecker's two volumes.

4. Richard N. Longenecker, *New Wine into Fresh Wineskins* (Peabody, MA.: Hendrickson, 1999), esp. chapters 6 and 7.

that is both faithful to Scripture and relevant to contemporary culture. Many of the issues in this debate center around defining how Scripture is relevant through changing times and locations.

WHAT IS THE NATURE OF SCRIPTURE?

The debate regarding how the Bible is relevant today touches the very core of the nature of revelation, the product of which is the Bible. The umbrella of evangelicalism provides a variety of perspectives on this issue, ranging from the Reformed to the charismatic. As you read the current volume and reflect on the views presented on how to use the Bible today, it is helpful to reflect on two major images used to explain how Scripture is relevant.

First, is the Bible a reference manual for life in the sense that it is a book of codes that apply the same way throughout all time? In this sense, the codes transfer from one culture to another in a concrete normative manner. The historical, cultural, and sociological settings of the original audience that the texts address are not really important since the Bible ultimately stands above all of this in its declarations. For this way of thinking, your decision-making method is to locate a "proof text" to resolve each issue that arises. Your methodology to argue your view is to assert what the text says in black-and-white print and leave it there. We adjust to biblical statements; biblical statements do not adjust to us. The challenge of this view is what to do when you cannot discover a "proof text" to cover your question. You either develop secondary suppositions about how to argue from the text to your issue, or you retreat into an assertive defensive mode.

A second imagery is this: Is the Bible more like a story that requires us to look behind the stage of players in order to discern the universal principles that drive the point God intends to score in the texts? The historical specifics are important nuances but are not binding since it is the underlying principles that drive the narrative's teaching. The Bible is more organic in its development. One context builds on another, and internal changes or progress may be discerned within the flow of the text and thereby indicate to us God's will about certain issues. Consequently, proof texts are subordinated to contexts and the lines of reason they provide that inform current questions that ancient authors may not have had in mind to address. Views that follow this methodology require a higher taxonomy of learning: you have to get "beyond" brute facts to the implications and constructs that the data provide. These kinds of approaches often develop methodologies that posit development in what the text teaches. They may posit trajectories of meaning in order to predict how an issue should be treated in the future, or develop figurative images that enable one to draw from the text to its implications.

A major challenge of a story type view is to ask the question, "When does the story end?" If Paul were alive today, would he adjust his statements, for example, about gender? When is the Bible speaking normative truth that never changes, and when is it speaking culturally conditioned statements? It is at this juncture that tension exists. For the code type view, the story is over ... next question! For a story type model, some of the views you read will end the story but continue to discern the principles the writers began. Others will suggest different ways in which the story continues within the contemporary believing community.

It is, of course, too simplistic to think that these two categorical images have clean lines of demarcation or that there are no combinations of the two or even other models to address the question. As you read the views and responses in this book, you will discover that this subject is very much a debate in process.[5] The purpose of this volume is to make the debate more prominent with a view to generating more discussion so that we can move the issues intrinsic to the debate forward.

It is important to affirm that the proponents of the variety of views within evangelicalism hold a high view of Scrip-

---

5. Counterpoints series volumes usually provide views that have become rather fixed representatives on a given subject. This volume, however, is providing an entrée into a subject that is currently emerging. Hence, the three final reflective essays are unique for a Counterpoints volume.

ture as God's Word, although their views of *how* Scripture is relevant in the contemporary setting may vary widely. It is a mistake to assume that disagreement over how the Bible teaches signals a greater or lesser view of the authority of Scripture. The current volume is merely a sample of a developing discussion within evangelicalism about the question of how the Bible has continuing authority. The last word has not yet been achieved on this subject.[6]

OTHER ISSUES TO CONSIDER

When we were children we sang the song, "Every promise in the book is mine, every chapter, every verse, every line." Now that we are adults, we know this is not true! The Bible is a progressive revelation and history of God's people over a long period, and God's ways of dealing with his people have changed. Israel was promised a land; Christians are not. Israel was promised blessings in relation to a physical temple; the church is a new kind of temple, and biblical authors can speak analogically about temple and body.

A study of the Bible quickly alerts us to change, and often change that is not forecasted or announced. We affirm change has happened by inductive analysis (and common sense), but we often cannot point to a particular text and say, "Aha! That text abrogates, explains, or advances that past teaching." Such judgments must be made from theological models. Consequently, you will read about "development" within and beyond the text, about the nature and validity of "trajectories," and assertions about "reading between the lines" of what an author said and what they might say today.

Another major question to probe is this one: When is a biblical statement normative for all time? We often deal

---

6. N. T. Wright's contribution on this subject asserts that it is not "the authority of Scripture" but "the authority of God exercised *through* Scripture" that is the way forward. See his *The Last Word: Beyond the Bible Wars to a New Understanding of the Authority of Scripture* (San Francisco: HarperSanFrancisco, 2005) and his fuller treatment in chapter five, "Theology, Authority and the New Testament," in *The New Testament and the People of God* (Minneapolis: Fortress, 1992).

with texts that raise this question with noncritical common sense. We realize that commands about day laborers, goring oxen, how to do evangelism, how often to observe the Lord's Supper, how to greet one another, or how to determine if a woman is pregnant need to be contextualized into our own time and space. But noncritical common sense can only carry us so far. We need more sophisticated paradigms to determine when the Bible is describing and when it is prescribing and when these two features have been adjusted because we have moved on in time and space. Hopefully, you will walk away from the reading of this volume with a deep realization that "How is the Bible relevant?" is no simple question, but it is one you cannot afford to avoid.

THE VIEWS REPRESENTED IN THIS BOOK
THE AUTHORS

The question of what Scripture means for contemporary culture is a topic of perennial interest in theology. This volume represents four views on the subject:

- a principlizing model by Walter C. Kaiser, Jr.
- a redemptive-historical model by Daniel M. Doriani
- a drama-of-redemption model by Kevin J. Vanhoozer
- a redemptive-movement model by William J. Webb

Each of these authors[7] has published on the interpretation and application of Scripture in a variety of arenas. Their footnotes and the bibliography at the end of this volume will provide you with the broader literature base. It is better that this introduction resist offering an overview or opinion of these views but rather leave that task between you, the reader, and the primary sources themselves.[8]

In addition to the four views and their responses, we have added three "reflections" from prominent scholars that give a broader analysis of the question of relating Scripture

---

7. Please consult the author page for a description of each participant.
8. The reflection by Mark Strauss starts with an interactive overview of the four views and thereby provides an introductory synthesis of the views.

to contemporary issues. These sections will probe issues in biblical and systematic theology as well as philosophy and missiology that inform the current discussion of the relevance of Scripture in the contemporary world.

One final comment before you launch into the core of this volume. The original working title for this book used the phrase "beyond the sacred page" rather than "beyond the Bible." The authors use the original phrase a great deal since their work was completed prior to a title change. While "beyond the sacred page" has a more poetic ring, "beyond the Bible" was deemed to be more direct speech for the title. These phrases are intended to be equivalent.

CHAPTER ONE

A PRINCIPLIZING MODEL

Walter C. Kaiser Jr.

ONE OF THE MOST IMPORTANT INTERPRETIVE TASKS, but the one most laypeople, teachers, and pastors often have had little training in, is the move from determining what a text meant in its original setting and context to *applying* that text in one's own day and culture. That move is filled with potential for great power in one's teaching and preaching, but it also possesses an equally great potential for mischief and harm to both the speaker and the audience. These moves are especially sensitive when the original text of Scripture involves cultural elements that are different from cultural elements in our own day. But as we will see, rather than viewing these elements as obstacles to understanding the text fairly, they are meant to actually help us in the task of applying that text to other times and places. The textual illustration of this kind of move used in a former day opens up the potential for our determining what the principle of the same issue being illustrated would be in our own day.

One proposal for bridging this gap between the "then" of the text's ancient context and the "now" application of that same text in our day was entitled "ethnohermeneutics,"[1] which recognized three horizons in this delicate cross-cultural interpretation: (1) the culture of the Bible, (2) the culture of the interpreter, and (3) the culture of the receptor. It is important to note that all three horizons have to be brought into the discussion of a scriptural text, yet without allowing the second and third horizons to override, or dictate, to the first horizon a new meaning; one that no longer serves as the basis for a common communication on the subject first introduced by the original context.

In the early church fathers, cultural matters in the Scripture were discussed under the topics of "condescension," "accommodation," and "acculturation." From their standpoint, the biblical writers did not make the interpretation of the text more difficult when they introduced cultural aspects; instead, they made it more accessible by showing us how it could be applied. To illustrate this point, notice how easily readers and interpreters of Philippians 4:2 handle "I plead with Euodia and Syntyche to agree with each other in the Lord." The particularization of the names and the specificity of some altercation that had taken place between these two ladies in the context of the church at Philippi should not cause us to pass over that statement in Paul's letter and say in effect, "Oh, neither Euodia nor Syntyche is a relative of mine, and I am not part of the church at Philippi, so that word is not for me in my day." Instead, most will see it for what it is—a good illustration of the principle Paul talked about in his letter to the Ephesians (4:32): "Be kind and compassionate to one another, forgiving each other, just as in Christ God forgave you." If that is a legitimate way to handle this *particularismus* in the New Testament, should not that same procedure work for

---

1. Charles H. Kraft, "Towards a Christian Ethnotheology," in *God, Man and Church Growth: Festschrift in Honor of Donald Anderson McGavran* (ed. A. R. Tippett; Grand Rapids: Eerdmans, 1973): 109–26, and Larry W. Caldwell, "Third Horizon Ethnohermeneutics: Reevaluating New Testament Hermeneutical Models for an Old Task," *Asian Journal of Theology* 1 (1987): 314–33. See my chapter entitled "Obeying the Word: The Cultural Use of the Bible," in Walter C. Kaiser Jr. and Moises Silva, *Introduction to Biblical Hermeneutics: The Search for Meaning* (2nd ed.; Grand Rapids: Zondervan, 2007), 222–39.

the Old Testament, which has many more instances of that same particularity and specificity involving people, places, times, and issues?

Therefore, what happens in this and similar cases where cultural issues intrude on the text can be handled by principlizing the text.[2] For example, in some cases in interpreting the Bible, we will keep the principle affirmed in the theology taught, along with the cultural-historical expression of that principle where the cultural expression remains similar to its meaning in our times as well. Such would be the case when Scripture taught lines of responsibility between husband and wife—both the theology of marriage and the cultural illustrations of it are rather closely proximate to one another.

On other occasions, we will keep the theology of the passage (i.e., one that is now embodied in a principle), but replace the behavioral expression with some more recent or meaningful expression from our contemporary world. To illustrate this instance, we would appeal to 1 Corinthians 5, where a mother and son were guilty of incest (a violation of the moral law of God), but the sanction for that law of stoning (as was true in the law of Moses) was replaced by temporary excommunication from the body of believers until there was genuine repentance and restoration to the church once again. Principles, then, must be given priority over accompanying cultural elements, especially when directed to the times and settings in which that text was written—times now different and separate from the contemporary manner of expressing that same principle.

Over twenty-five years ago I had occasion to put down in print what I meant when I had repeatedly urged Bible readers, teachers, and preachers to "principlize" the text of Scripture. My emphasis then, as now, was that the task of interpreting a text was not concluded until the reader or interpreter had carried what the text meant over to the present day and said what it now means. I had written in the past:

---

2. See Kaiser and Silva, *Introduction to Biblical Hermeneutics*, 233–37.

> To "principlize" is to [re]state the author's proposi-
> tions, arguments, narrations, and illustrations in time-
> less abiding truths with special focus on the applica-
> tion of those truths to the current needs of the Church.[3]

Later, in that same textbook, I explained:

> Principlization seeks to bridge the "then" of the text's
> narrative [or any other biblical genre] with the "now"
> needs of our day; yet it refuses to settle for cheap and
> quick solutions which confuse our own personal point
> of view (good or bad) with that of the inspired writer.[4]

This method of "principlizing" I had attempted to distinguish from several older and newer ways of making the
biblical text contemporary and relevant to our own times:

> Unlike allegorizing or spiritualizing, the method of
> principlizing seeks to derive its teachings from a care-
> ful understanding of the text [of Scripture]. Rather
> than importing an external meaning into the Bible (this
> includes pre-maturely using the analogy of subsequent
> doctrines [usually called "The Analogy of Faith"] and
> assigning these new meanings to the details of the ear-
> lier narrative, meanings which were not in the mind of
> the original author), we must receive only those mean-
> ings authoritatively stated by the authors themselves.[5]

The first step in principlizing a passage from the Bible is to
determine what the subject of the focal point of that passage
is. My colleague Haddon Robinson has called this focal point
"the big idea of the passage." Usually this focus can be found
expressly stated in the heart of the text selected (in a summarizing verse or clause thereof) for teaching or preaching.
It is necessary to get a fix on this first lest we are tempted to

---

3. Walter C. Kaiser Jr., *Toward an Exegetical Theology: Biblical Exegesis for
Preaching and Teaching* (Grand Rapids: Baker, 1981), 152.

4. Ibid., 198.

5. Ibid., 205. I distinguish between the "Analogy of Faith" and the "Analogy of [Antecedent] Scripture" in Walter C. Kaiser Jr., "Hermeneutics and the
Theological Task," *Trinity Journal*, n.s. 12 (1990): 3–14, and Henri Blocher's
careful study, "The 'Analogy of Faith' in the Study of Scripture," *Scottish Bulletin of Evangelical Theology* 5 (1987): 17–38.

impose a mold over the Bible by forcing it to answer one of our favorite questions, but one the text never encompasses in its purpose. A greater temptation is to introduce a truth taught in the New Testament and to read the Bible backwards (as in "eisegesis") and claim here was a "deeper truth" or something that is a *sensus plenior*, presumably encrypted between the lines and not in the grammar or syntax per se. Surely that imposition has given "eye-popping" New Testament types of truth to the Old Testament with plenty of contemporary relevancy, but the question is this: Did the Holy Spirit come to the same use of that text?

Once the topic/subject has been identified, then the emphasis must be sought from any terms that are repeated or are a key or part of the important words used in developing that same subject. Notice simultaneously has to be given to the connecting words in that pericope that link the phrases, clauses, and sentences, such as "because," "since," "therefore," or the like.

Once we have identified the subject, the emphasis, and the ways in which the passage is connected, we can move to see how each paragraph (in prose genres), scene (in narratives), or strophe (in poetical passages) can be expressed in propositional principles. It is always best to avoid using all proper names/nouns in stating the principle for each of these units of thought (e.g., the paragraph in the prose sections, the scene in narrative sections, or the strophe in poetical sections of the Bible) except divine names, for all such references to all other persons, places, or historic events will only lock the text into the past and handicap its application to the contemporary scene.

Likewise, all use of third person pronouns has the same inhibiting function on formulating useful principles for our day; instead of using third person pronouns, one is better advised to express the newly devised principles in terms of first person plural pronouns that have a hortatory function in the preaching and teaching situation—"Let us ...," "it's our job ...," or "we must...." Of course second person pronouns can likewise be used, but for teaching and proclamation purposes, it is always better if the speaker identifies with the audience rather than pontificating from on high against all of "you"!

Finally, it is likewise best if we use present tense verbs, present participles, or imperatives for our principles rather than past tenses, for once again putting the action descriptively in the past severely limits the statement of the principles' ability to lead the reader or interpreter into the present and the future or to view the text as directed to each one personally.

Before I leave the whole discussion of what is principlization and how it functions, it is important to mention as another illustration the use of the "Ladder of Abstraction."[6] The Ladder of Abstraction may be defined as "a continuous sequence of categorizations from a low level of specificity up to a high point of generality in a principle and down again to a specific application in the contemporary culture."

A good example of this is the appeal to the reason behind a case law (*ratio decidendi*) that on the surface (*prima facie*) appears to be no more than a prohibition for farmers, that they should not muzzle an ox treading out the husks on the grain (Deut. 25:4). Most of today's readers of Scripture do not own oxen, and even if they did, they would not use them in our day in place of combines for thrashing and separating the husks from the grain. Surely, therefore, here is a verse that apparently is culturally and contextually frozen in ancient times and not at all relevant to us in our day—unless there was a principle behind this specific illustration.

Nevertheless, Paul dared to use this text not just once but twice (1 Cor. 9:9–12 and 1 Tim. 5:18), to teach that persons who were ministered to with the Word of God should pay their pastors. How did Paul get from allowing oxen to take a swipe of grain as they went round and round tramping out the grain to paying pastors?[7] Paul could have gone to Deu-

---

6. I must indicate my indebtedness again to Michael Schuter and Roy Clements for the concept of the Ladder of Abstraction as it first appeared in my book, *Toward Rediscovering the Old Testament* (Grand Rapids: Zondervan, 1987), 164–66.

7. See Walter C. Kaiser Jr., "The Current Crisis in Exegesis and the Apostolic Use of Deuteronomy 25:4 in 1 Corinthians 9:8–10," *Journal of the Evangelical Theological Society* 21 (1978): 3–18; revised as "Applying the Principles of the Civil Law: Deuteronomy 25:4; 1 Corinthians 9:8–10," in *The Uses of the Old Testament in the New* (originally Chicago: Moody Press, 1985; now reprinted: Eugene, OR: Wipf and Stock, 2001), 203–20.

teronomy 24:14–15, which taught, "Do not take advantage of a hired man ... pay him his wages"; instead, Paul appealed to a text about oxen and then claimed that that text in Deuteronomy was not written for oxen (of course, oxen cannot read!), but it was written "for us."

What was Paul's point? Some scholars quickly concluded that the apostle was indulging in allegorical interpretation.[8] But to claim that Paul used an allegorical interpretation involved for most ignoring its original meaning and giving it a sense that was purely arbitrary. Others thought Paul used a rabbinic type of argumentation, or even a Hellenistic Jewish exegesis, but Paul did not suppress the historical or natural meaning of the text. His argument was a well-grounded, a fortiori type of logic that went from the lower relations (of the oxen themselves to the owners of the oxen) to insist that the same principle was true of the higher relations (of others who were being served and ministered to) as well.

Here is how the Ladder of Abstraction works: from the *ancient specific situation* (oxen that tread out grain) we move up the ladder to *the institutional or personal norm* (animals are God's gifts to humanity and should be treated kindly), to the top of the ladder, which gives to us *the general principle* (giving engenders gentleness and graciousness in those mortals who care for and can minister back to those who serve them as well, whether they are animals or people). As we descend the ladder on the other side, we meet *the theological and moral principle* behind our general principle ("love your neighbor" or just the injunction in the ninth commandment), to the contemporary or New Testament *specific situation* (pay those pastors ministering to you, including Paul, 1 Cor. 9:9–12).[9]

In this movement on the Ladder of Abstraction, we must move from the ancient specificity of the text (taking pity on those muzzled oxen who are going crazy walking round and round over top of grain they long to take a swipe at) up

8. W. Arndt, "The Meaning of 1 Cor 9:9, 10," *Concordia Theological Monthly* 3 (1932): 329–35.

9. See my diagram of this process in *Toward Rediscovering the Old Testament*, 166.

to the overarching general principle that applies and generalizes the particularity of the Scripture before we can once again apply that abstracted general principle in a new contemporary specific situation. Paul's point is not only one of being kind to animals; rather, it is about the special work of grace and generosity that takes place in the hearts and lives of those who express special concern and love for those who are ministering to them (whether as oxen threshing out the grain or as ministers of the gospel feeding the people the Word of God).

WHY GO BEYOND THE OBVIOUS?

If the Reformers correctly taught us that *sola Scriptura* was the proper boundary for authoritative teachings for the believing community, why are some now suggesting that we must go "beyond the sacred page" to get modern answers currently pressing for resolution in what is popularly called our postmodern era? If the Bible was able to communicate authoritatively in the day in which it was originally written, why must we in our day raise so many questions that seem to take us off, or beyond, the biblical page?

The answer to that query is readily at hand: because, so it is claimed, there is so much complexity in contemporary life that continues to pose more ethical, moral, doctrinal, and scientific questions than the Bible seems, at least at first glance, to be able to answer in a *direct* way for our generation. There are so many terms and so many new issues that were never even directly contemplated when the Scriptures were written that it would appear as if the biblical theologian and exegete is left with more questions than answers in this postmodern world.

Accordingly, in recent years, a new literature has arisen that suggests how, under carefully defined guidelines, it is possible, indeed necessary, to go "beyond" the sacred text to meet the challenges of our day. Some of the topics that fall under the category of cultural assessment involve the current fashion of wearing tattoos, involvement in transvestism, using reproductive technologies to compensate for infertility, advocating animal rights, treating the environment more carefully than before, revising names and functions of church officers, trying new hairstyles, advancing clothing taboos, insisting on new head coverings, and the like. But if going "beyond" is to be the recommended track for answering questions such as these, then what becomes of our much valued *sola Scriptura* ("Scripture alone")?

Our problem is not with our praiseworthy desire to offer help to a baffled church and laity on contemporary questions not directly dealt with in the Bible, but it now is: How can we establish procedures of interpretation that will take us outside of the boundaries of Scripture (if that is what it might take) while claiming the security and safety of possessing an authoritative source within those recently transgressed boundaries? Even if this is not the correct way to put the question, the point is this: How do we move from the day and times of the Bible to our day and age? How can we claim the biblical text for ourselves in a way that it applies to the problems we face in this present day with all of the new complexities, cultures, and content? Contemporary interpreters of the Word of God are said no longer to be content with moving from the *specificity* of the biblical text followed by a *generalizing principle* to apply to different types of people in different times and situations (as we have just advocated in the Ladder of Abstraction).

It is for this reason, then, that we are called upon to supply some examples of how the method of principlization is to be preferred over competing suggestions for helping us answer the very same questions.

IS EUTHANASIA MURDER?

The term *euthanasia* was coined by H. E. W. Lecky in 1869, meaning "good" (Gk. *eu*) and "death" (Gk. *thanatos*). Thus, this form of death was viewed as an easy death or the act or practice (either actively or passively) of letting or helping people die, especially those suffering from some incurable condition or disease. Scripture, however, does not directly mention, or give explicit guidance, on the issue of the *active* use of this form of death. Therefore, it is a good candidate for us to ask if this might be a case of where we need to go "beyond the sacred page."

Euthanasia has been defined as represented by four different types:

1. *Voluntary, passive euthanasia*, in which we allow the patient to choose to let nature take its course; we only give liquids and food where possible and make the person as comfortable as feasible, without any heroic steps to prolong his or her life, such as using a machine, medications, or surgery
2. *Voluntary, active euthanasia*, in which death is hastened by some *active* means by the individual or the physician
3. *Involuntary, passive euthanasia*, in which the patient has not expressed a willingness to die, and cannot do so, so that the medical personnel do not take any extraordinary measures to prolong the patient's life
4. *Involuntary, active euthanasia*, in which usually the physician or nursing staff do something to hasten death, whether for economic, genetic, or humanitarian reasons, regardless of the patient's wishes.

What concerns us here are all the cases involving some form of *active* role in bringing on death, whether by the patient or by medical personnel.

But this raises a necessary question: Is not causing a person's death with the intent of alleviating one's suffering and pain, or for similar reasons, the same as murder? Now that we have such enormous advances in medical technology, how does a Christian patient, or a Christian physician, determine what is the appropriate care for such an individual who is terminally ill, or who has suffered irreversible brain damage? What biblical teaching on matters of life and death apply to medical situations such as these?

The *principles* Scripture offers us for situations such as this are these:

1. God is sovereign over life and death, for he is the one who gives life and the one who takes it away (Job 1:21). Given the fact that all mortals are made in the image of God, human life is sacred and is therefore to

be valued and treated with dignity. Human interference with the time of a person's death would be an act of preempting God's right to set that time.

2. All *active* forms of life-taking are condemned in Scripture as falling under the injunction against murder (Ex. 20:13). This would include all active forms of euthanasia, whether carried out by a doctor, nurse, friend, or by the patient alone. Scripture does permit taking of life in some situations, such as in self-defense or in a just war, but *active* forms of euthanasia are not included as one of those exceptions in Scripture.

3. Even when a person is in the grip of a tragic situation, as King Saul was when he lay dying on the battlefield (see 2 Sam. 1:9–16), the soldier who claimed he accommodated Saul's unbiblical request to end his mortally wounded life was executed by David. This is not exactly a case of euthanasia, but it does illustrate the principle that extenuating circumstances do not change the prohibition against life-taking. It too is murder.

4. All arguments and societies that promote a "right to die" are likewise condemned by the Bible. Such arguments for a "right to die" deny God the opportunity to work on the patient's behalf and to control the day of our death.

5. Though death is unnatural, yet inevitable, it is more than a mere transition as humanism teaches. There is both "a time to be born and a time to die" (Eccl. 3:2; James 2:26). But death is more than a biological event; death occurs when the spirit leaves the body. This may not help or give a clinical diagnosis and a definition for medical personnel, but it would caution that a rigorous definition for death must be used by them. Accordingly, comatose patients may not be conscious, but they are very much alive and need continued treatment, unless critical vital signs and brain activity have ceased.

6. The use of drugs to relieve physical and emotional pain is biblically justifiable, for Proverbs 31:6 counsels: "Give strong drink to one who is perishing, and wine to those in bitter distress" (NRSV). The primary purpose here is to relieve pain, not directly to shorten life.

There does not appear to be a need to go beyond the principal teachings of the Word of God. Despite medical and other philosophical questions that may surround the issue of euthanasia, the principles of Scripture are adequate for guiding those who need help with the hard choices that arise in keeping up with the care of those who are perhaps terminally ill.

WOMEN AND THE CHURCH

Is there any hope that all who share the conviction that the Bible provides us with our source for a divine viewpoint on matters it raises will ever be able to come to some sort of agreement on a topic as sensitive as the issue of the biblical teaching on women? Alas, despite the acknowledgment that we all begin at the same point with Scripture, we surely show lots of differences when it comes to this topic of the place of women in the family and the church. However, even though a good deal of our disagreements have to do with certain pre-understandings that we all bring to the text of Scripture, the power of God's Word and the mighty work of God's Holy Spirit in assisting in the interpretation of that Word must not be forgotten. So, for all who have grown weary of this topic, let it not be the final resting point for the body of Christ. Our Lord did have some definite meanings in mind when he spoke so frequently on this area in Scripture.

POWER/STRENGTH ON THE HEAD OF A WOMAN

Both Genesis 2:18 ("I will make a power corresponding to the man," my trans.) and 1 Corinthians 11:10 ("The woman ought to have authority/power on her head," my trans.) ought to be considered together, since those are the two places in Scripture where the topic of "authority" or "power" are used in connection with woman.[10]

---

10. Much of the material used here comes from my article, "Correcting Caricature: The Biblical Teaching on Women," *Priscilla Papers* 19/2 (2005): 5–11; and an earlier contribution of mine entitled "Paul, Women and the Church," *Worldwide Challenge* (September 1976), 9–12; and idem, "Shared Leadership," *Christianity Today* 30 (October 3, 1986): 12.

Our Lord saw Adam as incomplete and deficient as he lived without the benefit of a companion. Therefore, God pronounced, "It is not good for the man to be alone" (Gen. 2:18). Surely, "two [were] better than one" (Eccl. 4:9–11). To end man's loneliness, God formed for the man, as the present translations read: "a helper suitable for him."

The use of the word "helper" is not to be taken in a pejorative way, for that same word (Heb. *'ezer*) is used of God, for example in Deuteronomy 33:26,29 ("he is your shield and helper [strength]"), so that is not the reason for examining this concept. But R. David Freedman argued convincingly that our Hebrew word *'ezer* is a combination of two older words from a Canaanite root: the one is *'-z-r* (with the initial Heb. letter of *'ayyin*, meaning "to rescue, save"), and the other is *ǵz-r* (with the Canaanite *ghayyin*, meaning "to be strong").[11] These two letters come in the alphabet right where our letter *o* comes in the English alphabet. We do know that both letters were originally pronounced separately, for presently we do have such place names as "Gaza," "Gomorrah," though today spelled with an *'ayyin*, yet reflecting the two separate letters since we remember some of the place names with a *g* type of laryngeal sound, as in Ugaritic, from the Canaanite tongue, which today shares about 60 percent of its vocabulary with Hebrew. Somewhere around 1500 BC the two phonemes merged into one grapheme and thus the two roots merged into one with only the textual context to indicate the difference. It is interesting to also note how many of the twenty-one times the word *'ezer* appears in the Old Testament that it is parallel to "strength" or "power," suggesting that in some cases, there were two words still being represented under a single spelling.

This rendering of Genesis 2:18 as "power" could explain what the apostle Paul was referring to when he argued in 1 Corinthians 11:10, "For this reason, a woman ought to have power/authority [Gk. *exousia*] on her head" (my trans.). Paul always uses *exousia* in its active, and not its passive, sense in 1 Corinthians (e.g., 7:37; 8:9; 9:4, 5). But in one of the weirdest

---

11. R. David Freedman, "Woman: A Power Equal to Man," *Biblical Archaeology Review* 9 (1983): 56–58.

twists in translation history, this one word *exousia* was rendered "a veil, a symbol of authority." But as Katherine C. Bushnell showed early in the twentieth century, the substitution of "veil" for "authority" went all the way back to the Gnostic Alexandrian teacher Valentinus, who founded a sect named after himself sometime around AD 140. In his native Coptic tongue, the word for "veil" and the word for "authority" were similar both in sound and in print (*ouershishi*, "power, authority," and *ouershoun*, "veil"). Both Clement and Origin, who also came from Alexandria, copied the same mistake, perhaps from the same Egyptian Coptic texts; thus the translation hangs on until our day ("a veil, a symbol of authority"). But it has no basis in fact at all. The NIV dropped the "veil," but it still rendered the one word *exousia* as *"a sign of* authority."

The result is that God gave to the woman a corresponding power or authority as that possessed by the man. Therefore, the woman was not man's "help*mate*," but a full power or authority corresponding to Adam.

MUST MEN RULE WOMEN AND WOMEN BE SILENT?

Genesis 3:16 is a command to men to "rule over [their wives]," which has long been held by many, with 1 Corinthians 14:34 being understood to confirm that injunction. But there are several things wrong with this so-called command and alleged parallel reference. Moreover, it must be noticed that the reference in 1 Corinthians 14:34 to the "law" has invariably been taken to point to Genesis 3:16. Both of these conclusions are faulty. (1) There is no imperative in the Hebrew word *yimshal*, which means "you will rule" over her, rather than "you must/shall rule" over her (using the English "shall" to translate the future Hebrew tense, but which can carry in English an imperative force). (2) The question raised in 1 Corinthians 14:33b–35 actually comes from a letter addressed to Paul from the Corinthian church and therefore is not normative teaching.[12]

---

12. D. A. Carson, *Exegetical Fallacies* (Grand Rapids, Baker, 1984), 38–40, classifies this solution as one of his "exegetical fallacies," but he does not tell us what "law" and where in the "law" the demand for women to keep silent is found. Paul answers four other times in the Corinthian letter questions

The tragedy of errors in this text begins with an Italian Dominican monk named Pagino, who published his translation that included Genesis 3:16 in AD 1528 with the meaning of "lust" in the phrase translated in the TNIV, "Your *desire* will be for your husband."[13] The Hebrew text here reads *teshuqa*, a word that only appears three times in the Hebrew Bible (Gen. 3:16; 4:7; Song 7:10), which simply means "turning." The Greek Septuagint rendered it *apostrophe*, "turning away." The Samaritan Pentateuch gave it the same rendering as did the Old Latin, the Bhairic Coptic, and the Ethiopic version of AD 500. Jerome's Latin Vulgate, produced around AD 382 with the assistance of the rabbis, rendered Genesis 3:16 this way: "Thou shalt be under the power of a husband, and he will rule over thee."

Instead of Genesis 3:16 darkly suggesting that a woman had a certain sexual "desire" or "lust" for her husband, which her husband had better take in hand before it all gets out of control, the text, in a *curse(!)* passage, predicts that the woman will turn (presumably away from God) toward her husband, and as a result some men will indeed rule over their wives. Eve should never have put her sole dependence on her husband, for he too was a fallen sinner just like she was. As a result, instead of a new gender hierarchy being instituted as God's new patriarchal norm, a curse fell over the husband-wife relationship—one that could only be healed in God and by his grace.

---

that had also been addressed to him; for example, in 1 Cor. 6:12 and 10:23, Paul is pummeled with "everything is permissible," but the apostle patiently responds "not everything is beneficial," or "not everything is constructive," or again, "but I will not be mastered by anything." In a similar manner, Paul responds to the question of women remaining silent by 14:36, "What! Did the word of God originate with you? Or are you the only ones (*masculine* plural) it [the word of God] has reached?" (my trans.). Note in some Western texts, verses 34–35 are placed at the end of the chapter. This also signals something was going on with regard to the teaching of these verses. While the substance of this silence tradition cannot be found in the biblical law, or anywhere else in the Old Testament for that matter, it can be easily found in the Jewish law of the Talmud and Mishnah.

13. See Katherine C. Bushnell, *God's Word to Women* (originally published in 1923 as Bible lessons of the Women's Correspondence Bible Class; now often reprinted privately), 128–45.

The principles here are again most straightforward and do not call for any cultural or exegetical moves outside or beyond the Scriptures.

WOMEN MUST BE TAUGHT AND ENCOURAGED TO PRAY AND PROPHESY IN PUBLIC

After Paul encouraged men everywhere to pray in public settings in 1 Timothy 2:8, but to be careful about their inwardly harboring hostility over some dispute or hidden anger, he went on to draw a strong comparison (*hosautos*, "similarly in a like manner")[14] in 2:9 for women, urging that they too should lead in public prayers ("lifting up holy hands in prayer"). But women are cautioned to dress modestly in such situations and not draw attention to themselves in this public venue.

But Paul also had advice for women who "prophesied" in 1 Corinthians 11:5. Paul defined what he meant by "prophesying" in 1 Corinthians 14:3: "But those who prophesy speak to people for their strengthening, encouragement and comfort." But if Paul did not want women leading in prayer and prophesying in public meetings, why did he speak in 1 Corinthians 11 only to the issue of whether their heads were covered or not? Why not prune the practice of women doing the forbidden act itself and cut it off at its very roots rather than troubling anyone with a mere incidental issue of how those engaged in a wrong practice were dressed?

But the radical part of Paul's teaching in the 1 Timothy 2 passage is missed by most: We must teach women (*gynē en hēsychia manthaneto en pasē hypotagē*, 1 Tim. 2:11). No one thought it was worthwhile or even necessary to teach women; not the Hebrews, not the Assyrians, not the Babylonians, not the Greeks, not the Romans—only the Christians! That is the only imperative in this text, but that apparently is the one most miss when they treat this passage. But that was the real bombshell of that day. Unfortunately, it is so familiar to us in our day that by now we assume what is

---

14. The TNIV weakly rendered this comparative expression as just "also."

already functioning, so we do not need to pause to reflect on the most startling aspect in Paul's instruction concerning women. But the thought of teaching women was seismic in its day; it shook up everything. Why would anyone want to do something so revolutionary as to teach women? What would one teach them? And for what purpose(s) would one teach them?

Why, then, does Paul go on to say that he did "not permit a woman to teach or to assume authority over a man; she must be quiet" (1 Tim. 2:12)? The answer comes in the *gar* ("because") clause that follows in verses 13–14: "For Adam was formed first." The Greek word for "formed" is *eplasthē*. Paul's usual word for "to create" is *ktizō*, but here Paul used *plassō*, which can also refer "to shaping or molding educationally, spiritually." If it is the latter, then instead of Paul basing his argument on the "orders of creation" (Adam came first, so by rights of primogenitor he must be over the woman), he bases it on the "orders of education" (Adam walked and talked with God in the garden before Eve was formed). Since the woman had not as yet been taught, she was all the more easily "tricked."

Notice this key verb that is usually used when people are unaware of aspects of what is being told to them (in this case by "the serpent"). Could that not have been the reason why "the serpent" took advantage of Eve? She had not walked and talked with God in the garden of Eden as had Adam, so she was at a disadvantage, as later on were the women all over the Mediterranean world who had not been taught. The Greek text insists that Eve was "thoroughly deceived" (using the preposition *ex* in front of the verb to emphasize the point). However, presumably, whenever any women were *first taught*, the injunction against their refraining from teaching and exercising any kind of authority would be lifted.

Once again, the exegetical principles derived from the text were adequate in and of themselves to cover the modern as well as the ancient situation. Women most certainly were to be taught and thereafter be permitted to pray in public and to prophesy in public, for that is exactly what God had ordered.

THE BIBLE AND HOMOSEXUALITY

The first person to use the word "homosexual" seems to be a Swiss doctor in 1869 named K. M. Benkert. The ancient world, of course, knew of the practice of homosexuality, as did the Greek philosophers, who often reported their involvement in such acts at their symposiums, where along with their drinking, young boys performed homosexual acts. But it became a modern issue on June 28, 1969, at a bar in Stonewall Inn, New York, when the police raided this establishment known to be frequented by persons of homosexual orientation. The customers retaliated and as a result police had to barricade themselves inside the bar for protection. This is usually given as the beginning of the modern "gay activist era." Later, in 1974, the American Psychological Association was forced by the gay lobby to remove "homosexuality" from its list of "pathological conditions," so it would no longer be regarded as a deviant perversion of normal sexual relations in its categories of psychological disorders.

Both male and female (also known as lesbianism) homosexuality is defined as the persistent and predominating disposition of a person to have forms of sexual relations with persons of the same sex. Today modern ethicists and researchers categorize homosexuality as "a sexual preference" and not as a specific act. Whether homosexuality is a behavior rather than a static orientation, or both, is still debated. Some argue from a non-Christian point of view that homosexuality is a *learned* preference and not the result of any biological factors in one's gene pool (still to this day no genetic factor has been identified as such); thus homosexuals are made, not born that way, from a confusion over their sexual identity. Nevertheless, homosexuality has moved from the margins (and closets) of society into the mainstream even though their actual numbers are decidedly small (some say 2 percent and at most 5 percent of the total population) in comparison with the political and ethical clout they bear in today's world.

There are seven biblical passages that treat the homosexual question, all from a negative point of view (Gen. 19:1 – 13; Lev. 18:22; 20:13; Judg. 19; Rom. 1:18 – 32; 1 Cor.

6:9–10; and 1 Tim. 1:8–11). But foundational to all of them is the plan God revealed in Genesis 1 and 2, that it was not good for man to be alone, so God formed a woman, also made in God's image, and brought the man and the woman together to become one and to fill the earth by procreation.

In the first of the seven texts, the "people of Sodom were wicked and were sinning greatly against the LORD" (Gen. 13:13); as a result, God sent two angels to investigate the sins of Sodom and Gomorrah. The men of the city, however, wanted "to know" these strangers (Gen. 19:5 KJV). According to what Derrick Sherwin Bailey argued in his 1955 *Homosexuality and the Western Christian Tradition*,[15] the Hebrew word "to know" (*yada^c*) only dealt with issues of hospitality, but not with any sexual references. Bailey challenged any reference to homosexuality or sodomy by saying that whereas *yada^c* appeared some 943 times in the Old Testament, only ten of those references carried any thought of the idea "to have intercourse/sex with." Therefore, what the men of Sodom wanted was merely to get acquainted with these strangers.

But if that were true, why did Lot surprisingly and unnecessarily offer his own daughters to the citizens of Sodom, especially in his description of the daughters as those who "have not known a man," a statement that implies sexual intercourse? Moreover, Jude 7 commented on this incident at Sodom and described it as one of "gross immorality and perversion." Bailey's case does not hold water.

Bailey handled the Gibeah story in Judges 19 in the same manner. But if the issue was only one of hospitality, then why did the homeowner in Gibeah, by whom the Levite and his concubine had been given lodging, beg his fellow countrymen not to act so "vile" (Judg. 19:23), as he too strangely offers his daughter to those beating down the door of his house?

Since the two texts in Leviticus (18:20 and 20:13) are located in the section of Leviticus known as the Holiness Code, pro-homosexual commentators want to claim that

---

15. Derrick Sherwin Bailey, *Homosexuality and the Western Christian Tradition* (London: Longmans, Green, 1955).

these verses apply only to priests and to a call for *ritual* purity, not to any moral issues as such. They argue that if Christians are going to demand adherence to these two texts against homosexuality, then they must also practice the other demands in the same context, such as refraining from sowing a field with two different kinds of seed (Lev. 19:19c), wearing clothes with mixed fabrics (19:19d), and having marital relations with one's wife during her menstrual cycle (18:19).

The principle that groups these laws together was a concern for what was "natural," that is, maintaining the created orders "after their kind."[16] It also involved a moral aspect, as well as the continued well-being of the populace. The mixing of the seeds, for example, could have resulted in certain forms of hybridization, which would have removed from the farmers and landowners of that day the ability to use a portion of their crops for next year's seed. Likewise, the menstrual period symbolically showed that only God had sovereignty over the woman and not the husband; therefore, a time of abstinence was mandated. Thus, the text does not address the priesthood or ritual provisions, but sees all of life within a moral context and one in which God is sovereign over the so-called secular and sacred. One simply cannot argue that having sex with animals (Lev. 18:23) or illicit sex with one's daughter (18:17) was morally irrelevant, as some pro-homosexual interpreters wish to view these texts; it certainly was a moral issue! In fact, the context of Leviticus 18:1 set the practices of the ungodly nations of Egypt and Canaan in juxtaposition with those challenges for a different moral behavior among the people of God.

The three New Testament texts on homosexuality (Rom. 1:26–27; 1 Cor. 6:9–10; 1 Tim. 1:10) call not simply for temperance and moderation (again the homosexual response to these texts), but for complete avoidance of all forms of homosexuality. The text in Romans warns of those who have

---

16. Walter C. Kaiser Jr., "The Book of Leviticus: Introduction, Commentary and Reflections," in *The New Interpreter's Bible* (Nashville, TN: Abingdon, 1994), 1:1134.

"exchanged natural sexual relations for unnatural ones" (Rom. 1:26). What Paul condemns are "perverts" (a modern distinction that describes those who indulge in homosexual acts in contrast to "inverts," those who may have a homosexual disposition but who do not practice it). Once again, however, some have unsuccessfully tried to define "natural" (*kata physin*) and "unnatural" (*para physin*) as being contrary to the *individual's* own nature and not as being contrary to the Creator's intention for them. But such word studies will not sustain this heroic effort to establish a toehold for the legitimacy of homosexual acts.

Paul gives a list of sins in 1 Corinthians 6:9–10 and 1 Timothy 1:9–10 in which "male prostitutes" (*malakoi*, lit., "soft to touch") and "homosexual offenders" or "perverts" (*arsenokoitai*, lit., "male in bed") will not inherit the kingdom of God. These principles are clear and straightforward. One does not need to go "beyond the sacred page" to see that God strongly dislikes the *practices* of such persons even while his love is sufficient to embrace these *same individuals* whose practices must be the grounds for repenting.

THE BIBLE AND SLAVERY

Human beings were made in the image of God and designed to be bound only to him. But in the rebellion of the fall, mortals rejected God as their Sovereign and wound up oftentimes with other mortals being masters over them. Accordingly, slavery had its roots in sin. Two forms of slavery need to be sharply distinguished: (1) biblical debt slavery, and (2) pagan slavery.[17]

The ordinances on slavery appear in first position in the Covenant Code of Exodus 21:2–11. This was natural enough since Israel had just been released from their Egyptian bondage. And the teaching on slavery was divided into two sections: male slaves in Exodus 21:2–6 and female slaves in 21:7–11.

---

17. I am indebted for many of my ideas in this section to James B. Jordan, *The Law of the Covenant: An Exposition of Exodus 21–23* (Tyler, TX: Institute for Christian Economics, 1984), 75–92.

Immediately a distinction must be made between a Hebrew slave and the type of slavery Israel had just experienced in Egypt. A Hebrew slave may only serve for six years and then he or she was to be set free with gifts to boot in the sabbatical year (Deut. 15:12–15). Since the land could not be used as collateral, for God was the owner of all the land of Israel (Lev. 25:23), the only collateral left for the indebted Hebrew was his or her labor power.

In contrast to this form of Hebrew debt slavery, there were other slaves who were purchased in their pagan state. And even though they also could be circumcised later on in their servitude, nevertheless, they were not to be released in the sabbatical year along with the Hebrew servants (Ex. 12:44; Lev. 22:11; 25:44–46). However, in these cases the law allowed that slave to save up his money and buy his freedom (Lev. 25:26, 49). So provision was made for manumission and release for all slaves, unless the slave had committed a crime.

Deuteronomy 15 makes it clear that there were two ways a Hebrew could become a slave: by committing a crime or by getting into debt. Even in the case of debt slaves, these Hebrews were to be released in the seventh year (i.e., the sabbatical year, not the slave's seventh year), and all debts were to be cancelled in that sabbatical year. When the slave was released, he took with him only what he brought with him to slavery; thus, if he came with a wife and children, they left with him. However, if he acquired a wife from his master and he had children, they either stayed with the master or they could be purchased with savings from the slave's time of work. The point seemed to be that if the Hebrew did not show himself responsible while serving his master, he might only land back in slavery once again in another serious debt situation, giving the newly acquired wife a rough life for one who had not been taught to work or to be responsible.

It is conceivable that some servants wished to remain in the service of their master because the slave loved his master. In that case, a ceremony of the piercing of the ear took place. The Hebrew slave renounced his freedom, and his master took him to a door or doorpost where he took an awl and pierced the slave's ear as a permanent sign of his lifelong service (Ex. 21:5–6). This was not due to any compulsion or pressure by the master; it was a free choice made by the Hebrew slave. He wanted to stay because he loved his master.

The slavery described here was not the same as that found in pagan society, where, especially in a monarchy, the assumption was made that all persons were *not* created equal; some bloodlines, some families, some mortals were called to be commoners. Added to this is our modern concept of slavery, which is an outcome of the seventeenth-century doctrine of the divine right of kings, designed originally to oppose the claims of the papacy. But this type of slavery was not designed to bring relief to those who had fallen into debt; it instead tacitly challenged God as King over all and therefore divided society on a class basis.

While much of the debt slavery was hard and difficult, a slave could gain instant freedom if he sustained any visible sign of injury or had been beaten by his master (Ex. 21:20; Lev. 24:17, 22). In fact, it could result in a capital offense if the slave died; however, if the slave regained his strength after a day or two, the presumption was to favor the master even while the injured would still be compensated for the lost time or for his medical bills. The threat of an instant loss of the master's investment no doubt had a strong mitigating factor on most potentially abusive situations, for in the event of proven abuse, the debt slave left immediately with the full capitalization, regardless of how few days or months he or she had worked to work off that hired loan.

Pagan society often kidnapped outsiders in order to make them slaves (a capital offense in Ex. 21:16), or they could be purchased from traders or through wars (Lev. 25:42, 44, 45; Num. 31:26–47; Deut. 21:10–14). But making mortals into slaves for other mortals could never be viewed in the Bible as being anything less than preempting God's lordship over all.

If that is so, why were there no attempts to stop or to hinder the slave business in the Bible? There was, but all too few get it. In the little book of Philemon, a book of only twenty-five verses and 335 words, Paul makes it clear to Philemon that he is sending back his runaway slave, Onesimus, who had indeed robbed Philemon as well, but now was being returned to Philemon "no longer as a slave" (v. 16). Here is the focus of the book: Onesimus was no longer to be a slave, "but better than a slave, as a dear brother" (v. 16b).

Onesimus, the slave and thief, was no longer to be a slave. Paul thereby taught the slave-holder Philemon, who lived at Colossae, as well as he now teaches us, that no one must be held as a slave, even though Paul will not take this action without having Philemon's consent first. Moreover, Paul is not recommending pure amnesty, with no payment, for he writes in this letter what Adolph Deissman labeled something comparable to a bank-draft when he adds in verses 18–19, "If he has done you any wrong or owes you anything [and he has, for this is what is called in Greek a "first class condition"], charge it to me. I, Paul, am writing this with my own hand." That last statement is equivalent to Paul's personal signature and has been found on other pieces of papyri in Koine Greek that were discovered early in the twentieth century.

Alas, despite the clarity of Paul's statements, many do not believe the Bible ever finally took a stand against all forms of involuntary, that is, pagan, slavery. This type of slavery should not be lumped together with debt slavery, which was a form of extracting oneself from debt when there was no other means of raising collateral to satisfy this financial emergency. Once again, the principles in the text are sufficient to help us answer similar questions in our day.

THE BIBLE, ABORTION, AND EMBRYONIC STEM CELL RESEARCH

More Americans elect to have an abortion than any other type of surgery. In fact, only three out of every four babies conceived in the United States escape a surgically conducted abortion; according to current statistics, the fourth one will be terminated by an abortion.

Abortion, however, is not a recent phenomenon; it was condemned by the Sumerians, Assyrians, Babylonians, and

Hittites, all of which regarded it as a serious crime. Classical Greece, by contrast, condoned abortion. Yet the Hippocratic Oath, which up until recently all doctors pledged as they graduated from medical school, stated: "I will not give a woman a pessary [i.e., a small soluble block inserted into the vagina] to produce an abortion."

Others joined in condemning abortion. The Jewish historian Josephus wrote around the end of the first Christian century: "The Law has commanded to raise all children and prohibited women from aborting or destroying seed; a woman who does so shall be judged a murderess of children, for she has caused a soul to be lost and the family of man to be diminished" (*Against Apion* 2.202). Likewise the early church stated its view in *Didache* 2.4 (a document also known as *The Teaching of the Twelve Apostles*): "Do not murder a child by abortion or kill a newborn infant."

In modern times, especially when in the 1820s the human ovum was discovered, it was argued that a woman was "with child" from the moment of conception. Modern laws against abortion in the United States remained in place until 1967, when a few states began to liberalize their abortion laws, with eighteen states following suit by the end of 1970. However, on January 22, 1973, the Supreme Court of the United States of America handed down its infamous ruling of Roe v. Wade, giving an even more permissive abortion law than that previously held in the United States.

The Bible, not surprisingly, has nothing to say directly on abortion. The reason, though, is not hard to explain. Abortion was so unthinkable that there was no need to even raise the topic in biblical law. Children were not a burden or a problem, but a "heritage from the LORD" (Ps. 127:3). The problem was not with a threat of pregnancy; it was the opposite threat—barrenness and childlessness, which would leave the family name extinct (Jer. 11:19). It was God who opened and closed the womb, so that conception was in his sovereign hand (Gen. 29:31, 33).

David celebrates God's secret work in the womb of his mother in Psalm 139:13–16, while he was being formed. It was God who "knit" him together in his mother's womb when he was "woven together" in the depths of her belly.

God's eyes saw David's "embryo" (Heb. *golmi*, v. 16) and poured his attention and love on him while he was being formed in the womb before David had lived even one day and done anything to attract the love of God. In like manner, God set Jeremiah apart for his life's work while he was still in the womb (Jer. 1:5), just as John the Baptist leaped in his mother Elizabeth's womb when Mary greeted her (Luke 1:41–44).

Another text that places the value of a full life on the baby in the womb is found in Exodus 21:22–25. "If men, who are fighting, hit a pregnant woman and [lit.] her children come out, but there is no harm [apparently to the mother or to the child], the offender must be fined whatever the woman's husband demands and the court allows. But if there is harm [to either the mother or the child] you shall take life for life" (my trans.).[18] The plural word "children" is used to allow for multiple births. Some suggest that word we have translated as "harm" in verse 22 (NIV, "prematurely") be rendered "miscarriage," but the Hebrew word for "miscarriage" (*shakhol*) is not used here (as it is in Gen. 31:38; Ex. 23:26; Job 3:16; Hos. 9:14).

Closely related to abortion is the more recent issue of human stem cell research, which surfaced in November 1998 at the University of Wisconsin, where scientists were able to isolate and culture human embryonic stem cells. The problem that arises with this research, despite its wonderful potential for supplying answers to human diseases such as Parkinson's, heart disease, and diabetes, is that to obtain these stem cells, the embryo must be destroyed. Human embryos can be obtained from three or four sources: (1) from in vitro fertilization to produce embryos, (2) from frozen embryos that are left over and not selected from the petri dish for in vitro fertilization, (3) from human cloning of embryos, and, more preferably, (4) from the human umbilical cord after gestation.

In addition to the moral problem that comes from using the first three sources for the stem cells (the same objections

---

18. The best short article on this topic and passage is Jack Cottrell, "Abortion and the Human Fetus," *Christianity Today* 17 (1972–73): 602–5.

that are made against abortion), so far embryonic stem cell research has also not been able to direct the embryonic cells so that they could effect the therapy wanted. Researchers deny the humanity of the unborn embryo and regard the embryo or fetus as only having "potential" human life and not being a real person, a conclusion that does not concur with the biblical assessment of these same types of situations.

The moral objections raised here, however, do not apply to human adult stem cells, which are usually obtained from those seeking the resultant therapy. Thus, adults have supplied bone marrow stem cells, which have been able to produce skeletal muscle, cardiac muscle, and liver cells. This nonobjectionable adult stem cell research has, as a matter of fact, already proven to be effective in the areas mentioned here.

There are, once again, enough biblical helps to formulate adequate principles for dealing with the issues of abortion and embryonic stem cell research without going beyond the Bible.

A SCRIPTURAL APPROACH TO THE PROBLEM AND THE DEVELOPMENT IN THE TEXT

I. Howard Marshall noted that the *liberal* method of interpreting Scripture is to measure it by what contemporary persons can believe and practice from it.[19] But Marshall insisted that evangelical readers of the Bible should not just concern themselves with the liberals' rejection of the Bible; we should also seek to learn what is their motivation for doing so and what principles have shaped that rejection. His hunch is that more of the problem may be with the contemporary mind that has been shaped by a totally different worldview and mindset.

Marshall calls for some new principled criteria to guide us in seeing fresh significance in the interchange between Scripture and its readers. Marshall has proposed that we can

---

19. I. Howard Marshall, *Beyond the Bible: Moving from Scripture to Theology* (Grand Rapids: Baker, 2004), 46.

obtain such criteria by noting three areas of development where the early Christians *not only built on* their sources, but as a matter of fact, *went beyond* them with the inevitable result that a pattern of diversity was seen between the earlier and later biblical materials.

The three areas of development that exhibited this phenomenon of moving beyond the text of Scripture were: (1) the use of the Old Testament by the early Christians, (2) the teaching of Jesus that took the early church not only beyond the Old Testament but was surpassed by the teaching of the gospel writers, and (3) the teaching of Paul that went beyond the "apostolic deposit" with further revelations and teaching that reacted against those teaching errors such as the Judaizers.

In the past, the term used to signify development in the biblical text was called *progressive revelation*. This term has not received much attention in recent times, since, as J. I. Packer put it, "[Recent theological fashions] view Scripture functionally, as a means of revelation in the present, rather than a revelatory process in the past."[20]

There are four negative ways in which progressive revelation has been used:[21]

1. From a *critical* standpoint, this label has been used to downgrade and label as inauthentic, truths about which some scholars are skeptical while elevating the "higher" truths of Scripture.

2. From an *apologetic* standpoint, this term has functioned as a way of excusing and justifying the more "primitive morality" of the Bible by means of a later revelation that allegedly corrected it.

3. From a *hermeneutical* point of view, progressive revelation became a slogan for the arbitrary and incon-

20. J. I. Packer, "An Evangelical View of Progressive Revelation," in *Evangelical Roots: A Tribute to Wilbur Smith*, ed. Kenneth S. Kantzer (Nashville, TN: Nelson, 1978), 143.

21. These four are dependent in part on James Barr, *The Bible in the Modern World* (New York: Harper & Row, 1973), 145, and Packer, "Progressive Revelation," 146–47. Also see my book *Toward Old Testament Ethics* (Grand Rapids, Zondervan, 1983), 60–64.

sistent process of selecting a few favorite teachings from the Bible while regarding the rest as "base" or "primitive."

4. From a *theological* standpoint, it was a way of removing the focus of attention from the divine act of disclosure and fixing it instead on human insight, discovery, and genius.

The upshot of this long history of discussion has often been to emphasize human discovery at the expense of divine disclosure in revelation. But such a conclusion is too heavy-handed and fails to meet the data from the text. There is little doubt that the Bible witnesses to a historical series of successive divine revelations. Did not Hebrews 1:1–2 explain: "In the past God spoke to our ancestors through the prophets at many times and in various ways, but in these last days he has spoken to us by his Son, whom he has appointed heir over all things, and through whom he made the universe"? That same succession of revelations is seen in our Lord's promise of the coming New Testament when he said to his disciples in John 16:12–13, "I have much more to say to you, more than you can now bear. But when he, the Spirit of truth, comes, he will guide you into all truth." Jesus had already noted in John 15:27, "And you also must testify, for you have been with me from the beginning." Therefore, instead of leaving us with analogies and scientific models, our Lord promised to supply his followers with a coming revelation (later called the "New Testament") to accompany what they already had in the Old Testament.

But there is more than historic development and succession here; there is also perfection of revealed truth at all stages along the process, even though that perfection was merely a perfection in seminal form with an incipient potentiality for increasing growth, clearness, and fullness. It was Geerhardus Vos who best described this seminal perfection. He taught:

> The organic nature of the progression of revelation ... [includes the] absolute perfection at all stages.... The organic progress is from seed-form to the attainment of full growth; yet we do not say that in the qualitative sense the seed is less perfect than the [grown] tree....

> In the seed-form the minimum of indispensable knowl-
> edge was already present.... Again, revelation ... does
> not proceed with uniform motion, but rather is ep-
> ochal.... The discovery of so considerable an amount
> of variableness and differentiation in the Bible [is not]
> fatal to the belief in its absoluteness.[22]

Accordingly, revelation in Scripture can be true, eternal
in its source, and organically or seminally perfect without
its being complete in its statements, its history, fully developed in its supporting doctrines, or fully apprehended by
all its readers or listeners. When these factors are properly
accounted for, the apparent conflict between progress/
development and revelation begins to give way, and ways
in which the tension can be resolved emerge for these very
same factors. Just as the historic process was necessary, so
too was the process of revelation necessary in order for it to
be pedagogically graded for learning as the race grew, stud-
ied, and profited from the earlier divine disclosures.

To return to Marshall's three categories of development,
he suggested that the first Christians went beyond what God
had offered in the Jewish Scriptures. He offered five examples
where these later New Testament believers went beyond: (1) in
the way God became more personal and parent-like to them;
(2) in their understanding of the three-foldness of God; (3) in
the way non-Jews would become not only part of the people
of God, but its majority group; (4) in the way concepts of the
afterlife moved from the fringe to the center of their thinking;
and (5) in the way the legislation of Pentateuch moved from
the center to less of an issue for Christians.

Likewise, Marshall observed that Christians moved
beyond the teaching of Jesus centering on the Old Testament,
and Jesus himself, to a proclamation of Jesus as the crucified
and risen one. Writers such as John selected, interpreted,
abridged, and elaborated on the words and works of Jesus
instead of merely repeating his words. There were four, not

---

22. Geerhardus Vos, *Biblical Theology: Old and New Testaments* (Grand
Rapids: Eerdmans, 1954), 15–16. William Brenton Greene Jr. made use of Vos's
quote in his "The Ethics of the Old Testament," *Princeton Theological Review*
27 (1929): 184–91.

just one, fresh gospels that told the Christian story. Whereas Jesus' central theme had been the kingdom of God, later teaching moved away from this center and reinterpreted the teaching with an emphasis on imitating Christ instead.

Finally, Paul further developed the apostolic deposit by also expressing the faith in new ways. Paul also had further revelations, part of which he referred to as a "mystery," that is, that which was previously hidden but was now revealed.

Rather than seeing a fairly "cut and dried" production, the New Testament writings offered perhaps a pattern that the church of our day can continue to follow. Marshall remarked that the closing of the canon was not compatible with the closing of the interpretation of the canon, for the process of doctrinal development goes on in our day just as it did in the days of the writing of the New Testament. In other words, perhaps we can do what the apostles did in the area of developing Scripture to newer forms of theology and practice.

In Marshall's five categories, where the New Testament believers went beyond Jewish Scriptures, all five illustrate basically the progress of revelation in Scripture itself. In like manner, for those who similarly argue that Paul's teaching went beyond Jesus' teaching, it can again be demonstrated that in each case it was an organic outgrowth of what Jesus had given, often in a more incipient form.[23] The case for disunity or a real division of theology between Jesus and Paul is rather weak. While it is to be admitted that Paul does use a different terminology from that used by Jesus, this is not to admit a discontinuity between the two. Often the differences can be traced to the fact that Paul was facing different times and a different culture. In fact, Paul did refer to our Lord's teaching directly (e.g., 1 Thess. 4:15) and by allusion in other passages (e.g., "a thief" in 1 Thess. 5:4, cf. Jesus in Matt. 24:23; or in 1 Cor. 11:23).

Even the case that claims that there are significant areas of expansion in the gospel of John over that of the

23. See David Wenham, *Paul: Founder of Christianity or Follower of Jesus?* (Grand Rapids: Eerdmans, 1996); idem, "Appendix: Unity and Diversity in the New Testament," in *A Theology of the New Testament*, ed. George E. Ladd (2nd ed.; Grand Rapids: Eerdmans, 1993), 684–719 (esp. 704–9).

three Synoptic Gospels (Matthew, Mark, and Luke) does not amount to a case of total disunity or discontinuity. It is true, of course, that John emphasized Jesus' extended discourses rather than his aphorisms, and John loved to point to the miracles of Jesus to make his summons to believe in the Lord Jesus Christ, but this is merely a difference in emphasis. Even the famous alleged difference in the timing of Jesus' eating of the Passover meal can be harmonized (for John's reference to "the day of Preparation of the Passover" [John 19:14]), as if it had occurred on Wednesday night with the crucifixion taking place on Thursday evening) when we realize that in John 19:31 Jesus' crucifixion took place on "the day of Preparation," followed by the very next day as a "special Sabbath" (i.e., the seventh day of Passover week). So John places the crucifixion on Friday as do the Synoptics.

Although we do see a progressive development of an organically related revelation, we do not agree that the apostles in any sense of the term went beyond what Scripture had taught, for they oftentimes developed what was already seminally present in the revelation that had preceded it. And even if these writers showed progress and development of doctrine, ethic, and thought, which we agree to so long as it has its roots organically anchored in the stream of disclosures they were continuing to unfold, we cannot agree that we, who are the subsequent readers of this text, can in some similar way "go beyond" the text based on an alleged apostolic example. Our interpretive contributions are not in the same stream as the revelatory words of God; we are but repeaters and appliers of what has already been communicated in Scripture.

Our best contribution is to move up the Ladder of Abstraction and state the general principle that embodies what is seen in the specificity, culture, and times of the text and then to apply it to our day in corresponding specifics that elaborate on that same general principle. May our Lord grant us his Holy Spirit in this task of interpretation and "illumination," rather than in an unauthorized work of creating new authoritative directives, which the Holy Spirit never promised to anyone beyond the prophets and the apostles.

A RESPONSE TO WALTER C. KAISER JR.

Daniel M. Doriani

THERE IS MUCH TO COMMEND IN WALTER KAISER'S concise presentation of what he has long called "a principlizing hermeneutic." An analysis of his essay can hardly divorce itself from Kaiser's body of work expounding and applying the Bible, especially the Old Testament. Kaiser's essay seeks to distill and apply to new questions the method he has used in numerous settings: the pulpit, conference podium, lecture hall, and graduate seminar.

The concept of principlizing has guided Kaiser through his varied interpretive work, which falls into three categories. The first is biblical exposition, which includes expository sermons for the church and commentaries, written especially for pastors, on books from Exodus to Malachi. Second, Kaiser has produced systematizing works, including surveys of Old Testament theology and ethics as well as studies of suffering and mission. Third, Kaiser wrote several works on interpretation, from his *Introduction to Biblical Hermeneutics* to the more practical *Preaching and Teaching from the Old Testament*. During his most productive years as lecturer and writer, Kaiser served as dean and then president of leading evangelical seminaries, so that he oversaw the broader enterprise of theological training. Throughout, Kaiser has manifested an energy, congeniality, and wit that adorn his work. Clearly, Kaiser is not merely advocating a theory in this essay; he is describing principles that both have guided his practice and were molded by that practice.

Given Kaiser's influence, it is right to appreciate the contributions he has made in the field of biblical exposition and application before we move to questions about his method. That is, a critical assessment of Kaiser's work must begin with the many points where his principlizing hermeneutic and the redemptive-historical approach share vital convictions. We first affirm the convictions that guide Kaiser's approach to the interpretation and application of the Bible, especially as he considers the question of development in Scripture and right and wrong ways to go beyond the sacred page.

We laud his affirmation that the Bible is the authoritative revelation of God's truth. Kaiser denies the destructive usage of the concept of progressive revelation—the skeptical approach that downgrades the "inauthentic" teaching or the allegedly "primitive morality" of some biblical teaching, the overconfidence that lets some theologians make "arbitrary" selection of "a few favorite teachings from the Bible." To use traditional evangelical labels, Kaiser affirms, explicitly or implicitly, the inerrancy, infallibility, sufficiency, progressive development, and christocentricity of the Bible. I share Kaiser's belief that God inspired Scripture's human authors so that the prime task of pastors and theologians is to discover, through careful reading, God's intended teaching in Scripture.

Because of these points of agreement, the distance between the redemptive-historical approach and the principlizing hermeneutic is not as great as a "four views" format might imply. This is clearest in his interaction with Marshall's proposal about ways to go beyond Scripture. Kaiser agrees with Marshall, as all must, that there is development within the canon. Citing Vos, however, he denies that development signifies deficiency or error. He rightly affirms that Scripture is perfect in all its stages of development. A seed can be perfect, even though it is far from its final form as a tree, flower, or vegetable. As a boy, Jesus was perfect, although immature. Similarly, Scripture can be God-given, true, and "seminally perfect without ... being complete in its statements."

The perfect-albeit-immature character of certain Scriptures is the concept that leads Kaiser to affirm the progress and development within the canon, as God brings the historical process of redemption to its climax in Christ's death and resurrection, while denying that the canon, in final form, is incomplete. At times, Kaiser's quest for principles seems to threaten to push this core truth into the background. Yet we must agree with Kaiser's assertion that God himself guided Scripture's authors, such as the four evangelists, as they "selected, interpreted, abridged, and elaborated on the words and works of Jesus," giving them a unique position in the divine economy. The "interpretive contributions" of contemporary Christians belong to a different category. We merely repeat and apply what has been delivered once for all to the church. Therefore we are "unauthorized" to go beyond the sacred page in the sense that we could add new truths or "directives." We applaud all these points.

Further, with the exception of Kaiser's comments on gender roles, and especially his unusual usage of possible Canaanite root words in his effort to explain Genesis 2:18, I generally agree with Kaiser's case studies, studies that take us beyond the sacred page in some sense of the phrase. Tempting as it is to comment on his particular work on euthanasia, gender, homosexuality, slavery, and abortion, I confine my critical remarks to his theory.

Despite its clear strengths, there are problems with a principlizing hermeneutic. First, principlizing treats the particularity and cultural embeddedness of Scripture more as a problem to be overcome than as something essential to the givenness of the Bible. Kaiser says cultural issues "intrude" on the text; the problem is "handled" by principlizing the text. Again, Kaiser says, "principles ... must be given priority over accompanying cultural elements, especially ... the times and setting in which" a text was written. A principlizing interpretation commendably "seeks to derive its teachings from a careful understanding of the text," but after careful work is complete, the interpreter "restates" his or her findings "in timeless abiding truths with special focus on the application of those truths to the current needs of the church." After identifying the subject and emphasis of a passage, the interpreter must "see how each paragraph (in prose genres), scene (in narratives), or strophe (in poetical passages) can be expressed in propositional principles."

Anyone who reads Kaiser's expository works knows that he is capable of handling the diverse genres of Scripture effectively. Nonetheless, his theory appears to affirm that what really counts is less the text itself than the principle expressed within the text. As a result, there can be no abiding interest in the genres of Scripture. Once the principle is extracted, the God-given form of Scripture falls away like a wheat husk or pea pod.

Second, and more seriously, principlizing's insistence on timeless, propositional truth privileges one form of divine communication above others. While we must never deny or even minimize the importance of propositional truth, we must remember that revelation comes in many forms. Alongside propositions, the Bible contains commands, questions, prayers, promises and curses, riddles, vows, parables, and more.

Consider Mark 8:14–27, for example. Both the disciples and Pharisees have witnessed a string of dramatic miracles described in Mark 6:30–8:10. Jesus has twice fed vast multitudes with a few loaves of bread, walked on water, and healed many sick. After all this, the Pharisees are, if anything, more confrontational, and the disciples more clueless than ever. When Jesus warns the twelve to watch out for the "yeast of the Pharisees"—that is, their faithless spirit—the disciples think he is rebuking them for failing to take an adequate supply of bread with them as they travel. This is most pitiable, since they twice recently saw Jesus' power to multiply food. But we must observe the *form* of Jesus' rebuke. Instead of presenting a proposition: "I can provide all necessary bread," or a command: "You must trust me to provide," Jesus upbraids them with a string of *eight* rhetorical questions:

> "Why are you talking about having no bread? Do you still not see or understand? Are your hearts hardened? Do you have eyes but fail to see, and ears but fail to hear? And don't you remember? When I broke the five loaves for the five thousand, how many basketfuls of pieces did you pick up?"
> "Twelve," they replied.
> "And when I broke the seven loaves for the four thousand, how many basketfuls of pieces did you pick up?"
> They answered, "Seven."

He said to them, "Do you still not understand?"
(Mark 8:17–21).

No matter how elegant the formulation of Jesus' point, no matter how compelling the ethical demand, it cannot have the effect of this series of "surely-you-must-know" rhetorical questions. Jesus expects them to know the answers! How devastating that they do not; how imperative that they search the matter out.

Third, Kaiser appears to claim a privileged position with regard to the text, as if he might be able to transcend both the original culture of the Bible and his own. How else can he attain his stated goal: "to restate the author's propositions, arguments, narrations, and illustrations in timeless, abiding truths." Just before he addresses the question of gender roles, Kaiser notes that many of our disagreements stem from "certain preunderstandings" that we bring to the text, but he fails to give this observation a role in his system. No human can achieve a timeless, culture-free posture. Nor, as my colleague Robbie Griggs says, should we want to. Our creatureliness and finitude are not evils to be overcome, but part of God's design. They do pose problems after the fall, problems both of ignorance and self-interested distortion. But these flaws should lead us to *terminate* the quest for timelessness and pure objectivity.

Alongside Kaiser's quest for *timeless truths*, there appears to be a quest for *timeless ethical principles*. As a corollary, he seems to ascribe particular injunctions a secondary status as "good illustrations" of principles. Beyond the aforementioned problems with timelessness, let us remember that we must not be wiser than God, who chose to give particular injunctions about sheep, food, buildings, and steps toward relational reconciliation. While it is possible to give certain principles, such as those found in the Decalogue, a kind of priority, we must admit that our grasp of broad principles would be intolerably vague if not for the particular commands that help define the broad principles.

A passage such as Jesus' denunciation of the hypocritical scribes and Pharisees in Matthew 23 illustrates the limits of the quest for principles. The principle is clear enough: "Don't be hypocritical." But how shallow that is compared

to the study of the frightening particularity of the hypoc-
risies of that day. The chronological distance and the cultural alienness of the sins Jesus denounced are not, I submit,
problems the interpreter must erase by locating timeless
principles. The alienness forces both intellectual reflection
and self-examination. The result of that self-examination
will be repentance at some points, but also, one hopes, a
realization that Christian readers are not hypocrites as the
Pharisees were. As great as the cultural and chronological distance between Matthew 23 and our day may be, the
redemptive-historical distance is greater. For at heart, a
believer is, *by definition*, not a hypocrite like the Pharisees.
They were self-justifying, impenitent foes of Christ, and we,
by God's grace, are at heart none of these — even if we have
the capacity to deny ourselves by lapsing into petty hypoc-
risies.

In sum, the redemptive-historical approach has substantive differences with the principlizing hermeneutic, along
the lines we have just explored. The redemptive-historical
theologian also wishes Kaiser made more of the christocentricity of Scripture and the Bible's character as the narrative
of God's redemptive acts. Yet we give thanks for the vital
points of agreement and the overriding sense of partnership
in gospel ministry.

A RESPONSE TO WALTER C. KAISER JR.

Kevin J. Vanhoozer

ONE'S FIRST DEAN, LIKE ONE'S FIRST KISS, is something you never forget. My memories of teaching at Trinity Evangelical Divinity School under Dean Kaiser are largely positive, not least because Dr. Kaiser created a protected space within which I enjoyed complete creative control over my syllabus, as long (of course!) as it was within the confessional bounds of the institution. We also share a common cause in defending the rights of authors to be heard as authors, though we have different approaches to this defense in the courtroom of academia. It is therefore a privilege to engage him as a coauthor.

Kaiser is not simply an author but a prolific one. He has literally written the book (or is it thirty?) on questions of hermeneutics, Old Testament ethics, exegetical theology, and Old Testament theology. Elsewhere he commends an integrative or "comprehensive" approach to questions of applying the Old Testament. My first thought, then, was to read his present chapter in light of everything else he has said on the subject, but that quickly proved impractical. I confine my remarks, then, to what he says in this chapter alone.

Kaiser's essay is a classic statement by an elder states-man of what has become in recent evangelical analysis "a consensus that the key to legitimate application involves ... 'principlizing.'"[24] The basic assumption of this approach is that underlying many of the commands or narratives in the Bible are fundamental truths that may be abstracted from

---

24. William W. Klein, Craig Blomberg, and Robert L. Hubbard, Jr., *Introduction to Biblical Interpretation* (rev. ed.; Nashville: Nelson, 2004), 483.

the culturally conditioned forms of behavior in which they were originally expressed. Kaiser views "principlizing" as restating what the authors say in terms of timeless abiding truths, the better to apply them to current needs of the church. Principlizing is the bridge that allows the interpreter to move from "there and then" to "here and now."

Principlizing requires exegetical discipline. For example, Kaiser insists that the principle in question must always be one that was in the mind of the original author (contrast this with Webb's authorless "redemptive spirit"). In particular, he resists the temptation to discover New Testament truth in Old Testament texts (presumably, Jesus was teaching the disciples on the road to Emmaus about the significance, not the original meaning, of the Old Testament prophets [see Luke 24:27]). Principlizing also involves a good deal of climbing. One has to climb up the Ladder of Abstraction to reach a general principle and then down again to reach the *terra firma* of specific application. (One wonders if Augustine is sitting on top of the ladder embracing the love of God as the Principle of Principles.)

The strength of this approach is that it represents a way to preserve the supreme authority of Scripture (*sola Scriptura*) while simultaneously demonstrating its contemporary relevance. Simply put, principlizing *preaches*. That people in the pew "get it" is an undisputed advantage of the approach. Any alternative to principlizing, if it is to serve the church, must be as readily intelligible. Further, principlizing *teaches*. Indeed, principlizing teaches, much as *Aesop's Fables* teach. This is not to suggest that Kaiser treats Scripture as anything other than historical and true, only that his process for making biblical narratives relevant resembles the way in which readers get the "moral" from the Aesop stories. Aesop explicitly formulates the moral for his readers. For example, the fable of Androcles concludes with this proposition: "Gratitude is the sign of noble souls." Aesop's didactic fables provide obvious narrative packaging to moral principles and proverbial wisdom.

Kaiser is unfazed by the maze of contemporary issues facing the biblical interpreter. Euthanasia, abortion, stem-cell research, slavery, homosexuality—no problem! In each case, Kaiser finds clear principles that enable him to make clean judgments. Even in the contested subject of women and the church, which also serves as his longest case study, Kaiser makes relatively short work of the matter. After a bit of linguistic legerdemain, he assures us that "the principles here are again most straightforward and do not call for any cultural or exegetical moves outside or beyond the Scriptures." He must be wondering what's wrong with the rest of us who don't seem to have his 20/20 exegetical vision.

To be sure, the principle that women too may exercise teaching authority depends on Kaiser's exegesis of texts such as Genesis 2:18 and 1 Corinthians 11:10, conjoined with some fancy etymological spadework in Canaanite roots. The net result is that Kaiser has God saying about Adam, "I will make him a *power* fit for him." I'd like to see that trick again, only this time in slow motion.

Kaiser may not go beyond the sacred page, but he certainly goes behind it, appealing to the Gnostic teacher Valentinus, in whose native Coptic tongue the words for "veil" and "authority" sound and look alike, in order to explain the mistranslation (as Kaiser sees it) of 1 Corinthians 11:10 in virtually all English translations. The principle behind women in the church may be straightforward then, but not the exegesis! Here Kaiser would do well to heed his own advice to those who would establish a biblical toehold for homosexuality: "Such word studies will not sustain this heroic effort...."

If I now raise some critical questions concerning the principlizing approach, it is largely because it is the default position of many evangelicals, as has previously been mentioned, and because I think we can do better. The question, though, is whether I can teach an old dean—and the disciples that follow him—new hermeneutical tricks.

The first volley of criticisms—cautions, actually—comes from David Clark.[25] (1) Principlizing is harder than it sounds because it is not always clear *which* general principle to draw from the text. (2) Principlizers are not always sufficiently aware of the cultural log in their own eye before they take

---

25. David K. Clark, *To Know and Love God: Method for Theology* (Wheaton, IL: Crossway, 2003), 91–98.

the cultural speck out of the eye of the biblical text: "principlizing obscures the fact that any articulation of the allegedly transcultural principles still reflects the culture of the
translator."[26] (3) Principlizers must guard against thinking
that their principles are purer than the Bible itself; *even the
statement of the principle is itself somewhat culturally conditioned*,
for interpreters are enculturated too.[27] Clark acknowledges
that a "soft" principlizing is necessary for evangelical theology. It is only the way of wisdom, however, to remember that
"they must speak softly who carry a big supracultural stick."

And now three further concerns of my own. First, is
there not a tension between affirming progressive revelation on the one hand and timeless principles on the other? If
one can deduce timeless principles from earlier instances of
revelation as well as later, then in what sense can we speak
of the "progress" of revelation? Where is the room for development if the principles undergirding even the earliest texts
are timeless? Kaiser cannot have it both ways: either there
is development, in which case the principles that guide us
are not as timeless as he claims, or else the principles are
timeless, and thus there is no meaningful development. He
tries to escape the dilemma by appealing to Vos's notion of
"seminal perfection," but I am still left with the question: Is
there progress *in the realm of principles* or not?

Second, does principlizing make too great a distinction
between theological principles (the kernel) on the one hand
and cultural practices / behavioral expressions (the husk)
on the other? At the limit, such a distinction can give rise
to an unhealthy, even docetic, dualism of head over body,
theological mind over cultural matter. But are principles
really more timeless than practices? Jesus' practices (which
John Yoder refers to as the "politics" of Jesus) embody the
Christian way, truth, and life—something that cannot simply be reduced to a set of abstract principles. Indeed, from
one perspective, the abstract principles are but the shadow

---

26. Ibid., 112.

27. It follows that the best principlizers are those who are culturally self-
aware and thus appropriately humble about their particular formulations of
the transcultural principles.

of the substance, the weaker brother of the concrete life of the incarnate Son of God.

Finally, and perhaps most radically, is "application" itself a biblical principle? Put differently, is "application" the best way to conceive of Christian discipleship, being biblical, following the Word, and doing the truth? The success or failure of principlizing depends on one's answer to this question to the extent that principlizing is a strategy for applying the text. Principlizing seems to work best with moralizing uses of the text (think Aesop). Too many sermons end with moralizing applications, even though Christianity is not primarily a system of morality. I therefore resonate with one observer of the present theological scene: "We are usually muddled when we talk about 'applying the Bible.'"[28] In my chapter I distinguish between "applying the text" and "living/performing the world implied by the text." The problem with principlizing is that it too often leads to moralizing, that is, to a way of reading the Bible that focuses on the search for transcultural principles of the ethical variety.

I believe that what is of transcultural significance is not some principle that we must distill from the biblical text but the text itself, precisely as a form of culturally concrete *sapientia* (wisdom).[29] Yes, the Bible was written for a particular culture, yet it has permanent (transcultural) value and authority precisely as a concrete instance of how to embody the mind of Christ in a particular situation. We need to focus not on abstract principles alone but on concrete (canonical) universals.[30] As I say in my chapter, principlizing risks de-dramatizing the Bible: going for the moral without the fable, the content without the form, the soul without the body of the text. In my dramatic model, the goal is not to obtain a

---

28. Richard Briggs, *Reading the Bible Wisely* (Grand Rapids: Baker, 2003), 84.

29. There is no little irony in a systematic theologian like me having to warn biblical scholars like Kaiser that their tendency to principlize may actually hinder our viewing the Bible itself, in all its literary diversity, as authoritative.

30. What's more valuable for moral and spiritual formation? Reading a book of universal principles or being mentored by a flesh-and-blood, particular human being?

set of timeless principles but to grow in wisdom by considering particular instances of truth, love, and wisdom in act. Again, I do see a modest role for something like principlizing, but the primary thing is to form and transform biblical interpreters through their apprenticeship to the particular habits of prophetic and apostolic judgment intrinsic to and embodied in the biblical texts.[31]

We need to change the picture by which we operate. The problem is not that of determining how to apply the text, as if the text were something external and remote to our present-day lives, but just the reverse: it is we who are external to the text. The challenge is not to abstract from the world of the text to the realm of timeless principles but to enter into what I called the world "implied by" the text. Instead of isolating a principle that we have then to make relevant to our situation, we need to explicate the main theodramatic action and to implicate our contemporary situation in it. In short, the task is not to transform the Bible (i.e., into timeless principles) so that it can enter our world, but to transform ourselves (i.e., our habits of vision) so that we can enter into the world implied by the Bible.

What I am proposing is not principlizing but *theodramatizing*—a form of typological or figural reading where what gets "figured" or worked out in the present is the old, old story of what God is doing in Jesus through the Spirit. To theodramatize a text—to go beyond the text theodramatically—is to understand what judgment has been embodied by a biblical author and then to embody that same judgment in a new conceptual or cultural form today. Jesus Christ is the substance of the faith, and he casts his shadow both backward (in the history of Israel) and forward (in the life of the church).[32] The relevance of Scripture in the present derives from its ability to provide concrete direction (theodramatic

---

31. I discuss the nature of judgment vis-à-vis concepts (and, by implication, principles) in my essay in this book.

32. This is not your great-great-great-great-grandfather's allegorism. "Bad" allegorism imports meaning into the text that the authors never intended. The kind of figural reading I am advocating assumes that there is an underlying theodramatic consistency and coherence that underlies and unifies the whole of redemptive history, Israel's and the church's alike.

precedent) for the church's right participation in what God is doing to renew all things in Christ through his Spirit.

I note in conclusion that all of Kaiser's case studies focus on moral and ethical issues rather than doctrine and theology. I therefore wonder how principlizing works when the church seeks to come to a common mind on such issues as the Trinity or the atonement. Does principlizing have a significant role to play with regard to the use of Scripture in theology? If not, how are we to go beyond the sacred page to *sacra doctrina*?

A RESPONSE TO WALTER C. KAISER JR.

William J. Webb

I WISH TO THANK DR. KAISER for his essay on a "principl-izing hermeneutic" (herein, PH) and for his many previous writings. While he is probably unaware of it, my own think-ing about a RMH (redemptive-movement hermeneutic) has been influenced by his PH approach in significant ways.[33] Thus I am much indebted to Dr. Kaiser and, as astute readers will recognize, I briefly use his PH method under the label "abstracted meaning" in conjunction with a RMH approach in the corporal punishment portion of my essay.

I could spend the whole of this response talking about ways in which I would embrace Kaiser's PH in a circum-scribed fashion. But that will have to wait for some other time. Far more pressing matters require attention, and I turn now to them.

THE BIBLE AND SLAVERY

At two important places I differ with how Kaiser presents slavery in the Bible. The first is a matter of optics or potential miscommunication, while the second is more serious and substantive in nature. The first problem is that Kaiser opens the discussion of slavery by presenting a contrast between *biblical slavery* as temporary debt slavery versus *pagan slavery* (by unstated inference) as permanent chattel slavery. While he later qualifies this contrast to include chattel slavery as part of the biblical portrait, the original juxtaposition of "biblical debt slavery" versus "pagan slavery" along with

---

33. For some of these influences and overlapping parallels see my response to Doriani's RH method.

the continued use of this stark contrast may confuse the matter for some readers. Since I have encountered a few Christian scholars who thought that the Bible accepted/ permitted only debt slavery, I want to be careful not to perpetuate this inaccurate portrait. Debt slavery was part of the pagan scene, and permanent chattel slavery was part of the biblical scene at least for non-Hebrew slaves.[34] Forgive my pedantic tweaking; this observation is more for the sake of readers than for Dr. Kaiser.

The second matter is more important for the purposes of this book, namely, Kaiser's understanding that Paul's letter to Philemon shows the apostle teaching the abolition of slavery. Kaiser writes, "Paul thereby taught this slave-holder Philemon, who lived at Colossae, as well as he now teaches us, that *no one must be held as a slave*" (emphasis mine). Kaiser makes his case for thinking that Paul is teaching abolitionism within the book of Philemon by citing Philemon 16a. I must say, however, that I enjoyed his well-couched acknowledgment that "all too few get it [Paul's abolitionist teaching]" as Kaiser does. So in what follows, I will briefly develop why I do not "get it" either. In other words, I do not believe Paul is instructing Christians in any explicit or direct sense that they need to embrace an abolitionist ethic (of course, a logical extension of the letter's redemptive spirit is quite another matter).

Within its literary and social context (contra Kaiser) I would argue that Philemon 16a "no longer as a slave" does not teach abolitionism, at least according to PH methodology. Does the letter improve the relationship and status for one particular slave, Onesimus? Yes. Does it teach abolitionism as a required social ethic for Christians? No. Well, at least not in any immediate, direct, or explicit sense. Several observations lead to this conclusion.

---

34. Permanent chattel slavery was also part of biblical slavery even for certain Hebrew slaves in a *qualified* sense. Some married Hebrew slaves probably made a choice (perhaps "quasi-voluntarily" or even "non-voluntarily" are accurate expressions in this instance) to stay permanently in their enslaved status when faced with the painful alternative of otherwise having to break up their family unit. The love of a Hebrew slave for his master was only one consideration in the decision about permanent enslavement.

First, the rest of verse 16 qualifies Paul's words "no longer as a slave" by saying "but better than a slave, as a dear brother." Paul certainly tempers the slave-master relationship in a radical sense. Yet, most likely he does not remove the slave status but instead sets the "brotherhood" status as more dominant in defining the relationship. In other words, Paul is saying, "no longer [purely!] as a slave" or "no longer as a slave [only!]." Such a contrastive ellipsis is common in Paul's letters and in the New Testament. The words about brotherhood that follow suggest that we move from overstatement or ellipsis to the transformed reality itself. The next six arguments confirm this nonabolitionist approach to exegesis.

Second, Paul directs Onesimus to return from where he, Paul, is in prison (probably Rome) to Philemon, his former master in Colossae (v. 12). It would appear that Onesimus was converted under Paul's ministry in Rome and now, as a Christian, there is a need for him to return to his master. Yet, returning a slave to his/her master is hardly an abolitionist action. This action implies the legitimacy of ownership, not the opposite.

Third, certain words further imply some sort of remaining ownership scenario that limits Paul's right to keep Onesimus with himself in Rome. Paul says he "would have liked to keep him" (v. 13), yet he is hesitant "without your [Philemon's] consent" (v. 14). There may also be a hint of this continued ownership within the twofold assessment of Onesimus's value in verse 16c—"as a man, and as a brother" (the reference to "man" [lit., "in the flesh"] *may* allude to his human/social value as a slave). Thus Paul seems to be asking Philemon to release Onesimus as one now-turned-Christian and as a close-to-my-heart coworker from his obligations in Colossae so that Onesimus can work in the ministry with Paul in Rome. This may amount to transfer of indentured service from Philemon to Paul. Yet it is not abolitionism. Note that Paul does not instruct Philemon to release *all* of his *Christian* slaves based on their new brotherhood status in Christ; Paul suggests the release of one slave who has become important to him in ministry.

Fourth, if we look at the other side of the faith question, Paul does not give instructions to Philemon to release his *non-Christian* slaves, who would not be considered "brothers" in Christ. While Christian brotherhood clearly transforms the slave-master relationship, an abolitionist perspective must reach beyond this framework to encompass the whole of humanity. There is no hint of this sort of abolitionist treatment of non-Christian slaves either in Philemon or in the rest of the New Testament. Along these lines, recall the lopsided treatment of Hebrew versus non-Hebrew slaves in the Old Testament.

Fifth, an abolitionist perspective on slavery does not worry about "debts owed," as Paul does in verse 17, for slaves who have escaped and made their way to freedom. The debts of which Paul speaks are most likely those of lost labor and perhaps lost articles often taken by runaway slaves to fund their escape. An abolitionist ethic compassionately understands that the greater good of achieving freedom from slavery will often, if not necessarily, incur a loss in these two categories. However, these two sorts of loss are legitimately and more than adequately compensated for, extraordinarily so, not in repayment by the escaped slave *after* the escape but in the previous benefits of slave labor to the master *before* the escape. Compare the underground railway story (in my response to Doriani) about runaway black slaves not gaining membership in white/free churches when they came to Canada.

Sixth, the ancient social context suggests that Paul is making strong hints, not about the abolition of slavery, but about easing the severe penalties for runaway slaves. The social climate of Paul's day often dealt brutally with runaway slaves. Escaped slaves, if caught, were frequently beaten, maimed, or put to death along with certain of their immediate family members as an object lesson. People who aided in the escape of slaves were at times treated in a similarly harsh manner. Within that ancient social context it is most likely that Paul simply "takes the edge off" the severe ramifications for a runaway slave. He also has the practical hopes of having Onesimus help him at some future stage in his ministry. Rather than offering any explicit abolitionist agenda or teaching, Paul may simply have wanted to avoid any scandal for the gospel should a runaway slave be caught while a functioning member of Paul's ministry team. Once again, this is not an abolitionist letter in the strict sense of exegesis, at least not an exegesis that does not value incremental movement and its logical and theological extension.

Seventh, any referent ambiguity about "good treatment" within the letter to Philemon must be understood in terms of the clear address to slaves and masters that came to the *same city* and probably at the *same time* and in the *same mail delivery* package, namely, the closely related instructions found in the letter to the Colossians. The words addressed to slaves and masters in that letter would have had a significant impact upon the household church, including Onesimus and Philemon. While Colossians contains an admonition to treat slaves fairly, it is only wishful thinking that could turn that letter's instructions into an abolitionist address. Read Colossians 3:22 – 4:1 and ask if these instructions command masters to free slaves or command slaves to pursue abolitionist emancipation. Imagine hearing the Colossians letter read aloud to numerous other slaves sitting beside Onesimus (the one "named" slave) in that church community, since *both* letters would have been read at this same house church. Such situational ponderings yield a strong probability that Paul does not teach abolitionism in the letter to Philemon — well, at least not in the PH manner that Kaiser suggests.

Now let me ask a "What if I am wrong?" question about one aspect of my development above. What if I am wrong about the ellipsis? My answer here is that it does not really matter to my broader thesis. Even if I am wrong about the ellipsis rendering of Philemon 16a, the next most probable understanding is that the *actual* release of Onesimus from slavery (1) was still procured in a transactional way — by Paul picking up the tab for Onesimus's past debts and by promising future service by Onesimus to Paul in view of Philemon's indebtedness to Paul — and (2) still included an informal, unlimited indentured service by Onesimus to Paul. This alternative view, which we might call a "transactional and informal indentured service" rendering of Philemon 16a, is strongly supported by six pieces (vv. 2 – 7) of the sevenfold discussion above and is still far more probable than Kaiser's view that Paul is teaching abolitionism. Of course, in this last sentence I am talking strictly about meaning derived from

Philemon through Kaiser's principlizing approach, which emphasizes abstracted principles that hopefully(!) have a starting point of solid exegesis within the immediate literary context. The same is true of attempts to discover abolitionist teaching by Paul using Doriani's face value approach.

Should a nonabolitionist reading of Philemon be the more exegetically convincing one (as I have argued), then Christians need to think through the hermeneutical and ethical implications. First, the difficult part. Start with an honest confession: not all biblical texts reflect an ultimate ethic in the treatment of human beings (both Old and New Testaments) in all of their concrete, specific particulars. Surely, Jesus himself tells us this in his own ethical reflection upon several texts of Scripture. It makes good sense that we expect this less-than-ultimate-ethic phenomenon in other texts than simply the ones Jesus suggests. Since I have made an extended case for this elsewhere, I will not develop the point any further here.[35]

Now the good news. Within this culturally limited and fallen-world development of the biblical text, a *Jesus* and a *dual-love ethic* redemptive core to Scripture function like a powerful spiritual magnet that pull in phenomenal ways toward something better. It is not that God *couldn't* move (contra Doriani's incorrect portrayal of a RMH view) the ball all the way downfield and across the goal line of an ultimate ethic. Of course, he could. Rather, he *chooses* to move the ball incrementally downfield, sometimes twenty, sometimes forty yards at a time.

God chooses to move incrementally, and not every play in the game is an ethical touchdown, for several possible reasons. (1) This is the "in between" time of a fallen world, and perhaps God wants to save something for the new heavens and new earth—the best is yet to come.

(2) Human beings are often slow as donkeys and have calcified hearts when it comes to even incremental change for good (Jesus talked about this in his reflection on Scripture).

---

35. For a lengthy treatment of this issue see, William J. Webb, "The Limits of a Redemptive-Movement Hermeneutic: A Focused Response to T. R. Schreiner," *Evangelical Quarterly* 75:4 (2003): 327–42.

(3) The far-reaching interconnected implications, like octopus tentacles extending from just one social structure issue, make enacting radical changes extremely difficult and slow within a real world (think about how the yearly incremental reduction in the import quota of foreign slaves in the 1800s adversely impacted the economy of the southern [non]United States, or think about all the complex factors that today make it so difficult to move toward renewable energy sources—incremental movement in ethics is tough, very tough).

(4) Surely God knows that radical social changes often bring about revolutionary bloodshed (let us not forget the French Revolution). This last factor ought to be fresh in our minds because of a growing awareness about how costly it is trying to change long-ingrained, totalitarian societies in the Middle East into democracies. While from an ethical perspective I might be inclined toward a qualified type of democracy as a better social structure than monarchy or a monoreligious totalitarian society (and I am),[36] the movement toward democracy can be extremely messy. At what cost should we do this? At what pace? Any combination of these factors may explain why God *chooses* (contra Doriani) often to use an incremental ethic, especially at the level of the concrete, specific expression of his instructions.

Having made a case for the improbability of Kaiser's abolitionist reading of Philemon, I dearly wish I could include an entire essay on the delightful and logically inspiring (but only incremental) redemptive movement within that little Pauline letter. But I will have to save that for another time.

GOD BLESS THE BRITS!

Here is a weekend adventure into the topic of slavery that readers might enjoy. Watch the movie *Amistad* (about a Spanish slave ship that winds up on the shores of England) and a second, more recent movie, *Amazing Grace* (about British

---

36. It would be nice to have a democracy that evidences healthy collective qualities and a capitalism that is generous towards the poor (rather than rugged/isolated individualism and rampant greed).

Parliament member William Wilberforce, who courageously led the charge to rid England and the entire trading world of slavery). You will discover that there are strong *Christian* and *British* components to the abolition of the slave trade. Then sit down and read Mark Noll's new book on *The [American] Civil War as a Theological Crisis*. It describes a house pathetically divided about how contemporary ethical reflection ought to be derived from Scripture. What a mess!

Some things have not changed. Unfortunately, the mess of the unresolved slavery debates continues to pervade much of American theological reflection today. Within the United States there was no unified theological voice (rather a crisis and paralysis), so that ultimately it was the sovereign "accident" of U.S. military history and not vigorous theological reflection or a true vision of biblical authority that spread abolitionism across American soil. By slow osmosis, abolitionism has become the adopted norm for American evangelical church doctrine today but with little biblical or hermeneutical understanding of why. It is my hunch, and just a hunch, that many Americans have *still* not come to terms with how to cogently argue from Scripture for an abolitionist ethic. In a sense, American theology has not caught up with the accident of its history. (What would you expect from a Canadian, eh?)

Since we have all benefited from the legacy of British theology in bringing an abolitionist ethic to our North American context (a solid "going beyond" case in my mind—i.e., taking Scripture's redemptive spirit to a logically greater realization), perhaps we could find it in our hearts to give a Brit a bit of a break. I speak of I. Howard Marshall.[37] As far as I can see in reading Marshall's work, he clearly views the New Testament as the end of the canon. In fact, Marshall writes, *"The closing of the canon is not incompatible with the nonclosing of the interpretation of the canon"* (emphasis his).[38]

---

37. When I think of British evangelical theology, I. Howard Marshall and F. F. Bruce immediately come to mind. My own *Slaves, Women & Homosexuals* book is dedicated to the memory of F. F. Bruce and to Craig Blomberg—both of whom (an egalitarian and a hierarchalist) embrace a redemptive-movement hermeneutic.

38. Marshall, *Beyond the Bible*, 54.

The italics should have helped to place this statement in the forefront of any reader. I am not sure how Kaiser missed it.

From this single statement alone I would surmise that Marshall holds that (1) the canon is closed; (2) Christians are no longer in the process of producing canonical pronouncements; and (3) Christians today are, for whatever "development" means to Marshall, interpreting canonical texts in a manner that does not amount to a new canon or any sort of new revelation. In view of this understanding of Marshall, I would have wished for greater charity and clarity within Kaiser's closing section.

While I do not take the same approach as Marshall, I appreciate his efforts. In short, I would differ from Marshall's work in several ways. (1) I personally desire a greater emphasis on Jesus as the christological center of all Scripture, which is a little different from what I sense in Marshall's development. (2) My methods are far more broadly sweeping—that is, involving redemptive-movement meaning between ancient cultural contexts and the biblical text and involving canonical-movement meaning between the Old Testament and the New Testament; I do not focus on development between authors or smaller chronological pieces. (3) I do not try to duplicate the apostolic process (but I am open to discussing certain similarities while emphasizing significant differences as well). (4) I dare not venture into the sacred halls of systematic theology, as that is not at all my discipline (though I take my hat off to Marshall for his courageous crossing of those well-guarded lines).

So, unlike Marshall, I do not attempt to replicate the hermeneutics of the apostles. But as for understanding Marshall, I suspect that if he were writing in this volume, he would simply say that extensive similarity (sameness?) in methodology does not equal sameness in revelatory or canonical result. If so, then Kaiser's own "seminal ideas" discussion is a lot closer to Marshall than Kaiser himself might think.

For the sake of clarity I should say again that a RMH does *not* hold to continued revelation beyond the NT canon. Let me make that crystal clear. I direct readers to a discussion of this matter under my response to Doriani.

CONCLUSION

I wish again to thank Dr. Kaiser for having had a formative impact on my own thinking. The concept of *abstracted meaning* in the biblical text (I prefer this terminology) or principlizing with a sufficiently circumscribed method is an extremely helpful way of going beyond the Bible biblically, particularly where the two horizons (ancient and contemporary) are very different. I did not have an opportunity to develop what provisions I would add in order to circumscribe the principlizing method, since more weighty issues absorbed my response time. To my mind, both an exegetical and hermeneutical wrestling with the slavery texts is an important first step for Christians to be able to think and argue cogently about an abolitionist ethic.

While I applaud Kaiser's principlizing method in general, his exegetical reasoning within the Philemon letter is not at all persuasive. Simply put: *one cannot principlize abolitionism out of a nonabolitionist text using the Ladder of Abstraction.* Such an approach to Philemon rests on exegetical improbabilities and correspondingly skewed or ill-formed principles.[39]

---

39. Ironically, principlizing from the particulars of Philemon, as understood from a more probable nonabolitionist rendering, yields the "principles" for how the churches in Toronto (wrongly!) handled membership of runaway slaves who had come to Canada through the underground railway. See my response to Doriani. Neither a face value (Doriani) nor a principlizing (Kaiser) approach can persuasively derive abolitionism from Philemon.

CHAPTER TWO

A REDEMPTIVE-
HISTORICAL MODEL

Daniel M. Doriani

LAST YEAR, MY SWEET, BEAUTIFUL DAUGHTER put on a wedding dress and said "I do." Careful observers saw that day coming in time to consider the wedding itself. As we planned, we realized that society provided several scripts or prototypes for the event. The first prototype is the grand wedding, the society event, the blowout, with its display of the family's status. A subtype features the princess-tyrant who says, "This is my day to shine even if the price is a year's wage and woe to all who stand in my path."

The second prototype is the simple wedding, where bride and groom don suit and dress, gather a few friends, go to the chapel, and quietly begin a new life. One subtype is the destination wedding that blends the simplicity of a small guest list with the splendor of a beach or mountain setting.

Third, many parents pine for the minimalist past: "We got married for $700 in a borrowed suit and borrowed dress. We drank fruit punch and munched celery sticks at the reception. We've been married thirty years, so it must have worked."

The Bible certainly was not, in any essential way, written to determine the right way to celebrate a wedding.

75

Nonetheless, redemptive-historical theology, as I understand it, has the resources to guide believers to live righteously even as they decide how to celebrate their weddings or seek to navigate similar questions.

The flash of this work, if there is any, arrives with its efforts to apply thin or problematic biblical data to questions such as wedding celebrations, gambling, spanking, gender roles, and polygamy. But our first concern is method, so we must examine some theory before I disclose what happened at our wedding.

FOUNDATIONS FOR A REDEMPTIVE-HISTORICAL INTERPRETATION
INTERPRETATION AS TECHNICAL SKILL AND SPIRITUAL TASK

The interpretation and application of Scripture is a matter of technical skill, art, and personal commitment. The technical component requires knowledge of biblical languages and of Scripture's historical, cultural, and intellectual backgrounds. We call this enterprise grammatical-historical exegesis. As interpreters consider a text's literary styles, its forms of argumentation and rhetoric, the shift toward art begins. Interpretation proceeds through proper procedures and years of practice, ideally under the guidance of mentors and within a coherent community. Among evangelicals at least, the goal is to read Scripture, with all its contexts and structures, in order to discover the author's ideas.

In many ways, redemptive-historical interpretation resembles a close reading of ancient and authoritative texts, such as constitutional documents or even dense poetry. Yet there are differences. The redemptive-historical theologian (RHT) is, for this essay, an evangelical who affirms the verbal or plenary inspiration of Scripture. We assert the inerrancy, infallibility, sufficiency, progressive development, and christocentricity of the Bible. Because we believe Scripture has a divine Author who inspires the human author, the discovery of the first Author's message obligates the ideal reader to believe and do certain things as a result, even if that should prove difficult.

THE AUTHORITY OF SCRIPTURE

It is said that a listener once interrupted one of Hegel's sweeping theoretical discourses to protest, "But Herr Doctor Hegel, the facts are otherwise," to which Hegel allegedly replied, "So much the worse for the facts." The RHT is no Hegelian. Because the Bible, in the autographs, unfailingly conveys God's history, songs, prayers, commands, theological propositions, and commitments, the RHT knows interpretation is as much a spiritual as a technical task. The right interpreter will yield to whatever he or she discovers, whether (in the short run) that brings joy or sorrow. Since Scripture has God's very authority, interpreters should be humble and open to correction.

To read the Bible is not to dissect a lifeless text—mere marks on a page. As we read Scripture, it reads us. We come to it humbly, expecting to learn. Since we know our minds are finite and (worse) prone to self-interested distortion, we expect to be corrected when we read the Bible. We study Scripture closely to know the personal Lord by hearing his Word. If the Bible says something we dislike, we do not say "It can't be" or even "I wonder," but "I stand corrected." If Scripture says something I do not prefer, then so much the worse for my preferences.[1]

In a similar way, entire cultures or societies should be open to correction. For example, a slave culture will tend to ignore or explain away certain teachings about the human race. Since every culture has strengths and weaknesses, insights and blind spots, we expect Scripture to correct every culture, including our own. The same applies to theological systems. We cannot claim such confidence in our theology that we exclude or explain away whatever fails to support it.

THE SUFFICIENCY OF SCRIPTURE

Redemptive-historical interpretation affirms the sufficiency of Scripture. Paul said, "The holy Scriptures ... are able to make you wise for salvation through faith in Christ Jesus. All

---

1. Daniel Doriani, *Putting the Truth to Work: The Theory and Practice of Biblical Application* (Phillipsburg, NJ: Presbyterian & Reformed, 2001), 62–67.

Scripture is God-breathed and is useful for teaching, rebuking, correcting and training in righteousness, so that the man of God may be thoroughly equipped for every good work" (2 Tim. 3:15–17). If Scripture is and does all this, we need nothing more. And there is nothing more. As Jude said, the faith "was once for all entrusted to us, his people" (Jude 3).

The RHT also believes the Bible regards itself as a document marked by finality. This is evident in many places. Moses surely believed that the covenant and law he delivered in Deuteronomy 4–11 was a sufficient guide for Israel's life in Canaan. The gospel writers also believed they gave the Christian community all it needed for faith, salvation, discipleship, and obedience (Matt. 28:18–20; John 20:31; 21:25). Matthew wrote self-referentially: In his final charge, Jesus said, "Make disciples ... teaching them to obey everything I have commanded you." If readers wanted to know how to do this, they could reread his gospel.

Of course, Scripture is not sufficient in the sense that it tells us everything we need to know. Farmers and engineers must study the physical and technological world, athletes must know the rules and techniques of their game, fathers must know their children, and theologians need their lexicons, grammars, and histories. But we need no God-given revelation beyond the biblical canon.

This concept of the sufficiency of Scripture finds strong expression in the Westminster Confession of Faith 1:6: "The whole counsel of God concerning all things necessary for His own glory, man's salvation, faith and life, is either expressly set down in Scripture, or by good and necessary consequence may be deduced from Scripture." After a fashion, this volume debates that claim: Does Scripture contain everything necessary for "faith and life"? Should we take this, and 2 Timothy 3, to mean the Bible offers sufficient guidance for every moral or spiritual question?

Yes and no. No, the Bible is not a legal code that minutely prescribes the proper action in vexed cases such as end-of-life medical care or the arcana of copyright protection. Indeed, minute prescription is rare in Scripture. Furthermore, the more specific the prescription, the less likely that it will apply directly today. Specific case laws about goring oxen, the sons of less-loved wives in polygamous families,

.and meat sacrificed to idols illustrate the limits of minute prescription and suggest why it is uncommon (Ex. 21:28–30; Deut. 21:15–17; 1 Cor. 10:27–30). So, no, the Bible is not a book of minute legal prescriptions.

But yes, the Bible does provides sufficient direction "for every good work" if we meditate on it wisely. Vanhoozer compares the Bible to a script that expects actors to improvise within the parameters set by playwright and director; in that regard, it contains sufficient direction for believers to speak and act faithfully. Again, it is like a collection of maps, interpretive frameworks of reality that enable disciples to live faithfully.[2]

Scripture is sufficient in the sense that it accomplishes all that God intends, that his people should "love the LORD ... and walk in all his ways" (Deut. 11:22; 30:16; 1 Kings 8:58; Pss. 86:11; 89:15; Rom. 4:12). It provides guidance sufficient for faithful living. Skeptical scholars explicitly deny this.[3] But evangelicals who appeal to the "trajectory" of Scripture appear to deny it implicitly. When dealing with topics such as gender roles, hell, or homosexuality, they point out the constraints placed on the authors of the texts we have—such as unusual local contexts, immature audiences who could not bear the whole truth—and conclude we cannot take Scripture at face value. Of course, some revelation is partial and some contexts are unusual. The problem arises when trajectory analysts try to guess what Scripture would have said next—about gender or hell or whatever—if there had been more revelation.

Someone once told me, "We don't know what Paul would say if he were alive today." That is true, but moot. No one knows what he *would* say. But we do know what he *did* say, and we know Scripture itself says its content equips believers for every good work.[4]

---

2. Kevin Vanhoozer, *The Drama of Doctrine: A Canonical Linguistic Approach to Christian Theology* (Louisville: Westminster John Knox, 2005), 295–97.

3. I use the term "skeptical" rather than "critical" to denote biblical scholars who deny the Bible's veracity. As Bob Yarbrough notes, we all aim to be critical thinkers.

4. C. S. Lewis imagines a theologian in hell, but still theologizing, wondering what Jesus would have said—how he might have matured!—if his life hadn't been cut short at such an early age. See *The Great Divorce* (New York: Collier, 1946), 46.

If Scripture is sufficient, then *the Bible contains what God wants it to contain.* God does not gaze ruefully at the church and its canon and long for what might have been. God does not think:

- if only historical circumstances had not required Jesus to accommodate his teaching to the views of his age,
- if only circumstances had allowed Paul to write in a setting free from prejudices,
- if only the Gentile churches had been more mature,

the apostles could have said what needed to be said. But alas, there was no opportunity to label which teachings were temporary concessions and which were permanent! Now if my people are to discover the truth about slavery, gender, homosexuality, war, and hell, I can only hope that they follow the trajectories of the books they have and realize where they lead.

THE CLARITY OF SCRIPTURE

The paragraph above leads us to consider whether the Bible clearly says everything God wants us to believe. While the Bible itself concedes that parts of it are obscure (Matt. 13:10–17; 2 Peter 3:16), orthodox theologians have long affirmed that Scripture does clearly state the fundamentals of faith and life. But some evangelicals seem to hesitate to affirm the clarity of Scripture. For example in *Beyond the Bible*, I. H. Marshall says this about hell: "The imagery used by Jesus is sometimes what his audience would understand, but this accommodation may lead to misunderstanding."[5] That is, "in a number of parables spoken by Jesus the protagonist condemns unworthy servants to horrendous fates." Marshall finds such imagery unacceptable: "There would be universal agreement among civilized people that no human being should perpetrate horrors of the kind in the parabolic imagery."[6] This remark certainly appears to undermine the

---

5. I. H. Marshall, *Beyond the Bible: Moving from Scripture to Theology* (Grand Rapids: Baker, 2004), 66.
6. Ibid., 66–67.

authority of Scripture insofar as Marshall hints that the consensus of "civilized people" rules out certain biblical teachings. We wonder who these "civilized people" might be?[7] Marshall and his peers perhaps?

But Marshall also seems to undercut the clarity of Scripture when he tries to say that Jesus does not subscribe to the barbaric behavior of the people in his parables. Jesus merely created a parabolic "protagonist" who used horrific images. Yet if the parable's imagery for divine punishment is insufferable, then what is it saying? Marshall affirms "the reality of divine judgment." But after he says we must use "the mind of Christ" to rule out a literal interpretation of the words of Christ, he fails to say what the proper interpretation of the parable's language is.[8] Marshall suggests that we certainly cannot take Jesus' statements about hell at face value.

The evangelical egalitarian Craig Keener also seems to deny that Scripture is clear enough that we can take it at face value. Commenting on Ephesians 5, Keener says Paul commanded women to submit to their husbands not because he genuinely advocated it, but "because he was smart."[9] He had to show his Greco-Roman readers that Christianity upholds the social order.[10] But Paul "subordinates wives so weakly ... that it is difficult to believe that he is arguing for their transcultural subordination."[11] So Paul's instructions are a temporary measure to make Christianity sound inoffensive: "Paul is responding to a specific cultural issue for the sake of the gospel, and *his words should not be taken at face value* in all cultures." Paul only asked women "in his day"

---

7. The appeal to the mind of civilized people may be read as a sign of broad-mindedness, but if we ask "Whose definition of 'civilized people'" we see that it can mask another form of provincialism.

8. Ibid., 67. His massive *New Testament Theology* (Downers Grove, IL: InterVarsity Press, 2004), with one glancing reference to hell on p.559, sheds no light on the question.

9. Craig Keener, *Paul, Women and Wives* (Peabody, MA: Hendrickson, 1992), 139.

10. Ibid., 144–47.

11. Ibid., 169–70. I cannot see why Keener thinks the nuance in Paul's call to subordination makes it "difficult to believe" that he meant his words to apply transculturally.

to conform "to the general social ideal without fighting it."[12] Thus Keener thinks Paul did not believe he was free — on this or any other occasion! — to write what he truly believed. Since Keener is committed to the *authority* of Scripture, he has taken the only path that is open to him as an egalitarian scholar: he denies its *clarity*.

Similarly, John Stackhouse says: "It is abundantly clear that there are hierarchies in the church and in the home in the … New Testament. The complementarians are simply right about that."[13] Stackhouse then cites seventeen "complementarian" passages. But, he explains, the Spirit was simply giving the church "prudent instruction as to how to survive in a patriarchal culture that he thinks will not last long."[14] Because it was intent on spreading the gospel, the early church simply went along with its patriarchal culture to avoid scandal. Thus, the biblical teaching on gender and on slavery are the same. Slavery is absolutely wrong, but the Bible didn't say so, because the church would have to wait to overthrow it at the right time.[15]

Here our commitment to follow Scripture wherever it leads may be helpful, for close exegetical study shows that the analogy between slavery and patriarchy fails because it overlooks crucial facts. Paul flatly tells slaves, "If you can gain your freedom, do so" (1 Cor. 7:21).[16] Further, he directly forbids free Christians to become slaves: "Do not become

---

12. Ibid., 171. Emphasis mine. Keener believes Paul's summons to mutual submission rules out male leadership.

13. John Stackhouse, *Finally Feminist* (Grand Rapids: Baker, 2005), 50.

14. Ibid., 51–54.

15. Ibid., 55–60.

16. A few scholars render the verse differently. Literally, the Greek says, "But if you are able to become free, rather make use [of it]." Some say Paul wanted slaves to make use of their slavery, not their freedom, by remaining slaves and making the best use of it. The rationale: Paul generally urges the Corinthians to stay where they are in chapter 7. But this is untenable: (1) The sections for singles and marrieds state exceptions to the principle of staying put (7:9, 15); this is the exception for slaves. (2) "Make use [of it]" is an ellipsis, to be completed from the context. The nearest noun is "freedom," in the immediately preceding phrase. Therefore, make use of freedom is correct. (3) The Bible often commends liberation of slaves; only Exodus 21:6 considers voluntary continuation in it.

slaves of men" (7:23; the context shows that he means literal, not spiritual, slavery). And Paul's letter to Philemon (11–21) seeks to persuade the slave owner to free Onesimus. Paul's opposition to slavery is not stated in the form of a frontal assault on the institution, but he clearly wants Christians to avoid or escape it if they can.

But when we come to gender roles, we see nothing like this testimony about slavery. No passage tells women to avoid the trap of patriarchal marriage or to escape it if they can. There is no parallel between slavery and male leadership. The parallel is between male leadership of marriage and parental leadership of children. Both are grounded in creation. Both continue after the fall—supplemented by instructions that rein in potential abuses of power (Deut. 24:1–4, 21:15–18; Eph. 5:25–30, 6:4).[17] Both are reaffirmed after Christ accomplishes redemption.

Meanwhile, frankly skeptical biblical scholars affirm the clarity of Scripture in their own way. They think Paul did mean what he said, that his words mean precisely what they seem, that Paul is dangerously wrong, and that he must therefore be opposed.[18] One of this book's coauthors, William Webb, appears to agree with Marshall, Keener, and Stackhouse when he writes:

> What we should live out in our modern culture, however, is not the isolated or "on the page" words of the text but the redemptive spirit that the text reflects as read against its original culture. In applying the text to

---

17. Stackhouse rightly says, "Jesus presses against the gender expectations of his day ... without actually overturning them" in *Finally Feminist*, 40. Jesus was a reformer, not a revolutionary.

18. See, e.g., Elizabeth Schüssler Fiorenza, *Bread Not Stone: The Challenge of Biblical Egalitarian Interpretation* (Boston: Beacon, 1984); Luke Timothy Johnson, *The First and Second Letters to Timothy* (New York: Doubleday, 2001), 206–11. See especially Francis Watson in "Strategies of Recovery and Resistance: Hermeneutical Reflections on Genesis 1–3 and Its Pauline Reception," *Journal for the Study of the New Testament* 14:45 (1992): 79–103. He notes (87–91) that egalitarian interpreters sometimes try to "recover" the true meaning of a text but concludes that even if there is some uncertainty about the precise meaning of Genesis 1–3, "recovery" is finally "a lost cause" so that it is best to "resist" Paul's teaching.

our era, we don't want to stay static with the words of
the text. Rather we need to move on, beyond the text.[19]

Several scholars seem therefore to agree that if we simply
read the words of the biblical text, we do not necessarily find
the mind of God. Webb decries "static" readings of "isolated
texts."[20] At a formal level, the redemptive-historical exegete
agrees. But Webb and others want to trace the arc of movement through and *beyond* the biblical text or canon, while
the RHT seeks to trace movements *within* the canon. We do
not deny that biblical authors accommodate to their culture.
Indeed, we affirm that God's self-revelation unfolds through
the covenants over a period of centuries, sometimes because
God's people could not receive all the truth at once. But we
also affirm that the revelation is sufficient, clear, and complete at the close of the canon.

Those who imply that the canonical writers were so constrained by their age and audience that we lack sufficient
direction on vital matters say more, in the end, about their
view of God than about their view of Scripture. They deny
that the Lord had the capacity to say what he wished before
the canon closed. He lacked the power to overcome local
conditions. Therefore he could never fully state his will
before the apostolic age ended.

THE REDEMPTIVE-HISTORICAL METHOD AND ITS WAY BEYOND THE SACRED PAGE

STEP 1: CLOSE, ACCURATE INTERPRETATION

The first aim of a redemptive-historical interpreter is to
read Scripture closely and accurately. Calvin rightly said
the chief virtue of an interpreter is "lucid brevity." Further,
"since almost his only responsibility is to lay open the mind
of the writer whom he has undertaken to explain, to the
degree that he leads his readers away from it, he goes astray

---

19. William Webb, *Slaves, Women & Homosexuals: Exploring the Hermeneutics of Cultural Analysis* (Downers Grove, IL: InterVarsity Press, 2001), 33.
20. Ibid., 33–37.

from his own purpose."[21] However interesting the reader's questions, however interesting the author's subpoints, the search for the author's main point is the first task.

The RHT is, therefore, fully committed to reading the Bible in context in every sense of the word. We attend to the immediately surrounding verses, the entire book, and the corpus of men like Moses, Luke, and Paul. We examine the cultural-historical milieu. We labor over the structure of a passage and its grammar, syntax, and lexical features. We also consider its genre—narrative, law, prophecy, visions, wisdom, or epistle—knowing that each genre has its sub-types and each one has its modes of expression.

STEP 2: SYNTHESIS OF BIBLICAL DATA

When RHTs synthesize biblical data into doctrinal or ethical statements, we proceed inductively, paying close attention to its place in redemptive history. After all, Jesus himself said that Moses made concessions to the capacity of his hearers, so that the full disclosure of God's plan came later (Matt. 19:3–12). Therefore we shun flat, decontextualized use of "Bible verses" and consider the way biblical concepts develop, whether in bursts or slowly and organically.

Still, RHTs do not claim that we simply read while everyone else adds their system. Like other interpreters, we seek master texts to guide our reading. Like almost all evangelicals, we believe that there is unity within the diversity of Scripture. We believe that God's plan of redemption for the nations through the line of Abraham is the unifying theme of Scripture (e.g., Gen. 3:16; 12:1–3; 22:18; 26:2–5; 2 Sam. 7:1–17; Ps. 132:11–18). The Gospels self-consciously describe the fulfillment of that promise. John selected his materials and wrote that his readers might "believe that Jesus is the Christ" and so "have life in his name" (John 20:31). Luke wrote so that "repentance and forgiveness of

---

21. John Calvin, "Epistle Dedicatory" (to Simon Grynaeus) in *Epistle to the Romans*, trans. by Henry Beveridge (Grand Rapids: Baker, 2003), xxiii. See also John L. Thompson, "Calvin as a Biblical Interpreter," in *The Cambridge Companion to John Calvin*, ed. Donald McKim (New York: Cambridge Univ. Press, 2004), 60.

sin will be preached" in Jesus' name to all nations, for Moses and all the prophets say the Christ must "suffer these things and then enter his glory" after rising from the dead (Luke 24:25–27, 45–47). These and similar passages, located at climactic moments in the Gospels, lead us to believe redemption through the Lord Jesus is the unifying theme within the diversity of Scripture.

STEP 3: APPLICATION OF SCRIPTURE

As we seek to establish the meaning of Scripture, we inevitably consider its application to daily life. Unlike a few members of my school, I maintain that the imitation of God / imitation of Christ motif pervades Scripture and is a leading source of ethical guidance (e.g., Gen. 1:27; Matt. 10:24–25; Mark 8:34; Luke 6:40; John 13:14–15; Acts 4:13; Rom. 8:29; Eph. 4:24; 5:1–2; Phil. 2:1–11). Since the character of God — his love, justice, righteousness, and patience — is supremely manifest in the death-resurrection nexus, the redemptive focus of Scripture produces guidance for the Christian life. It promotes the character that is the core of all action.[22] Of course, mere creatures cannot attempt to imitate God's character and action in every way. Yet we have a point of departure for any attempt to live beyond the sacred page: the Bible is the narrative of God's action, accomplished in Christ and applied by the Spirit, to redeem a people to be reconciled to him and conformed to his image.[23]

STEP 4: ADJUSTING A TRADITIONAL VIEW OF APPLICATION

In the last three paragraphs I barely diverged from standard Bible interpretation. But I do believe we can constructively go beyond the sacred page if we make more use of biblical narratives. A standard statement declares, "Unless Scripture

---

22. Doriani, *Putting the Truth to Work*, 46–47, 201–7.

23. Some RHTs so stress the centrality of God and redemption that any move to draw moral lessons from biblical narratives is viewed as moralism and a betrayal of the principle of God-centered reading. See S. G. De Graaf, *Promise and Deliverance*, trans. by H. E. Runner (Phillipsburg, NJ: Presbyterian & Reformed, 1977), 17–23; Geerhardus Vos, *Biblical Theology* (Grand Rapids: Eerdmans, 1948), 18.

explicitly tells us we must do something, what is merely narrated can never function in a normative way."[24] Of course, heedless imitation of narrative causes problems. But why should ethical assertions have priority over narrative? The principle itself is extrabiblical.

More important, the Bible doesn't *have* narratives, it *is* a narrative. Why then should narrative supply less data for theology or ethics than any other genre?[25] Since the prophets and apostles constantly draw conclusions about covenantal living from narrative, we could argue that narrative is foundational and ethics derivative. As Christopher Wright says, the character of God, revealed in narrative, teaches believers how to walk in the ways of the Lord.[26] When narratives show that God's actions demonstrate imitable attributes, we surely should imitate them.

Narrative shows us what moral excellence means. Consider the statement, "God is compassionate" (cf. Ps. 86:15), and the command, "Be ... compassionate to one another" (Eph. 4:32). The doctrinal statement can hardly take precedence over narratives manifesting God's compassion. We discover what "God is compassionate" means through narratives. Jesus' compassion moved him to heal and feed people (Matt. 9:36; 14:14; 15:32; 20:34). Thus, the narratives demonstrate what "God is compassionate" and "Be compassionate" mean.

The same holds for other facets of God's character. Indeed, we could argue that the narrative of Jesus' life can precede the doctrinal statement: "While we were still sinners, Christ died for us" (Rom. 5:8). At a minimum, narratives, doctrinal discourses, and ethical demands are mutually defining.[27] This is not to deny the value of propositional truth; it is to remember that revelation comes in many forms. Alongside

---

24. Gordon D. Fee and Douglas Stuart, *How to Read the Bible for All Its Worth* (Grand Rapids: Zondervan, 1982), 97.

25. A point Craig Blomberg makes and practices in *Neither Poverty nor Riches* (Grand Rapids: Eerdmans, 1999), 163.

26. Christopher Wright, *Living as the People of God* (Downers Grove, IL: InterVarsity Press, 1983), 26ff.; idem, *Old Testament Ethics for the People of God* (Downers Grove, IL: InterVarsity Press, 2004), 24–47.

27. Doriani, *Putting the Truth to Work*, 193ff.

propositions, the Bible "contains commands, questions, exclamations, promises, vows, threats and curses."[28] Why should doctrinal propositions and direct ethical imperatives gain primacy over other modes of revelation?

This has implications for the call to go beyond the Bible. If narratives present paradigmatic individuals whom the faithful should emulate or avoid, then we have guidance for proper conduct in areas that direct teaching never covers. And narratives do portray paradigmatic individuals. Scripture instructs readers to learn from acts of faithfulness or unfaithfulness described in narratives.

For example, Hebrews 10:35–12:2 reviews the lives of old covenant heroes in order to exhort the church to run the difficult race set before it. Likewise, Paul tells the Corinthians to learn from Israel's rebellion in the wilderness: "Now these things occurred as examples.... [Therefore] do not be idolaters ... and do not grumble, as some of them did" (1 Cor. 10:6–10). The Gospels also commend and condemn characters as they respond to Jesus. Matthew praised several agents in his narrative: the centurion of unparalleled faith (Matt. 8:5–10), the persistent Syro-Phonecian mother (15:21–28), and the woman who anointed Jesus in Bethany (26:6–13). Luke praises the faithful and blames the faithless in the accounts of a paralytic and his friends (Luke 5:17–26) and of the healing of ten lepers (17:11–19). He chides his host for a cool reception at one dinner (7:36–50) and praises a warm one at another (10:38–42). Although most narratives let readers draw their own conclusions, few offer no hints to guide assessment.[29]

This principle lets us responsibly go beyond the sacred page. For example, when a government produces a critical mass of flawed policies and moral lapses, Christians ask: "Is it possible for a Christian to work for that government?" In business, they ask: "Can I work for a major media corporation that is generally constructive, but also produces some salacious or degrading programs? For an advertising agency

---

28. John Frame, *The Doctrine of the Knowledge of God* (Phillipsburg, NJ: Presbyterian & Reformed, 1987), 200–201; see also Vanhoozer, *Drama of Doctrine*, 87–91, 278–81.

29. For example, Matt. 14:13–21; 15:32–39; 17:1–8 make no editorial comment.

whose leading client is a brewer? For a software designer charged with enhancing the profitability of state lotteries? For a pharmacy that distributes abortifacients?"

No law addresses these questions, but there is a clear narrative pattern. Israelites often worked, with God's blessing, for pagans—Joseph for Pharaoh, Daniel for Nebuchadnezzar and Belshazzar, Nehemiah for Artaxerxes—or for godless Israelites (Obadiah for Ahab). Therefore withdrawal is not mandatory. Yet we cannot take every post. Joseph served one pharaoh, to save lives, but Moses refused to serve another, who took lives. Daniel and his friends discovered how risky it is to work for godless kings and refuse them total obedience (Dan. 3:1–30; 6:4–24), as did Obadiah (1 Kings 18:7–12).

The principle is clear: Where a series of acts by the faithful create a pattern, and God or the narrator approves the pattern, it directs believers, even if no law spells out the lesson.[30] For our project, the capacity of narrative to guide believers suggests another way to go beyond the sacred page and to address issues that never attract the direct interest of Scripture. As for our questions about work, we see that believers may labor in compromised settings, if they can effect good and resist evil from their post.

WEDDINGS REVISITED

So, can the Bible teach us to how to celebrate a wedding? Apparently not, for no passage tells us how to do so. Yet we are not directionless, largely because of certain narratives. Clearly, if we "love our neighbors as ourselves" and "count others more significant" than ourselves, as Christ did (Phil. 2:3), we can rule out the princess-tyrant and the pecunious but penny-pinching paterfamilias because their agendas are selfish.

Can we say more? Apparently not, for three reasons. First, no passage has the form for wedding celebrations as its central interest. Second, some say we must never make the incidental features of a passage the focal point of our

---

30. As the case of Gideon and the fleece illustrates, acts that are isolated or disapproved cannot have normative value.

teaching. That leads to the legalism that reads our wise counsel into a passage, then passes it off as biblical mandate.[31] Third, a focus on incidentals leads to arbitrary, senseless imitation of biblical characters (wearing robes, traveling by foot).

Because we are committed to the discovery of the author's intended meaning through grammatical-historical exegesis, RHTs feel the weight of these arguments. Besides, we have seen the sour result when a secondary point of the text becomes the primary point of a sermon.

Nonetheless, as an absolute, "One must not make the secondary point of a passage the primary point of a sermon" cannot stand, for Jesus himself "violated" this principle on several occasions. In Matthew 12:1–4, Jesus (applying a narrative!) finds that David's action in taking consecrated bread reveals the principle that God desires "mercy, not sacrifice," and that is by no means the main point of 1 Samuel 21. In Matthew 22:29–32 Jesus cites Exodus 3 when he tells the Sadducees that they missed the truth about the resurrection in part because they failed to attend properly to verb tenses: "I *am* the God of Abraham" rather than "I *was* the God of Abraham." Thus Jesus makes a minor point from Exodus into his main point.

Evangelical interpreters and homileticians should agree: We must not articulate principles that put us in the right and Jesus in the wrong. Therefore we should admit the role of biblical models, even if they are secondary features of a passage.

In the case of weddings, longstanding church practice agrees. For centuries, Christian weddings have used a secondary feature of John 2 in a normative way when Christians notice that Jesus honored marriage by attending a wedding at Cana (John 2). Actually, he did more than attend; he promoted the festivities. If the narrative of Christ's life provides a model for ours, we have a potent clue about the right way to celebrate weddings. The way to celebrate is not "expressly set down in Scripture," but Westminster 1:6 rightly leads us to seek something that "by good and necessary consequence may be deduced from [it]."

---

31. Haddon Robinson, "The Heresy of Application," *Leadership* 18:3 (Fall 1997): 21–22.

Weddings appear tangentially about fifteen times in the Bible. Weddings are a time of "gladness of heart" and "mirth" (Song 3:11; Jer. 7:34; 16:9; 25:10), a time for processions and feasting (Judg. 14:10–14; Matt. 25:1–13; Luke 12:35–36; 14:8). Biblical weddings feature an adorned bride (Rev. 21:2; cf. Eph. 5:27) and love songs (Ps. 78:63). Jesus assumes that weddings feature a feast (Matt. 9:15; Mark 2:19; Luke 5:34). Sometimes the wedding feast lasted a week (Judg. 14:12–17; probably Gen. 29:27; but these cases derive from flawed weddings, possibly limiting their probative value). In biblical weddings, friends and family gather for a feast, with music and joyful celebration, before bride and groom go off to bed (Gen. 29:22–23; Deut. 22:13ff.).

Is this normative? The characters in biblical narratives and the authors of biblical texts certainly assume that weddings feature celebration. Moreover, they reason from that assumption. It could be, however, that our texts simply acknowledge a fallen or neutral human custom. But no, our pattern holds through creation, fall, redemption, and restoration. At creation, Adam and Eve rejoiced at their union. When he met Eve, Adam burst into poetry: "This is now bone of my bones" (Gen. 2:23). Again, Jesus did not just attend a wedding, he supplied fine wine to promote the festivity (John 2:1–12). The Lord even chose to describe the inauguration of eternity as the wedding feast of the Lamb (Rev. 19:7–9; 21:9).

This pattern certainly doesn't tell us exactly what to do. We may not even have any categorical imperatives. For example, it may be a blessed custom, yet not mandatory, to celebrate with a feast, especially if a family is poor.[32] Still, the biblical data seems to rule out two extremes. First, the identification of a wedding with joy and feasting shows that however disordered the wedding-industrial complex may be, the primary goal of the paying parties is not to control costs. Weddings call for celebration. Second, the strong participation of groom, families, and community, not to mention the Bible's opposition to egoism, forbid domination by a princess-tyrant. At a wedding, therefore, family and friends

---

32. Scripture makes concessions for the poor. See the laws on substituting doves for lambs.

should gather for feasting, joy, and song. After that, we can improvise.

Since wedding practices vary widely from culture to culture, interested parties can appraise their culture's practices critically yet fondly. In our family's case, everyone agreed to avoid the forms of commercialization that can make weddings a financial and logistical burden. We also agreed that, just now, weddings have probably become bloated in part as a compensation our culture has settled on: since premarital cohabitation is the norm, lifestyle hardly changes. Therefore, amplify the party!

So we had reasons to shun excess. But we also wanted to have a party or two so everyone could eat, drink, and dance ("And not just one song, Dad!"). So we embraced a robust celebration and did not resent paying for it.

The Bible never squarely addresses our issue, never prescribes the way to celebrate a marriage, but it does describe enough weddings to offer real guidance. We avoid the miser and the princess-tyrant and celebrate, drawing on historical accounts and on images of feasting and song. This is not standard grammatical-historical interpretation, but it is plausible redemptive-historical exegesis that goes beyond the sacred page. If we now have at least some idea of the way RHTs go beyond Scripture, it is wise to consider how other theologians do it.

SURVEY: HOW THEOLOGIANS GO BEYOND THE SACRED PAGE
CONSTRUCTIVE WAYS TO GO BEYOND THE SACRED PAGE

The phrase "beyond the sacred page" sounds somewhat like an I. H. Marshall title, *Beyond the Bible*. In it, Marshall says he searches for ways to go beyond the Bible in a biblical way. He observes that while the canon is closed, "the interpretation of that canon" is not, so that the "development of doctrine and practice" continues.[33] But there is more than one way to go beyond the Bible in doctrine and practice, and

---

33. Marshall, *Beyond the Bible*, 48, 54–55.

some are more benign than others. First, a theologian may use formulations that go beyond biblical language to enunciate latent theological ideas more clearly. Thus, we speak of the Trinity and of substitutionary atonement, although these precise phrases never appear in Scripture. Such terms accurately summarize biblical teaching, often in the face of heresy. This is constructive.[34]

Second, we go "beyond the Bible" when we seek answers to questions the Bible never addresses or never addresses in their current form. For example, the Bible addresses church government but not formulations for books of church order. It tackles gender roles but not in the form of each culture's urgent questions. For example, in many times and places, men have asked if they should physically discipline their wives.[35] Today that question seems absurd. We debate the way husbands and wives should collaborate in domestic duties; in other places and times that question would seem absurd. We may also go beyond the Bible when we apply it to questions that could not arise in the past—when we apply "You shall not steal" not to sheep but to intellectual and digital property.

GOING BEYOND SCRIPTURE IN THE SENSE OF GOING AGAINST IT

But there is another way to go "beyond" the Bible, or any authoritative source, and that is to go against it. Comedian Gilda Radner went beyond/against the conventions of humor when she told this story to an audience that knew she was dying of ovarian cancer:

> A woman with cancer sees her oncologist, who says, "Well, I'm afraid we're finally at the end of the line. You only have eight hours to live. Go home and make the best of it."
> The woman goes home, gives the news to her husband, and says, "Honey, let's just make love to each other all night long."
> The husband says, "You know how sometimes you're in the mood for sex and sometimes you aren't?

---

34. Ibid., 42–43.

35. In 1620, the Protestant William Whately still said yes in *A Bride Bush* (London, 1617, 1623) and *Care Cloth* (London, 1624).

Well, I'm just not in the mood tonight."

"Please," his wife pleads. "It's my final wish, darling."

"I just don't feel like it," the husband says.

"I beg you, darling!"

"Look, it's easy for you to say. You don't have to get up in the morning."[36]

The story seems more interested in forcing people to contemplate death than in amusing them. Contemplation of death is a worthy goal, but hardly a typical aim of comedy. Yet a debate could emerge. Some people think the joke is funny. Besides, it might appeal to one strand in the tradition of comedy: the jester as truth-teller. Similarly, Rembrandt went beyond/against his day's conventions of portraiture.

Some evangelicals apparently want to go beyond Scripture in the sense that Rembrandt and Radner "go beyond." As we saw, Marshall finds graphic language about God's punishment intolerable and hints the concept is too: "We can no longer think of God that way" — even if the imagery comes from Jesus. Marshall believes he knows how to escape these images: "a mind nurtured by the Spirit, the mind of Christ" or "a mind nurtured on the gospel" can enable Christians to "go beyond the Bible at certain points" and yet do so in a biblical way.[37]

How can an evangelical Christian go beyond/against Jesus' words? Marshall appeals to "a combination of the apostolic deposit and Spirit-given insight." This can "promote true development in Christian doctrine and practice."[38] Therefore, Christians can no longer advocate genocide or slavery, as the Bible seems to do, and can no longer exclude "women from some forms of ministry." Such teachings "are no longer binding on Christians today in their original form."[39]

In important ways, this is unexceptional. Self-identified Christians, whom orthodox evangelicals typically call liber-

---

36. Thomas Cathcart and Daniel Klein, *Plato and a Platypus Walk into a Bar: Understanding Philosophy through Jokes* (New York: Abrams Image, 2006), 124–35.

37. Marshall, *Beyond the Bible*, 45–48, 66–70.

38. Ibid., 71.

39. Ibid., 35–37.

als, critics, or skeptics, have rejected biblical teachings for centuries. It is certainly common to question the biblical teaching on slavery. On slavery, we must observe that the Bible never commands or endorses it. Rather Moses' law tolerated it, regulated it, restrained its worst features, and (ordinarily) limited its duration to six years.[40] But we take note when an evangelical, who affirms the authority of Scripture, says he must use the mind of Christ to go beyond/against the words of Christ. Marshall is not alone.

A self-identified evangelical, Bart Campolo, stated his position on difficult biblical concepts in bold terms. Campolo declared that he has misgivings about "God's sovereignty, wrath, hell" — especially the idea that people "are going to hell because they failed to believe the right stuff" about Jesus. Indeed, if the doctrine of hell is valid, "then God might as well send me to Hell ... I am a free agent, after all, and I have standards for my God, the first of which is this: I will not worship any God who is not at least as compassionate as I am." He explained, "I required no Bible to determine [this], and — honestly — I will either interpret away or ignore altogether any Bible verse that suggests otherwise."[41] Campolo is aggressive in his willingness to say that "the Bible is wrong." This is one way to go beyond the Bible.

GOING BEYOND SCRIPTURE BY APPEALING TO ARCS AND TRAJECTORIES

The tone and explicit commitments may be different, but evangelicals who appeal to the arc, trajectory, or movement of Scripture appear to go beyond Scripture in a similar way. Christian feminists in particular are apt to appeal to the trajectories of biblical teaching. The reasoning may go like this:

---

40. Perhaps we wish the Bible had explicitly called for its termination. It is not our place to guess why the Bible did not say what we wish, but we can note that slavery was an all but universal human phenomenon until roughly two centuries ago. In that context, many called for reform of slavery, but no one called for abolition of the institution. See Thomas Sowell, *Black Rednecks and White Liberals* (San Francisco: Encounter, 2005), 111–69.

41. Bart Campolo, "The Limits of God's Grace," *The Journal of Student Ministries* 1:3 (September/October 2006): 1–4.

We cannot linger over every obscure passage in Leviticus specifying punishments for the abuse of betrothed slave girls (Lev. 19:20–22). If a particular passage such as 1 Timothy 2, found late in the Pauline corpus, seems to restrict women, then it is fraught with such difficulties as to be incomprehensible. Or it is directed at local, temporary problems.[42] Such problems cannot obscure the Bible's trajectory toward liberation.

Tracing the trajectory of Scripture is judged superior to swapping proof texts, which, everyone knows, is no way to read the Bible. But opposition to proof texting is hardly adventurous. Indeed, the appeal to trajectories over proof texting looks like an attempt at victory by definition: we follow the progress of ideas; you grab ideas out of context to "prove" what you already believe.

But it is all too easy to toss the accusation of "proof texting" on what may be the fruit of painstaking exegesis. Besides, when we tackle biblical teaching that appears to counter contemporary sensibilities, we should discern the trajectory of Scripture inductively, studying one text at a time. A hasty appeal to trajectories may tempt us to smooth out unexpected bumps in the biblical data.[43]

Analysis of trajectories also founders on human ignorance. If we had exhaustive knowledge of the economy, we could predict the future. If erroneous economic forecasts cause trouble, how much greater the peril to guess what the apostles might have said about hell, gender roles, or homosexuality if they were writing today. Indeed the conclusion of Revelation warns against such things (Rev. 22:18–19). Moreover, if trajectory analysis exaggerates our knowledge, it also minimizes God's power. As we saw, it implies that God would have said something more acceptable—to modern sensibilities—but circumstances made it impossible.

Herman Ridderbos has shown that when Jesus entered history, he called, trained, and commissioned the apostles to be

---

42. See Susan Sumner, *Men and Women in the Church* (Downers Grove, IL: InterVarsity Press, 2003), 207ff.; Keener, *Paul, Women and Wives*, 111–15, respectively.

43. Trajectories are rarely smooth in ordinary life. Consider how we might chart the progress of a marriage, an economy, defeat of an addiction, or the growth of a church.

his agents, to record what happened and what it signified.[44] We have the canon that God intended and that the church needs.

CONSTRUCTIVE WAYS TO GO BEYOND THE SACRED PAGE, REVISITED

What then shall we do when we encounter difficult teachings? What if the topic is hell or the conquest of Canaan—a divinely sanctioned total war? First, the idea that something is unthinkable is better suited to the start than to the conclusion of a discussion. The Bible constantly teaches things that are unthinkable to some group. Monotheism was once almost universally unthinkable. The Bible's prohibition of premarital sex is unthinkable to many college students. When we read an unpalatable text, we may ask if we have properly understood it. We also seek to fit the passage in the context of the whole of Scripture. But if the message is clear and remains offensive, we ought to change our thinking, not the message.

This doesn't mean we refuse to explore ideas. So, for example, we may concede one aspect of Marshall's point about hell. Some of the imagery—a king slaying his adversaries—that perhaps sounded inoffensive in other ages does seem harsh today (Luke 19:27). What can we learn if we explore biblical images of hell? For one thing, a literalist might see a conflict between some of them: it is "the darkness" and "the lake of fire," and fires give light (Matt. 8:12; Rev. 20:14–15). Do we have contradiction, then? No, we have diverse images, which we should examine for consistent themes.

The central problem for many who reject Jesus' teaching—on hell, for example—is that they are too quick to accept their judgment and too reticent to accept the Bible's. The Western mind balks at hell for various reasons, not least because some perceive a contradiction between the love and the judgment of God. But we constructively go beyond the sacred page when we explore the coherence of biblical ideas that seem antithetical.

---

44. Herman Ridderbos, *Redemptive History and the New Testament Scriptures* (Phillipsburg, NJ: Presbyterian & Reformed, 1988), 12–30; cf. Kevin Vanhoozer, "Imprisoned or Free," in *Reading Scripture with the Church*, ed. A. K. M. Adam et al. (Grand Rapids: Baker, 2006), 62–64.

Bible-believing apologists and theologians like C. S. Lewis, Miroslav Volf, Tim Keller, and Oliver O'Donovan have been doing that for decades as they explore the doctrine of hell rather than abandoning it.

- Lewis argued that people choose hell rather than repent of their selfishness and submit to God.[45]
- Volf argued that the doctrine of final judgment provides necessary restraint on human violence: "The certainty of God's just judgment at the end of history is the presupposition for the renunciation of violence in the middle of it." Besides, a God who is not angry at injustice and does not finally end it "would not be worthy of our worship."[46]
- Keller observed that a loving God can be filled with wrath, not despite his love but because of it. It is right to be angry when people bring injustice or violence to someone we love.[47]
- O'Donovan argued that without the judgment of God, even the "unbridled acts of war" in the conquest narrative, the cross is incomprehensible: "The transcendent fire of election and judgment had to be shown … in all its possible hostility to the world, if we were to learn what it meant that in Christ the Word of God became flesh and took the cause of the world as his own cause." Without clear demonstrations of God's wrath toward sin, O'Donovan says, we would never grasp the love and redemption manifest in incarnation and atonement. (This argument appeals to RHTs because of its link with soteriology.)[48]

These authors go beyond the Bible in the best sense. They show that they submit to the authority of Scripture and acknowledge its clarity when they take the difficult biblical teaching on hell at face value. Then they move beyond

---

45. C. S. Lewis, *The Great Divorce*, 72–73, 32–46, passim.

46. Miroslav Volf, *Exclusion and Embrace: A Theological Exploration of Identity, Otherness, and Reconciliation* (Nashville: Abingdon, 1996), 301–4.

47. Tim Keller, *The Reason for God* (New York: Dutton, 2008), 73–74.

48. Oliver O'Donovan, *Resurrection and Moral Order* (Grand Rapids: Eerdmans, 1994), 158.

exegesis by exploring the way that doctrine (1) might make sense to a contemporary doubter or skeptic, and (2) might cohere with other doctrines that we readily accept. Lewis links hell to the fallen human will, Keller ties hell to the love of God, Volf joins it to the cause of peace, and O'Donovan connects it to the cross of Christ. Each concedes that their culture is quick to question the doctrine. As Keller says, we should expect the Bible to "contradict and offend every human culture at some point because human cultures are ever-changing and imperfect."[49] But no one flinches from the countercultural elements of biblical teaching, even if fellow believers object to them.

In a case like this, the RHT goes beyond the sacred page first by going *back* to it, bringing every exegetical resource to bear to verify the doctrine. Next we take our culture's questions and objections to Scripture, looking for biblical and theological resources that make it easier for people to understand and accept it. Thus we go beyond the page by hearing the questions people raise and by engaging in theological reflection, perhaps not so tightly tied to Scripture, so as to advance biblical ideas in a new setting.

There is also a more practical way to go beyond the pages of Scripture. This time the source is not skeptical theologians but humble Christians, seeking guidance on matters that the Bible doesn't seem to answer.

GOING BEYOND THE SACRED PAGE THROUGH CASUISTRY

Christians have been going beyond the Bible in search of guidance for a long time, even if they never thought of it as going beyond the Bible. Still, it is a form of movement beyond Scripture when believers seek pastoral counsel or spiritual direction on matters the Bible did not or could not directly address: Shall I make a final attempt at reconciliation with this woman? Stay in this job? Marry this man? Some of these questions are prudential: the man in question

49. Keller, *Reason for God*, 72–73.

is a Christian, single and unencumbered, but his height, weight, hair, smell, or romantic spirit don't meet the woman's standards. It is serious pastoral work to help a woman sort out the relationship between biblical, cultural, and personal dreams about marriage.

Yet such questions can belong to the most challenging areas of this project. For example, Christian women outnumber Christian men in many nations, but the gap is so acute in some eastern European nations that for Christian women the choice is between singleness and an "unequal yoke." They ask their pastors — and visiting speakers: "I am thirty-five and there are no godly men to marry. But the man who shows interest in me is moral and a nominal Christian. What should I do? I want to have a family, children. Can I marry him?" Like some of the earlier questions about compromise at work, this conversation raises questions of competing ethical norms in vexed cultural conditions. The questioner may believe she is seeking the voice of wisdom and experience. Vanhoozer, drawing on the imagery of dramatic performance, might call it improvisation.[50] Christian ethicists used to call it casuistry.

"Casuistry" is virtually an epithet in some circles as a result of past abuses, especially the way certain casuists, as far back as Matthew 15, found "rules for getting around the rules." Yet casuistry may be defined as the "art of resolving particular cases of conscience through appeal to higher general principles," especially when one must act at a time when principles seem to be in conflict or when a new problem has emerged.[51] We are all casuists in the sense that we apply principles to the riddles and "shifting circumstances of daily life."[52] The choices may be wrenching: Should a woman with small children leave a husband who strikes her occasionally? When is it time to turn off a respirator? Or mundane: Must we obey irritatingly low speed limits for smooth, deserted ribbons of blacktop? Is the answer dif-

---

50. See his book, *The Drama of Doctrine*.

51. Thomas Merrill, "Introduction" to *William Perkins, 1558–1602: His Pioneer Works on Casuistry* (Nieuwkoop, Netherlands: De Graaf, 1966), x–xi.

52. Geoffrey Bromiley, "Casuistry," in *Baker's Dictionary of Christian Ethics*, ed. Carl F. H. Henry (Grand Rapids: Baker, 1973), 85.

ferent if someone in the car is sick and desperate to get to a physician?

Casuistic questions appear and are answered in the Bible: What are the grounds for divorce (Matt. 19:3–9; 1 Cor. 7:10–17)? Must we pay taxes to Caesar (Matt. 22:15–21)? May Christians eat meat that has been offered to idols (1 Cor. 8)? Some cases persist, while others change. The Pharisees asked, "Is it lawful to heal on the Sabbath?" We ask, "Is it lawful to go shopping on Sunday?" At its best, the motive for casuistry is a desire to live righteously.[53]

Biblical principles don't fully answer most such questions. Sometimes no rule covers a question. Or perhaps several norms may apply but appear to point in different directions.[54] Wise pastors enlist the person bringing the question, for we seek to develop their moral judgment and character, not simply dispense a decision.

Centuries ago, the Puritans' passion for holiness led them to a casuistry that carefully explored questions about faithful living. For example, William Ames answered this question: If we have a sinful thought, should we keep it to ourselves or express it? Ames distinguishes the senses in which we can keep something to ourselves. First, if someone maintains silence in order to commit the sin more easily, then it is evil. If we utter an evil thought to bring it to completion, it is evil. But if someone remains silent regarding a sin because it is evil and shameful, silence is good. An evil thought is not a sin until the mind approves it. But if "we begin to nibble upon it and are tickled with it," if we contemplate it with delight or complacency, then we sin. If we entertain impure thoughts with pleasure, we have approved the evil, even if there is no intent to act upon it.[55] Whether we fully agree with Ames or not, we see the value of his deliberations.

---

53. J. I. Packer, "Situations and Principles," in *Law, Morality and the Bible*, ed. Bruce Kaye and Gordon Wenham (Downers Grove, IL: InterVarsity Press, 1978), 155.

54. This is the procedure for casuistry in medical ethics. See Mark Kuczewski, "Casuistry," in *Encyclopedia of Applied Ethics*, ed. Ruth Chadwick (San Diego: Academic Press, 1998), 1:425–30.

55. William Ames, *Conscience with the Power and Cases Thereof* (Norwood, NJ: Walter J. Johnson, 1975 [facsimile, 1639]), Book 3, ch. 20, 94–96.

The spiritually inert may think casuistry looks like excessive rigor, but the godly recognize meditative casuistry as a friend, not an enemy, of holiness.

Casuistry does have dangers, however. The questioner can become dependent on the spiritual guide and the guide may think too highly of his judgments. Casuistry can go constructively beyond the pages of Scripture if it follows a few principles. (1) The guidance given must never contradict Scripture; it must never go against the sacred page. It must remain within the law's parameters. (2) The guide should never present his advice or counsel as law or mandate. Vanhoozer's concept of improvisation may have the potential to minimize that problem, since it implies that the actor is responsible to develop his character, not merely follow directions.

In casuistry, spiritual leaders answer questions that people bring to them. But every leader knows that some questions are better than others. Indeed, some should never be asked (e.g., what is the best way to destroy my rival?), and others might never be asked unless the leader proposed it (how can you best love your rival?). This leads to another way to go beyond the sacred page: by improving the questions we bring to Scripture.

GOING BEYOND THE SACRED PAGE BY ASKING THE RIGHT QUESTIONS

When a supplicant came to Jesus with a question or request, he gave a direct reply roughly half the time. The rest of the time, he bypassed or revised it and answered the question the petitioner *should* have asked (see, e.g., John 6:1–59). Clearly then, we should try to ask questions God approves.

Let us assume that every sincere moral or spiritual question has some level of validity and that leaders should help people bring their questions to God. But some questions are more helpful than others when people face ethical choices.[56] We might call them "questions the Bible endorses." These questions help us gather, summarize, and apply biblical

---

56. For example, "What will happen if I get caught?" is not a helpful question.

data to life's issues. They fall into four categories, questions of duty, character, goals, and vision.

1. What is my duty? What should I do? What do I owe to others?
2. What are the marks of good character? Who should I be? What kind of person?
3. What goals are worthy of my life energy? Where should I go alone? Where with my community?
4. Given that people have different perspectives on ethical questions, how can I see the world as God does? How can I gain a biblical worldview?

The Bible's interest in these questions is often visible. For example, see duty in Exodus 20–24 and Romans 12; character in Romans 6–8 and Ephesians 4:17–32; goals in the assignments or callings God gave Moses, Solomon, and Paul; discernment in Proverbs and Ecclesiastes.[57] We can test the value of these questions by considering gambling.

BRINGING THE RIGHT QUESTIONS TO THE TOPIC OF GAMBLING

Gambling is widespread enough that Christians regularly pose questions about it. Few doubt the church's opposition to gambling addictions and the concomitant human and economic costs. But Christians do ask if all gambling is immoral: Nickel card games? Lotteries and raffles where the proceeds go to good causes? Is it wrong, in a friendly athletic contest, for someone to call "loser buys," referring to the post-game beverage? What if a Christian gambles as social entertainment, expecting to lose a little money, just as we expect to "lose" a little money at a restaurant?

The Bible never expressly assesses gambling. It does describes the casting of lots often enough (1 Chron. 26:13–16; Neh. 11:1; Jonah 1:7) that it could be informative. The Bible sometimes says lots reveal God's will (Josh. 7:10ff.; 18:6–10; Prov. 16:33), and once even prescribes their use (Lev. 16:8). Yet lots often appear in decidedly negative situations (Matt.

---

57. I develop this in *Putting the Truth to Work*, 97–157.

27:35; John 19:24; cf. Job 6:27; Joel 3:3). And lots, while used in Acts 1:26, disappear after Pentecost. Lacking a clear pattern, we seem to have no guidance.

Yet we can go beyond the Bible's apparent silence and make a case against gambling, by asking the four questions. First, gambling appears to violate our duty. It subverts the fourth command and the creation order by promising wealth without toil. The gaming industry violates the ninth command by deceiving the gullible with false promises of wealth. Gambling violates the tenth command by fostering a desire for a neighbor's money. It sabotages love of neighbor, since one gambler's gain is another's loss. It subverts the first command, since it promotes love of money. Gambling can lead to additional failures of duty. Since gambling inevitably leads to loss in the long run, it impedes our ability to provide for our families (1 Tim. 5:8) and to give to the poor (Lev. 25; 2 Cor. 8–9; James 2:14–17). Further, the Bible assumes that funds should be put to use, not frittered away (Matt. 25:14–30). Finally, we should work six days to earn our bread, but the gambler hopes to gain without labor (Ex. 20:9; Eph. 4:28; 1 Thess. 3:10–12).

Second, gambling also promotes flaws in character. The desire to get rich is a chief motive for gambling, but Paul says the desire for riches leads to ruin (1 Tim. 6:9–10). The gambler is greedy and greed a form of idolatry (1 Cor. 5:10; Eph. 5:5). It leads to dissension (Prov. 15:27; 28:25), to bribery and injustice (29:4; cf. Jer. 6:13), and the perversion of one's calling (1 Sam. 2:12–17). By character, God is a giver (John 3:16; James 1:5), but the gambler seeks to take from others.

Moreover, the goal of the gambler is to get rich at the expense of others. Unlike other economic activity where money changes hands, the winning gambler takes money from the loser and offers no goods or services in return. Even at the casino, the winner ultimately takes nothing from the "house." All winnings come from the losses of other patrons.

Finally, the gambler's worldview is contrary to God's. The gambler's world is ruled by chance, by luck. The Bible says the sovereign Lord rules over all.

These notes on gambling show how the right questions enable us to go beyond the Bible's surface data. They can also help us tease information out of thin biblical resources, as the next case shows.

BRINGING THE RIGHT QUESTIONS TO ARCHITECTURE

Suppose that a group of Christian architects seeks a theological consultation: "In our field, we constantly face tradeoffs between aesthetics, economy, and safety. Can the Bible offer us any insight on the relative value of this trio?" On this occasion, we will locate a Mosaic case law, exegete it by appealing to the cultural context, distill the principle that drives the case law, then apply the principle to contemporary cases that parallel the original law.

We appeal to Deuteronomy 22:8: "When you build a new house, make a parapet around your roof so that you may not bring the guilt of bloodshed on your house if someone falls from the roof." The original intent of this law is safety. Given that Israelites worked, entertained, even slept on their roofs, a retaining wall was a sensible way to keep Joshua, a reckless child, or Abishag, an overactive sleeper, from tumbling off the roof and wounding themselves. The law prevented the "guilt of bloodshed."

Because Westerners rarely use their roofs, we need not require parapets today, unless the roof is used, as in the case of rooftop spaces in some city buildings. But the principle applies to other situations.[58] To make a parapet is to love a neighbor and preserve life by preventing accidental injuries. We apply the principle most closely today when we install safety railings on flat roofs and place banisters by staircases. We extend the principle if we install speed bumps in residential neighborhoods.[59] The rule for parapets shows that we rightly extend the sixth command, "You shall not murder," by promoting the positive counterpart; we should act to preserve life.

---

58. See Walter Kaiser's call for "principlizing" in, for example, *Towards an Exegetical Theology* (Grand Rapids: Baker, 1981), 149–63.

59. John Goldingay, *Models for Interpretation of Scripture* (Grand Rapids: Eerdmans, 1995), 92.

This readily leads to the four questions. Our duty is clear, but the parapet law also informs our worldview. It teaches us to see ourselves as our brother's keeper, even if he is reckless and should know how to care for himself. Our goal is a life-preserving environment for our community, even if it costs us money. This fits our values and character. We are willing to expend wealth to protect others, even if they are prone to bring troubles on themselves by doing foolish things like toppling off a roof.

The RHT gladly notices the law's hints of God's redeeming grace. The law's concern to preserve life echoes the character of the life-giving, life-preserving Lord. Indeed, God's concern for foolish, reckless, and self-damaging people motivates his work of salvation. Unless God were interested in the kind of people who need parapets, the kind of people who destroy themselves, the race would be lost. This law summons us to imitate God's compassion for all who suffer from foolish and self-inflicted wounds.

This study cannot tell our architects precisely what to do, but it does direct them to privilege safety over aesthetics and cost control when the three values compete. The principle also applies to engineers, designers, and construction workers. Designs should protect life. This will hardly answer every question of our earnest architects, but we do see a way to go beyond the sacred page.

The cases we have taken up so far—wedding celebrations, gambling, and building safety—are relatively simple. They show how the redemptive-historical approach can work in less controversial cases. But what of more difficult cases, such as gender roles? Can the redemptive-historical method lead us to good results?

First, a personal word: I grew up in a church that ordained women; my mother is an ordained minister. I have three daughters, no sons. My local church, located near a major university, has numerous highly talented women. Thus, personal history and motives push me toward evangelical feminism. But the data in Scripture lead me in another direction. I will address just one aspect of the gender debates, the roles of women in the church. Let me affirm the obvious: women and men are equally created in the image of God, equally redeemed by faith, and equally stewards of God's gifts. I explore roles, not ontological or soteriological categories.

THE SACRED PAGE, WOMEN, AND MINISTRY

After reading the next pages, a skeptical reader may conclude that I never stepped an inch beyond the sacred page. But I go beyond by reflecting on the reception of Scripture in my culture and among my peers. In exegesis, I delve into history and grammar to elucidate the sense of Scripture. Throughout, my trust in its authority, clarity, and sufficiency keeps me from going beyond/against Scripture and capitulating to our culture's dominant paradigm for gender relations.

As we saw, the redemptive-historical method is committed both to close exegesis of crucial passages and to analysis of the sweep of Scripture. That analysis looks for progress, development, or other patterns through epochs of redemption. The process can begin anywhere, so long as we cover the data. We begin with 1 Timothy 2:9–15, a passage the church once thought to be clear and final.[60]

In 1 Timothy, Paul teaches believers how they should "conduct themselves in God's household" (1 Tim. 3:14–15). Proper conduct includes proper gender roles (2:8–15) and properly functioning church leaders (3:1–13). These will be connected if Paul wants men to teach doctrine and fight heresy.[61]

Paul says: "I ... want women to dress modestly ... not with braided hair or gold or pearls or expensive clothes, but

---

60. On the history of interpretation, see Daniel Doriani, *Women and Ministry* (Wheaton, IL: Crossway), 147–74.

61. Strong egalitarian explanations of 1 Timothy 2 include Craig Keener, *Paul, Women and Wives*, 101–32; I. H. Marshall, *The Pastoral Epistles* (Edinburgh: T & T Clark, 1999), 436–71. Among complementarians, see Douglas Moo, "What Does It Mean Not to Teach or Have Authority over Men: 1 Timothy 2:11–15," in *Recovering Biblical Manhood and Womanhood*, ed. John Piper and Wayne Grudem (Wheaton, IL: Crossway, 1991), 179–93; William D. Mounce, *Pastoral Epistles* (Nashville: Thomas Nelson, 2000), 94–149; Thomas R. Schreiner, "An Interpretation of 1 Timothy 2:9–15: A Dialogue with Scholarship," in *Women in the Church: A Fresh Analysis of 1 Timothy 2:9–15*, ed. Andreas Kostenberger, Thomas R. Schreiner, and H. Scott Baldwin (Grand Rapids: Baker, 1995), 105–54.

with good deeds" (1 Tim. 2:9–10).[62] For both Greeks and
Jews, extravagant dress could signify promiscuity or disregard of a husband's authority.[63] "Rejection of external adornment was part of a woman's submission to her husband."[64]
Most likely, the context for 1 Timothy 2:9–15 was worship.[65]
If so, then elaborate displays take attention from the God
who is worshiped to a well-dressed worshiper.[66]

Instead, Paul commands, "Let a woman learn in quiet-
ness and full submission" (1 Tim. 2:11).[67] Greek and Jewish
cultures commonly judged the education of women a waste
of time and a cause of temptation. The Mishnah advised
men "not to talk much to womankind" lest they neglect the
law and finally inherit damnation.[68] Philo said Satan wisely
attacked Eve through her senses, for "mind corresponds
to man, the senses to woman." Thus the masculine soul
devotes itself to God the Creator, while the feminine soul

---

62. A few scholars believe γυνή (gynē), rendered "women" in almost all
translations, should be translated "wives." See Gordon Hugenberger, "Women
in Church Office: Hermeneutics or Exegesis? A Survey of Approaches to
1 Timothy 2:8–15," *Journal of the Evangelical Theological Society* 35 (1992):
341–60. Greek does use the same word for women and wives, but "women"
seems right: (1) When γυνή (gyne) indicates a wife, the context mentions marriage or husbands. (2) Paul would hardly forbid wives to dress ostentatiously
but permit single women to do so (see Schreiner, "Interpretation," 115–17).
Further, "I want" indicates a virtual command. βούλομαι (boulomai) means "I
counsel," not "I wish."

63. After a long complaint about the luxuries of women, Juvenal adds,
"Meantime she pays no attention to her husband." See Juvenal, "Satire 6," in
Juvenal and Persius, trans. by C. G. Ramsey (Cambridge, MA: Harvard Univ.
Press, 1965), 121–25.

64. David Scholer, "Women's Adornment: Some Historical and Hermeneutical Observations on the New Testament Passages," *Daughters of Sarah*
6:1 (1980): 5.

65. Doriani, *Women and Ministry*, 189, note 3.

66. Paul does not ban all hairstyling; braids could be simple. The problem is elaborate hairstyles. See James B. Hurley, *Man and Woman in Biblical
Perspective* (Eugene, OR: Wipf and Stock, 2002), 198–99, 257–59; David Gill,
"The Importance of Roman Portraiture for Head Coverings in 1 Corinthians
11:2–16," *Tyndale Bulletin* 41.2 (1990): 244–60.

67. The verb is an imperative.

68. *The Mishnah*, trans. by Herbert Danby (New York: Oxford, 1933), 446
(*Aboth* 1:5).

attends to things created.[69] But Paul, violating the views of his day, said women should listen and learn in a quiet, submissive, teachable way.

Paul says women should learn, but he says they should not teach or exercise authority over men: "I do not permit a woman to teach or to have authority over a man; she must be silent" (1 Tim. 2:12). This certainly seems to be a categorical prohibition. Nonetheless, virtually every word is contested or requires comment. First, Paul sometimes lets women teach men. He let women prophesy in Corinth (1 Cor. 11:5). Besides, if women were to exercise the gifts that all Christians share, it would seem that they would often need to speak to do so. We can reconcile Paul's prohibition here with his permission elsewhere in two ways: the prohibition is either temporary or partial. Egalitarians say it is temporary. Noting that "I permit" is in the present tense, some say Paul prohibited teaching in the present, when women were uneducated. When that changed, they could teach.[70]

But this view ignores the way Paul explains his prohibition: women may not teach because of the order of creation, not a lack of education. Besides, some wealthier women *were* educated.[71] Further, Paul could have said, "Women may not teach *until* they are educated." And the present tense of "I do not permit" hardly means the injunction is temporary. Does the present tense of "I don't permit you to hit your brother" suggest that the injunction is temporary?[72]

---

69. Philo, "On the Creation" 1:131, and "The Special Laws" 7:581–83, in *The Works of Philo*, trans. by F. H. Colson (Cambridge, MA: Harvard Univ. Press, 1929 and 1937).

70. Aida B. Spencer, *Beyond the Curse: Women Called to Ministry* (Peabody, MA: Hendrickson, 1989), 84–86; Keener, *Paul, Women and Wives*, 109–13.

71. Stephen Baugh, "A Foreign World: Ephesus in the First Century," in *Women in the Church: A Fresh Analysis*, ed. Kostenberger, Schreiner, and Baldwin, 45–47.

72. Paul uses ἐπιτρέπω (*epitrepo*), "permit," two other times (1 Cor. 14:34; 16:7). Neither records a mere preference. See George Knight, *Commentary on the Pastoral Epistles* (Grand Rapids: Eerdmans, 1992), 140. Or look at it this way: If I tell my children, "I don't permit you to lick your plates" on Monday and I see them licking again on Wednesday, I am hardly likely to accept this excuse, "But Dad, you used the present tense and now we're in the future."

Therefore Paul's prohibition is permanent but *partial*. As our survey of Scripture will show, women may teach privately and informally, but they should not serve as the church's authoritative teachers.

Three factors indicate that Paul forbids women authoritatively to teach core doctrines in the church assembly. First, the task of guarding the gospel, so crucial in Paul's letters to Timothy (1 Tim. 6:20; 2 Tim. 1:12–14), belongs to the elders or "overseers" (the terms are interchangeable; cf. Acts 20:17, 28; Titus 1:5–7). These are males—"the husband of one wife" (1 Tim. 3:2). Second, other Scriptures show women teaching (below), but none show them preaching or teaching in the assembly. Third, Paul's language and grammar show that he specifically forbade women to teach doctrine and to exercise ruling authority in the church. We must now develop this last point.

The verb "teach" can be a general term for instruction, but in Paul's letters, especially the Pastorals, what is taught is ordinarily foundational doctrine.[73] Consider 2 Timothy 2:2, "The things you have heard me say in the presence of many witnesses entrust to reliable men who will also be qualified to teach others." Paul also says elders must "hold firm to the trustworthy word as taught, so that he may be able to give instruction in sound doctrine and also to rebuke those who contradict it" (Titus 1:9 ESV).

The noun "teaching" is similar. Paul says, "So then, brothers, stand firm and hold to the teachings we passed on to you" (2 Thess. 2:15). The teachings or "traditions" (ESV) are the apostolic message, preserved in speech and writing

---

73. In the fifteen Pauline texts that use "teach" (διδάσκω, *didaskō*), three certainly refer to basic doctrine (1 Cor. 4:17; Gal. 1:12; 2 Thess. 2:15) and six almost certainly do (Rom. 12:7; Eph. 4:21; Col. 1:28; 2:7; 1 Tim. 2:12; 4:11), leaving six that refer to other teaching. There are two cognate nouns for teaching, διδαχή (*didache*) and διδασκαλία (*didaskalia*). The first word refers to Christian doctrine in four of its six uses in the NT (Rom. 6:17; 16:17; 2 Tim. 4:2; Titus 1:9; but not 1 Cor. 14:6, 26). The second word typically refers to false teaching (Matt. 15:9; Mark 7:7; Eph. 4:14; Col. 2:22; but not Rom. 15:4); until we get to the Pastoral Epistles. There Paul specifies if it is sound doctrine or not (1 Tim. 1:10). See Knight, *Pastoral Epistles*, 88–89, 140–41; J. N. D. Kelly, *The Pastoral Epistles* (Peabody, MA: Hendrickson, 1993), 50; Schreiner, "An Interpretation of 1 Timothy 2," 127–28.

(Gal. 1:6–12). So, when Paul says, "I do not permit a woman to teach," he means that men who are tested, approved, and consecrated must proclaim and defend the core truths of the faith (2 Tim. 2:24–26).

Paul also says women must not "exercise authority." The Greek word (*authenteō*) appears just once in the NT and about a hundred times in extant ancient Greek literature. The term can have negative connotations, leading egalitarians to say Paul means women must not usurp or abuse authority, but most evidence indicates "rule" or "exercise authority" is the best definition.[74] In a telling example, Chrysostom said women must not teach men because Eve "once taught Adam wrongly" and must not exercise authority over man because "she once *exercised authority* wrongly." "Exercise authority" is our word; when Chrysostom adds "wrongly" to it, it shows that he (a Greek speaker) knew the word did not intrinsically have negative force. If *authenteo* does not intrinsically mean to abuse authority, then Paul is forbidding women to rule, not to rule badly.[75]

The grammatical structure supports this view. The terms "teach" and "exercise authority" are joined by the Greek conjunction *oude*. *Oude* means "and not," "neither," or "nor." *Oude* also has an interesting grammatical feature. When it links two verbs, either both are bad in themselves or both are good in themselves. It never links a negative and a positive verb.[76] In 1 Timothy 2:12, Paul links "teach" and "exercise authority" with *oude*. This means both are positive or both are negative. Since "teach" is clearly positive,

---

74. For "exercise authority" see H. Scott Baldwin, "A Difficult Word: ΑΥΘΕΝΤΕΩ in 1 Timothy 2:12," and "Appendix 2: ΑΥΘΕΝΤΕΩ in Ancient Greek Literature," in *Women in the Church: A Fresh Analysis*, ed. Kostenberger, Schreiner, and Baldwin, 65–80 and 269–305. See also Leland E. Wilshire, "The TLG Computer and Further Reference to ΑΥΘΕΝΤΕΩ in 1 Timothy 2:12," *New Testament Studies* 34 (1988): 120–34; and idem, "1 Timothy 2:12 Revisited: A Reply to Paul W. Barnett and Timothy J. Harris," *Evangelical Quarterly* 65 (1993): 54. Wilshire's first article is amenable to Baldwin; his second is not.

75. John Chrysostom, *Sermons in Genesis*, cited in Greek and English in Baldwin, "ΑΥΘΕΝΤΕΩ in 1 Timothy 2:12," 73–74, 283.

76. Andreas Kostenberger, "A Complex Sentence Structure in 1 Timothy 2:12," in *Women in the Church: A Fresh Analysis*, ed. Kostenberger, Schreiner, and Baldwin, 84–104.

"exercise authority" must be positive too.[77] Thus in 2:12 Paul does not forbid women to rule wickedly—by domineering or usurping authority; he forbids that they rule in general in the church. Men bear responsibility for the doctrine and direction of the church.

Next, Paul says male leadership rests on the created order and is not a concession to our fallen condition: "For Adam was formed first, then Eve" (1 Tim. 2:13). Knowing it is a slight hyperbole, Charles Cosgrove says "the purpose or justification behind a biblical moral rule carries more weight than the rule itself."[78] That is, when we encounter a command that seems irrational (to eat no pork) or outdated (to slay bulls that have a habit of goring), we ask why it is given. Today (yet surely not in other days) and at first impression Paul's dictum—"I do not permit a woman to teach"—seems irrational and outdated. But the form of Paul's argument forbids that we rest on first impressions, for the command is grounded in creation. When Jesus appealed to creation regarding divorce, he considered it a conclusive argument (Matt. 19:4, 8). The same holds for David in Psalm 8, Solomon in Proverbs 8:22–36, Isaiah in 40:18–25, Paul in 1 Corinthians 11:3–10, and Hebrews in 2:5–15. Paul's claim that male leadership rests in creation means his teaching rests on something essential to men and women. Scripture says the order of creation will not change until Jesus returns to judge and restore creation. Then bodies will change and marriage will end (Matt. 22:30; 1 Cor. 15:22–23).

Space forbids that we continue the close analysis of 1 Timothy 2. We have concluded that the text means what it seems to mean: Women should learn the faith and share their knowledge in some settings, as Paul says in Titus 2:4. But they should not become primary public instructors and defenders of the faith in the local church's pastoral positions, as Paul envisioned them in his instruction to Timothy. This

---

77. Paul uses another word, ἑτεροδιδασκαλέω (*heterodidaskaleo*), for false teaching (1 Tim. 1:3; 6:3).

78. William Cosgrove, *Appealing to Scripture in Moral Debate: Five Hermeneutical Rules* (Grand Rapids: Eerdmans, 2002), 12–50.

division of gender roles has been God's design from the beginning. So there is no reason to go beyond/against the plain sense of 1 Timothy 2 if we seek Paul's guidance for the role of women in the church.

However an egalitarian may question this or that point of exegesis, the main rejoinder does not lie there. Rather, the egalitarian will say three things. First, the teaching in 1 Timothy applies to temporary local conditions. But Paul's decision to argue from creation refutes this. Second, traditionalists neglect the equality of male and female before the gospel (Gal. 3:26–28). All parties agree on the equality of men and women, soteriologically speaking. But that is not the point under discussion. Third, traditionalists fail to account for the whole biblical testimony and for the arc of the biblical narrative, which tends toward the equality of women. This demands a careful reply.

First, we concede that the biblical narrative tends toward the equality or liberation of women in vital ways. Chiefly, the gospel liberates women from sin, and since the gospel is identical for all people, it proves again what we knew since Genesis 1: men and women are fundamentally equal. The end of polygamy and changes in divorce law from the Old Testament to the New Testament benefit women (cf. Deut. 24:1–4 and 1 Cor. 7:10–16). When the old covenant closed, the Old Testament penal code lost its civil authority. This certainly gave women more options in cases of rape and seduction, among other things (Ex. 22:16–17; Lev. 19:20–22; Deut. 22:22–29).[79]

Second, however, we deny that there is a shift or a developmental arc in which women steadily exercise more authority. On the contrary, throughout biblical history the picture is quite consistent and the final texts, 1 Timothy 2 and 1 Peter 3, are among the strongest for male leadership in church and family.

---

79. Some of these laws seem onerous to us, but protection of the family's integrity and inheritance were leading values. See Christopher Wright, *Old Testament Ethics*, 293–94. The discussion of Leviticus 19 in Richard Bauckham, *The Bible and Politics* (Louisville: Westminster John Knox, 1989), 34ff., demonstrates the subtlety of these laws.

WOMEN'S ROLES: A SURVEY OF BIBLICAL HISTORY

But the traditional or complementarian view of gender roles hardly rests on two late New Testament texts. Indeed, the same view permeates Scripture, from its last pages to its first.

Adam and Eve are fundamentally peers in the creation narratives—God created both in his image and both rule his creation. But there are three hints of Adamic leadership from the start: Adam is created first, leading to thoughts of primogeniture; Adam names Eve, and naming is a function of authority; and God calls Adam, not Adam and Eve, to account for the first couple's rebellion.[80]

A naïve survey of Scripture shows God appointing men to most leadership positions after the fall. The law appointed male priests (Ex. 29:30) and male monarchs (Deut. 17:14–20; 2 Sam. 7:12–16). Jesus chose twelve male apostles (Matt. 10:2–4). Paul assumes all elders are male (1 Tim. 3:1–7). The first missionaries and church planters in Acts were male. All of Paul's named traveling companions were male: Barnabas, Silas, Luke, Timothy, Titus, John Mark, Epaphras, Epaphroditus, and others.

A more careful survey reveals women led in various ways. The great majority of prophets and judges were male, but Deborah was a judge (Judg. 4–5) and Huldah a prophetess (1 Kings 22:14–20). Women prophesy in public (1 Cor. 11:5) and instruct leaders like Apollos in private (Acts 18). Paul praises women for crucial assistance in his churches, mentioning Euodia, Syntyche, Mary, Junia, Tryphena, Tryphosa, and Persis for singular aid (Rom. 16:6–13; Phil. 4:2–3). Lydia, Andronicus, and Junia had vital roles (Acts 16:14; Rom 16:7). He also urges older women to instruct younger women (Titus 2:3–4). Clearly, *women do all sorts of things. But they do not do everything.*

Among the prophets, another pattern emerges. The writing prophets (Isaiah to Malachi), miracle-working prophets (Moses, Elijah, Elisha), and leadership prophets (Moses, John the Baptist) were all male. There are prophetesses, but they reveal God's truth in private settings.

---

80. Again, some skeptical egalitarian scholars, who feel free to say the Bible is wrong, agree with this interpretation of Genesis 1–3.

In a dark hour in Josiah's reign, a temple restoration led to a rediscovery of the law, which revealed sin and foretold judgment. Hilkiah the high priest took the case to Josiah, who ordered Hilkiah to inquire of the Lord, a task they asked Huldah the prophetess to lead (2 Kings 22:8–14). Speaking to four men who visited her home, she declared impending judgment (22:15–20). Hearing this, the king led the response: covenant renewal and a program of iconoclasm (23:1–16). Thus the king and his officials genuinely consulted Huldah, who profoundly influenced events. She neither initiated the action nor determined the action, but she shaped events by declaring God's word to her visitors.

Another prophetess, Moses' sister Miriam, led the women of Israel in a song of praise after the Egyptian army drowned in the sea. But her song followed that of Moses and used his very words (Ex. 15:1–3, 20–21). Similarly, in Luke 2, Anna the prophetess is paired with Simeon. He first praises God, then reveals God's word to Mary, but Anna also speaks of Christ in the temple "to all who were looking forward to the redemption of Israel" (Luke 2:25–38). A survey shows that none of the prophetesses mentioned in Scripture teaches independently and publicly. None leads a general assembly.

Hannah and Abigail also declared revealed truth and Scripture preserves it (1 Sam. 2; 25), but the speech, again, is private, not public. Abigail's case is representative: when David foolishly vows to slay Nabal for insulting his men, she intervenes so that David repents. She reasons from the *law* of God, the *nature* of God, and the *promises* of God to persuade a man of God to act like one. She persuades David although he has formal authority and she does not. Abigail did not publicly instruct men in theology; she did use theology to instruct a public man. David heeded Abigail and repented at her *private* counsel.

Priscilla's instruction of Apollo, in tandem with her husband, Aquila, is similar. She teaches in private, beside a man. The cases of Deborah, judge and prophetess, and Paul's colaborers in Rome follow the same pattern.[81]

---

81. Doriani, *Women and Ministry*, 23–40.

The ministry of Jesus deepens but does not alter this picture. Jesus broke with the prevailing view that women were intellectually and spiritually inferior to men. He assumed that women were made in God's image (Matt. 19:3) and capable of robust discipleship. Women followed him, supported his ministry materially (Luke 8:3), remained with him at his crucifixion (John 20:25–27), and were the first to witness his resurrection (20:1–18). He violated norms by freely speaking to women (4:7, 27) and calling them to discipleship. He blessed his friend Mary for sitting and listening at his feet instead of preparing a meal (Luke 10:38–42).

Later, a woman called to Jesus, "Blessed is the mother who gave you birth and nursed you" (Luke 11:27). This statement reflected the notion that women find greatness by connection to a great husband or son. She meant this as oblique praise to Jesus. He accepted, yet corrected her remark, "Blessed rather are those who hear the word of God and obey it" (11:28). "Rather" means the declaration is correct, but not exhaustive.[82] Mary is blessed to have Jesus as son, but the blessing surpasses the physical bond. He blesses all who hear God's Word, believe it, and act on it (Luke 1:45; 8:21). Women find supreme blessing through discipleship, which knows no gender.

Jesus healed, touched, befriended, instructed, and discipled women, but he did not eliminate all distinctions between men and women. He chose twelve males and no females as his apostles and foundational witnesses. He trained them to preach and to write what they heard and saw (Acts 1:8; 4:20; 1 John 1:1–4).[83]

Evangelical egalitarians deny that Jesus' choice of male apostles sets a precedent.[84] They say he accommodated to a

---

82. The sometimes ambiguous Greek particle μενοῦν (*menoun*) means, "Yes, but rather," not "No, rather" (see Margaret Thrall, *Greek Particles in the New Testament* [Grand Rapids: Eerdmans, 1962], 35).

83. Ridderbos, *Redemptive History*, 12–24.

84. Nonevangelical Christian egalitarians dispute gospel accounts, alleging that an emerging male hierarchy suppressed information about early female leadership; see Elizabeth Schüssler Fiorenza, *In Memory of Her: An Egalitarian Theological Reconstruction of Christian Origins* (New York: Crossroad, 1983), esp. 40–92.

culture that could not have accepted female apostles, leaders, and traveling companions. Besides, egalitarians say, women were uneducated and considered intellectually inferior, so no one would accept their leadership. They argue that since women are educated today and contemporary cultures do accept female leaders, Jesus' concessions to his day are irrelevant.[85]

This feeble argument conveniently forgets that Jesus defied cultural conventions whenever he saw fit. He touched lepers, called tax collectors and prostitutes his friends, and violated sacrosanct Sabbath codes. After shattering so many conventions, why should he quail at one more? Educationally, furthermore, neither Jesus nor the Twelve were highly educated (Matt. 13:54–57; John 7:15; Acts 4:13), yet the early church accepted their leadership. Besides, it is at best precarious to assert that Jesus yielded to social pressure when a moral issue is at stake—and egalitarians insist that it is a moral issue.

Thus, Paul's teaching in 1 Timothy 2 coheres with testimony from Genesis onward. Women can be full disciples, can teach women and children, and can instruct men privately, but they may not preach or teach authoritatively among God's assembled people. First Corinthians 11:5 assumes that women did prophesy in Christian gatherings, but when the prophecy was tested—an authority function—women were to be silent (1 Cor. 14:26–36).[86] When women did lead, it was beside men and under their authority. No woman approaches the rank of Abraham, Moses, David, Elijah, Isaiah, Peter, or Paul. When Miriam aspired to equality with Moses, God chastised her (Num. 12). When Barak tried to avoid leadership in battle, Deborah urged him on and refused to proceed without him (Judg. 4).

There are three ways to view the data. Critics say the Bible is erroneous. Evangelical egalitarians say male leadership

---

85. Rebecca Groothuis, *Good News for Women* (Grand Rapids: Baker, 1997), 109–11; Stanley Grenz, *Women in the Church: A Biblical Theology of Women in the Ministry* (Downers Grove, IL: InterVarsity Press, 1995), 211–12.

86. Constraints of space forbid that I develop this, but see James Hurley, *Man and Woman in Biblical Perspective* (Grand Rapids: Zondervan, 1981), 188–94; Doriani, *Woman and Ministry*, 81–86.

was a temporary concession to ancient cultures. Evangelical complementarians say God ordained men to be the principal leaders of church and family.

The Bible does make concessions to cultural realities. Notably, biblical law regulates and undermines the institution of slavery but does not forbid it. But our survey of Scripture indicates that male leadership is no concession. Even if many passages are complex, we have no mere heap of texts. From beginning to end, Scripture is univocal: in the church, as in analogous Old Testament administration of God's people, men must lead and teach. In the categories of redemptive history, this is suggested at creation—and Jesus himself affirms the strength of arguments from creation in Matthew 19:3–9. Then it is established in positive Mosaic law, not merely penal or case law. It is also presented as normative in Old Testament narratives from all eras of redemptive history, from the Abrahamic, Mosaic, and Davidic covenants.

Jesus and the apostles maintain the standard during the era of the Gospels. In Acts, after the gift of the Spirit, men still lead the church. Finally, Paul and Peter reaffirm the principle in their letters (in 1 Cor. 11; 14; Eph. 5; 1 Tim. 2; 1 Peter 3, not to mention shorter texts). There is no movement toward new roles for women and no reason to doubt the clarity of Scripture, therefore no valid reason to resist the plain teaching of God's Word. Unless we love the culture more than we love the Scripture, there is no reason to go beyond/against the sacred page.

CONCLUSIONS

The scope of this project has led me to say next to nothing about the RHTs commitment to the christocentricity of Scripture and far too little about the issue of slavery. Nonetheless, I hope I have contributed something to a vital debate. I argued that there are constructive ways to go beyond the sacred page without going against it, without appealing to conjectured trajectories or pitting the mind of God against the words of God.

My modest proposal is essentially a call to return to diligent exegesis and the orthodoxies of interpretation.

We study Scripture one text at a time. Yet we also believe Scripture is unified, so that its ideas develop organically. If a passage says something we dislike, we have every right to ensure that we have understood it correctly. But if Scripture genuinely clashes with our convictions, then so much the worse for our convictions. Surely the sovereign and righteous Lord has the right to correct his fallen, finite children. Indeed, we must expect it.

This essay makes two theoretical points. First, we can make more use of narrative in our ethic. Second, we must try to bring the best questions to the Bible, questions of duty, character, goals, and worldview. But in most ways, the essay restates the classic evangelical view of the way interpretation ought to be practiced. When I say we have the resources to respond faithfully to questions about weddings and gambling or hell and gender, I restate an old idea. Today, however, it is a contested idea, even among evangelicals.

So-called evangelicals question ever more biblical teachings that they judge unpalatable. Consider that a leading egalitarian can reel off seventeen passages and say, "The complementarians are simply right," and hardly anyone blinks as he goes on to argue another view, despite all the texts he just cited.[87] If evangelicals can question the complementarian position despite the textual evidence, we cannot profess surprise if they support "faithful" homosexuality, despite the Bible's overwhelming opposition to it.[88]

If evangelicals can question what certainly seems to be clear teaching about homosexual unions, questions about polygamy are bound to come next. It is easy enough to see how the defense of polygamy will unfold (especially since there is always a theologian who will supply the rationale for a new trend that can claim to be "loving"). First, it is hard to see why, if "male and female" is irrelevant to marriage, the central, immutable feature of marriage should be the number of participants.[89] Second, one could easily argue

---

87. Stackhouse, *Finally Feminist*, 50.

88. Robert Gagnon, *The Bible and Homosexual Practice* (Nashville: Abingdon, 2001)..

89. Mark Steyn, "The Marrying Kind," *Atlantic Monthly* (May 2005), 142–43.

that polygamy is more natural than a homosexual union. Third, polygamy appears to be compassionate, insofar as many Christian women long to marry but cannot find a suitable mate because men are immature, immoral, and faithless. Fourth, while polygamy falls short of God's ideal, we hardly live in an ideal world. Besides, polygamy promotes other ideals—marriage and procreation. Finally, we might hear a call to relinquish chronological and geographical bias: it's time to learn from the polygamists of the old covenant and of the African church today. Surely, someone will argue, polygamy is preferable to a life of loneliness or marriage to an unbeliever. Yes, some will recoil from such arguments, but on what basis? Personal distaste? How long can that last? We shudder today and acquiesce tomorrow.

But we have not even mentioned the greatest issues. If one "evangelical" retreats from the Bible's view of hell because it seems unthinkable, another can shrink from the concept of blood atonement. That, of course, takes us to the core of orthodoxy. So we see that orthodox theology depends in measure on orthodox methods of interpretation and a willingness to follow them wherever they lead. It is imperative that interpreters look outside Scripture. We read the grammars, histories, and lexicons that make the past accessible to us. We observe our culture so we can grasp and respond winsomely to the questions of the hour. And we must always look to apply the principles of Scripture to old and new questions, such as the right way to celebrate a wedding or to erect a building in the city. But it is no tragedy if, in our effort to follow the Lord, there is a sense in which we never go far beyond God's sacred page.

A RESPONSE TO DANIEL M. DORIANI

Walter C. Kaiser Jr.

THE FOUR FOUNDATIONS OF A REDEMPTIVE-HISTORICAL METHOD

THE FOUR FOUNDATIONS that Professor Doriani establishes for his redemptive-historical method of interpreting the Bible are usually assumed by all conscientious interpreters of the Bible. He correctly noted what is called for: (1) technical skill and spiritual sensitivity, (2) a high view of the authority of Scripture, (3) a view that the Scriptures are sufficient in and of themselves, and (4) a view of the clarity of Scripture. There is no need to comment further on those areas or to contest his challenge to I. Howard Marshall on the imagery used by Jesus for the doctrine of hell, for I agree with Professor Doriani.

But what I want to focus on is his use of the redemptive-historical method as a way of going beyond the sacred page. His initial steps, of course, are no-brainers, for indeed we must, as step one, read Scripture closely and accurately. Daniel rightly emphasizes the fact that we must "search for the author's main point [as] the first task." That is a welcome note in this day of hermeneutical confusion.

The second step is also usually adopted by most serious readers of the Bible. It proposes a synthesis of the biblical data, in which we must "proceed inductively, paying close attention to its place in redemptive history." He sees the unifying theme, even within the examples of diversity in the Bible, to be part of God's plan of redemption that passes through the line of Abraham and David (Gen. 3:16; 12:1–3; 22:18; 26:2–5; 2 Sam. 7:17; Ps. 132:11–18).

His third step is less perspicuous, the application of Scripture to daily life. He proposes to do this by "the imitation of God/imitation of Christ motif" as the major source for ethical guidance. This cannot be done completely, of course (for who can fully imitate our Lord?), but we should attempt to imitate God/Christ as best as we can in all of our actions. Daniel called this a "point of departure," as "God's action accomplished in Christ [is] applied by the [Holy] Spirit."

It is Doriani's fourth step that promises to take us beyond the sacred page, especially if we are to make more use of biblical narratives. For him, the narratives have a paradigmatic force that has equal value to propositional truths, ethical imperatives, or doctrinal statements. In fact, if we are ever to get beyond the Bible, we will need to learn from the narrative passages. Even though most narratives allow their "readers [to] draw their own conclusions, few offer no hints to guide assessment." This Professor Doriani puts into a principle: "Where a series of acts by the faithful create a pattern, and God or the narrator approves the pattern, it directs believers, even if no law spells out the lesson."

USING CASUISTRY TO GO BEYOND THE SACRED PAGE

The commitment here begins with the discovery of the author's intended meaning, which is exactly where we need to begin. But then even the secondary point of a passage can be made the primary point of a sermon, for it is claimed that is what Jesus did in Matthew 12:1–4 when David used the consecrated bread. But Doriani does not think that 1 Samuel 21 exhibited the primary principle that God desires "mercy, not sacrifice." Here and in Matthew 22:29–32, the modeling role of Jesus must not be subsumed to a primary principle in the text, he urges. Doriani suggests that it is the method of "casuistry" that is to be used at this point to take us beyond Scripture.

To be sure, "casuistry" for many people means being overly subtle, perhaps even fallacious and dishonest in one's reasoning. But in its *secondary meaning* it refers to the application of general ethical principles to particular cases of conscience or conduct.[90] Applied to Scripture, the questions must be what the higher or general ethical principles are and how they are derived, if at all, from within Scripture itself.

Doriani's goal is to "go beyond the sacred page without going against it, without appealing to conjectured trajectories or pitting the mind of God against the words of God." The assumption is that "we all are casuists in the sense that we apply principles to riddles and [to] 'shifting circumstances of daily life.'" So how is this done while avoiding the obvious dangers such as (1) asserting principles that contradict Scripture, and (2) presenting our principles as law or a mandate?

Four topics are briefly explored to illustrate how casuistry works for Doriani: wedding celebrations, gambling, building safety in architecture, and women in ministry. Feeling that the Bible never expressly takes up the topic of gambling, Doriani asks a series of four questions that concludes that the gambler violates our *duty*, promotes flaws in our *character*, supplies wrong *goals*, and gives us a *vision*[91] or a "worldview [that] is contrary to God's." So where did we go beyond the surface of what the Bible expects of us? Nowhere, as far as I can see. The method seems to be identical to my method of principlization, only under a different rubric. His four criteria of "duty, character, goal, and vision" are helpful, but they seem to get at the same type of application process that principlization gets at.

My conclusion is the same for his illustration from Deuteronomy 22:8, about making sure that there is a parapet or railing around a flat roof to avoid an accidental death or injury. We apply the same principles in our day when we put a fence around a backyard swimming pool, as well as banisters on staircases, or put speed bumps in residential neighborhoods. These are merely contemporary illustrations

---

90. This is according to *Random House Webster's College Dictionary* (New York: Random House, 1992), 213. Bromiley, "Casuistry," 85–86, cited p.100, n.52 summed it up as "in essence casuistry is the application of law or laws in the shifting circumstances of daily life."

91. The italicized words are Professor Doriani's four criteria.

of the ancient practice that is now made into a principle that calls for avoiding injury or accidental death, even though most homes today do not have a flat roof or easy access to their rooftops as they did in the ancient Near East.

His final example is much more detailed: women in ministry. From my own essay on 1 Timothy 2:9–15, it should be clear that here our differences come from diverging exegesis of the text. For example, verses 9–10, which advise against "braided hair or gold or pearls or expensive clothes," are treated by Doriani as signs of "promiscuity or disregard of a husband's authority," but that does not seem to be their function here. They are, however, put here as a caution for women who were praying or prophesying in public so that they did not call attention to themselves in this public act of worship, but allowed all attention to be focused on the Lord himself.

Doriani also argues that there was a permanent prohibition on women teaching publicly because of the orders of creation in 1 Timothy 2:13–14, "not [because of] a lack of education." But Paul does qualify this ban when he supplies the reasons for the prohibition: women have not yet been taught (he has just mandated that they *must be taught*, which is the only imperative in the passage!) and because Eve was herself "tricked" (Gk. *exapatetheisa)* by the evil one exactly for the same reason: she had not been taught as yet (see my chapter on this matter). The same reasons apply for the prohibition on temporarily banning a woman from "exercis[ing] authority": she has not been taught as yet.

I agree that "the text [of 1 Timothy 2:9–15] means what it seems to mean." Our only disagreements are: (1) What does this text mean? (2) Are the "orders of creation" in vogue here, or are these "orders of education" (Gk. *eplasthe)* commanded for the moral, spiritual, and educational formation of women? (3) Is the church mandated by our Lord to teach women regardless of what the rest of the culture thinks is only a waste of time and effort? (4) Is it not true that the woman was "tricked" or "deceived" (Gen. 3:13; "The serpent deceived me, and I ate") because she had not as yet been taught, whereas Adam was not "deceived" or "bamboozled" by the serpent because, even though he knew better, he was still just plain persuaded by the woman (3:12, "The woman you put here with me—she gave me some fruit from the tree, and I ate it")?

Nevertheless, despite the fresh command to the church that the church must teach women, some still want to know where Scripture says that God has given to women any kind of "authority" or "power." The answer is in 1 Corinthians 11:10: "For this reason, a woman ought to have *authority* on [her] head" (my trans. of the Greek: *dia touto opheilei he gyne exousian echein epi tes kephales*). The source of that teaching is Genesis 2:18, as I have argued in my chapter.

CONCLUSION

I like Doriani's conclusion: we must return to diligent exegesis, treating one text at a time, believing Scripture is unified and develops organically. We must not retreat from biblical teaching because its views on hell or other personally disagreeable teachings are "unthinkable," as Doriani rightly contests. Instead, "we must always look to apply the principles of Scripture to old and new questions." That is where I end up as well in this argument. God's Word is not only authoritative, but it is thoroughly sufficient as well for all the burning issues of our day and all those yet to come.

A RESPONSE TO DANIEL M. DORIANI

Kevin J. Vanhoozer

FULL DISCLOSURE: DAN AND I were at seminary together, and because he graduated before me, he is my academic elder. This is not the only reason I endorse his chapter, however. His essay, perhaps the most practical of the lot, is a fine exhibit of the wisdom gleaned from years serving the church as both teacher and pastor and is a worthy sequel to his important book *Putting the Truth to Work: The Theory and Practice of Biblical Application*.

Doriani's approach represents the redemptive-historical, biblical-theological face of the Reformed tradition. It is a Reformed approach primarily because it affirms what we could call the tradition's *formal* conviction about the supreme authority (and sufficiency) of Scripture for faith and life as well as its *material* conviction that despite the many kinds of writing in Scripture, there is a unified redemptive history whose center is Jesus Christ. Both convictions are instrumental in the way Doriani seeks to move beyond explicit biblical formulations in order to address new pastoral situations or "cases."

One strength of the redemptive-historical approach is that it recognizes a progress both of redemption and revelation. Indeed, both Doriani and Webb view redemptive movement (for what is history but a kind of movement?) as the unifying theme of Scripture (see my response to Webb for a fuller development of this point). However, Doriani's framework allows him to describe this development somewhat differently than Webb (he speaks, for instance, of patterns that emerge through epochs of redemption). I suspect that Doriani would agree with Calvin when it comes to what exactly develops in the history of redemption: the substance of Old Testament and New Testament history is the same (the covenant of grace), but the form grows clearer until it reaches its definitive statement in Jesus Christ. In other words, there is one history of redemption that becomes ever more glorious, and it reaches its climax within the pages of the New Testament itself.

A second strength: Doriani rightly describes the process of interpreting and going beyond the words on the biblical page as a matter of technical skill, art, and spiritual commitment. This is a key point, but also one that is easily missed. As with any tool, an interpretative approach is only as good as the person using it. Understanding, I believe, is as much a spiritual as an intellectual challenge. Moreover, the closer we get to matters that ultimately concern us — our existential and theological bottom lines, as it were — the more tempting it is to read the text, and go beyond it, in ways that suit our own agendas. I therefore resonate with Doriani's acknowledgment that individual interpreters and even whole cultures must open themselves to correction by Scripture rather than reading Scripture in ways that are perceived to be politically, culturally, or even theologically correct. Going beyond the sacred page requires sanctified, virtuous readers with clear heads and humble hearts.

A third strength, while not unique to Doriani, is typically not found, or not found as often as it should be, in evangelical writing on these matters. It is his desire to apply not only didactic material but also other kinds of texts that communicate less directly. Narratives, for example, portray "paradigmatic individuals" whose actions speak louder than words (i.e., explicit principles) and can contribute to the formation of Christian character. Of particular significance are patterns of actions on the part of paradigmatic individuals that show up in all parts of Scripture — creation, fall, redemption, and restoration alike — as in the example of a pattern of wedding celebrations.

By and large, I see more continuity than discontinuity between our two approaches. Vos himself recognizes that "the Bible is not a dogmatic handbook but a historical book full of *dramatic* interest."[92] So: what's in a word? In what way is thinking in terms of a "drama" of redemption superior to thinking in terms of a "history"? Interestingly enough, I think many of the advantages of the "drama" model (if it is only a model!) are pastoral. Jesus' death and resurrection are in the past, to be sure, but God continues to be active. "Drama" emphasizes the church's role in the ongoing redemptive action. Yes, redemption has been accomplished (to use John Murray's phrase), yet the gospel continues to progress through the nations. And, if one of theology's tasks is to minister faith's understanding in new situations, then we must prepare to play our parts in new scenes, perhaps with unfamiliar cultural props. Still, the history of redemption approach gets the most important thing right: Christians today must learn to view themselves, and their cultures, in the framework of redemptive history rather than viewing redemptive history as a slice of history writ large.

Doriani scores high marks when it comes to employing the six criteria I propose for developing canon sense and catholic sensibility, particularly with regard to the first three. My first quibble pertains to the last of my criteria: Does it resonate? Doriani has near-perfect pitch when it comes to attuning his position to Scripture. His ear is not so good, however, when it comes to listening to *tradition* (though as a Reformed thinker, he is less prone to tone-deafness than are Kaiser and Webb).

Let me say a bit more about why I find my colleagues to be lacking in catholic sensibility. The reason is fairly straightforward. Along with a good portion of the evangelical guild of Old and New Testament scholars, they display little interest in the history of biblical interpretation, at least not in their respective essays. Gerhard Ebeling's observation that the history of the church is the history of biblical interpretation serves as a salutary reminder that our generation is hardly the first that has been called to go beyond the letter.

The local church is a particular instance of the universal church and therefore has much to gain from a famil-

---

92. Geerhardus Vos, *Biblical Theology* (Grand Rapids: Eerdmans, 1948), 26. Emphasis mine.

iarity with the church's early ecumenical consensus ("masterpiece" theological theater) and later Protestant confessions ("regional" theological theater). The history of the church is replete with what Doriani calls "paradigm narratives" — accounts of how Christians in other times and places went beyond the Bible. The so-called Great Tradition is a history of great performances, a history of Christian saints obeying — doing — the Word of God. We can learn from their example, lessons positive or negative as the case may be, just as the church is to learn from the history of Israel (1 Cor. 10:6). The same could be said about the history of Christian missions.

While Scripture is the supreme authority for Christian life and faith, tradition exercises a ministerial authority to the extent that it enlarges our understanding precisely by showing how faithful interpreters have responded obediently in new situations to what the Bible says. Moreover, because no single interpretative approach or community discerns all there is to be gleaned from the Scriptures, there is a need to develop a catholic sensibility that attends not only to the way believers have read the Bible in the past, but also to the way Christians in the global South and East demonstrate their understanding through the lived performance of faith. A canonically centered, catholically bounded approach that hearkens to voices from past and present, North and South, East and West, corresponds to the vocal unity-in-diversity of the Bible itself, and speaks with a ministerial authority that merits the attention of future generations. It takes many interpretative communities spanning many times, places, and cultures in order fully to appreciate all that God is saying to the church in Scripture, and our methods need to acknowledge this.

Doriani proposes two ways of going beyond the sacred page constructively. Both resemble my own approach in striking ways. One of his ways is "asking the right questions" (e.g., What should I do? Who should I be? How should I view the world?). These queries closely resemble my own suggestions for achieving canon sense and theodramatic understanding by directing our attention to figuring out where one is in the drama of redemption, what's going on, and how one is to fit in. As Dan and I are on the same page in this matter, there is no need for me to go "beyond the sacred Doriani."

His other proposed way of going beyond involves casuistry, and here I have a second quibble (i.e., a slight concern). Let me first commend him for rightly recognizing the nature of the challenge of applying or going beyond the letter of the text: it's all about prudence or good judgment. What we're ultimately after, I think, are ways of inculcating good canonical judgment, judgments that move beyond Scripture into the contemporary context without missing a biblical beat.

My worry, however, is that a particular picture of casuistry—as the art "of resolving particular cases of conscience through appeal to higher general principles"—holds him captive. I have no problem with his stated goal (i.e., forming right judgments with regard to particular cases). I do, however, question the means: "through appeal to higher general principles." What I like in his chapter is the way he improves upon the tradition by "adjusting" the traditional view of application. Yet, having begun by prudence, is he now falling back into principlizing? Something more is needed to bridge the gap between principles and particular cases. Principles are largely theoretical and are the object of *episteme*, theoretical knowledge. What we need, however, is Christian *phronesis*: practical reasoning about what to say and do in situations for which no explicit biblical guidance is given.

I would encourage Doriani to explore the potential of a distinctly redemptive-historical casuistry rather than viewing casuistry as an appeal to principles abstracted from the history of redemption. I think he begins to do this in the section where he underlines the importance of asking the right questions. My own view would be that the right questions are the ones that help us further the main theodramatic action: Who are the principal *dramatis personae*? What is God doing to move the plot forward? How can I (we) participate so as to speed the play to its God-directed end? While Doriani does well to incorporate biblical narrative into the process of prudential reasoning (casuistry), I think all the other literary forms of the Bible have an equally important role to play in inculcating the mind of Christ in disciples who seek to follow God's Word into strange new worlds.

As I have argued elsewhere, the literary diversity of the Bible is not a problem to be solved by distilling culturally purified propositions. On the contrary, the various forms of literature in the Bible exist to form and transform our habits of perception and thinking. We become better prepared to carry the action forward when we are able to see the history of redemption through the lens not only of narrative, but of genres such as wisdom and apocalyptic as well.

I mentioned at the outset that both Webb and Doriani acknowledge a certain redemptive movement or progress through the Scriptures. As a complementarian, Doriani confronts head-on the claim that the clear development over the "arc of the biblical narrative" is in the direction of equality of women.

In light of the postmodern suspicion that we read as we are, it is notable that, at least in this case, Doriani reads Scripture not only against the cultural grain but also against the grain of his own personal upbringing. It is also worth noting that he does not use his method as an excuse for not grappling with the exegetical details of specific texts. After all, the whole (i.e., the full sweep of redemptive history) is made up of many parts, and to understand the whole correctly one must do justice to the individual parts as well. (Of course, Kaiser also appeals to "language and grammar" in arguing for egalitarianism.) Doriani's reading of redemptive history leads him to affirm the equality and liberation of women in everything except leadership in church and family. Though Jesus was a cultural revolutionary about many things, on this latter point Doriani sees no movement, though whether this is a function of the method itself or his own employment of it was not entirely clear to me.

A final comment. The issues Doriani examines are broadly ethical (or in the case of architecture, aesthetic) rather than doctrinal. The one exception may be women in ministry, but even this question, important though it be, is not at the ecclesiological core. The development of basic Christian doctrine is an important testing ground of hermeneutical methods that do more than repeat what the Bible says. Might there be more light yet to come from examining the ways in which the church fathers from East and West were able to come to a consensus over the potentially empire-breaking confession of the deity of Jesus Christ? How did they go beyond the Bible at Nicaea?

A RESPONSE TO DANIEL M. DORIANI

William J. Webb

AFTER READING DORIANI'S ESSAY on the "Redemptive-Historical Method" (herein, RH), I went for a long walk in the woods. It was a beautiful day and, as is my custom, I talked to God as I walked. I asked God these sorts of questions: How is it that some Christians, genuine Christ followers, can live out their lives with merely a static understanding of Scripture? How is it that they can think their views strongly uphold biblical authority when in fact (at least from my perspective) they severely diminish it? How is it that they can so vigorously commend the "face value" instructions of the Bible without exploring what an ultimate ethic ought to look like in human relationships? How can they claim that their method affirms the sufficiency of Scripture when Scripture is sufficient to cast a far grander ethical vision than their method permits?

Of course, my prayer to God was a lament of sorts. I did not expect or ask God for revelatory answers, nor would I ever do so. But I did ask that God's Spirit would help me respond gently. I surely want the mind of Christ to prevail, even within my own deficient version of it, as I try to express my views in this dialogue format. Here are a few reflections that I hope readers will find helpful.

BABY AND BATHWATER

Please do not throw out the baby with the bathwater. Anyone who holds to hierarchy on the gender issue I would encourage to question Doriani's alignment of a RMH (redemptive-movement hermeneutic) or trajectory approach exclusively with an egalitarian position. There are leading evangelicals who endorse a RMH approach (contra Doriani) and yet maintain some sort of contextually configured hierarchy,[93] generally of a soft or light version, for today. Three well-known evangelical scholars who within their own hierarchical framework have endorsed a RMH approach are Darrell Bock, Craig Blomberg, and Mark Strauss.[94]

Even if for logical and theological reasons one does not take an extension of redemptive-movement meaning all the way to egalitarian soil, at the very least one might consider its application in the numerous biblical texts where the treatment of women surely does not represent an ultimate ethic. Also, the canonical movement meaning within Scripture on this subject is powerful—it ought to be given at least some weighting within contemporary application. This shared use of a trajectory or RMH method provides some healthy common ground between egalitarians and hierarchalists. Whatever a person may think about egalitarianism, it would be a mistake to disavow a RMH method because of fondness or dislike for that position.

THE SLAVERY TEXTS

A number of times throughout his essay Doriani describes his RH method as a "face value" approach to the biblical text. For most readers this functional description is probably more easily understood than the redemptive-historical label. For this reason I will use his face value description below.

Let's start by talking about a foundational exegetical problem. Doriani seems to think that Christians can simply "exegete" their way to an abolitionist ethic. For instance, he cites 1 Corinthians 7:21c, "If you can gain your freedom, do so," in a manner that gives the impression that the apostle Paul was providing support here for abolitionism. But such face value aboli-

---

93. A RMH certainly pushes the envelope within hierarchal conclusions about the nature and expression of that hierarchy.

94. William J. Webb, "A Redemptive-Movement Hermeneutic: Encouraging Dialogue among Four Evangelical Views," *JETS* 48:2 (June 2005): 334–340. Darrell Bock wrote the foreword to *Slaves, Women & Homosexuals* because of his appreciation for a RMH even though he does not come to the same conclusions as myself on the gender issue. Similarly, Craig Blomberg gave written consent for me to include his name in the dedication of the book (dedicated to Blomberg and F. F. Bruce) in view of his shared endorsement of a RMH.

tionism is not a part of our Bibles—Old or New Testament—let alone a tiny ripped-out-of-context portion from Paul.

First, in the previous verse (1 Cor. 7:20) Paul calls for the Corinthians to remain in the situations in which they were called—even for slaves to do so—unless circumstances or opportunities arose where they were able to gain their freedom. Second, 1 Corinthians 7 has marriage as the central topic and slavery is a sidebar illustration of what it means to "remain as you are," whether married (paralleling slavery) or single (paralleling free). Notice in 7:32–35 that Paul wants single men to remain single because it affords greater opportunity to serve the Lord. The reason for slaves to gain their freedom if possible is so that, like unencumbered "free" single persons, they would have greater opportunity to serve God (7:22–23). In sum, the text is hardly an apostolic call for abolitionism. The same point can be made about the letter to Philemon. Despite reshaping the relationship of a master and a slave in wonderful, redemptive ways, Paul does not issue a call for all Christians to emancipate all their slaves or for slaves to seek their freedom even if it means running away (nonviolent emancipation).[95] For an exegetical discussion of Philemon, see my response to Walter Kaiser.

Likewise, the household codes addressing slaves and masters in Ephesians, Colossians, and 1 Peter could be paraphrased as follows: "Slaves, obey your masters and even endure hardship and abuse; Christian masters, treat your slaves well." Once again, this is hardly abolitionist teaching. There is no call for Christian masters to free their slaves and certainly no freedom or permission granted to slaves to run away at first opportunity. There exists incremental improvement to be sure, but hardly abolitionism.

Now come with me to two downtown black churches in Toronto, Canada, today. Both black evangelical churches are set in the core of the old, historic district of the city. When I have spoken at these churches, I have asked senior members

---

95. I do not want to discount Doriani's broader point where he cites 1 Cor. 7:21c about some of the dissimilarities between the slavery texts and the women texts. Yes, I am aware of these differences. Unfortunately, Doriani ignores the key similarity between these two case studies in relation to a RMH, namely, that many biblical texts (like the slavery texts) do not present an ultimate ethic in terms of the treatment of women. But that is another discussion.

who keep their black history archives and memorabilia this question: "Why did you not join the existing Baptist and Presbyterian white churches when you [your grandparents and great grandparents] came north on the underground railway?" The answer in both cases was the same, "We tried to join the white churches. But we were not permitted to become members." In fact, what happened was that these black runaway slaves were not permitted to become members unless (1) they had a letter from their church in the south affirming that they were members in good standing, and (2) they could show documentation from their former slave owner that they had obtained their freedom in "legitimate ways" — that is, a letter of payment or permission.

What a sad joke — a religious travesty! So how were white/free Christians reading their Bibles? The answer is quite simple: with a face value approach. I am not suggesting that Doriani or all who use a face value approach would necessarily arrive at this same handling of runaway slaves. My point is much broader, namely, that a face value reading of the slavery texts can easily lead Christians to the ethical conclusions encapsulated in this story. Despite what is claimed about the text being clear, one might say that *clarity within the face value method is not always clear.*

For that matter, it is extremely hard to reach an abolitionist conclusion using a face value reading of the biblical text. One might propose that according to the biblical story line slavery is not part of the first garden, nor is it part of the final eschatological garden. Fair enough. But during the in-between time, known as our fallen world, the face value approach to the words on the page (without any concept of redemptive-movement meaning) must accept the instruction of Scripture for what it is. On a purely face value level of meaning, Scripture clearly teaches slaves to make the best of it and serve their masters obediently, and for masters to treat their slaves well. The often-cited texts of 1 Corinthians 7:20 and Philemon simply do not teach abolitionism.[96]

---

96. Neither does the New Testament carry Old Testament corporal punishment texts (the second example within my RMH essay) to an ultimate ethic. While little is said at a concrete level, the New Testament seems to adopt Old Testament attitudes towards corporal punishment with an "as is" affirmation through theological analogy.

Ah, but maybe we have missed some crucial meaning here. From a RMH perspective I do think that there is *far more meaning* to these slavery texts than simply their face value meaning as it is derived from reading the text up and down the page in an isolated sense (see the discussion of slavery in my RMH essay). These texts are not simply there to regulate society, as Doriani suggests. We need to celebrate the *incremental redemptive movement* of both Old and New Testament slavery texts and permit their underlying spirit to carry us to an abolitionist position—using a logical and theological extension of Scripture's redemptive spirit found within the slavery texts themselves. I am convinced that Doriani's face value method, although often popular, is biblically deficient and ethically dangerous.

THEOLOGICAL REFLECTION AND RIGOROUS REASONING

Under this heading I am not quite sure how to articulate my concerns with Doriani's method other than to say that it sounds as though he thinks that Christians ought never to reflect critically about Scripture, not even in what might be considered a good sense. For instance, he states as a broad methodological point: "If the Bible says something we dislike, we do not say 'It can't be' or even 'I wonder,' but 'I stand corrected.' If Scripture says something I do not prefer, then so much the worse for my preferences." This minimization of what we might call "rigorous Christian reasoning"[97] comes across at numerous points throughout Doriani's essay.

Please do not misunderstand me. I applaud Doriani's emphasis on the need for radical submission to Scripture. I agree that at every point within the process of engaging the biblical text Christians need to be saying to God, "Thy will be done (not mine)." Furthermore, we need to embrace a hermeneutic of suspicion, not against Scripture, as some have proposed, but against ourselves as interpreters with all of our various biases. I am with Doriani all the way here.

---

97. "Rigorous theological, ethical, and hermeneutical reasoning" is probably a better term than "critical thinking" simply because of misunderstandings associated with the latter expression.

The problem, however, is that Doriani's method lacks sufficient balance. First, an emphasis on (1) the depravity of human interpreters of Scripture (a theme Doriani plays to the fullest) must be balanced with (2) a strong belief in, prayer for, and expectation of the Spirit's role in renewing the minds of Christians so that they can read Scripture with the tenderness of God's own heart and not with hearts of stone. Accordingly, Doriani's depiction of Christian minds is a little too dark for an accurate biblical understanding (see Vanhoozer's essay on the subject of acquiring the mind of Christ). Moreover, balance is also needed between (1) submission to Scripture and (2) a rigorous Christian reasoning about Scripture. The problem here is a catch-22—without rigorous Christian reasoning the version of biblical authority that we submit to may well be wrong (see below). So Christians desperately need balance in this area.

Doriani's overly lopsided focus on an "I stand corrected" posture misses out on the crucial and refreshing balance of rigorous Christian reasoning. Doriani's approach to what he discovers on the sacred page sounds strikingly similar to the words of John Henry Hopkins, a proslavery advocate whom I cite in my RMH essay. Of course, we must submit to the authority of Scripture, but let us not do so in a naïve manner, as can easily happen, so that we wind up getting wrong what God through Scripture truly wants of us. In discussing the slave-beating text of Exodus 21:20–21, I make three evaluative comments (using theological and ethical reflection) about a face value reading of that text. I say that a face value understanding of this text *ought to disturb contemporary Christians* for three reasons: (1) It enshrines the right of masters to beat their slaves; (2) it permits a latitude of punishment that could well have included very bloody and brutal beatings of slaves; and (3) it does so by positively invoking (instead of rejecting) the notion of people as property. If one cannot think and speak such ethically/theologically evaluative thoughts about a biblical text like Exodus 21:20–21 and instead one has to say, "I stand corrected" (as Doriani suggests), then Christians are in a great deal of trouble.

There must, to my mind, be a better way. On the one hand, Christians need to be able to think deeply about where Scripture does not reflect an ultimate ethic in the treatment of human beings as expressed in its concrete-specific instructions. On the other hand, Christians need to ponder persistently where the text forges new and exciting incremental movement (relative to the cultures of its first readers) as it gently and lovingly moves people toward something better. Both of these tough-minded tasks are essential. Both require a thankful use (not denigration) of the minds that God has given us, along with a dependence on his Spirit and a canonical embracing of the mind of Christ. Surely discovering aspects of incremental redemptive movement ought to be expected exploration by Christians within a text that has *Jesus* and a *dual-love ethic* at its redemptive core. Even if concrete-specific biblical instructions in some component or partial sense reflect the fallenness of this world and/or reflect the culturally restrictive horizons of an ancient world, often they evidence magnificent (praise God!) incremental movement toward a greater realization of Scripture's core ethic.

While we do not want to be anachronistically judgmental of a biblical social ethic, we surely do not want to promote a naïveté that treats Scripture as if it at every point presents an ultimate ethic. Only by wrestling hard with the incremental nature of Scripture's ethic and by listening to its redemptive spirit do we appreciate the much grander scope of Scripture's ethical vision. Christians ought to think rigorously and deeply about the biblical text with theological, ethical, logical, and hermeneutical reasoning with respect to what they find on the sacred page. The face value method seems lacking at this last crucial point.

REVELATION AND ILLUMINATION

I will address two problems under this "revelation and illumination" heading: (1) an incorrect understanding of Revelation 22:18–19 and, correspondingly, (2) an incorrect understanding of a RMH.

AN INCORRECT UNDERSTANDING OF REVELATION 22:18–19

Doriani mentions Revelation 22:18–19 in his critique of trajectory methods because from his perspective those who hold

such methods "add to" and/or "take away from" God's revelatory Word—that is, canonical Scripture. Although I cannot
speak for all trajectory methods (I will own only the faults
of mine), I assume that Doriani has my RMH essay as the
ultimate target or referent since (1) I represent such thinking
in this volume (though my preferred articulation is not "trajectory" but "movement meaning"), (2) his essay explicitly
links me with trajectory methods, and (3) in the context of
his Revelation 22 comments he talks about trajectory methods
without any stated exceptions that would spare me and my
particular RMH approach from his indictment. For these reasons I understand Doriani to be saying that trajectory/RMH
proponents like myself violate Revelation 22:18–19. To make
the point, he states:

> Indeed the conclusion of Revelation warns against
> such things (Rev. 22:18–19 [i.e., against people add-
> ing to or taking away from Scripture]). Moreover, if
> trajectory analysis exaggerates our knowledge, it also
> minimizes God's power. As we saw, it implies that God
> would have said something [further revelation] more
> acceptable—to modern sensibilities—but circum-
> stances made it impossible.

Since his indictment (if it be true) is extremely serious,
I will cite the entire portion of the Revelation text to which
Doriani refers:

> I warn everyone who hears the words of the prophecy
> of this book: If anyone adds anything to them, God
> will add to him [or her] the plagues described in this
> book. And if anyone takes words away from this book
> of prophecy, God will take away from him [or her]
> his [their] share in the tree of life and in the holy city,
> which are described in this book. (Rev. 22:18–19)

Clearly, whatever "adds to" or "takes away from" means,
the context is a prophetic curse—an imprecation of sorts with
heavy prophetic weighting. Obviously, the anathema falls on
any individual who has done an extremely evil deed(s) and presumably continues to do so. Commentators have often noted that
the curse comes from or is at least related to curses and admo-
nitions to obey God's commands in the book of Deuteronomy

(Deut. 2:1–4, 29–32; 4:1–6; 28:15–68).[98] The curse pronouncement in Revelation 22 is indeed serious because it identifies the erring individual as now living outside the covenant community and as subject to the full wrath of God. The penalty is the most severe eschatological consequence imaginable for human beings, namely, that the indicted individual becomes subject to the most awful of the curses of Revelation (including the eternal flames of hell) and forever forfeits eating from the Tree of Life (i.e., participation in the new heavens and new earth—eternal life with God). As Beale and Osborne convincingly argue,[99] the most likely persons (and activity referents) within the book of Revelation that the author John has in mind are the Balaam-like and Jezebel-like false prophets named in chapters 2 and 3. Like their Old Testament namesakes, these false prophets have led people away from worshiping Yahweh/Jesus, have encouraged the worship of idolatrous gods, and have promoted the related sexual immorality.

Perhaps that clarifies why, after reading Doriani's essay, I went for a long walk in the woods. Here are some of my woodland reflections. If Doriani's handling of Revelation 22:18–19 exemplifies his face value method, a method he describes as "close exegesis," "diligent exegesis," and "painstaking exegesis" that avoids proof texting,[100] then it would appear that we have a problem. Use of his face value method has produced an argument that turns on an artificial level of correspondence. It hears Revelation 22:18–19, picks up on the English idioms "add to" and "take away," and then rushes to an application without having grasped their true referential meaning

---

98. For two excellent discussions of Revelation 22:18–19, see Grant R. Osborne, *Revelation* (Baker Exegetical Commentary on the New Testament; Grand Rapids: Baker, 2002), 794–97; G. K. Beale, *The Book of Revelation* (New International Greek Text Commentary; Grand Rapids: Eerdmans, 1999), 1150–56.

99. To begin with, note the emphasis on false prophets in the seven churches and *the* false prophet *par excellence* who emerges as part of the evil trilogy. Also, there are connections between Balaam and the curse formulas of Deuteronomy.

100. Doriani pleads that we understand his method not as a proof texting method but as a method that evidences hard, painstaking labor. Along these lines he writes, "it is all too easy to toss the accusation of 'proof texting' [against my/Doriani's face value method] on what may [actually] be the fruit of painstaking exegesis."

within the book of Revelation, namely, what exactly the Jezebels and Balaams of chapters 2–3 were doing. Ironically, Doriani's indictment against RMH/trajectory proponents, by his citation of Revelation 22:18–19, provides an example of what he claims his method vigilantly avoids, namely, any sort of fallacious reasoning based on proof texting.

AN INCORRECT UNDERSTANDING OF A RMH METHOD

I cannot answer for other trajectory methods, but I will speak for the RMH model that I am proposing here and have used elsewhere. Doriani repeatedly suggests that trajectory methods attempt to provide Christians with *revelation* that exceeds the boundary of the canon. Perhaps some trajectory proponents argue this. I do not, however, know of any such persons. I for one am utterly appalled at the idea of attempting to provide extracanonical revelation.

A couple of considerations ought to bring some correction of this misunderstanding. First, the RMH model argues that any ethical development is simply an expression or further realization of the (abstracted) redemptive spirit within the text. So while there is a going beyond the concrete specificity of the text, there is *no* going beyond the spirit of the text. Here we "stay within" the biblical text. Now I must admit to poor communication at times on my part. For instance, this important "staying within" the meaning of the biblical text and its envisioned ethic was not presented as clearly as possible in the original RMH diagram (published in 2001). The method here is exactly the same as that earlier version (except perhaps that in this volume I have voiced the benefit of using multiple methods together), but the diagram in my present RMH essay much better depicts both the *going-beyond* the concrete and the *staying-within* the abstracted, redemptive-spirit meaning. Hopefully this greater emphasis on the "staying within" will demonstrate that I am *not* at all talking about new revelation or some enlarged canon beyond the New Testament.

Second, I would like to discuss "revelation and illumination" as they relate to the RMH approach. This ought to alleviate concern that I am somehow arguing for new revelation. Perish the thought! Below is a depiction of how "revelation and illumination" interface within a RMH model:

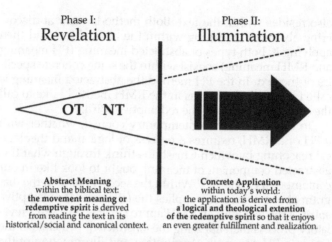

Phase I:	Phase II:
Revelation	**Illumination**

OT NT

Abstract Meaning
within the biblical text:
the movement meaning or redemptive spirit is derived
from reading the text in its
historical/social and canonical context.

Concrete Application
within today's world:
the application is derived from
a logical and theological extention
of the redemptive spirit so that it enjoys
an even greater fulfillment and realization.

What I call "movement meaning" or "redemptive spirit" is meaning found within the biblical text itself and thus part of phase I: *Revelation*. With the close of the New Testament canon there is no more revelation. What I refer to as "a logical and theological extension" of the redemptive spirit is not revelation but rather standard application by Christians and illumination of the Spirit—this is phase II: *Illumination*.

For Christians familiar with the Ladder of Abstraction from Kaiser's principlizing hermeneutic (PH), the RMH is simply a specialized development of that method, namely, the movement from *abstract* meaning (in the text) to a significantly modified *concrete* application (in our world). In fact, as I acknowledge in my response to Dr. Kaiser's essay, part of my thinking for a RMH model came from Kaiser's abstraction-to-particularization method, which I like to use in my hermeneutical toolbox in conjunction with a RMH approach.

The primary difference is that a principlizing method (PH) takes its cue from a *nonmovement (static) dimension of meaning in the concrete particulars* of the biblical text (derived from reading the words in their literary context) in order to discover a component of abstracted meaning that resides within the text, whereas a redemptive-movement method (RMH) takes its cue from a *movement dimension of meaning in the concrete particulars* of the biblical text (derived from reading the words in their ancient historical/social and canonical contexts) in order to discover another aspect of abstracted meaning that also resides within the text. Both methods work at discovering abstracted meaning within the biblical text and then applying it; both types of abstracted meaning (PH meaning and RMH meaning) coexist within the same concrete specifics of the text. In the PH method the abstracted meaning is called a principle, whereas in the RMH method I like to call the abstracted meaning the redemptive spirit.

To move into our contemporary context, whether with a PH or a RMH, requires a process of logical and theological reasoning by which Christians think through what this abstracted component of meaning ought to look like in our contemporary context.[101] Within the second phase in the diagram above, where one applies the (abstracted) redemptive spirit of the text with an RMH approach, it is no more a revelatory process than applying the (abstracted) principle of the text in a PH approach. Application and illumination of the Spirit? Yes. Revelation? No.

Here is the final clincher for putting to rest misgivings about a RMH developing new revelation, namely, a practical

---

101. With the *PH method* one has to give rigorous thinking to (1) similarities and differences in order to determine how high to go on the Ladder of Abstraction before crossing over between two worlds—differences between the ancient and contemporary horizons push one up the ladder to a more abstracted articulation of one's principle, while similarities ought to bring one down the ladder. Then (2) further hard thinking is needed with the PH method to reason through how to bring the abstracted meaning (the imbedded principle) back down the ladder into a contemporary context. Because this is a human reasoning process, not all will agree with the PH results and the strength of one's application is only as good as the reasoning in both steps—(1) and (2)—is cogent. With the *RMH method* rigorous thinking is required in (1) looking at the biblical text within its ancient historical/social context and canonical context in order to get a sense of abstracted redemptive spirit with respect to its strength, incremental movement, and direction of movement. After this abstracted meaning is ascertained, the next step (2) involves further thinking and reflection, given the logic of extension (some prefer calling this step trajectory) and various other theological factors, about how far one ought to take the underlying or embedded redemptive spirit within the new contemporary context. Once again, the conflicting results arrived at by different people using the PH method must likewise be expected using the RMH method. Since the RMH, like the PH, involves a human reasoning process, not all RMH proponents will agree with each other's results, and the strength of anyone's RMH application is only as good as the reasoning in both steps—(1) and (2)—is cogent.

case study with differing results. Darrell Bock, who wrote the foreword to my *Slaves, Women and Homosexuals* book, is a happy supporter of a RMH approach. Yet he is a hierarchalist and I am an egalitarian. (We are praying for each other to see the light.) On the issue of slavery he utilizes a RMH to discover within the concrete particulars of the biblical slavery texts a component of (abstracted) movement meaning or redemptive spirit. This in turn permits him through an application process of logical and theological reflection to show that such abstracted meaning, if naturally or logically or theologically extended, ought to take the shape of an abolitionist ethic in our contemporary context.

We see eye-to-eye here. In fact, he could have written my slavery essay and would probably have done a better job. Nevertheless, Dr. Bock and I take the logical and theological extension of the redemptive spirit within the women texts to different endpoints—he is a light or ultra-light hierarchalist (not a heavy hierarchy by any means) and I am a complementary egalitarian. Now one of us in the process of RMH application is wrong! But this should demonstrate that we are definitely into application and not revelation. The same thing is true when using the PH process and taking the abstracted meaning (principle) into a contemporary culture. Not everyone is going to agree on (1) how high up the Ladder of Abstraction to cross over, and (2) exactly how the principle should be fleshed out in a new context. Whether using a RMH or a PH, the validity of the result always depends on the cogency of the reasoning across a couple of logical and theological steps.

METHODOLOGICAL HUMILITY AND PREDICATED ARGUMENTS

Doriani adopts what in my view is faulty argumentation at the core of his essay because he utilizes predicated arguments.[102] In other words, his arguments based on biblical

---

102. By "predicated arguments" I mean arguments against a competing view that are correct if and only if one's own view, from which those arguments are made, is correct. To say it another way, the arguments against the opposing viewpoint are "predicated" upon or require the validity of one's own position in order to be true.

authority, biblical clarity, and the sufficiency of Scripture work as arguments only if his underlying predications and assumptions about his method are correct. If we begin reading his essay and find ourselves aligning with his face value approach or with his gender conclusions (wrongly polarized) because that is part of our preunderstanding coming into the essay, we will be more vulnerable to accepting his reasoning without critical reflection. His arguments work only because they are predicated upon (hence "predicated arguments") the correctness of his face value view. However, to the degree that I am correct about a RMH and he is incorrect about his face value method, then all of his loaded charges flip back upon himself and virtually torpedo his method.

In effect, Doriani's use of predicated arguments betrays a lack of methodological humility. He may well be a very humble man in *all* other aspects of his life. I am speaking here *strictly* of methodological and epistemological humility. Let me illustrate the problem by putting his shoes on my feet and walking a block or two in a reversed manner. For instance, I am fully convinced that Doriani's view undermines biblical authority because it squelches an element of movement meaning embedded within the biblical text. I am strongly persuaded that Doriani's face value approach harms a robust understanding of the sufficiency of Scripture — it causes theological impotence in the formation of a contemporary ethic. And I think that Doriani's understanding and appreciation of the Spirit's illumination within the Christian community to enable reflection upon a biblical ethic are highly deficient. I could go on.

Should I say such things about Doriani's face value approach? Should I put my convictions about Doriani's method "undermining biblical authority" into an expanded argument form and publish them in order to persuade readers of my position? Absolutely not![103] First, in writing any going-beyond essay I would want to estab-

---

103. Given that Doriani included these predicated arguments about a theology of Scripture within his original essay, I have little choice but to respond to them and show why they are problematic.

lish the validity of my approach on its own merits. To a large extent, Doriani's chapter did not fulfill his assignment, in that it was an attack on other positions instead of a positive argument for his own position. Rather than addressing difficult interpretive problems and giving better methodological answers than others do, Doriani seeks to discredit others with pejorative language that tends to prejudice the reader rather than engage the real issues. On this note, I would have loved to see a lengthy discussion by Doriani about how he would argue with his face value method in a persuasive manner for an abolitionist ethic. Such was lacking.

Second, even if I were convinced that Doriani's face value method undermines biblical authority (and I am), it would be unkind of me to focus on "undermining biblical authority" arguments in critiquing his method, because I know that, like me, he personally expresses at a confessional level a sincere belief in this important aspect of a theology of Scripture. I wish to guard, not destroy the integrity of his theological confession.

Third and most important, if I grounded my case on predicated arguments, I would be betraying an inflated sense about the rightness of my position (and wrongness of his). By using such predicated arguments, I would be demonstrating a lack of epistemological and methodological humility. Perhaps one might think there is no need to be humble when protecting the Bible. Yet, such good "protecting the Bible" motives lie behind my own use of and argumentation for a RMH, whether Doriani is aware of these intentions or not.

Aside from reasons based purely on methodological assessment, I also do not care for a face value approach because I see it as extremely damaging to Scripture. While such underlying motives on my part may be honorable, they ought to be held in check within my critique of other competing approaches lest I be guilty of holding my own interpretive method at the same level of affirmation as Scripture itself (not to mention the above two considerations). Affirmation of method ought not to be equated with affirmation of Scripture. Our very best attempts at discerning meaning from Scripture ought not to be equated with Scripture itself. The absence of such scholarly (and I think Christian) humility leads well-meaning people, myself included at times, to make such faulty arguments.

CONCLUSION

I conclude my response to Doriani's essay by voicing some of my own liabilities. In all of my efforts to understand and apply the sacred page, I have sought to be faithful and true to Scripture and to its authority upon my life. I really *do* think there is a component of redemptive-movement meaning (redemptive spirit) embedded within the concrete particulars of the biblical text that I am responsible for embracing as a Christian. I need to give applicational expression to that redemptive spirit if I am to obey Scripture in the fullest sense.

Unlike Doriani and Kaiser, I am not inclined to see the New Testament as resolving either the slavery or the corporal punishment issue in terms of a *concrete specification* of the text (RM meaning is an entirely different matter). So, we are naturally going to see contemporary ethical formation derived from the New Testament in different ways. The basic idea of redemptive-movement meaning and how it is derived from the text is quite simple. But working with that meaning to produce a model for going beyond is not as simple. I will be the first to admit that I have not always communicated the model as clearly as I ought. Furthermore, in my present construction of the RMH method I may not yet have everything exactly right. I am open to ways of improving the model, for in the final analysis I am primarily committed to God and to Scripture and not to the model.

In many respects I entered into this response to Dr. Doriani with great reluctance and a heavy heart. Nevertheless, our dialogue has been beneficial inasmuch as it helps us clarify the issues distinguishing our respective views. I am hopeful that this interaction may clear the way for future dialogue of a more constructive sort where we can simply put our models on the table for mutual inspection and reflection. On such an occasion we could discuss the strengths and weaknesses (yes, even a RMH has weaknesses!) of our respective methods while vigilantly guarding the genuineness of our shared affirmations and earnest convictions about Scripture. I will guard his confessional integrity and he can guard mine.

CHAPTER THREE

A DRAMA-OF-REDEMPTION MODEL

ALWAYS PERFORMING?

Kevin J. Vanhoozer

It may be that when we no longer know what to do we have begun our real work and that when we no longer know which way to go we have come to our real journey. The mind that is not baffled is not employed. The impeded stream is the one that sings.[1]

OF PATHWAYS, WRONG WAYS, AND OTHER WAYS OF GOING BEYOND

The Bible, God's Word written, is "a lamp to my feet and a light for my path" (Ps. 119:105), but there is some confusion over how to switch it on and some debate over how far ahead it shines.

---

1. Wendell Berry, *Standing by Words: Essays* (Berkeley, CA: Shoemaker Hoard, 2005), 97.

THE WAY OF THE WAY

The early Christian movement was dubbed "the Way" (Acts 9:2; 19:9) for good reason: these believers were disciples committed to the one who said, "I am the way and the truth and the life" (John 14:6). Jesus told his disciples that they could understand him by reading the Scriptures: the Old Testament interprets Jesus and Jesus interprets the Old Testament (Luke 24:25 – 27). Similarly, those who would continue to follow Jesus today have no recourse but to interpret the Old and New Testament Scriptures.[2]

The challenge of present-day Christian discipleship is to follow the way of Jesus Christ in a very different space and time in which the prevailing ways of life (cultures) bear scant resemblance to the preindustrial, agrarian settings of ancient Israel. John the Baptist had to prepare the way of the Lord (Matt. 3:3); our task is to *continue* it. How can a young church keep its way straight as it wends its way through contexts that the Word of God never mentions? What does it mean to be biblical in the twenty-first century? We begin with a cautionary tale.

A WRONG WAY

In the summer of 2005 A. J. Jacobs put into storage any of his clothes that were made of mixed fibers (Lev. 19:19) as the first step in what he termed Project Bible: a year-long experiment of living strictly according to the Scriptures. Jacobs, an agnostic wanting to reconnect with his Jewishness, kept a day-by-day record of his experience, which he eventually published as *The Year of Living Biblically: One Man's Humble Quest to Follow the Bible as Literally as Possible.*[3] Jacobs spent eight months trying to live according to the Old Testament and four months according to the New. He conducted his experiment with tongue planted firmly in cheek, demonstrating the "righteous idiocy" of literal interpretation by taking legalism to its logical extreme. For example, on Day Sixty-Two he stoned Sab-

---

2. See Eugene Peterson, *The Jesus Way: A Conversation on the Ways that Jesus Is the Way* (Grand Rapids: Eerdmans, 2007).

3. New York: Simon & Schuster, 2007. See also A. J. Jacobs, "By the Book: An Experiment in Biblical Living," *Christian Century* (October 16, 2007), 24 – 33.

bath breakers and adulterers in Central Park. Not wanting to be arrested for criminal assault, however, he decided to toss pebbles surreptitiously at the small of an offender's back.

Even failed experiments sometimes yield interesting results. Jacobs' attempt to stick to the original intent and follow it "to the letter" ends up mocking not literal interpretation but his own shaky grasp of what this involves. He equates "living biblically" with following rules but fails to recognize the bigger picture in which the rules are (or are not) to be applied. He does not see that living biblically is a matter not only of volition, but of cognition, affection, and imagination as well, or that living biblically is ultimately a community project, not the accomplishment of an individual. Jacobs is unable to see past the letter into the subject matter, or spirit, of the text, nor does he display any awareness of developments within the Bible itself. Though creative in its parody of fundamentalist interpretation, his experiment is ultimately unimaginative and uninspired. The Bible, in Jacobs' hands, is but an obsolete guide to etiquette, not a living and active force that cuts through human hearts (Heb. 4:12).

A STILL MORE EXCELLENT (HERMENEUTICAL) WAY

I. Howard Marshall has conducted a similar experiment, examining from the perspective of a New Testament scholar how thinking and living biblically might require one to go *beyond* the Bible with principles sanctioned by the Bible itself.[4] How, and to what extent, can first-century discourse and discipleship exercise an authoritative role on twenty-first century discourse and discipleship?

What Marshall knows, and Jacobs does not, is that we cannot live biblically without engaging in biblical interpretation. It's all about right interpretive reason, about knowing how to move from *sacra pagina* (holy Scripture) to *sacra doctrina* (holy teaching). The issue is not *whether* but *how* the Bible exercises its authority despite its historical and cultural distance. We can eliminate the two extremes: that what the biblical authors say has antiquarian interest only, and that

---

4. I. Howard Marshall, *Beyond the Bible: Moving from Scripture to Theology* (Grand Rapids: Baker, 2004).

everything the biblical authors say is transculturally normative. What we need are biblical principles for discerning the
Word of God in the words of man, the theologically normative from the anthropologically relative.

The process of biblical interpretation is itself a means of
discipleship. One cannot follow the way without following
the way the words go. Who is in the best position to lead
us to the promised land of right reading, to use the Bible
to illumine our pathway through territories known and
unknown? Who holds the keys to the kingdom of biblical
interpretation? There are many academic pretenders to the
theological throne. My own view is that theological interpretation of Scripture—reading the Bible in the church to hear
God—is a joint project. We need all the theological disciplines working together in order to think and live biblically.
Left to its own devices, each single discipline falls short of
cultivating the godly wisdom that is the end of theological
education: the ability to know and love God rightly.

Being biblical is ultimately an ecclesial rather than an
academic project, however. It is a matter of knowing how
to speak, and do, the truth in love; of becoming mature,
growing up in every way into Christ (Eph. 4:13–15). Biblical studies alone are not enough, especially when they bog
down "behind the text."[5] Yes, it requires application, but as
we saw above with the example of stoning, it is not always a
straightforward matter to know how "what it meant" bears
on the present. This is where church history helps inasmuch
as it is simultaneously the history of biblical interpretation,
for what else is the church but the community that seeks
to follow the Word of God? Similarly, pastoral counseling,
missiology, and systematic theology are all forms of biblical interpretation to the extent that they too foster biblical
thinking and living in individuals and families in this and
in other cultures.[6]

---

5. By "behind the text" I am referring to the interest not in what the text
says but in questions concerning historical background (i.e., the world from
which the text was produced).

6. See Paul Ballard and Stephen R. Holmes, *The Bible in Pastoral Practice: Readings in the Place and Function of Scripture in the Church* (Grand Rapids:
Eerdmans, 2006).

We would do well to keep in mind the apostle Paul's mission statement for the Bible: "All Scripture is God-breathed and is useful for teaching, rebuking, correcting and training in righteousness" (2 Tim. 3:16). *Sacra pagina* is profitable for *sacra doctrina*, which in turn is profitable for *sacra vita* (holy living), which includes sanctification and *shalom*. Theology is "practical" in the fullest, most robust sense: it is a matter not of building systems of ideas so much as it is of world-building, or rather, of building up the world into the fullness of Christ (Eph. 1:22–23). Being biblical, then, ultimately refers to what may be termed a "political" task: building the city of God amidst the ruins of the city of Man.

FAITH SEEKING (AND DISPLAYING) UNDERSTANDING: THE DIVINE DRAMA OF REDEMPTION

In order to continue biblical Christianity into the contemporary context, it is important to know what kind of road we are traveling. What/who are we trying to follow? To what/whom are we trying to be faithful: a person, a philosophy, a moral code, a tradition, an ancient culture?

The subject matter of the Bible, and hence of Christian faith and thought, is intrinsically dramatic. The gospel is the good news that God the Father has said and done things in Jesus Christ through the Holy Spirit for the salvation of the world. What the church seeks to understand is essentially a true story: the history of God's dealings with his creatures. By story I am thinking not of a particular kind of literary genre so much as a series of events that, when taken together as a unified drama, serve as a lens or interpretative framework through which Christians think, make sense of their experience, and decide what to do and how to do it.

In employing a theatrical model I am not subscribing to a particular theory of drama but rather deploying a number of themes and concepts that will prove fruitful in our search for Christian understanding.[7] Going beyond the Bible

---

7. I range over various drama theories and theater traditions in much the same way that I do with philosophy and literary theory, making ad hoc use of

biblically is ultimately a matter of participating in the great drama of redemption of which Scripture is the authoritative testimony and holy script. The Bible communicates divine *doctrina* that instructs the church in the way of the divine drama. Theology involves not only theoretical but *theatrical* reasoning: *practical* reasoning about what to say and do in particular situations in light of the gospel of Jesus Christ; practical reasoning about what to say and do in order "to present yourself to God as one approved, a worker who ... correctly handles the word of truth" (2 Tim. 2:15).

THEODRAMA

Drama reminds us that we should not draw too fine a distinction between "word" and "act"; the theater is, after all, the language of action. The sacred page exists to direct our attention to the divine play: "The play's the thing."[8] Theology is merely the shadow cast by the theodrama; God's doing—God's speech and action—is prior to the church's response. The gospel that assembles the church is a divine comedy in which followers of Jesus Christ have a privilege and responsibility to take part.[9]

Theater occurs when one or more persons "present" themselves to others.[10] And so it is with the drama of redemption. Everything begins with revelation, the self-presentation of God on the stage of world history: "Revelation in the Bible means the self-unveiling ... of the God who by nature cannot be unveiled to men."[11] Theodrama is precisely a matter of God's taking the initiative to make himself known to others, of God's own parting of the secular curtain in order to reveal and redeem. Unlike philo-

---

only those elements that help me conceptually to elaborate what is going on in Scripture. The theologian is, after all, a minister of understanding and is free to use any and all concepts insofar as they serve the ministerial cause.

8. Shakespeare, *Hamlet* (act 2, scene 2).

9. For a fuller treatment of these themes, see my *The Drama of Doctrine* (Louisville: Westminster John Knox, 2005), part 1.

10. Bernard Beckerman, *Dynamics of Drama: Theory and Method of Analysis* (New York: Knopf, 1970), 8.

11. Karl Barth, *Church Dogmatics*, I/1, 315.

sophical systems where the medium is ideas, or film where the medium is celluloid images, the medium of drama is living persons in dialogical interaction. Drama involves external, bodily activity that makes known one's inner life or spirit.[12] But this is precisely what happens in the history of Jesus Christ: the living God presents himself through the medium of the words and deeds that comprise a particular human life. It is theodrama all the way down. God's being is in Christ, revealing and reconciling himself to the world.

The drama-of-redemption approach has certain advantages over its history-of-redemption, narrative-of-redemption, and logic-of-redemption rivals. Though these approaches rightly recognize that the Bible is "the great story and plot of all time and space,"[13] they differ over how best to understand what makes the story authoritative.

The great merit of a redemptive-historical approach, such as that of Geerhardus Vos, is that it rightly identifies the content of revelation as forming not a dogmatic system but a book of history that unfolds organically.[14] He is thus able to treat the diverse words and deeds of God under a unifying redemptive-historical context.[15] If there is a weakness, it is that Vos does not show the church how to go beyond the sacred page, for the simple reason that the church today shares the same redemptive-historical context with the

---

12. Paul Kurtz uses Aristotle's categories to analyze the formal, material, efficient, and final cause of dramatic theater. The *form* of drama, for example, is story; the *material* of drama is the human being. See Kurtz, *The Fiery Serpent: A Christian Theory of Film and Theater* (Enumclaw, WA: Pleasant Word, 2007).

13. Amos Wilder, *The Language of the Gospel* (New York: Harper & Row, 1964), 64–65.

14. Interestingly, Richard Gaffin cites two programmatic statements from Vos, one from his Princeton inaugural lecture and the other written after his retirement, in which he mentions both the historical nature of biblical revelation and its "dramatic interest" (see Gaffin, "Introduction" to Geerhardus Vos, *Redemptive History and Biblical Interpretation: The Shorter Writings of Geerhardus Vos* [Phillipsburg, NJ: Presbyterian & Reformed, 1980], xv).

15. "Biblical Theology, rightly defined, is nothing else than *the exhibition of the organic process of supernatural revelation in its historic continuity and multiformity*" ("The Idea of Biblical Theology as a Science and as a Theological Discipline," in ibid., 15).

authors of the New Testament: "We ourselves live just as much in the N.T. as did Peter and Paul and John."[16] Whether *other* contexts (i.e., technological, cultural, intellectual) have a bearing on the church's life and thought is something that Vos does not explicitly address.[17]

Narrative-of-redemption approaches similarly recognize that what unifies the diverse books of the Bible is an over-arching story, a story that begins with creation and ends with restoration, re-creation, and consummation. However, drama does better in reminding us that the whole into which we are to participate is a unified action, and that we are to participate in *active* faith. It is not enough to be spectators or hearers of the Word only; we must be actors and doers as well. While narratives can be told in the third person at something of a distance from oneself, drama is "dialogue in action" and calls for first and second person discourse, the language of interpersonal relations. Story becomes drama when one enters into it, body and soul.

What we may term the "logic of redemption" approach seeks underlying abstract principles or universal truths (e.g., "God punishes disobedience") that can serve as premises for theological arguments in new contexts. One abstracts such principles, however, only by extracting them from the particular scene in which they make sense. Those who de-dramatize the Bible in this way want the "point" without the parable, the content without the form, the "soul" without the body of the text. It is not always easy, however, to decide *what* the principle behind the text is or *how* to apply it anew.[18] In a dramatic paradigm, by way of contrast, the point is not to extract a principle through some *procedure*

---

16. Geerhardus Vos, *Biblical Theology* (Grand Rapids: Eerdmans, 1948), 325–26.

17. The drama-of-redemption approach makes room as well for a consideration of what we will term below the world "in front of" the biblical text, and for the way in which the text has been received in the church.

18. For a critique of the principlizing approach, see David Clark, *To Know and Love God: Method in Theology* (Wheaton, IL: Crossway, 2003), 91–98. Clark's main worries are two: that the principles will be seen as better than the Bible, and that the principlizer will fail to recognize his or her own cultural conditionedness.

but to become a wiser *person* precisely by considering particular instances of canonical wisdom: not abstract truth but concrete wisdom-in-act. In the words of David Clark: "Abstracted propositions will not inspire new ways of living nearly as well as the concrete poetry, story, and apocalyptic in which God saw fit to inspire the Bible."[19]

In sum: the drama-of-redemption approach affirms God's actions in history, preserves the emphasis on story, and incorporates a canonically attuned, wisdom-oriented "chastened" principlizing, while better integrating the interpreters into the action. The superiority of theodrama as a model for thinking about biblical authority and interpretation thus consists in its awareness that understanding is a matter not only of cognition but of action; moreover, it insists that there are biblical texts whose meanings are only fully "realized" as something is *done* with them or on their basis.[20]

SCRIPT

The theatrical analogy opens up a fresh perspective on what it means to live biblically (performance) and thereby gives us new purchase on the nature of the Bible itself. The Bible is the church's holy script. Although it displays an overarching narrative structure, it includes a variety of literary genres and authorial voices. As to form, the Bible is polyphonic discourse: what someone (prophets and apostles) in particular situations at particular times says about something ("the gospel of God" [Rom. 1:1]) to someone in some way (literary genres).[21] To confess that the Bible is God's Word is to hold that God so guides and coordinates the human authors as to render them a canonical cloud

---

19. Ibid., 97.

20. Trevor Hart, "Introduction: Art, Performance and the Practice of Christian Faith," in *Faithful Performances: Enacting Christian Tradition*, ed. Ivan P. Khovacs, Trevor Hart, and Steven R. Guthrie (Aldershot, UK: Ashgate, 2007), 6.

21. See my "The Apostolic Discourse and Its Developments," in *Scripture's Doctrine*, ed. Markus Bockmuehl and Alan Torrance (Grand Rapids: Baker, 2008).

of witnesses who together communicate the divine playwright's intention.

The drama *is* the discourse, we might say, and this in three senses. First, the prophetic and apostolic discourse is the authorized memory of and testimony to the theodrama. Second, Scripture is *divine* discourse: the medium of God's own spoken action, the means through which God continues to address and engage the church. It follows that what is transcultural is not some principle behind the Bible but the biblical discourse itself. Third, as discourse, the Bible is not a dead textual body to be exegetically dissected but a Spirited letter that is living and active and demanding of response. The church's script is not an inert object for critical analysis but an invitation to dialogue and participation. Biblical discourse — what the writers say about what they have seen and heard — is the basis for fellowship with the authors and, ultimately, with the triune God (1 John 1:1 – 3).[22]

PERFORMANCE

Those who read Scripture are called to be "doers of the word, and not merely hearers" (James 1:22 NRSV). To look into the mirror of the text only to forget what one sees there is to be a hearer only, thus short-circuiting the process of interpretation that is intended to produce "doers who act" (1:25 NRSV). The script exists to tell the church about the drama and to solicit its participation. Biblical interpretation is incomplete unless it issues in some kind of performance, for, as Calvin says, "All right knowledge of God is born of obedience."[23]

It follows that the most important form our biblical interpretations take is that of lived performance. "No one can appreciate the full truth of the Christian revelation unless he or she is a player within its distinctive

---

22. See Philip F. Esler, "New Testament Interpretation as Interpersonal Communion: The Case for a Socio-Theological Hermeneutics," in *The Nature of New Testament Theology: Essays in Honour of Robert Morgan*, ed. Christopher Rowland and Christopher Tuckett (Oxford: Blackwell, 2006), 51 – 74.

23. John Calvin, *Institutes*, 1.6.2.

dynamics—participating in the drama of God's self-communication to the world and living out its implications in committed action."[24] Hans Urs von Balthasar only slightly exaggerates when he says that the lives of the saints are themselves interpretations of the gospel, more true and more convincing than all exegesis. From a Protestant perspective, of course, all believers are player-saints in the company of the gospel.[25]

"Do this" (1 Cor. 11:24–25). The church performs her faith and participates in the theodrama each time people come together and share the Lord's Supper. In eating the bread and drinking the cup, the church commemorates the climax of the theodrama and anticipates its end.

DIRECTION

Theology exists to help the church creatively and faithfully to continue the way, the truth, and the life of Jesus Christ until he comes. Theology is God-centered biblical interpretation that issues in performance knowledge on the world stage to the glory of God. Briefly stated: theology exists to minister theodramatic understanding of what God has said/done in the world for us and of what the church must say/do for God in response.

To understand is to acquire "a set of capacities for action in relation to something."[26] That which faith seeks

---

24. Ben Quash, "Real Enactment: The Role of Drama in the Theology of Hans Urs von Balthasar," in *Faithful Performances*, ed. Khovacs, Hart, and Guthrie, 13. J. I. Packer agrees: "The basic form of obedient theology is applicatory interpretation" ("In Quest of Canonical Interpretation," in *The Use of the Bible in Theology: Evangelical Options*, ed. Robert K. Johnston [Eugene, OR: Wipf and Stock, 1997], 44). According to Packer, some truths—mainly about ourselves—we only know and perceive as truth "in the process of actually obeying it", 54.

25. Old Testament prophets like Jeremiah (Jer. 19:1–13) sometimes performed mini-dramas that illustrated by enactment the content of their message. See David Stacey, *Prophetic Drama in the Old Testament* (London: Epworth, 1990), and William Doan and Terry Giles, *Prophets, Performance, and Power* (New York and London: T & T Clark, 2005).

26. David Kelsey, *To Understand God Truly* (Louisville: Westminster John Knox, 1992), 124–29.

to understand is, as we have seen, the theodrama — what God is saying and doing and what the people of God must say and do in response. *Doctrina* thus resembles theatrical direction, that is, sacred teaching given for the purpose of communicating the main idea of the play and hence for providing instruction on how rightly to participate in the drama of redemption.[27] Kierkegaard is well aware, however, that sinners resist doctrinal direction: "We pretend to be unable to understand [the Bible] because we know very well that the minute we understand we are obliged to act accordingly."[28]

To play our parts rightly, it is not enough theoretically to know what the play is about; we must also be the kind of persons who have the will and the capacity to play. Doctrine exists not to increase the church's inventory of information but to cultivate theodramatic wisdom: the ability to make right judgments, to say and do the right think, vis-à-vis not only the created but the re-created or eschatological order of things, the order of things "in Christ."

The purpose of doctrine, then, is to make us wise unto Christ: the center, climax, and central content of the theodrama.[29] Doctrine helps the church to move forward with her script by providing answers to the following questions:

1. Where are we in the theodrama? What kind of scene are we playing?
2. Who are we? In what kind of plot are our lives entangled?
3. What time is it? What act and scene of the drama of redemption are we playing?

---

27. Cf. Kierkegaard: "Doctrines are descriptions which propose to be actualized in human experience" (cited in Alister McGrath, *The Genesis of Doctrine* [Grand Rapids: Eerdmans, 1997], 79).

28. *Søren Kierkegaard's Journals and Papers*, ed. and trans. Howard V. Hong and Edna H. Hong; 7 vols. (Princeton University Press, 1967–78), 3:270–73.

29. For an excellent treatment of how Christian wisdom is connected to virtue and thus to the pedagogy of the Holy Spirit that renews and transforms our minds and hearts, see Daniel J. Treier, *Virtue and the Voice of God: Toward Theology as Wisdom* (Grand Rapids: Eerdmans, 2006), esp. 200–202.

4. What is happening? What is God doing?
5. What should we say or do?[30]

Together, these five add up to a single, comprehensive question: *Why are we, the church, here?* The answer to that question takes the form of a mission statement: we are here to participate rightly in God's triune mission to the world. Doctrine, as direction for right doing in the drama of redemption, is thus a matter of formation as much as information. The privilege and responsibility of theology is to form not merely theoretical systems of belief but theatrical systems or designs for living. *Doctrina*, lived understanding, ultimately involves not only concepts but the church's whole way of life: beliefs, values, and everyday practices. In the final analysis, doctrine enables the church to *do* the truth and thus fulfill her vocation "to live as Jerusalem in the midst of Babylon."[31]

PERFORMING THE SCRIPT: DISCOVERING THE WORLD IN FRONT OF THE BIBLICAL TEXT

The Bible, I have claimed, is theodramatic discourse: something someone (prophets and apostles, the Holy Spirit) says about something (the drama of redemption) to someone (the church) at some time (past, present) in some way (a variety of literary forms). This raises a pertinent question: Is the notion of "performing" discourse really the best model for describing the way the Bible functions authoritatively in the church?

---

30. I am modifying these from N. T. Wright, *The New Testament and the People of God* (Minneapolis: Fortress, 1992), 122–23, who in turn got them from J. Brian Walsh and Richard Middleton, *The Transforming Vision: Shaping a Christian World View* (Downers Grove, IL: InterVarsity Press, 1984). The four questions Wright poses are: 1. Who are we? 2. Where are we? 3. What is wrong? 4. What is the solution?

31. William Stringfellow, *An Ethic for Christians and Other Aliens in a Strange Land* (Waco, TX: Word, 1973), as cited by Rowland and Tuckett in *The Nature of New Testament Theology*, 197.

IS PERFORMANCE REALLY THE BEST TERM?

Theologians have been exploring the parallel between interpreting texts and performing scripts since Nicholas Lash's seminal 1982 essay "Performing the Scriptures."[32] The essential insight is that there are some texts — musical scores, play scripts — whose interpretation, and perhaps meaning, depend on *doing* something with them. To perform a script is to give a text the kiss of life; only when we take up our script and walk (talk) do we "actualize" and bring it to completion.[33]

Much in the life of the church resembles performance: "When we read or sing the Psalms together, we perform them. When we enact scenes from the life of Jesus, breaking bread and washing feet, we are performing. When we obey a direct commandment, we are, in some sense, performing that commandment."[34] Yet not everyone is convinced. Samuel Wells points out that it is not clear how the church is to enact the script in unfamiliar circumstances: "The script does not provide all the answers."[35] In the second place, the script is not yet finished: "There is more to the Christian story than the pages of the Bible disclose."[36] Finally, the idea that the church is to perform a holy script and thereby re-create a golden era of the gospel suggests that the church need not engage with the contemporary intellectual and cultural context.

Dan Stiver raises additional concerns in relation to my book *The Drama of Doctrine*.[37] He asks what it would mean

---

32. Nicholas Lash, *Theology on the Way to Emmaus* (London: SCM, 1986). See also Frances Young, *The Art of Performance: Towards a Theology of Holy Scripture* (London: Darton, Longman and Todd, 1990); Stephen Barton, "New Testament Interpretation as Performance," *Scottish Journal of Theology* 52 (1999): 179–208; Khovacs, Hart, and Guthrie, eds., *Faithful Performances*.

33. The etymology of the term is instructive: *par* ("through, to completion") + *fournir* ("to furnish, provide").

34. Shannon Craigo-Snell, "Command Performance: Rethinking Performance Interpretation in the Context of *Divine Discourse*," *Modern Theology* 16 (2000): 480.

35. Samuel Wells, *Improvisation: the Drama of Christian Ethics* (Grand Rapids: Brazos, 2004), 62.

36. Ibid., 63.

37. I am grateful to Dan for making his unpublished paper available to me. His "Appropriating Drama: Reply to Vanhoozer" was originally pre-

to perform *Huckleberry Finn* as a script. Even if it were not Mark Twain's intention, would not performing the script involve some form of racism? Similarly, how should Christians perform the conquest of Canaan, the story of David and Bathsheba or, to return to A. J. Jacobs's experiment in living biblically, the command to stone to death a rebellious son (Deut. 21:21)? There are difficult cases closer to church home (i.e., the New Testament) as well. How do we "perform" Jesus' command to the rich young man to sell his possessions and give the proceeds to the poor (Mark 10:21), the story of God's healing the sick via contact with Paul's skin (Acts 19:11–12), or Paul's analogy between the first and second Adam (Rom. 5:12–21)? The question, in each case, is whether interpretation really is a species of the genus *performance*.

THE NATURE OF PERFORMATIVE UNDERSTANDING

These questions rightly identify the key issue: *How do the biblical texts generate understanding and what is the nature of that understanding?* Biblical scholarship is a necessary but not sufficient condition for the understanding that faith seeks. Yet there is something further to be *done* with the holy script after exegesis and analysis, not least because the holy script contains more than information. Indeed, the biblical discourse is part and parcel of the theodrama, for the Bible both recounts the action and is itself an element in the action. *Strictly speaking, however, we do not perform the discourse per se but the theodrama it describes and enacts.* We can best respond to the objections raised against the performance metaphor by first understanding discourse and then discoursing on understanding.

Understanding Discourse

To understand written discourse, says Ricoeur, is to "follow its movement from sense to reference: from what it says, to what it talks about."[38] Even fiction refers in its own way to

---

sented at a regional AAR meeting in 2006 that focused on my book *The Drama of Doctrine*.

38. Paul Ricoeur, *Interpretation Theory: Discourse and the Surplus of Meaning* (Fort Worth: Texas Christian Univ. Press, 1976), 87–88.

some place and time where something happens. According to Ricoeur, what the understanding reader ultimately grasps is neither the author's intention nor what an author says (the sense) but rather what the author is talking about (the referent). This may or may not coincide with the author's own historical context (the world "behind" the text); some authors write about what might or ought to be as well as about what actually is. Ricoeur himself focuses on the way in which texts project a possible world, that is, a possible way of being human with others: "What is to be interpreted in the text is a proposed world which I could inhabit and in which I could project my ownmost possibilities."[39]

Discourse projects a world "in front of" the text—a possible state of affairs or a possible way of looking at things that readers can contemplate or imagine. To understand a text, then, is to engage the world "in front of" it, the world it dangles in front of the reader's wondering eyes. So, too, with Scripture: we achieve understanding not by processing its information but by "inhabiting" the world it projects.

Discourse on Understanding

To understand a discourse is to grasp what an author is doing with his or her discourse and what that discourse is about. It is a matter of "appropriating" the vision the author lays out "in front of" the text. The moment a discourse is made truly our own is the moment we commit to following both its "direction of thought"[40] and its "design for living."

To return to the initial objection that biblical interpretation is not a matter of performing texts: strictly speaking, *we do not perform the text/script but the world/theodrama that the text/script presupposes, entails, and implies.* The task of understanding is to "unfold" (to open or spread out) what has been "infolded" (implied) in the discourse—the world "of" the text. "The unfolding of your words gives light; it gives understanding to the simple" (Ps. 119:130). Readers gain

---

39. Paul Ricoeur, *Hermeneutics and the Human Sciences: Essays on Language, Action and Interpretation*, trans. John B. Thompson (Cambridge: Cambridge Univ. Press, 1981), 112. The technical term, from Heidegger, is a way of being-in-the-world (*Dasein*).

40. Ricoeur, *Interpretation Theory*, 92.

understanding when they appropriate—perform!—the worldview proposed by the biblical text by actively following its direction of thought and its design for living. Performative understanding is therefore not a matter of replicating the author's situation (the world behind the text), or of repeating the author's words, *but of unfolding what the author says (about the theodrama) into one's own situation (the world in front of the text).*

To understand *Huckleberry Finn* is to grasp what Twain is proposing readers *do* in *their* world on the basis of what he is saying about Huckleberry's world. There is racism in the world of (and behind) the text of *Huckleberry Finn*, but Twain does not want his readers to perform *that*. On the contrary, to understand Twain is to follow the direction of his thought about racism, to unfold *that* proposal (i.e., a way of being-in-the-world-with-others that transcends racism), and to perform *that*.[41]

Speaking of rafts: even Plato noted the importance of having a framework for understanding and urged his readers to "use it as a raft to ride the seas of life."[42] Christians have a holy script as their raft. It is not enough to admire it; one has to ride it. This is also the point of Jesus' parable of the sower (Matt. 13:14–15, 18–23), which may be read, among other things, as a blast against the inadequacy of theoretical understanding alone.

WHICH WORLD? WHOSE APPROPRIATION? INTRODUCING THE IMPLIED CANONICAL READER

What Christian readers of Scripture are ultimately trying to understand are not principles so much as the divine play described, implied, and projected by the script. Which textual world in particular carries divine authority: the world *behind, of,* or *in front of* Scripture? We have already identified the world of the text with the biblical authors' take on the

---

41. Some authors, of course, *are* racists, and readers are right to resist them. Yet Christians believe that God is the ultimate author of Scripture and thus are willing to trust the mode-of-life proffered in the text. Thanks to Dan Treier for helping me to clarify this point.

42. Plato, *Phaedo* 85d.

theodrama. The world of the biblical text is ultimately the issue of divine discourse, and it is this which the church is to perform/appropriate/understand in its own time and place. Reading Scripture in the church is not merely a matter of replicating authorial intentions but of *realizing* them.

While the present situation (the world "in front of" the text) is relevant to the task of interpretation, it is not authoritative. The church lives in the everyday world but is not of it (John 15:19). The world of the text — which is to say, the world *implied* by the text — is in fact a description of the way the world really is and is becoming. For the world implied — or to use a more familiar theological term, *revealed* — by the biblical texts is in fact the real world, the only world there is, as it already/not yet *is* "in Christ."

It is just here that we may begin to appreciate the contribution of Scripture's diverse literary genres. Though the Bible is always about what is real, it does not always refer to reality in the same way. The book of Revelation, for example, is not a description of the past, like history, but an apocalyptic glimpse of the future. As such, it shows us that the theodrama at the heart of biblical discourse is not simply a matter of what was or of what is but also of what is to come. The world implied by biblical apocalyptic is the real world as it will be "in Christ."

To read the book of Revelation with understanding means adopting an apocalyptic way of being in the world. This means being aware that our theodramatically charged present looks both to the past (the "already" or historical aspect of Christ's work) and to the future (the "not yet" aspect of Christ's work). What God communicates with sundry voices and in diverse ways through Scripture is ultimately this theodramatic vision of the world being made new. In speaking of "performing" the script, then, I have in mind not reproducing the world behind the text or of recreating the scenes depicted in the text but rather of living in a way that conforms to the world as it is being transformed "in Christ."

Not every performance by the church correctly enacts the world implied by her script. Misunderstanding happens. Some interpreters will misconstrue the discourse and move beyond Scripture in ways that miss the Way. The criterion for normative appropriation, I submit, is a function of what I shall term the implied canonical reader.

It is commonplace to distinguish ideal and actual readers. Church history is the story of how Christians, actual readers, have appropriated the text and gone beyond it, for good or for ill. The ideal reader, however, is the one implied and intended by the discourse itself: one who completely understands not only the explicit message of the text but its implications as well; one who has the linguistic and literary competence to follow all the author's directions.[43] According to Markus Bockmuehl, the ideal reader of the New Testament (1) has a personal stake in the truthful reference of what the text asserts, (2) has undergone an intellectual and spiritual conversion to the gospel, (3) acknowledges the texts as authoritative, (4) belongs to a church, and (5) is illumined by the Holy Spirit.[44] In short, the ideal reader is a disciple, one "drawn into an act of reading that involves an active part on stage rather than the discreet view from the upper balcony."[45] Genuine understanding is indeed performative.

The implied reader is a disciple who believingly inhabits the world implied by the biblical text, thereby exhibiting an appropriate "fear of the Lord."[46] The church should be that community that conforms to the implied *canonical* reader who knows how to follow the direction not only of specific texts, but of the larger story of Scripture of which they are a part. Taking the implied canonical reader as our norm, then, we may say that understanding involves grasping

---

43. Wolfgang Iser defines the ideal reader as the imaginary person who should completely understand a text as the author intended and who should therefore respond as the author expects. See his *The Implied Reader: Patterns of Communication in Prose Fiction from Bunyan to Beckett* (Baltimore: Johns Hopkins Univ. Press, 1974).

44. Markus Bockmuehl, *Seeing the Word: Refocusing New Testament Study* (Grand Rapids: Baker, 2006), 69–72.

45. Ibid., 72.

46. Anthony Thiselton rightly grasps the pragmatic or performative nature of *believing* by viewing it as a disposition to respond to situations in action appropriate to belief (*The Hermeneutics of Doctrine* [Grand Rapids: Eerdmans, 2007], 21).

the author's communicative intent, discerning meaningful patterns, and relating each canonical part to the canonical whole.[47] The implied canonical reader knows that each passage, book, event, person, and speech act must be viewed in relation to the whole drama of redemption. Specifically, the implied canonical reader knows where she is in the theodrama—in which scene and which act—and how she should respond.

CANONICALLY CULTIVATING THE MIND OF CHRIST: ACHIEVING THEODRAMATIC VISION

It should now be clear that "performing the script" is in fact shorthand for living in the world implied by the script. Note that "living the Bible" is not quite the same thing as "applying the Bible." How can we "apply" the story of Paul and Silas in prison (Acts 16:16–34) today? It's straightforward—if one is ever in first-century Philippi in prison for exorcising the demon of a slave girl and there was an earthquake during your midnight hymn-sing! A canonical performance, however, is neither strict replication of a prior blueprint nor application of a principle. It is rather a lived demonstration of theodramatic understanding. The story in Acts 16 shows us the kind of world we live in and the kind of thing God does in the world and the kind of people we are to be in response. To read this passage wisely is not to apply but to appropriate its message and hence "of being transformed by watching/hearing it properly, as a word about who this God is that we are trying to know and love."[48]

We move beyond the script and become faithful performers of the world it implies by cultivating minds nurtured on the canon. The aim of the drama-of-redemption approach is to train and discipline the believer's mind, heart, and imagination to think, desire, see—and then *do*—reality as it is in Jesus Christ. Moving "beyond" the sacred page involves

---

47. I believe that the notion of the ideal canonical reader can forestall objections that readers who submit to the text may simply conform themselves to the situated human author's personal ideology.

48. Richard Briggs, *Reading the Bible Wisely* (Grand Rapids: Baker, 2003), 95.

more than applying it; it involves renewing and transforming people's habits of seeing, thinking, and acting. Scripture is not merely a vehicle for conveying information. It is rather a medium of divine communicative action whose purpose is not only to inform but to transform: to nurture right vision, right attitudes, right actions.

My approach here parallels that of Richard Hays in his *The Moral Vision of the New Testament*, though I prefer to speak of a *theodramatic vision* of both Old and New Testaments. Minds nurtured on the canon must read the text carefully (Hays's descriptive task) and place it in canonical context (Hays's synthetic task). As to relating the text to our situation (Hays's hermeneutic task), this requires "an integrative act of the imagination" whereby the community views itself as indwelling the world implied by the biblical texts.[49] It is just here that the norm of the implied canonical reader comes into its own. Finally, what Hays calls the pragmatic task ("living the text") we have treated under the rubric of performative understanding.

Canonical reading fosters theodramatic vision — the "mind of Scripture"[50] and, ultimately, the "mind of Christ" (1 Cor. 2:16). Jesus is the embodiment of the ideal canonical reader, the full measure of theodramatic vision. Jesus is able to answer the key questions — Who am I? What am I to do? — because he knows the answer to the prior question: Of what story do I find myself a part?[51]

Disciples learn from their master: "Have this mind among yourselves" (Phil. 2:5 RSV). The apostle Paul wants those in the church to adopt the same attitude — the same theodramatic vision, the same disposition to act — as Jesus Christ. What we have to learn is a whole pattern of thinking, feeling, and acting that corresponds to the nature of the

---

49. Richard Hays, *The Moral Vision of the New Testament* (San Francisco: HarperCollins, 1996), 6.

50. The phrase comes from Athanasius. See Frances Young, "The 'Mind' of Scripture: Theological Readings of the Bible in the Fathers," *International Journal of Systematic Theology* 7 (2005): 126–41.

51. These questions concerning narrative understanding come from Alasdair MacIntyre, *After Virtue* (Notre Dame, IN: Univ. of Notre Dame Press, 1981), 216.

coming kingdom of God, where "what [God] wants done is done."[52] This is, after all, the main action of the play: the coming of the kingdom of God in Christ through the Spirit. Disciples must practice the three Ds: they must *discern, deliberate on*, and *do* what citizens of the kingdom of God would do in this or that situation. To be sure, it is not a matter of literally replicating what Jesus did; we don't need to die on wooden crosses as criminals in order to be crucified daily. But we do need to discern, deliberate on, and do what it means to be crucified with Christ (Gal. 2:20) and to die daily (1 Cor. 15:31).

IMPROVISING WITH A SCRIPT: TRAINING IN CREATIVE CANONICAL REASONING

What should a disciple on the Way do when she comes to an unfamiliar crossroads? One of the first crossroads in the early church had to do with the very identity of Jesus as the Son of God. Was the Son a creature or literally "of God"? In a monotheistic framework such as Judaism, there were few conceptual resources to help resolve this issue, and there were no "scripted" answers in the Bible either. Theological necessity was the mother of theological invention, and the Council of Nicaea improvised a way forward: *homoousios*.

We can't always address contemporary disputes by reciting Scripture, much less the Nicene Creed. Sometimes, to be faithful, we have to be creative. Persons with theodramatic vision will have the mind of Christ, which, as we have seen, is a matter of adopting the same attitude and pattern that characterizes the life of Jesus. When disciples find themselves in strange new territory, they will spontaneously *extend* the pattern. It is but a small step from the notions of performing the world implied by the text and extending the pattern of Jesus Christ to that of improvising with a script.

---

52. Dallas Willard, *The Divine Conspiracy* (San Francisco: HarperCollins, 1998), 25.

IMPROVISING

Doctrines do not always tell us exactly what to say and do. Their purpose is not merely to give us "answers" but to instill in us habits of seeing, judging, and acting in theodramatically appropriate manners. This is how doctrine nurtures understanding: "But solid food is for the mature, who by constant use have trained themselves to distinguish good from evil" (Heb. 5:14).[53]

Christians demonstrate the measure of their theodramatic understanding by how well they are able to participate in what God is now doing in Christ in new situations, amidst different cultural props and changes of scenery. Doctrines, by fostering deeper understanding of the drama of redemption, help us to discern what new things we have to say and do in order to be faithful to our canonical script and so move the *same action* forward in *different contexts*.

What is authoritative about the Bible, I have suggested, is its theodramatic vision. What this chapter sets forth is a framework for biblical interpretation — for living biblically — within which the church's improvisation of what to say and do in order to be faithful witnesses to and participants in the drama of redemption can take place.[54] Doctrine serves the project of faithful improvisation. Improvising well — knowing how to act both spontaneously and fittingly — requires both training (formation) and discernment (imagination). It is not a matter of being clever and original but of learning "to act from habit in ways appropriate to the circumstance."[55]

... WITH A SCRIPT

Lest anyone object that improvisation is inappropriate, let me humbly suggest that Jesus' life was itself an improvisation of an Old Testament theme: covenant. What Jesus did

---

53. I am grateful to Stephen Williams for calling my attention to the appropriateness of this verse.

54. Note that Hays (*Moral Vision*, 6) says something similar about New Testament ethics as a framework for improvising moral judgments.

55. Wells, *Improvisation*, 65.

was both creative ("new"), yet entirely in keeping ("faithful") with what God had done in Israel previously. Likewise, the apostle Paul "improvised" the gospel for non-Jewish listeners in Asia Minor and Rome. The key to good improvisation is knowing how to continue the same action in new situations.

Tom Wright has thrice put forward a model for conceiving biblical authority that trades on the notion of biblical improvisation.[56] He compares the drama of redemption to a Shakespeare play, most of whose fifth act is missing. The church has the first four acts (creation, fall, Israel, Christ) but must work out the fifth act (church) for herself, all the while remaining in character. It is not enough for the actors "merely to parrot what has already been said";[57] they must go beyond the sacred page and find — improvise! — the conclusion. Still, the first four acts are the "authority" for the fifth act, hence the idea of "improvising with a script."

This suggestive model has much to commend it. However, I see the fall not as its own act, but as the conflict in the first act, creation. I prefer to see each of the five acts of the theodrama as set in motion by a divine act. Hence: creation, election of Israel, Christ, Pentecost and the church, consummation. On my dramatic reckoning, the church does not have to work out the ending so much as to live in its light. The essential thing is to play the right act. The church is no longer in Act 2, under the law, nor in Act 3, in which case it would have to do the work of Christ. Nor is it already in Act 5, as some in the first-century church at Thessalonica with an overrealized eschatology mistakenly thought. No, the church is in Act 4, an in-between the first and second comings of Christ time, marked by the firstfruits of the end time but not yet at the end.[58]

---

56. The original suggestion appeared in N. T. Wright, "How Can the Bible Be Authoritative?" *Vox Evangelica* 21 (1991): 7–32. Reprises appear in *The New Testament and the People of God*, 140–43, and in *The Last Word* (San Francisco: HarperSanFrancisco, 2005), 121–27.

57. Wright, *The New Testament and the People of God*, 141.

58. For a similar correction of Wright, see Wells, *Improvisation*, 52–57.

DETERMINING THE WAY FORWARD: MARKS OF THE CHURCH ITINERANT

Christians in every age must improvise both their doctrine and discipleship. But they are not without resources. In addition to an authoritative script, there is also a great tradition of classic productions: masterpiece theater (i.e., ecumenical councils). Nor should we ignore regional theater: confessional theology (i.e., denominational theology). The church has been playing Act Four for centuries, though the scenes, characters, and plot complications have varied greatly.

All this variety prompts the question: Is the church always performing, but "never able to arrive at a knowledge of the truth" (2 Tim. 3:7)? There are two parts to this question. First, how can we tell whether the church has found or lost its Way? Clearly, we need a set of criteria with which to distinguish scriptural from unscriptural improvisations, faithful from unfaithful performances. Second, should we expect an absolute knowledge of the truth, a single great performance by some local church to which the church universal must conform?

In my view, right understanding involves grasping the relationship between what the Bible says about God and what we know about the contemporary situation, and then acting accordingly (i.e., according to the world implied by the script). As we will see, it is all about fittingness—a concordant relation between diverse parts and a larger whole—both textual/canonical and contextual/situational fittingness. In order to determine what is textually and contextually fitting, the church needs canon sense, catholic sensibility, and a sensitivity to circumstance.[59]

THEODRAMATICS: FROM CANONICAL REASON TO CONTEXTUAL JUDGMENT

The drama of redemption is replete with scenes of God's people making decisions about what to say and do in new

---

59. See my "'One Rule to Rule Them All'? Theological Method in an Era of World Christianity," in *Doing Theology in a Globalized World* (ed. Craig Ott and Harold Netlands; Grand Rapids: Baker, 2006), 85–126.

situations, an aspect of their "true worship". (Rom. 12:1) to the Word of God. Both "performance" and "improvisation" capture this sense of how the church is summoned to participate in a drama not of its own making: "Choose for yourselves this day whom you will serve" (Josh. 24:15).

The operative term here is *judgment*. Actors in the drama of redemption make judgments that demonstrate either their wisdom or their folly. Theology's aim is to cultivate persons with theodramatic wisdom: the ability to know what to say and do in order to advance the main action of the play.

It may help to distinguish a broader and a narrower meaning of the term. Broadly speaking, "to judge" is "to identify this as that," "to relate this to that," or "to distinguish this from that." Making connections and drawing distinctions are basic mental operations. Such everyday judgments identify what, for the purposes of practical reason, it is relevant to know about a given situation before one can act. As we will see, would-be disciples need to make judgments about truth, goodness, beauty, and, above all, fittingness.

More narrowly, we think of judgments as decisions rendered by judges regarding guilt or innocence: this is just; that is unjust. The judiciary renders judgments as to what is lawful and unlawful [judic = *jus* (law) + *dicere* (to say)]. Living biblically involves this type of judgment too. Indeed, Oliver O'Donovan notes that Scripture often combines both senses when it speaks of executing "judgment and justice" (2 Sam. 8:15 KJV).[60]

Sincerity is no excuse for bad judgment; it is not enough to do what is right in one's own eyes only (Judg. 17:6). Though the church is not performing Act Two, those things were written for our instruction (1 Cor. 10:11), and our situation today is uncomfortably similar to that depicted in the book of Judges. Then, as now, large swaths of the people of God followed charismatic leaders, many of whom fell into idolatry. Then, as now, the people of God fraternized with the inhabitants of the cultural land. Then, as now, the people of God faced a drastic choice: to talk in the way of the Word

---

60. Oliver O'Donovan, *The Desire of the Nations* (Cambridge: Cambridge Univ. Press, 1996), 38.

of God or in the way of the other nations. Both the judges and the prophets were advocates of theodramatic faithfulness, as should pastors be today.

God is the ultimate judge, who not only declares what is right but will also "set things to right."[61] Indeed, the drama of redemption is in large part the story of divine judgment or right-doing, of God doing "judgment and justice."[62]

The canon is the Christian's rule for making good theodramatic judgments. The challenge of moving beyond the sacred page is to render judgments about what is "meet and right"[63] to say and do as disciples of Jesus Christ. It is not enough to think God's thoughts after him. We need practical understanding: the ability to judge God's judgments after him. Something is "meet" if it is fitting or befits. Something is "right" if it corresponds to the righteousness of God. We turn now to examine criteria for making judgments about what is "meet" (true, good, beautiful) and "right" (just) so to do.

RIGHT THEODRAMATIC JUDGMENT: AIMS, OBJECTIVES, AND CRITERIA

The mission of the church is to put feet on the gospel and demonstrate to the world the reconciliation made real in Jesus Christ. The church is to be a living parable of the kingdom in the midst of the kingdoms of this world; this means witnessing to, and participating in, what has already been done through the cross and resurrection.

"According to the Script": Exercises in Theodramatic Fittingness

Christians perform the kingdom of God by continuing Christ's way, staging scenes of love and justice, holy living

---

61. J. A. Motyer, "Judgment," in *New Dictionary of Biblical Theology: Exploring the Unity and Diversity of Scripture*, ed. Brian S. Rosner et al. (Downers Grove, IL: InterVarsity Press, 2000), 613.

62. Cf. O'Donovan: "Judgment is an event, a performance" (*Desire of Nations*, 39). The point, to cite Oliver O'Donovan once more, is that justice is an "effective performance, the act of 'judgment,' which sets wrong right" (*The Ways of Judgment* [Grand Rapids: Eerdmans, 2005], 7).

63. From the 1662 *Book of Common Prayer*. See also the corresponding phrase in the Latin Mass: *Dignum et justum est* ("It is right and fitting").

and forgiving, wherever two or three are gathered in his name. The church makes known the theodrama—the good news of God *doing*—by staging what for lack of a better term we could call *world-for-world translations* of the Bible, unfolding the world implied by the canonical text in terms of its own contemporary context.

There is no slide-rule or computer program for good translation, nor is good judgment arrived at by mere calculation. No procedure or method can guarantee the right result, for the simple reason that good judgment is a capacity that involves the heart and will as well as the intellect. The purpose of doctrine is not to give us the answers (i.e., how the universal principles apply) but to shape our habits of thinking and imagining so that we become people who habitually make good theodramatic judgments—judgments as to who God is, what God is doing, and what we must do in response.

There are no shortcuts. The drama-of-redemption approach takes the detour of sanctification: what we need more than high-tech procedures is the low-tech passion for becoming a discerning and an obedient people, a people with the capacity to recognize what God is doing in Christ and the will joyfully to fit in.

Living biblically is all about fittingness. Making judgments that are "meet" and "right" is ultimately a matter of discerning what best fits with our holy script and our secular situation. Fittingness is the warp and woof of understanding: we grasp the whole when we see how the parts are joined together.[64] Often we require the imagination—the power of "synoptic vision"—in order to discern a meaningful pattern in what to the untrained eye is only a hodge-podge of unrelated elements.

The "whole" that Christians must discern and to which they must conform it not a system of ideas so much as it is a

---

64. I am hardly the first to argue for the centrality of fittingness as a mode of theological reasoning. Aquinas, for example, argues that it was "fitting" [Lat. *conveniens*—"comes together"] that God should become incarnate (*Summa Theologiae* 3.1.1). See also Frederick Christian Bauerschmidt, *Holy Teaching: Introducing the* Summa Theologiae *of St. Thomas* (Grand Rapids: Brazos, 2005), 163, n.1.

unified, already/not-yet-complete action: the triune drama. Hence Christian fittingness is ultimately a matter of theo-dramatic consistency. The overarching whole that serves as a rule for decisions about fittingness is nothing less than God's being-in-act: the whole economy of Father, Son, and Spirit.

Is there any biblical warrant for thinking in terms of theodramatic fittingness? There is indeed: "For it was fitting [*prepō*] that he, for whom and by whom all things exist, in bringing many sons to glory, should make the pioneer [*archēgos*] of their salvation perfect through suffering" (Heb. 2:10 RSV). In context, the author is making a case for the superiority of the Son over angels, Moses, and Aaron, and for the necessity of the cross. What we have in this single verse is a kind of précis for the entire theodrama, alluding as it does to the creation, the incarnation and death of Jesus, the church, and the consummation. Even more striking is the author's explanation of both the person and work of Jesus Christ in terms of the *fittingness* of divine action: "The incarnation and death of Christ were fitting as the effective means to the achievement of the Creator's grand design, namely, the restoration of all things."[65]

Canon Sense: Fittingness to the Script

The canon is a measuring rod that helps us discern which of our words and acts "measure up" to the word and acts of God that comprise the theodrama. The following three imperatives for developing "canon sense" also serve as guidelines for determining theodramatic fittingness.[66]

1. *Determine who is speaking and how what they are doing with their words relates to the main idea and action of the whole triune drama.*

The biblical authors are historically conditioned and culturally located human beings who need to be understood in

---

65. Philip Hughes, *A Commentary on the Epistle to Hebrews* (Grand Rapids: Eerdmans, 1977), 98.

66. Other authors have proposed related sets of criteria for determining whether our understandings and improvisations are Word-authorized and Spirit-led. See, for example, N. T. Wright, *The Last Word*, 127–42; Packer, "In Quest of Canonical Interpretation," 49–55; Robert Schreiter, *Constructing Local Theologies* (Maryknoll, NY: Orbis, 1985), 113–17.

their own contexts. At the same time, the divine playwright uses their diverse voices as the medium for communicating a unified drama. The believing reader should thus be alert for interesting connections—echoes, allusions, type-scenes—because plots often move forward by reincorporating past elements. To read with canon sense, then, is to read figurally or typologically, which is to say with the conviction that there is an underlying theodramatic consistency and coherence that underlies and unifies the whole. For example, a reader with good canon sense will "hear" the conceptual connection between Jesus' favorite self-designation ("Son of Man") and the apocalyptic figure of Daniel 7:13–14.[67]

2. *Know who, when, and where you are in the drama.*

Judgments about theodramatic fittingness are hardly arbitrary. "It is scripted": there is an authoritative account of what God has done, is doing, and has promised to do. Canon sense means being able to locate oneself in relation to the overall creation-fall-redemption-consummation story line of the Bible. What is "fit" finds its right place in a larger whole. Patterns of speech and action will be fitting, then, to the extent that they discover and display a real similarity to the theodrama in spite of the culturally dissimilar. It's all about continuing the same play in different situations. The interpreter/performer of Scripture is above all a "worker in fittingness."

3. *Put on the canonical spectacles of faith in order to see, judge, and act in the spectacle of faith now playing in a world theater near you.*

Living biblically involves more than biblical information-processing. So does canon sense. We develop canon sense not by learning bits of historical or textual information but by becoming apprentices to the diverse authorial voices that individually and together, in their different literary registers, communicate God's Word. The various discourses of the canon discipline and disciple our minds, hearts, and imaginations, less by stating universal truths than by demonstrating the ways in which the prophets and apostles said and did what was fitting for their situations. The Bible trains

---

67. Thanks to Gary Meadors for suggesting this example.

us to see things not simply from the perspective of eternity (*sub specie aeternitatis*) but from the perspective of the theodrama (*sub specie theodramatis*).

Those with canon sense can make what are essentially canonical judgments, though in different linguistic-conceptual form. This is a matter not of extracting an abstract universal principle but of emulating concrete canonical wisdom. What we learn from our apprenticeship to the canon is not a specific language (e.g., Hebrew) or even particular concepts (e.g., Son of God) but a *pattern of judgment* that can be expressed in other languages, other situations, other concepts.

Catholic Sensibility: Fittingness to the Situation

Perhaps the most effective way of guarding oneself from hermeneutical idolatry—the omnipresent danger of making a god of one's own interpretations—is to be aware of how other saints demonstrate canon sense. Christians have been staging the theodrama in their respective contexts for centuries.[68] Jesus' promise that the Spirit will guide us into all truth (John 16:13) has reference not to this or that denomination or individual, but to the whole (*kath' holou* = "catholic") church. The Spirit-led tradition of the church extended in space and time provides a rich resource of case studies in how other performers have made judgments concerning contextual fittingness.

African, Asian, Latin, and North American theologies are best seen as types of regional theater—performance traditions that show how to embody the biblical text in contrasting contexts. Those who cannot see their own cultural conditioning are doomed to repeat it.

Genuine theodramatic understanding involves knowing not simply "what they said/did, there and then," but "what we should say/do, here and now." Christians from all parts of the world can learn from the past and from other Christian communities how best to put on Christ in new contexts. Local theater (individual congregations) should draw upon

---

68. We might say that theodramatic improvisation is a species of what Hiebert calls "critical contextualization" (Paul G. Hiebert, "Critical Contextualization," *International Bulletin of Missionary Research* 11:3 [1987]: 104–12).

the resources of regional theater (confessional traditions) and masterpiece theater (the ecumenical creeds). For the local church is a contextualized performance of the catholic church: it is the universal church made particular, visible, and concrete. Churches seeking the wisdom of their cousins and elders may find the following three questions useful.

1. *Does it translate?*

This is perhaps the core question when it comes to judgments of sameness. Has the interpreter, in rendering the biblical text in a new language, remained faithful—said the same thing? Obviously the words will be different; the whole point of translating is to move from one language into another. It is important to keep in mind that what we are trying to keep the same is not the external form but the judgment that it embodies. Judgment, we saw, is an act—a basic mental operation in which something is identified, distinguished, or connected. What stays the same in good translation is the underlying judgment.

As Andrew Walls has observed, the wonderful thing about translating the gospel into other languages and cultures is that these translations lead to an *enlarged* understanding of the gospel itself. When Paul translates the story of Jesus Christ into a Hellenistic world, "it is as though Christ himself actually grows through the work of mission."[69] No single translation will discern all that there is to be gleaned from the Scriptures; there is wisdom therefore in a catholic tradition that includes voices from past and present, from North and South, from East and West.

2. *Does it modulate?*

What ultimately gets transferred from context to context is not only verbal meaning (content) but patterns of communicative action (forms of life, practices) as well. Perhaps, then, it would be better to speak of "transposing." Dramatic transposition, like its musical counterpart, is a matter of preserving the same melodic line (speech) and harmony (action) in a different key (culture). To transpose or modulate is to change from one mode, key, or form to another while pre-

---

69. Andrew Walls, *The Missionary Movement in Christian History* (Maryknoll, NY: Orbis, 1996), xvii.

serving the same subject matter. The mode of gesture, dress, and the like may be different when *Romeo and Juliet* is transposed into the twentieth-century New York City setting of *West Side Story*, for example, but the story is the same.

Again, the challenge is to formulate criteria for recognizing sameness. To ask whether something modulates is to determine whether it displays "cross-modal similarity."[70] Loudness, for example, is a mode of sound, but most people have no problem associating it with largeness, a mode of size, rather than smallness. "Modes" refer not only to qualities of things, however, but to ways of doing things as well. How, for example, does one transpose the practice of greeting one another with a holy kiss—something Paul commands no less than four times (Rom. 16:16; 1 Cor. 16:20; 2 Cor. 13:12; 1 Thess. 5:26)—into twenty-first century North America? Church tradition is in large part the history of attempts to make such transpositions.

The challenge is to transpose the world implied by the biblical text—canonical patterns of judging and acting—into different places and times. There are, then, two dimensions to theodramatic fittingness: the first sees a particular act as part of a greater story; the second perceives an even greater similarity between two dissimilar acts. The imagination is indispensable in both cases—for making synthetic judgments concerning part-whole relationships; for making analogical judgments concerning cross-modal (i.e., cross-cultural) relations. Whatever one calls this process—transposition, contextualization, contemporizing—it is essentially a matter of discerning the sameness-in-difference that characterizes faithful yet fitting performances of the drama of redemption.

3. *Does it resonate?*

Resonance refers to "the sound produced by a body vibrating in sympathy with a neighboring source of sound."[71] This is a wonderful image of the faithful church, the body of Christ. The faithful church resonates the Word

---

70. Nicholas Wolterstorff, *Art in Action* (Grand Rapids: Eerdmans, 1980), 99.

71. From *Collins English Dictionary* (New York: Collins, 2008).

of God to the extent that it continues to sound deeply and clearly the divine voice speaking in its holy script. To return to Hebrews 2:10: what is fitting is that which is resonant or "consonant" with God's character — with God's being-in-act displayed in Jesus Christ.

Resonance is not repetition. To live biblically is not to re-create the past but to resonate in the present. The church "resounds" to God's glory not by replicating the self-same sound again but by filling space and time with booming, echoing sympathetic vibrations — sound and shock waves from the big bang of resurrection. Subsequent church performances resonate with the script when they "ring true" — to use the motto of my Cambridge college — even at a distance.

The Word of God has resounded in the church through the centuries. We get more light yet from our holy script with each new faithful performance. Call it *creative understanding*: the progressive discovery of the full meaning potential of biblical discourse precisely through the process of making Scripture resonate in new contexts.[72]

Here, then, are six tests for discerning right theodramatic correspondence.[73] Canon sense keeps us centered; catholic sensibility keeps us bounded. No single method can guarantee successful world-for-world translation, however. In the final analysis, discerning how to embody the gospel in new contexts requires not methodical procedures but sanctified persons, persons whose minds and hearts and imaginations are captive to the Word.

RULE OF LOVE; WAY OF WISDOM

The scripted theodrama, the sum total of those acts that reveal God and the human good, is the standard by which all judgments of fittingness must be assessed. Doctrines state acts, not merely facts, and give us the understanding to participate in these acts as faithful performers. God's very being is in his acts: God is as God does. Moreover, God is

---

72. See my *Drama of Doctrine*, 350–54 for a fuller treatment of creative understanding.

73. Look, Ma: no speech acts!

the creator of everything that is, so that everything that has being—everything that *is*—also has a measure of his truth, goodness, and beauty. It follows, then, that truth, goodness, and beauty, as characteristics of God's being-in-act, are also forms of theodramatic fittingness.

Why not make things even simpler and tie fittingness—speaking and doing the truth (and the good and the beautiful)—to the Rule of Love? Does not Augustine indicate the way forward when he says, "Love God, then *do* as you please"? Surely the church will not go wrong as it moves beyond the sacred page so long as it loves first and remembers its first love, for God is love (1 John 4:7–8).

To espouse an abstract Rule of Love without further qualification, however, is to open the Pandora's box of situation ethics. What *is* love? The notion of theodrama comes into its own as a response to this question. For the Bible defines love in terms of obedience to Jesus' speech (John 14:21, 23) and paradigmatically in terms of Jesus' action: laying down one's life for one's friends (John 15:13) and enemies (Matt. 5:44; Rom. 5:10). Indeed, the drama of redemption begins and is propelled forward by God's love, by God's willing the good for creation. To love rightly we have to know who people are and what has already happened. Love without theodrama is blind, but theodrama without love is empty.

Fittingness is ultimately a matter of "rightly ordered love," of love that has been trained to know truth, do good, and sense beauty. These so-called "transcendentals" are first and foremost characteristics not of being-as-such but of God's being-in-act. Truth, goodness, and beauty are not abstract universals but concrete "theatricals" (i.e., forms of God's being-in-act). Truth involves *apprehending* fittingness (i.e., that which corresponds to the theodrama); goodness involves *acting* fittingly (i.e., in a way that corresponds to the theodrama); beauty involves *appraising* fittingness (i.e., the way the parts of the theodrama correspond to one another).

In the final analysis, however, "transcendental" meditation is not enough: disciples must not only admire but appropriate the truth, goodness, and beauty of Jesus Christ for themselves. The way forward is the way of wisdom—to walk in such a manner that one corresponds in one's whole being-in-act to God's prior being-in-act. *The wise disciple is the one who discerns, deliberates, and does the truth, goodness, and beauty that is the love of God in Jesus Christ.* It now only remains to put Christian wisdom to the test by setting the drama-of-redemption approach to work on two case studies.

HOW TO MAKE CANONICALLY CORRECT JUDGMENTS: TWO CASE STUDIES

The first case study concerns doctrine (dogmatic theology), the second ethics (moral theology). Yet both have to do with discipleship—with following the script beyond the sacred page—and are thus indicators of the measure of our theodramatic understanding.

MARY, MARY: THE QUITE CONTRARY DOCTRINE OF THE MOTHER OF GOD

John Henry Newman's idea of the "development" of doctrine began as a sermon on Luke 2:19: "But Mary treasured up all these things and pondered them in her heart." It is only fitting, therefore, that we take as a case study in going beyond the Bible the development of the doctrine of Mary.[74] The goal is to make a right theodramatic judgment, this time with respect to Mary's person and work. Where does Mary "fit" in the canonical script? Where should she "fit" in the church's subsequent performance?

The Roman Catholic Church has been pondering Mary for centuries. The result is a collection of practices and beliefs grouped under the rubrics of Marian devotion and Mariology. Here we have scope to examine only two developments, one ancient and one modern, and to suggest some general guidelines as to theodramatic correctness in the church today with regard to Marian devotion.

---

74. The Gk. verb for "pondering" is *symballō*—"to put it all together." It is even more fitting (!) to begin with Mary, then, because she is herself a worker in fittingness.

Theotokos (Council of Ephesus, 431): "God-Bearer"

Does it translate? This question takes on special significance with regard to the phrase *theotokos*: "mother of God" or "God-bearer" or "the one who gave birth to the one who is God."[75] This honorific title, given to Mary in Eastern Christianity during the fourth and fifth centuries, represents what is likely "the greatest quantum leap in the whole history of the language and thought about Mary."[76] Whether Mary is *theotokos* is very much an "in front of" the text kind of question that necessarily takes us beyond the sacred page. Does it is also take us beyond the sacred pale?

To set the historical context: Nestorius, patriarch of Constantinople, attacked the popular epithet *theotokos* in a series of sermons out of a concern not to confuse the divine and human natures. A more biblical title, he suggested, might be *anthropotokos* ("man-bearer") or *christotokos* ("Christ-bearer"). Mary bore the manhood of Jesus but not the divine Son himself. (Here we may recall the wise saying that "thinkers are more likely to be right in what they affirm than in what they deny.") This was no mere dispute about words, but about how correctly to understand the identity of the baby born to Mary.[77]

Though the Bible does not use the Greek term *theotokos*, it does not follow that the term is unbiblical. As we have seen, what counts is preserving the basic judgments enacted in biblical discourse, not the exact terminology: "The same judgment can be rendered in a variety of conceptual terms."[78] The Council of Ephesus made the right call: the Greek concept *theotokos* reflects a canonical judgment. The

---

75. So Jaroslav Pelikan, *Mary through the Centuries* (New Haven, CT: Yale Univ. Press, 1996), 55.

76. Ibid., 57.

77. For the record, when presented with the historical dispute regarding *theotokos*, most students in my introductory theology course inevitably vote with Nestorius. However, whereas Nestorius may have been worrying about pagan goddess worship, my students are nervous about excessive Marian devotion among Roman Catholics!

78. David Yeago, "New Testament and the Nicene Dogma," in *The Theological Interpretation of Scripture*, ed. Stephen E. Fowl (Malden, MA: Wiley-Blackwell, 1997), 93.

one to whom Mary gave birth was not merely a man, much less a detached human nature, but God in the flesh, the incarnate second person of the Trinity. *Theotokos* not only displays good canonical judgment, but it clarifies further the identity of some of the key *dramatis personae*. For what is ultimately at stake in calling Mary "God-bearer" is Christology: the identity of Jesus Christ, one person in two natures.[79]

Immaculate Conception (Vatican City, 1854): The "Great Exception"

In 1854, Pope Pius IX pronounced the Immaculate Conception—the notion that Mary was preserved free of original sin by a special grace from the moment of *her* conception in *her* mother's womb—to be a doctrine that "has been revealed by God, and on this account must be firmly and constantly believed by all the faithful."[80] The dogma was intended "to translate into doctrine the understanding of Mary that had developed through the centuries in the church's prayer and liturgy."[81] The relevant question here is whether these developments, the doctrine and the practices, were indeed "according to the Scriptures." Is Mary, to use Pelikan's phrase, "the Great Exception" to the rule that "all sin"?[82] And is the postulate of Mary's sinlessness necessary to preserve the integrity of Jesus' identity as the sinless Son of God?

We begin by stating the obvious: the doctrine of the Immaculate Conception has no explicit biblical basis.[83] This

---

79. Cf. Joseph Ratzinger's remark: "Thus in Mariology Christology was defended" (*Daughter Zion: Meditations on the Church's Marian Belief* [San Francisco: Ignatius, 1977], 36).

80. In Henry Denzinger and Roy Deferrari, *Sources of Catholic Dogma* (Fitzwilliam, NH: Loreto, 2002), no. 1641, 413. A similar statement had been issued by the Council of Basel in 1439, but for various reasons this was not canonically binding. In 1858, just four years after the papal bull, a "lovely lady" appeared to a young French girl in the village of Lourdes and announced, in the *patois* of the area, "I am the Immaculate Conception."

81. Alain Blancy and Maurice Jourjon and the Dombes Group, *Mary in the Plan of God and in the Communion of Saints* (New York: Paulist, 1999), 96.

82. Pelikan, *Mary through the Centuries*, ch. 14.

83. The chief proof text is Luke 1:28: "Hail [Mary], full of grace [Lat. *gratia plena*; Gk. *kecharitomene*]." Interestingly, earlier Catholic theologians such as Bonaventure and Thomas Aquinas rejected this teaching on the grounds that

has not deterred the tradition from amplifying Mary's role along the lines of Duns Scotus's principle that "it seems preferable to attribute greater rather than lesser excellence to Mary," as long as one does not contradict the authority of Scripture.[84] Again, what is required is good theodramatic judgment formed and informed by the holy script. Hence the key questions: Who is Mary in the theodrama, where is she in the overall story line, and what is she doing there? Who should we say that *she* is?

A full answer to these questions is beyond the scope of the present chapter, but the following points are germane to making a right theodramatic judgment. First, Mary occupies a key role in the center of the theodrama: the birth of Jesus Christ. Second, she plays a key transitional role in salvation history: she represents both the faithful remnant of Israel ("daughter of Zion") and the first member of the church ("daughter of her son" [Dante]). Her significance is perhaps best understood when her story is set beside that of John the Baptist. According to Jesus, John is both the greatest born of women, yet least in the kingdom of heaven (Matt. 11:11), for John the Baptist exits the stage before Act Four. Mary, by contrast, stands in a long line of pious mothers who give birth to children of the promise (Sarah, Hannah) and, more importantly, with the remnant of Israel who believe God's promise of salvation. Mary thus represents both the faithful remnant of Israel and the firstfruits of Pentecost, as she is last seen at prayer in the upper room with the apostles (Acts

---

it contradicted what Paul says concerning the universality of sin (Rom. 3:23). Later Protestants pointed out that Luke 1:28 should be translated "favored one"; the text does not say that grace extends throughout Mary's being but that God extends her, in Calvin's words, "a singular distinction" (Calvin's *New Testament Commentaries*, ed. David W. Torrance and Thomas F. Torrance [Grand Rapids: Eerdmans, 1972], 1:32). Note also that Stephen is said to be "full of grace" in Acts 6:8.

84. Cited in Pelikan, *Mary through the Centuries*, 196. Cf. the guidelines for assessing doctrinal development in Mariology proposed by Tim Perry: (1) Is this development explicitly taught in Scripture? (2) Is it implicitly taught in Scripture? (3) Is it logically related to another doctrine implicitly or explicitly taught in Scripture? (*Mary for Evangelicals* [Downers Grove, IL: InterVarsity Press, 2006], 262).

2:14). She is also depicted at the foot of the cross, but only in the fourth gospel (John 19:25–27).

Mary is thus the only figure in the Bible who plays a role in Acts Two, Three, and Four alike: she represents the believing remnant of Israel; she is the mother of Jesus who remains with him to his death; she is a follower of the risen Jesus and gathers together with other believers to pray. Throughout, she is an exemplary disciple who listens responsively to and obeys the word of God. Mary is a model of theodramatic faithfulness, who understands what God is doing in Jesus and responds accordingly.[85]

Did Mary need to be preserved from the stain of original sin in order to perform her role? Thomas Aquinas anticipated the objection of the Reformers in saying that if Mary were free of original sin, she would not need the salvation which is by Christ: "But this is *unfitting*, through implying that Christ is not the Savior of all men, as he is called (1 Tim. 4:10)."[86] The doctrine lacks fittingness, in other words, because it detracts from the unique glory of Jesus Christ. Nevertheless, Aquinas goes on to assert Mary's actual sinlessness on the basis that "she would not have been worthy to be the Mother of God, if she had ever sinned."[87] However, God repeatedly elects people not on the basis of their holiness but in order to be holy (Eph. 1:4). To the extent that Mary is *not* a sinner, then, she is less a paradigm for the rest of us.

Where does Mary fit in evangelical performances of the New Testament? Scot McKnight suggests that we would do well to start an "Honor Mary" day.[88] But there already is an appropriate day: the Feast of the Annunciation ("Lady

---

85. Timothy George notes that Scripture also depicts Mary as exemplary in her not always understanding God's purpose: "The Blessed Virgin Mary in Evangelical Perspective," in *Mary, Mother of God*, ed. Carl Braaten and Robert Jenson (Grand Rapids: Eerdmans, 2004), 106–7. Moreover, given Mary's transitional status, one is on stronger theodramatic grounds identifying her with the "new Israel" than with the "new Eve." She is not the font of a new humanity but a type of faithfulness to her divine vocation (so Perry, *Mary for Evangelicals*, 297) as one who is *simul iustus et peccator.*

86. *Summa Theologiae* 3.27.2, emphasis mine.

87. Ibid., 3.27.4.

88. Scot McKnight, *The Real Mary: Why Evangelical Christians Can Embrace the Mother of Jesus* (Brewster, MA: Paraclete, 2007), 144.

Day"), traditionally celebrated on March 25 (i.e., nine months before Christmas). This feast should appeal to evangelicals because it marks the first explicit announcement of the gospel recorded in the New Testament. Of course, Mary is a prominent figure in Advent too. Augustine regularly celebrated Mary in his Christmas homilies: "He was created from a mother whom he had created."[89] Augustine displayed good theodramatic judgment as to Mary's final theological significance. Mary, while blessed, is not as great as the church: "Why? Because Mary is part of the Church ... a quite exceptional member ... but still a member of the whole body."[90]

What, then, should we say and do about Mary? When evangelicals display negative attitudes towards Mary, they are not performing the script but reacting to the tradition of Marian interpretation. Karl Barth declares: "Mariology is an excrescence, i.e., a diseased construct of theological thought. Excrescences must be excised."[91] It is important, however, not to confuse subsequent doctrines of Mary with the biblical figure herself. Barth has no desire to write Mary out of the New Testament, but he is under no illusion as to who is the central character of the theodrama: "Every word that makes her person the object of special attention, which ascribes to her what is even a relatively independent part in the drama of salvation, is an attack upon the miracle of revelation."[92] The greatness of Mary's character according to the New Testament is that "all the interest is directed away from herself to the Lord."[93] There is perhaps no greater model of Christian discipleship than Mary's "May it be to me according to your word" (Luke 1:38).

TRANSSEXUALITY: TOWARD ORDINATION OR INSUBORDINATION?

This next case study stretches our capacity for good judgment to the limit. What should we say/think/do about

89. *Sermones* 188.2.
90. *Sermones* 72A.7.
91. Barth, *Church Dogmatics*, 1.2.139.
92. Ibid., 140.
93. Ibid.

people who want to have sex-change operations? This question concerns not only bioethics but our very understanding of what it is to be human. It is a question of ethics and of theological anthropology. Who do we say that *we* are?

The Next Big Issue: Transordination?

Transsexuality may soon be the new homosexuality — the latest hot button dispute about sexuality to send shock waves through society, the courts, and the church. Because this may be an unfamiliar topic to many readers, we begin with some basic definitions and a brief history.

Transsexuals (also called "transgendered") are people "who do not fit comfortably into society's traditional understandings of sex and gender."[94] For example, a biologically normal person may feel that they actually belong to the opposite sex.[95] Here we need to distinguish "sex," which is physically, hormonally, and genetically characterized as male or female; "gender," which is "the social appropriation of sex and its meaning at the level of conceptualization, i.e., in the life of the mind";[96] and "gender identity," which is one's psychological sense of self. In brief: *sex* is something biological (chromosomal marker); *gender,* something sociological associated with perceptions of masculinity and femininity (cultural marker), and *gender identity,* something psychological (consciousness marker).

Until fairly recently, transgendered people could only go as far as transvestism: dressing like the other sex.[97] Now, those who are so inclined can undergo "sex reassignment surgery," also known as sex-change operations. In Britain,

---

94. Justin Tanis, *Trans-Gendered* (Cleveland: Pilgrim, 2003), 18.

95. This is what distinguishes transsexuality from "intersex" — the condition of being born with ambiguous sexual characteristics. There is a growing literature concerning intersexuality as well, but that is beyond the scope of this chapter. See, for example, Julie A. Greenberg, "Defining Male and Female: Intersexuality and the Collision between Law and Biology," *Arizona Law Review* 41 (1998): 265 – 328.

96. *Transsexuality: A Report by the Evangelical Alliance Policy Commission* (Carlisle, UK: Paternoster, 2000), 63.

97. Virginia Charles Prince, born male in 1912, was a self-proclaimed "transgenderist": a biological male living as a woman, but without benefit of a sex-change operation.

the Gender Recognition Act of 2004 allows a biologically normal man to become a woman (and vice versa) and then to obtain a new birth certificate, thus overturning a 1972 ruling (*Corbett v. Corbett*) that sex is to be determined biologically and that birth certificates could not be changed as this would be to rewrite history.[98]

The repercussions of transsexualism are far-reaching. Especially since the 1980s, the transgendered have positioned themselves as the next chapter in the civil rights movement. One of the chief battle grounds is the public restroom. The Transgender Law Center in San Francisco has launched a Safe Bathroom Access Campaign: "Bathrooms are the single most common public place where the gender binary is strictly enforced." Some public universities now have transgender bathrooms alongside traditional "Men" and "Women."

Transsexuality raises other contested issues with regard to marriage and ordination, as has homosexuality. Under the aforementioned Gender Recognition Act, a man can have male-to-female transsexual surgery and then legally marry another man, even though for all biological (chromosomal) purposes, he is still male. This raises the prospect of whether the church would recognize such a marriage, if it were not strictly speaking between "a man and a woman."[99] A further issue in the church is whether ministers who undergo transsexual surgery may remain ordained. The United Methodist Church is presently addressing that very question with respect to the Rev. Ann Gordon's decision to become the Rev. Drew Phoenix. His/her congregation has been supportive, and the only action the denomination took was to ensure that the name change was duly reported.

Perhaps the greatest challenge to biblical thinking and living posed by transsexualism is not the political one but the ontological.[100] At the heart of the matter is a frontal

---

98. See *Transsexuality*, ch. 4.

99. For an excellent treatment of this issue, see Oliver O'Donovan, "Transsexualism and Christian Marriage," *Journal of Religious Ethics* 11 (1983): 135–62.

100. The French philosopher Lucy Irigary agrees with Heidegger that each age has one big issue to think through. She suggests that sexual difference is the issue for our time ("Sexual Difference," in her *An Ethics of Sexual Difference* [Ithaca, NY: Cornell Univ. Press, 1993], 5).

assault on the very idea of the "naturally given" as opposed to the "culturally graven." In particular, the notion that human sexuality is dimorphic (consisting of two forms: male and female) is ripe for deconstruction. An increasing number of thinkers from different disciplines contend that the male-female binary division is neither a fact of life nor a wholly arbitrary development, but the product of a non-necessary social construction.[101]

Which Role? Whose Creation? Sex Change as Exchange of Truth for a Lie

Transsexuality is a particularly difficult case for a drama-of-redemption approach to consider, not least because the Bible maintains a discrete silence with regard to the modern distinctions between "sex," "gender," and "gender identity." Nevertheless, it is not without its canonical resources, not least because one of the key factors in making good theo-dramatic judgments is knowing *who* you are.

The plot thickens, however, for some critics of the traditional position themselves make use of the language of the theater. Feminist philosopher Judith Butler, for example, argues that male and female are not ontological categories because gender "is real only to the extent that it is performed."[102] Indeed, the *International Bill of Gender Rights* defends a kind of radical improvisation of sexuality when it claims that "individuals have the right to define, and to redefine as their lives unfold, their own gender identities." To the extent that the body is the medium for the theater as the "language of action," then, the ultimate issue concerns our human identity as embodied persons. The stakes are indeed high.

---

101. See esp. Christine E. Gudorf, "The Erosion of Sexual Dimorphism: Challenges to Religion and Religious Ethics," *Journal of the American Academy of Religion* 69 (2001): 863–91. Gudorf argues for a more fluid sexual polymorphism with a spectrum of possibilities for conceiving sexual and gender identity.

102. Judith Butler, "Performative Acts and Gender Constitution: An Essay in Phenomenology and Feminist Theory," in *Performing Feminisms: Feminist Critical Theory and Theater,* ed. Sue-Ellen Case (Baltimore: Johns Hopkins Univ. Press, 1990), 278.

Several Shakespeare plays turn on a member of one sex pretending to be a member of the other (e.g., Rosalind in *As You Like It* or Viola in *Twelfth Night*), but these changes are only provisional and it is clear that they depend on artifice. The question for transsexualism, similarly, is whether it ever gets beyond artifice: the technologically induced artificial.

As Oliver O'Donovan has noted, it is only thanks to new medical techniques that some are able to "choose" their sex.[103] This new technology, when combined with a social constructivism that sees identity and roles as social creations only, provides considerable grist for the mill-to-power, to the illusion that we are our own creators: "I think (male/female), therefore I am (male/female)." Ironically enough, the very material procedures of medicine serve the very idealist project of making the "outer" body conform to one's true "inner" self. This is not, however, how the Bible scripts the self.

We do not have to become materialists to insist that the body is integral to who we are. Human beings are psychosomatic unities. The person—what makes me "me"—is not located in one "part" only (e.g., the body, the soul). It follows that one's personhood cannot be divorced from one's sex. A little lower than the angels, human beings are not abstract but embodied souls and ensouled bodies. As a recent House of Bishops study says: "From a Christian point of view, it has not traditionally been possible to separate the question 'who are you?' from the question 'what sex are you?' The two necessarily go together."[104] In short, it is embodied persons, not mere bodies, who are male or female.[105]

One's true self is not, therefore, hovering above or within one's body. At the limit, the idea that we are men trapped in women's bodies or women trapped in men's bodies collapses the distinction between sex and gender and flirts with a gnostic, even docetic, disregard for bodily reality (he only

---

103. Oliver O'Donovan, *Begotten or Made?* (Oxford: Oxford Univ. Press, 2004), 19–21.

104. *Some Issues in Human Sexuality: A Guide to the Debate* (London: Church House Publishing, 2003), 244.

105. I am indebted to an unpublished paper by Joshua Malone, "Only Skin Deep? A Theological Interpretation of Male/Female Differentiation and Gender Identity," for this point.

seems [*dokeo*] to be male). By contrast, the body has an important part to play in all Acts of the theodrama: "belief in the
resurrection of the body ... shows that our bodies are integral
to who we are before God. We are not simply people who
inhabit bodies, rather our bodies are part of who we are."[106]

Our true theodramatic vocation is to discern, deliberate
on, and do those possibilities that are given to us with our
biological sex. After all, the body is a temple of the Holy
Spirit and therefore not our own (1 Cor. 6:19). In refusing
one's biology, the creature refuses what is ultimately not
merely a natural given but a gift of God. And in doing that,
the creature exchanges the truth for a lie—and not for the
first time. Paul in Romans 1:18–28 speaks of sinners as those
who prefer to have it their own way, thus worshiping the
creature rather than the Creator. The Gentiles "exchanged"
the truth about God for a lie; others exchanged natural relations with members of the opposite sex for relations with
their own sex: "The language of exchange suggests that the
acts that are a consequence of the root sin also somehow
reflect it."[107] Paul goes on to say that these men and women
"did not see fit to acknowledge [have a true knowledge of]
God" (Rom. 1:28 RSV).

Sin is and has always been the denial of reality: the serpent
in the garden not only questions God's word ("Did God really
say?" [Gen 3:1]) but contradicts it ("You will not certainly die"
[3:4]). It is hard not to see the transgender liberation movement as transgression: an overt rebellion against the binary
divide between male and female bodies and behavior.[108] The
sex-change operation is a radical surgical intervention into
an otherwise healthy body. As such, it is a bad improvisation
in which, forgetting what happened in Act One (creation),
one strikes out in one's own technologically clever (but self-
determined) direction, ontologically ad-libbing, laughing
all the way to the organ bank. To perform sex reassignment

---

106. *Some Issues in Human Sexuality*, 249.

107. Allan Verhey, *Remembering Jesus: Christian Community, Scripture, and the Moral Life* (Grand Rapids: Eerdmans, 2002), 236.

108. Virginia Mollenkott says that "contemporary transgender people have no desire to reinforce [or respect!] the binary gender construct" (*Omnigender: A Trans-Religious Approach* [Cleveland: Pilgrim, 2001], 134).

surgery is to encourage the worst kind of playacting: hypocrisy. The irony, as with all sin, is that in trying to find oneself, one loses oneself. Those who seek to rewrite their roles make God a bit player in a drama that exchanges the gospel for the pottage of self-determination.[109]

Who do we say that we are? How does God see us? The transsexual belief that male souls are trapped in female bodies and vice versa has little to justify it other than one's own subjective feeling: "What it *is* to be male or female becomes a matter of what it is to *feel* male or female."[110] Even after a sex change operation, however, there is a conspicuous lack of real-world fittingness: a male-to-female transsexual could not conceive a child, and a female-to-male transsexual could not father one. In the final analysis, human creativity is unable to alter the created order.

It all begins with Act One, God's good creation: "male and female he created them" (Gen. 1:27). When viewed in theodramatic perspective, we see that we are but actors who have received divine casting calls. To be or not to be male or female is not for us to decide. Our identities "are fundamentally determined, not by human social construction, but by the creative and redemptive activity of God."[111] It is the producer's call. Our task is to respond to our vocation as embodied creatures and to play our parts as well as we can to God's glory: "Man has the double obligation to live as man *or* woman and as man *and* woman."[112]

CONCLUSION: GETTING ON WITH THE "REAL WORK"

To ask how one should move beyond the sacred page to doctrine and ethics is, to return to Berry's phrase, the "real

---

109. To be sure, all of us have sinned and have manifested a tendency to script-write our own lives. Transsexuals are not "worse" sinners than anyone else, though the symptoms of their self-alienation may be more conspicuous.

110. *Transsexuality*, 59.

111. *Some Issues in Human Sexuality*, 183.

112. Paul Jewett, *Man as Male and Female: A Study in Sexual Relationships from a Theological Point of View* (Grand Rapids: Eerdmans, 1975), 49.

work" of the church in this, and every, age: to deliberate well the course of discipleship. The case studies I have just examined are difficult, even "mind-baffling."

To state the drama-of-redemption method — or at least its abbreviated acronym — is simplicity itself: AAA (attend; appraise; advance). We must *attend* (see) to what is going on in Scripture: to the words; to all the things the authors are doing with their words; to the actions represented by the words. We must *appraise* (judge) where we are in the theodrama. To appraise is to determine a thing's praiseworthiness or blameworthiness or, in terms of the present essay, a thing's fittingness or unfittingness vis-à-vis the theodrama. We must display whatever understanding we have gained; we must *advance* (act), script in hand, and move into the world in front of the text — to the glory of God.[113] My hope is that minds nurtured on the canon to conform to the mind of Christ will see, judge, and act on the way forward.

Two final points must suffice by way of conclusion. The first point is purely formal. There is no guarantee that everyone who employs the drama-of-redemption approach will reach the same conclusions with regard to the two cases above. But this alone should not trouble us, for no theological method can guarantee that every person who uses it will arrive at the same result (e.g., universals, principles, absolutes, meanings, etc.).[114] Not even the vaunted grammatical-historical method can do that. Methods may be flawless — not so the men and women who employ them.

Second, and more to the material point: the church must get on with the principal work of commemorating, celebrating, and continuing the theodrama, performing the world projected by the script in faithful yet creative fashion. When the church demonstrates faith's understanding, she does what is true, good, and beautiful "in Christ." Though I have focused on disputed topics here, the real work is to under-

---

113. The attend-appraise-advance triad may look sequential, but it often isn't. It belongs instead to the "I believe in order to understand" school of hermeneutical circles.

114. Cf. Terrance Tiessen, "Toward a Hermeneutic for Discerning Universal Moral Absolutes," *Journal of the Evangelical Theological Society* 36:2 (1993): 189–208, esp. 189.

stand the main topic—the gospel—and all that it entails. In sum, our real work as church members is to follow the sacred page where no church has gone before by entering into the theodrama with all our heart, soul, mind, and strength.[115]

---

115. Thanks to Dan Treier, Steve Garrett, Adam Johnson, Hans Madueme, and Armida Stephens for their helpful comments on an earlier draft, and to my wife, Sylvie, for suggesting the Wendell Berry passage.

A RESPONSE TO KEVIN J. VANHOOZER

Walter C. Kaiser Jr.

PROFESSOR VANHOOZER BEGINS BY ASKING, "What does it mean to be biblical in the twenty-first century?" Since this century has little resemblance to "the pre-industrial, agrarian settings of ancient Israel," does this mean that we no longer need to "stick to the original intent [of the biblical author] and follow it 'to the letter'?" Will that procedure end up "mocking" the biblical text without allowing us to "[live] biblically," as Vanhoozer suggests? If so, what can replace that procedure? Kevin suggests that the kind of living and interpreting needed is one that comes as a "community project," that "see[s] past the letter into the subject matter, or spirit, of the letter."

A MORE EXCELLENT HERMENEUTICAL WAY

In order to learn what is transculturally normative in the Bible, "we need ... biblical principles for discerning the Word of God in the words of man," argues Professor Vanhoozer. In order for the Bible to be heard properly, it must be jointly read in the church and be the benefactor of all the theological disciplines. By themselves, biblical studies tend to "bog down [by trying to get] behind the text." "It is not always a straightforward matter to know how 'what it meant' bears on the present."

Therefore, "practical" [systematic] theology is "not [about] building systems of ideas so much as it is of world-building ... building the city of God amidst the ruins of the city of man."

FAITH SEEKING AND
DISPLAYING UNDERSTANDING

What the church seeks to understand "is intrinsically dramatic," a "series of events that, when taken together as a unified drama, serve as a lens, or interpretive framework, through which Christians think, make sense of their experience, decide what to do and how to do it," advises Professor Vanhoozer

He allows that we can go "beyond the Bible biblically" by "participating in the great drama of redemption of which Scripture is the authoritative testimony and holy script." This is unlike the medium of ideas; it is "living persons in dialogical interaction." How this takes place and what the criteria are, are not at all clear. We are assured the drama-of-redemption method has advantages over several similar methods, including the history-of-redemption, the narrative-of-redemption, and the logic-of-redemption, which exhibit these faults (taken respectively as listed here): it "does not show the church how to go beyond the sacred page," it makes hearers "spectators" without requiring them to be "actors and doers," and it seeks "underlying abstract principles or universal truths" that give us only "the content without the form" and without any guidance on how "to apply it anew" to our contemporary context.

How this redemptive drama works is not altogether clear, for while it begins with the prophetic and apostolic discourse of Scripture, what engages the actors is not "a dead textual body to be exegetically dissected but a Spirited letter" that demands a response. The Bible gives us an invitation to dialogue, but there is "no guarantee that everyone who employs the drama-of-redemption approach will reach the same conclusions." But if that is so, where then is the authority and sufficiency of Scripture?

DISCOVERING THE WORLD
IN FRONT OF THE BIBLICAL TEXT

Kevin asks, "Is the notion of 'performing' discourse really the best model for describing the way the Bible functions authoritatively for the church?" Surely the Bible calls us to be doers of the word and not hearers only, but what is this talk about our "performing" the text and actualizing it? Professor Vanhoozer claims that "the script [Scripture] is not yet finished"; it is an ongoing text and perhaps an ongoing canon. Can interpretation really be "a species of the genus *performance*"? Here we come to the central question.

To answer his own question, Kevin turns to Paul Ricoeur, who taught that understanding "neither [seeks] the author's intention nor what an author says [the sense] but rather what the author is talking about [the referent]." Instead, discourse projects a world "in front of" the text, which means "understanding [comes] not by processing its information, but by 'inhabiting' the world it projects."

Now if I apply that same theory to Kevin's words, I suppose I should play down or forget about what he intends by his words and "project my ownmost possibilities" from my own experience and framework of reference. But this in-front-of the text world turns out "not [to be] authoritative." It is not even an application of the text, but only an appropriation of its message for me as one of its actors. It is like having a five-act play in which the first four acts are authoritative and scripted, but for the fifth act we must go beyond the script, "improvise" the ending of the play, and carry on as best we can, I suppose! But the critical move is the one that deliberately turns away from the *author's intentions*, even though *doing* the Word is where the text wants us to end up.

MARY, GOD-BEARER, IMMACULATE CONCEPTION

Mary's person and work are used by Professor Vanhoozer to demonstrate how in the development of doctrine we must go beyond the Bible. Though Scripture never directly tackled the question as to whether Mary was only a "Christ-bearer," "man-bearer," or "God-bearer," the Council of Ephesus in AD 431 did take up the challenge and correctly settled for "God-bearer," because God in the flesh did not detach himself from his deity.

The second notion that Mary was preserved free of original sin by God's special grace, as Pope Pius IX concluded in 1854, however, is not a correct inference, for Scripture speaks of no explicit exceptions that all have sinned and all need a Savior.

However, in neither of these two cases is it clear *how* the drama of redemption operates for us in these particular instances. Instead, both are good examples that there are legitimate theological inferences that can be made from the text. Thus, if Jesus is the God of Abraham, Isaac, and Jacob, the God of the living and not of the dead, then the resurrection from the dead is inferred by our Lord. As George Bush persuasively argued:

> If *inferences* are not binding in the interpretation of the divine law, then we would ask for the *express* command which was violated by Nadab and Abihu in offering strange fire [Lev 10:1–3], and which cost them their lives. Any prohibition in set terms on that subject will be sought for in vain [in the Bible]. So again, did not our Saviour tell the Sadducees that they *ought to have inferred* that the doctrine of the resurrection was true, from what God said to Moses at the bush?[116]

TRANSSEXUALS AND TRANSGENDERED EXAMPLES

Here Vanhoozer correctly notes that this problem is "a frontal assault on the very idea of the 'naturally given' as opposed to the 'culturally graven.'" He answers this issue by stating the principle that "to be or not to be male or female is not for us to decide. Our identities 'are fundamentally determined, not by human construction, but by the creative and redemptive activity of God.'" There does not appear to be room for a drama here, in which the interpreters play their parts in order to go beyond the Bible for their meaning; instead, one goes right to Scripture for a determining principle.

---

116. George Bush, *Notes, Critical and Practical, on the Book of Leviticus* (New York: Newman and Ivison, 1852), 183, emphases his.

204 Four Views on Moving beyond the Bible to Theology

The rebellion against the binary division between male and female attempts to strike down, not a human social convention by some undergoing sex reassignment surgery, so that they can go from a biologically defined man to become a woman and vice versa; rather, it is a revolt against the creative activity of God himself. As such it goes against the manufacturer's instructions and specifications, which in this case is God's manual of functions. But this is to argue from a biblical principle. It is not clear how this can be cast into any role in a drama that thereby extracts and extends the meaning process or the continuance of the canon of Scripture.

CONCLUSION: WHAT IS THE REAL WORK?

If what is wanted here is a tracing of the course of discipleship, the "fit" would be great. However, we are actually trying to find out how we answer contemporary (and some past) questions of a fixed canon. Kevin's illustration of A. J. Jacobs' "religious idiocy" of attempting to live by what he thought was a "literal interpretation" of the Bible sets us off on the wrong foot. By no stretch of the imagination can such an example even begin to illustrate what is normative for those of us who derive principles from the "vaunted grammatical-historical method" to answer questions that do not appear directly on the page, but for which Scripture holds us responsible for adequate applications of the truth of God.

After reading and rereading Kevin's chapter many times over, for the life of me I cannot explain to anyone else, much less myself, how the "drama-of-redemption approach" works or really solves any of the crucial questions being put to the Bible in our day. I think he must use principles from the Bible, but place them in the hands of players in the drama to practice rather than to stop with a cognitive acknowledgment of their existence. If that is the case, then I too am with Kevin.

A RESPONSE TO KEVIN J. VANHOOZER

Daniel M. Doriani

IT IS A CHALLENGE to attempt a critical assessment of Kevin Vanhoozer's essay on the drama-of-redemption hermeneutic, since I so rarely disagree with him. Perhaps this is no surprise, since we both attended Westminster Seminary during the late 1970s. On occasion we even shared a ride, a meal, a drama (!), or a tennis court before our paths diverged and we lost contact for two decades. At Westminster, we learned the virtues of covenant theology while John Frame proposed measures to mitigate the weaknesses of Westminster's redemptive-historical traditions.

The weaknesses were epitomized by two sayings. The first was a wistful gibe about preaching: redemptive-historical preachers have only one sermon, but at least it's a good one. That is, every sermon ends the same way and has the same main point, but at least it's about Christ. The second saying is the earnest but overused-unto-exhaustion call to "think God's thoughts after him." What had once been a summons to discipleship of the mind began to sound like a call to disciple the mind and forget the will and the emotions.

Frame attacked these problems by declaring, somewhat cryptically, "the meaning of Scripture is its application." That is, we understand Scripture only when we know how to use it. According to Frame, an inability to *live out* "You shall not steal" shows that a reader never really understood "You shall not steal." For Frame, the separation of meaning and application perverts the purpose, even the nature, of theology, since theology does not seek to discover abstract truth but the application of Scripture to godliness in every area of life.[117] He knew that some seminaries are prone to churn out what one friend called "brains on a stick." Here, then, Frame stood in line with Calvin's conviction that "all right knowledge of God is born of obedience."[118]

Vanhoozer has other influences, probably stronger than these, not least Ricoeur, Austin, and Balthasar. And he surely is a creative thinker in his own right. But he doesn't stand alone when he says the purpose of doctrine "is not merely to give us 'answers'" or information, but to instill in disciples "habits of seeing, judging, and acting in theodramatically appropriate manners" (notice that "theodramatically" could be excised without apparent loss of meaning). Vanhoozer's proposals essentially cohere with cardinal tenets of the best version of redemptive-historical or covenantal theology: Scripture describes the drama of redemption, a drama in which divine action inaugurates each new phase of the drama. He agrees with Geerhardus Vos that "the content of revelation" is not "a dogmatic system but a book of history that unfolds organically." The difficulty is "that Vos does not show the church how to go beyond the sacred page" since "the church today shares the same redemptive-historical situation with the authors of the New Testament."

Vanhoozer seeks to rectify this problem by proposing that we see both Scripture and the life of Christians through the master metaphor of drama. The Bible, he says, is not written to increase our "inventory of information"; it is a drama we can enter. The ultimate goal of study is action, participation in the divine drama: "Theology exists to minister theodramatic understanding of what God has said/done in the world for us and of what the church must say/do for God in response." Doctrine exists to shape our habits of speech, thought, judgment, and life, all in response to God's prior performance mediated through Scripture. This Scripture, the canon, "is the church's holy script."

Vanhoozer's proposal for movement beyond the sacred page flows logically from his view of Scripture. Starting from

---

117. John M. Frame, *The Doctrine of the Knowledge of God (A Theology of Lordship)* (Phillipsburg, NJ: Presbyterian & Reformed, 1987), 67–97.

118. John Calvin, *Institutes* 1.6.2.

an orthodox conception of Scripture's inspiration, he proposes that we view Scripture as a record of God's covenantal performance. It is a divine drama, for the subject matter is "intrinsically dramatic" and because it serves as a script directing our contemporary performance. God the Father, who is playwright and producer, has acted through Jesus Christ, the Son and principal actor. Beneath the Holy Spirit, pastors can help direct us through the script. But we must enter the plot as characters, as players and "doers of the Word." Indeed, the very lives of saints, who are fellow members of a large ensemble cast, help interpret Scripture. That is, they show the right way to perform, actualize, or complete it. We must know who we are and where we are to play our part correctly. Where are we? We "inhabit" the world of Scripture. Who are we? Believers are actors in the divine drama.

Here Vanhoozer modifies the familiar fourfold grid we place on the Bible: creation, fall, redemption, and restoration. Vanhoozer doesn't reject this grid but proposes some new terminology and a fifth element: (1) creation, (2) the election of Israel (supplanting the fall with God's positive, post-fall action), (3) Christ and redemption, (4) Pentecost and the church, (5) consummation. Today, disciples live in the fourth act, the era of the Spirit and the church. The Bible's mission and story are ours. Indeed, in the Bible we have what Ricoeur called a habitable text. It is also a script that expects actors to "improvise both their doctrine and discipleship" within the parameters set by playwright and director. Scripture contains sufficient direction for believers to "make judgments" about speaking and acting faithfully in contemporary situations.

Vanhoozer seems to believe that disciples generally know the content of biblical ethics. Yet it is possible to know God's law without knowing (switching metaphors) how "to transpose the world implied by the Bible ... into different places and times." At that point, the disciple needs to improvise in light of the whole canon. Neither love nor abstract wisdom is quite enough: "The wise disciple ... discerns, deliberates, and does the truth ... that is the love of God in Jesus Christ." That is how a character develops, how we "do the reality as it is in Jesus Christ."

I find myself in agreement with virtually every point here and have advocated a number of them in somewhat different terms. Curiously, I happened to read Vanhoozer's *Drama of Doctrine* just as I returned to acting after a decades-long hiatus. On this occasion, while I served as theological consultant to Compass Cinema's Modern Parables project, the writer/director decided I should play the teacher/preacher role in the first short film. In the script—received two days before filming—I had eighty lines. Alas, I had little time and even less inclination to memorize them. The director, bowing to reality, let me improvise as long as I hit my mark, looked into the camera, and delivered the cues that linked one scene to the next. Above all, my improvisation had to fit the scene and advance the goals of the project. It worked. The director and I were (literally and figuratively) on the same page, and I delivered my lines to reasonably good effect. The experience only enhanced my appreciation of Vanhoozer's thesis. Nonetheless, I have a few questions and friendly criticisms.

My principal question for Vanhoozer will be familiar to him: What is the warrant for constructing a theological system that rests on such a slender biblical basis? To be sure, Scripture is always in the background for Vanhoozer, suffusing his thought, but its presence is understated. It is a trait of his work that he neither quotes nor exegetes the Bible very much. I believe his work would be stronger if he presented additional biblical evidence for his proposal.

Consider, for example, the emphasis he places on "theodramatic fittingness." As biblical warrant for this concept, he (fittingly!) cites Hebrews 2:10. But there is more data than that. The phrase "it is fitting" appears eight times in the NIV translation. The Greek verb *prepō* appears in precisely Vanhoozer's sense in Matthew 3:15, touching Jesus' baptism; in 1 Corinthians 11:13, touching prayer postures; and in Ephesians 5:3, touching coarse talk. He could also have cited 1 Timothy 2:10; Titus 2:1; and Hebrews 7:26. The same concept, although not the same vocabulary, appears in 1 Corinthians 14:40; Ephesians 5:4; and Colossians 3:18. On each occasion, there is a lack of constraint, command, or necessity. It is possible to do otherwise, but the agent who understands God's will and this world realizes the need to act a certain way.

Would Vanhoozer's presentation be stronger if he limited his jargon? Rereading his essay, I found, for example, that most uses of "theodrama" and "theodramatically" could be deleted without altering the meaning (I cited one example earlier). Would his innovations command more respect if he explored the roots of his work in earlier theologians (per his own advice about the dramaturge in *Drama of Doctrine*, 244–47)?

But my principal question comes from another direction. Vanhoozer seems to have spent modest time teaching, preaching, and leading in the church; how might his work differ if he, like many seminary professors, had been a pastor or even an interim preacher for an extended period? The church is the more indebted to Vanhoozer because of his long labors in linguistic theory and his potent, painstaking analysis of Derrida, Nietzsche, Ricoeur, and Rorty. Nonetheless, a mentor might urge him to labor in a particular church most weeks for a year or so. I am sure he would bless the chosen church, and I suspect that the experience would deepen and refine his theories. Through regular teaching, he might find more support for his theory. I think of passages such as John 7:15–17 and 13:14–17 or the concept of walking in the ways of faithful kings.

A stint in the church might also remind him how much some people need direction. Although I still teach every semester in a seminary, my primary calling is to pastor a large and diverse church. Some have walked with the Lord for fifty years, some for mere months, and some are still inquiring. The latter groups often need direct commands.

But perhaps most of all, Vanhoozer would find satisfaction as he watched his theories bear fruit. He would find people joyful in their imaginative participation in the Scripture's habitable texts, striving to enter the story of redemption and to imitate the noble *dramatis personae*.

A RESPONSE TO KEVIN J. VANHOOZER

William J. Webb

THE ESSAY "DRAMA OF REDEMPTION" (herein, DOR) can be described as vintage Vanhoozer. After reading it, I find myself asking, "What is there not to like?" I have long been an admirer of the Vanhoozer "way," inasmuch as it resonates well with the Way of Jesus. The DOR method provides a wonderful synthetic approach to the whole "going beyond" issue. Even if one were not fond of Vanhoozer's method, surely his masterful control of the English language, along with his wit, wisdom, and metaphorical genius would soften the most ardent critic. Since I am much at home with a DOR approach, readers will be best served if I focus the bulk of my reflection on the other two views. Nevertheless, I would like to suggest two ways in which the Vanhoozer approach and one of his examples (transsexuality) could be further strengthened.

HERMENEUTICAL TOOLS

The greatest strength of the Vanhoozer approach may also be its greatest weakness. While Vanhoozer offers an essentially global or comprehensive perspective and a crucial character emphasis that guide the process of interpretation holistically, Christians often need additional good hermeneutical tools for slogging their way through tough textual trenches. Followers of Christ on both sides of the slavery debate certainly *thought* that they had the mind of Christ. Both sides *thought* that they were honoring biblical authority. Both sides *thought* that they were more righteous than the other in terms of character and cause. So, alongside a more mystical/spiritual content or a strictly canonical content to the mind of Christ is the need for Christians to reason rigorously about the process of hermeneutics.

Lessons from the hermeneutics of the past and from what I like to call "more neutral" cases such as the slavery texts and other examples where the church has substantial agreement ought to guide us with methodological insights for our present interpretive struggles.[119] From these more neutral cases we can derive a set of hermeneutical tools for discerning what are cultural or accommodated (sometimes, less-than-ultimate-ethic) components within the biblical text and what are transcultural components. A few time-tested tools forged in the slavery debates or on other past occasions can help Christians think through the process of applying Scripture today.

In sum, it is easy to subsume my "hermeneutical toolbox" within the Vanhoozer global approach. Over the years a number of Vanhoozer students, in addition to my own, have expressed to me that they like a blending of our two approaches. They are probably right.

SAME CONCLUSION BUT SOFTER/BROKEN TONE

While I agree with Vanhoozer's conclusions in the transsexuality example, I hope that upon reflection we might all incorporate a softer and more broken tone. Two things temper my own thinking on this issue. First, I have a son, Jon, with a degenerative brain disease (Leukodystrophy)—a disease that progressively destroys his cognitive and muscular abilities. Marilyn and I have watched him slowly go downhill for the past seven years. He was normal up to age fourteen; now at age twenty-one he reasons at the level of a preschooler, and his days of walking have just about come to an end. His behavior has changed dramatically for the

---

119. Before moving to the debated subjects of women/gender and homosexuality, I start each of my eighteen criteria with a focus on more neutral examples first. Thus the title of the book, *Slaves, Women & Homosexuals*, is not simply three subjects but a philosophy of approach, where one moves from examples of greater interpretive unity to the more debated issues today.

worse, and we use medications to keep aggressive violence at bay. Jon has taught me a lot about the brokenness of our world and *even more about my own brokenness*. I sometimes tell my students that they should get a half-tuition refund on my courses because I am such a messed-up person! Our frequent trips to Toronto to see leading geneticists and metabolic doctors have also led me on a journey in understanding genetics within our fallen world. This whole area of research is growing at a phenomenal rate, and clearly genetics and genetic mutations *do* impact behavioral traits to some extent for good or evil.

Second, my research on homosexuality has uncovered similar findings at least in terms of the *possibility* of genetic influences in the sexual domain. Recent twin studies have made the case for the possibility of some genetic influence on this behavior. Moreover, social-scientific studies reveal with *certainty* a vast array of broken-world environmental factors that influence sexual preferences. While from a Christian perspective we may view these genetic and/or environmental components as part of a fallen world, they are, nonetheless, important mitigating circumstances. They offer a lens of compassion and empathy through which we, as broken people ourselves, should view others who are at least in part impacted by this fallen world, whether they are aware of that theological category or not.

Even if we also see the "natural/God-given" body as the essential rudder that ought to steer the course of our conclusions (I agree with Vanhoozer here), such does not mean that other nature-imposed and/or nurture-imposed factors of a fallen world might not also be present. Given our own brokenness as human beings and the possibility of fallen-world factors impacting transsexuality, perhaps a more gentle, compassionate, and even broken tone would be appropriate.

CONCLUSION

In thinking about Vanhoozer's essay, I can happily look beyond matters of tone and additional hermeneutical tools. Far weightier for our consideration are the benefits of his method — an overarching philosophy and theology of approach combined with a beautiful infusion of character and community for shaping the process. I might restate my conclusions by saying that Vanhoozer's approach is just a little too much in the clouds — the theological stratosphere — for it to function as a *completely stand-alone* method especially for tough, "in the trenches" textual and hermeneutical issues.

But that grand perspective is also its central strength; it provides an excellent umbrella approach (along with Wright and Hays) for the task of going beyond. Following suggestions by a number of Vanhoozer's students as well as from my own students, perhaps the DOR method could function as a surrounding safety net within which the RMH (redemptive-movement hermeneutic) approach can thrive. Meanwhile, the RMH along with other cultural/transcultural criteria (see my *Slaves, Women & Homosexuals*) may offer the drama of redemption some helpful staging tools for wrestling with the concrete specifics of the biblical text.

CHAPTER FOUR

A REDEMPTIVE-MOVEMENT MODEL

William J. Webb

MOVING *BEYOND* THE BIBLE. I must confess to a certain amount of discomfort with that little word "beyond." Obviously, there is a sense in which we should never move beyond the Bible. If I say to my wife, Marilyn, "Honey, I really need to move *beyond* you," should I be stupid enough to say that, I suspect that the damage I might incur in our relationship could be, well, *beyond* repair. In one sense, then, we should never move beyond the Bible for it contains the sacred and cherished covenant with the God we have come to love deeply.

My preferred way to avoid such misunderstandings, though far from failsafe, is to insert crucial qualifiers between the words "beyond" and "the Bible." I encourage Christians to embrace the redemptive spirit of the text, which at times will mean that we must move beyond the *concrete specificity* of the Bible. Or, we must move beyond the *time-restricted elements* of the Bible. Or, we must be willing to venture beyond simply an *isolated* or *static* understanding of the Bible.[1] Or, we

---

1. A static understanding is reading the words of the Bible *only* within their immediate literary context, up and down the page. That is a good start. But, it still creates an isolated or nonmovement understanding of the Bible's ethic inasmuch as it neglects to understand its words within their larger ancient social context.

must progress beyond the *frozen-in-time aspects* of the ethical portrait found within the Bible.

Nevertheless, while I have taken great pains to qualify the notion of "going beyond," my efforts to be clear have failed miserably with some readers of my earlier work. My most hostile critics do not seem to care one wit about my qualifiers. They simply toss the qualifications away and create a fictional piece that I do not remember ever writing.

However, I suspect that it does not really matter whether you adopt the classy and subtle terminology of Kevin Vanhoozer, "Continuing Scripture," or the rugged, bold wording of an I. Howard Marshall, "Beyond the Bible," or the cautious, qualified wording of William Webb, "Beyond the Concrete Specificity of the Bible," or even the delightfully punned wording of Gary Meadors, "Moving beyond the Bible Biblically."[2] It does not really matter which wording you adopt. One thing is certain. You will need to find yourself a well-padded flak jacket. Many Christians do not want to venture beyond the Bible in any sense. Many would much rather stay with the concrete specificity of the biblical text because it offers a sense of safety. Listen to the words of the nineteenth-century author John Henry Hopkins (1792–1868), who could not bring himself to accept an abolitionist viewpoint on slavery. Hopkins wrote:

> If it were a matter to be determined by personal sympathies, tastes, or feelings, I should be as ready as any man [sic] to condemn the institution of slavery, for all my prejudices of education, habit, and social position stand entirely opposed to it. But as a Christian ... I am compelled to submit my weak and erring intellect to the authority of the Almighty. For then only can I be *safe* in my conclusions.[3]

Like Hopkins, many Christians today are looking for safety and certainty in their interpretive conclusions. They feel that

---

2. See I. Howard Marshall, *Beyond the Bible: Moving from Scripture to Theology* (Grand Rapids: Baker, 2004), which also contains a response chapter by Kevin J. Vanhoozer. Gary Meadors creatively used the conference title "Moving beyond the Bible Biblically" for the Midwest ETS meeting in March 24–25, 2006.

3. As cited by J. Albert Harrill, *Slaves in the New Testament: Literary, Social and Moral Dimensions* (Minneapolis: Augsburg Fortress, 2006), vii, emphasis mine.

if they root their conclusions for a contemporary ethic within the concrete specificity of the biblical text, such a move has the approval of God and thus the safety they are looking for. Yet, maybe Scripture was not written in order to establish a utopian society with complete justice and equity at every turn of the page. I suspect it is we who want a fully packaged ethic with all of its glorious details at the drop of a dime. Instead, Scripture seems to gives us an ethic that needs in some ways to be developed and worked out over time. It would appear that many biblical texts were written within a cultural framework with limited or *incremental movement* toward an ultimate ethic. If so, then possibly "movement meaning" within the text itself ought to tug at our heartstrings and beckon us to go further.

A REDEMPTIVE-MOVEMENT APPROACH: AN OVERVIEW

In broad terms Christians often tend toward one of two ways of approaching the Bible: (1) with a *redemptive-movement* (RM) or *redemptive-spirit* appropriation of Scripture, which encourages movement beyond the original application of the text in the ancient world, or (2) with a more *static* or *stationary* appropriation of Scripture that locks itself into the concrete specificity of, or as close as possible to, exactly what is found on the page. The latter understand the words of the text in isolation from their cultural/historical and canonical context and with minimal—or no—emphasis on their underlying spirit, thus restricting contemporary application to how the words of the text were applied in their original setting. But to do so often leads to a *mis*appropriation of the text precisely because one has failed to extend further or reapply the redemptive spirit of the text in a later cultural setting. As will be argued, it is a trajectory or logical extension of the Bible's redemptive spirit that carries Christians to an ultimate ethic.[4]

In the diagram below, notice the strikingly different facial expressions of the person reading the Bible. It is the

---

4. This overview section has been adapted from my *Slaves, Women & Homosexuals* (Downers Grove, IL: InterVarsity Press, 2001). Used by permission of the publisher. All rights reserved.

same person but looking at the Bible from two different perspectives or horizons. When someone views the Bible from the left side of the diagram, they are reading Scripture through the lens of its ancient-world context, namely, the ancient Near East (ANE) for the Old Testament (OT) or the Greco-Roman (GR) and the Second-Temple Judaism (2TJ) for the New Testament (NT). When a person shifts to the right side of the diagram, they are reading the Bible through the lens of their contemporary culture and in particular (for purposes of this diagram) in a situation where our present-day ethic happens to have advanced beyond the static forms of the biblical text to something better.

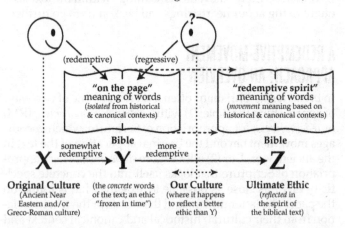

Now you can understand why the person from the right-side perspective looks perplexed or disturbed. For instance, imagine a contemporary Christian in our Western context reading the text of Deuteronomy 21:10–14. I will cite the passage in full:[5]

> When you go to war against your enemies and the LORD your God delivers them into your hands and you take captives, if you notice among the captives a beautiful woman and are attracted to her, you may take her as your wife. Bring her into your home and have her shave her head, trim her nails and put aside the clothes she was wearing when captured. After she has lived in your

---

5. Cf. Num. 31:25–32; Deut. 20:14.

house and mourned her father and mother for a full month, then you may go to her and be her husband and she shall be your wife. If you are not pleased with her, let her go wherever she wishes. You must not sell her or treat her as a slave, since you have dishonored her.

One might say that this war text is "exposure challenged" in Christendom today and that it has in effect been banned from public readings in our contemporary churches. The reason should be obvious. As Christians read this text, it begins to dawn on them that the Bible contains a war ethic that includes "grabbing hot-looking women" as wives. This should rightly be a disturbing feature within the text as we read our Bibles today. It is unlikely that Christians will mount a lobby group that attempts to bring this text into legislation through Congress or Parliament (for us Canadians) as a way in which we ought to treat female POWs in our modern war context.

So what is happening as Christians today read a text like Deuteronomy 21:10–14? Well, most contemporary readers of the biblical war texts (often unknowingly) are reading these texts through the lens of the Geneva or Hague war conventions. Our everyday, street-level discussions about the treatment of war captives are very much governed by these documents. Whether people are aware of it or not, even recent media coverage about the ethics of taking pictures of war captives is dominated by these emerging treatises on war ethics. I call them emerging treatises for two reasons. (1) There has been a long history of development in military ethics, a summary of which is easily accessible on the Web.[6] (2) I do not want to give the impression that even these latest war conventions, as good as they are, have somehow reached an ultimate war or violent-force ethic (diagram position "Z").

But let us come back to the other side of the diagram (position "X"). Sometimes I get a chance to talk with Christians and non-Christians alike who are extremely disturbed when they encounter the "grabbing hot-looking women" war ethic of Deuteronomy 21:10–14. While not abandoning a right-side reflection on the text through the lens of the Geneva

---

6. For the Geneva War Convention and other treaties governing our conduct of war, see "The Avalon Project at Yale Law School: Rules of War," www.yale.edu/lawweb/avalon/lawofwar/lawwar.htm (accessed February 10, 2008).

and Hague war conventions, I encourage them to begin by reading Scripture from an entirely different vantage point, namely, the ANE historical contexts within which they originally emerged. I will get them reading ancient extrabiblical war documents from Egypt, Assyria, Babylonia, and so on. Once they do this, they discover that the treatment of women in ancient war practices was utterly horrendous—it often included the bodily mutilation of women (cutting off their breasts and displaying them on poles), torturous deaths, multiple rape, and a type of concubine enslavement where women would be required to perform perpetual sexual favors and/or produce offspring for their owners.[7] In ancient siege warfare the fate of female captives was considered so dreadful that, if it looked like a city was about to fall, the men at times killed their own wives. What an utterly ugly world—the treatment of humanity by humanity is sometimes staggering. In our present-day context this ancient war portrait shares some commonality with the rape camps of Rwanda.

Pondering the biblical text within that sort of ancient-world war context places Deuteronomy 21:10–14 in an entirely different light. The Israelite warriors were not permitted to rape or mutilate the women captives; they had to wait at least a month as a minimum delay—a cooling-off period—before any sexual contact. Furthermore, in order to have sexual intercourse with a captive woman, they had to marry her. Should the marriage not work out, the foreign woman went free; she could not be held or sold as a slave.

By reading the biblical text within its ANE context, one begins to hear its redemptive movement—the sound is rather sweet. Combined with good ethical reasoning and reflection, it is a logical trajectory of this "better treatment of female POWs" ethos that ought to carry Christians forward in forging new documents that help offset or minimize the atrocities of war. The redemptive-movement meaning within the text, which I alternatively call its "redemptive spirit," ought to inspire Christians to venture into contemporary war discussions with the intention, wherever possible, of "going beyond" even the Geneva and Hague conventions.

---

7. See William J. Webb, *Brutal, Bloody and Barbaric: War Texts That Trouble the Soul* (Downers Grove, IL: InterVarsity Press, forthcoming).

In sum, the essence of a RM model can be captured succinctly in three or four words: "Movement is (crucial) meaning."[8] To be sure, movement is not the only meaning within the text. But movement provides absolutely crucial meaning that is often lost by contemporary readers as we wrestle with how to apply the text in today's setting. We might alternatively depict an "on the page" or "isolated" type of meaning as one derived *only* by reading the words of a text within its immediate literary context—up and down the page. This sort of meaning is also important. But it is movement meaning, captured from reading a text in (1) its ancient *historical and social* context and (2) its *canonical* context, which yields a sense of the underlying spirit of the biblical text. (Canonical movement will be illustrated in the slavery discussion below.) It is this redemptive-movement or redemptive-spirit meaning that ought to radically shape the contours of our contemporary ethical portrait.

Along these lines, my essay will primarily develop a redemptive-movement or redemptive-trajectory model. Through the use of two primary examples—slavery and corporal punishment—I will seek to show how "movement meaning" helps us understand the redemptive spirit of the biblical text and thus yields an important consideration for applying Scripture today.

THE SLAVERY TEXTS

Let us explore the concept of "movement meaning" through the lens of several slavery texts. We begin with that seldom-preached text of Exodus 21:20–21, "If a man beats his male or female slave with a rod and the slave dies as a direct result, he must be punished, but he is not to be punished if the slave gets up after a day or two, since the slave is his property." One might paraphrase this text as follows: "A Hebrew slave owner must not kill a slave during a beating (such would bring an undefined penalty), but otherwise the slave owner is legally free to beat the 'living daylights' out of a slave, provided the

---

8. Movement between the ANE context (cf. GR or 2TJ contexts) and the biblical text is an extremely crucial component of textual meaning that is frequently lost or not given sufficient weighting in a nonmovement (static) approach to our present/contemporary application of Scripture.

slave is able to get up after a day or two."[9] This text ought to disturb contemporary Christians for it enshrines the right of slave masters to beat their slaves, it permits a latitude of punishment that could well have included bloody and brutal beatings, and it does so by positively invoking (instead of rejecting) the notion of people as property. Such "on the page" meaning of this text can be easily detected from its immediate lexical and grammatical literary context.

This slave-beating text is at times cited by those opposed to the Christian faith today. Although I have never heard this beating text preached from a church pulpit, I have heard this portion of the Bible cited to me by several non-Christians —by my neighbors at a New Year's Eve party, by students on a Canadian university campus after I had given a lecture on social ethics, and by secular ethicists who would want to dispose of the Bible altogether as a basis for contemporary social ethics. They often ask a similar question, "You believe in a God who would say it is okay (no judicial recrimination) to beat a slave within a hairbreadth of their life provided they walk after a day or two? That's the God you believe in? That's the Bible you follow?"

When responding, I genuinely empathize with their position. I spend a good deal of time talking in detail about the way in which a text such as this troubles my soul. But eventually I will get around to making the point that I do not think they (my non-Christian opponents) have read the text correctly. On one such occasion a person actually grabbed a nearby Bible and read it to me just to show me that they had indeed cited the Bible correctly. There it is, right on the page! After a deliberate and lengthy pause, I responded again, "No, I still think that you have not read that text correctly."

Now given an opportunity to explain myself, I generally talk about how we need to read the slave-beating text of Exodus 21 within its ancient historical and social context in order to capture its movement meaning. This is the first

---

9. There is nothing within the NT that would automatically or directly rescind the biblical authority and ease-of-applicability of this OT verse (Ex. 21:20–21) if a NT slave owner were looking for explicit advice from God about how to interact with disobedient slaves.

component of movement meaning—the historical or ancient social movement.[10] What I argue is this: if we are going to read the biblical text with all of its intended meaning and not lose important components of that meaning, then we must read the text within the ancient-world context and its canonical context.

For example, in the ANE setting there was nothing holding back a master from beating a slave to death if they wished.[11] The only consideration, which curtailed such a brutal act, was the obvious loss of the slave's productivity. Yet, such utilitarian value often gave way to making a point to the larger slave community. Beating a slave to death was not an unheard of practice, and some masters exercised such rights in order to send a clear message to the rest of their slaves. It was often a harsh and cruel method of social control for the larger slave community. Now one reads the text of Exodus 21:20–21 in that sort of ancient social context and you have to say, "Okay, I see some movement. I see distinct redemptive movement away from the original cultural context and toward something better."

To this slave-beating portrait one must add another group of texts within the Bible (Ex. 21:26–27; 27:3–4) that say, if in beating a slave, the slave is injured physically (e.g., if he/she loses a tooth, an eye, an ear, etc.), then the slave must go free. Once again, the current of meaning runs far deeper than an isolated understanding of words on the page. We must read these slave-beating texts within the ancient-world context where masters often in punishing slaves (both ANE and GR) intentionally left physical mutilations in all kinds of horrendous ways in order to make a lasting visual statement to the rest of the slave community and to give the disobedient slave a perpetual reminder that something similar or worse might happen in the future.[12]

Within this kind of a harsh ancient-world setting one again senses a wonderful aspect of movement meaning. Yes, the Bible allows beatings, but if any physical mutilation occurred,

---

10. At some later point, if possible, I will also introduce the idea of movement meaning as it relates to the larger canonical context.

11. For space considerations I will generally not cite ancient sources throughout this discussion of slavery. For a more detailed development of ANE/GR sources, see Webb, *Slaves, Women & Homosexuals*, 30–55, 73–81, 162–72.

12. Ibid.

such mutilation meant that the slave went free! This RM meaning derived from reading the Bible within its broader ANE context can be captured in one English word, "Wow!" These OT biblical texts not only regulate social behavior, they do much more. They provide a crucial element of movement meaning within them that captures and conveys the Bible's redemptive spirit—the integral heartbeat of the text as it incrementally moves people toward an ultimate ethic.

We could go on with the text of Deuteronomy 23:15–16 (cf. Isa. 16:3–4) that provides safety and refuge to slaves who run away from foreign countries and forbids returning them to their country of origin. This text sounds rather ho-hum and blah just reading the isolated words on the page, especially for contemporary Western readers who intuitively are listening to the biblical text with abolitionist assumptions. But understanding this biblical text within the ancient-world environment yields for us the depth of its movement meaning. In the ancient world runaway slaves were sought for bounty. Captured slaves were at times executed in a brutal and torturous fashion along with their families and/or accomplices. The ancient Code of Hammurabi prescribed the death penalty for even aiding and abetting a runaway slave. Most nations held extradition treaties for the return of slaves.

In a radical departure from these prevalent views, Israel became a safety zone or a "city/country of refuge" for foreign runaway slaves. I read the Bible within this ancient-world environment, and once again I have to say, "Wow! Redemptive-movement meaning." That is my God. He *is* concerned about social ethics beyond simply regulating society and maintaining its current standards. He is concerned to move a much-entrenched social institution with incremental steps toward a better treatment of human beings.

To this emerging slavery portrait we must add the powerful components of canonical development, especially as we read texts like Galatians 3:28 ("neither slave nor free"; cf. Col. 3:11) against the backdrop of the OT itself and 2TJ/GR. The radical concept of equality within the new "in Christ" society, like the underlying ideology that transformed Jew and Gentile relationships in the first century, was eventually heard by the church with an awakened sense of realized ethic. It is important for our discussion about "going beyond" models that it is the movement meaning within the slavery texts themselves (thus a distinct advantage to the RM methodology) that serves as a strong connection in meaning between the biblical text and an ultimate, abolitionist ethic.

Consequently, the slavery texts ought to be understood from two distinctly different perspectives or horizons. Both of them are legitimate. On the one hand, there is a difficult or painful side to the portrait. As one reads the biblical texts on slaves, an overwhelming impression emerges: *a less-than-ultimate ethic in the treatment of slaves/people is a major part of our Bible*. If we clear away the technical language, we might simply say that there is a problem with the treatment of slaves in the Bible. There exist numerous "not so pretty" components within the slavery texts that illustrate a less-than-ultimate ethic in the treatment of slaves/people:

- Human beings/slaves are considered to be property (Ex. 12:44; 21:20–21, 32; Lev 22:11).
- Foreign slaves in Israel did not experience the seventh year of release (Lev. 25:39–46).
- Slaves within Israel were used to produce offspring for their infertile owners (Gen. 16:1–4; 30:3–4, 9–10; cf. 35:22).
- Sexual violation of a betrothed slave woman led not to death, as in the case of a free woman (Deut. 22:25–27), but to a mere payment/offering for damages (Lev. 19:20–22).
- A bull owner's liability for their animal goring a slave to death (compared to a free person) shows tremendous inequality in terms of the value of human life (Ex. 21:28–32).
- Slave owners were permitted to beat their slaves without any penalty, provided the slave survived and could get up after a couple of days (Ex. 21:20–21).

To call the biblical treatment of slaves "abusive" in terms of the original culture would be anachronistic. Relative to the ancient culture many of these texts were in some measure progressive. Nevertheless, the above practices are problematic and in need of movement toward an ultimate ethic. A much more humane treatment of persons can be legislated and lived out in our modern civil-law settings.

The idea of a RM hermeneutic is not that God himself has somehow "moved" in his thinking or that Scripture is in any way less than God's Word. Rather, it means that God in a pastoral sense accommodates himself to meeting people and society where they are in their existing social ethic, and (from there) he gently moves them with incremental steps toward something better. Moving large, complex, and embedded social structures along an ethical continuum is by no means a simple matter. Incremental movement within Scripture reveals a God who is willing to live with the tension between an absolute ethic in theory and the reality of guiding real people in practice toward such a goal.

On the other hand, fortunately, there exists a wonderful and inspiring side to the biblical portrait of slaves. It is this positive side that establishes *redemptive movement as crucial meaning within the biblical text*. This RM meaning or redemptive-spirit meaning must profoundly shape the course of our contemporary appropriation of the Bible in a way that often carries us beyond the bound-in-time components of meaning within the biblical text. In the next set of examples the hermeneutical task is to "listen to" and "hear" the slavery texts within their cultural/historical context (relative to the ancient world) and their canonical context (with movement to the NT). In both cases, by hearing the biblical text in this manner, the reader begins to sense wonderful "movement meaning" as part of the biblical words about slavery:

- Holidays granted to slaves for festivals and for the weekly Sabbath rest, compared to the ancient world, were generous (Ex. 23:12; Deut. 16:10–12).
- In both OT and NT slaves are included in the worship setting (Ex. 12:44; Deut. 12:12, 18; cf. Col. 3:22–25; 4:16), and the NT church community profoundly raised a slave's status yet further to equality "in Christ" (Gal. 3:28). Some ancient cultures (such as the Roman Empire) restricted slaves from involvement in the sacred rituals and religious festivals because they were thought to have a defiling or polluting influence.
- No interest loans within Israel were a preventative attempt to reduce the occurrence of debt slavery (Lev. 25:35–36; Deut. 15:1–2, 7–11); this compares with

loan rates within the surrounding foreign nations that were often well in excess of 20 percent interest.

- The legislated release of Hebrew debt slaves after a certain number of years, when compared with most of the ancient world, is a highly redemptive aspect to biblical legislation (Lev. 25:39–43; cf. Jer. 34:8–22).
- Material assistance for released slaves stands out as a generous act of biblical law (Deut. 15:12–18).
- Limitations were placed on the severity of physical beatings (Ex. 21:20–21), and freedom was granted to any slave who was physically damaged (21:26–27). Other ancient cultures did not limit the slave owner's power in this way. In fact, torturous abuse of select slaves and intentional maiming/disfiguring often became an object lesson for others.
- Masters are admonished to turn away from harshness and to show genuine care for their slaves (Eph. 6:9; Col. 4:1), transforming the slave-master relationship with a new sense of Christian brotherhood (Philem. 16).
- Scripture denounces foreign countries (Gaza and Tyre) for stealing people in order to trade them as slaves (Ex. 21:16; Deut. 24:7; cf. 1 Tim. 1:10).
- In the ancient world runaway slaves were sought for bounty. Captured slaves were often executed along with their families and/or accomplices. In a radical departure from these prevalent views, Scripture outlawed any extradition so that Israel became a safety zone and refuge for foreign runaway slaves (Deut. 23:15–16; cf. Isa. 16:3–4).

When the Bible's slavery texts are read against the ANE/GR context, redemptive movement becomes increasingly clear. These biblical modifications to the existing social norms brought greater protection and dignity for the slave. This improvement in the conditions of slaves relative to the original culture was clearly a redemptive action on the part of Scripture. Admittedly, it was not redemptive in any absolute sense. Scripture only moved the cultural "scrimmage markers" so far. Yet, that movement was sufficient enough to signal a clear direction in terms of the possibility of further improvements for later generations. RM meaning was (and is) absolutely crucial to contemporary application of Scripture. It is this movement meaning within the biblical texts—yes, even within the slave-beating texts—that should by logical extension of their underlying redemptive spirit take us to an abolitionist ethic. In so doing, an aspect of meaning from words within the slavery texts (not simply from without) becomes the basis for our contemporary convictions about the abolition of slavery.

In sum, a sense of the redemptive spirit or incremental development in ethic ("movement meaning") within the slavery texts of the Bible is discovered through reading these texts relative to their ancient historical/social setting. Such ancient context movement is often augmented by further canonical movement between the Testaments. This often-missed aspect of movement meaning is a crucial part of biblical authority for Christians wanting to apply the text today. Ultimately, a logical extension or trajectory of the redemptive-spirit meaning is what carries Christians in a credible fashion from the slavery texts to our contemporary affirmation of an abolitionist ethic.[13]

THE SPANKING/CORPORAL PUNISHMENT TEXTS

A second example of a RM approach will be illustrated within the spanking texts and, more broadly, the corporal punishment (CP) texts of Scripture. The brief treatment of this subject herein is a glimpse into a couple of chapters within a forthcoming book on the subject: *The Rod, the Whip and the Meat Cleaver: Corporal Punishment Texts That Trouble the Soul.*[14]

---

13. For an in-depth development of a redemptive-movement approach to the slavery texts and one that provides ANE/GR slavery sources, see the above noted discussion in *Slaves, Women & Homosexuals*. See also Webb, "A Redemptive-Movement Hermeneutic: The Slavery Analogy," in *Discovering Biblical Equality: Complementarity without Hierarchy*, ed. Gordon D. Fee, Rebecca M. Groothuis, and Ronald Pierce (Downers Grove, IL: InterVarsity Press, 2004), 382–400.

14. I must express thanks to InterVarsity Press for granting permission to publish a highly condensed version of two chapters from a forthcoming book: William J. Webb, *The Rod, the Whip and the Meat Cleaver* (Downers Grove, IL: InterVarsity Press, forthcoming).

None of us read Scripture in isolation from life experience. So, I probably should confess my own personal background that I bring to this subject. I was raised in a home with wonderful Christian parents who endeavored to do what Scripture taught about raising children, and so they naturally endorsed spanking. My father was a medical doctor, a scholar in the field of public health, and an avid lay "academic" when it came to biblical studies—he has a mammoth library of Christian books. I suppose that both his medical background and his love for biblical studies attracted him to Dobson's materials on raising children. Thus I grew up in a family of four boys (no girls) and, as you might guess, Dad and Mom took each of us boys on more than one occasion to the proverbial woodshed.

Not surprisingly, in our own home my wife, Marilyn, and I continued in the tradition of spanking that was handed down to us—no pun intended—from both our parents and from Scripture. We have now been married for many delightful years and together have raised three children, the youngest of which is now sixteen years old. With our oldest two children we read every Dobson book on parenting available and basically adopted his method for ourselves.[15] Only with the youngest did we start to wrestle through and begin to move away from CP, although still embracing alternative forms of child discipline.

Some of our journey as a couple can be attributed to my wife's educational and skills development in teaching (B.Ed. from University of Western Ontario and an M.Ed. from University of Toronto) and her growing abilities at good classroom management in a Canadian context where CP is not permitted in our schools. Her role in special education and in dealing with behavioral issues involving severe disciplinary cases, often with complicating medical components, made our own "normal parenting" through noncorporal means look comparatively easy. Of course, another part of our journey as a couple is related to our own pilgrimage in understanding Scripture and what it means to be faithful to its teaching and ethic. With a RM hermeneutic we no longer think about these matters the same way that we did twenty years ago.

---

15. For the most recent edition of his classic work, see James Dobson, *The New Dare to Discipline* (2nd ed.; Carol Stream, IL: Tyndale, 1992).

I have introduced this personal journey section for several reasons. First, I do not want you to think that I am trying to discredit Dr. Dobson or the Focus on the Family ministry. They have played a helpful role in our family—their materials have always been on our reading tables for Marilyn and myself. Our children have benefited greatly from their videos and publications through each stage of their development.

Second, I surely do not want to discredit my own parents—they did the best that they could do within their own context as parents. In fact, I think they were wonderful parents.[16]

Third, while I will strongly disagree with and oppose certain evangelical scholars in this essay—Andreas Köstenberger, Al Mohler, and Paul Wegner—I do so with something of sheepish embarrassment because I held to and lived out their perspectives for many years. Some readers might get the impression that I am disappointed with their perspectives on Scripture. Yes, that is so. But the brunt of my disagreement and disappointment is not with them but with myself! When it comes to understanding and applying the spanking texts of the Bible, I often wonder how I could ever have been so blind.

Several things happened that helped me open my eyes, if you will, and look at Scripture differently. First, I began to understand the handful of spanking texts (Prov. 13:24; 19:18; 22:15; 23:13–14; 29:15, 17) within the larger discussion of what the Bible says and teaches about the corporal punishment of both adults and children. I have become increasingly aware that I was formerly reading and applying the spanking-children texts through a contemporary Western perspective and not really engaging the biblical text and what it teaches at the concrete-specific level with regard to the subject of CP. For instance, Scripture clearly teaches CP for adults as well as children. So, what does it mean for Christians to be faithful to the CP teaching of Scripture today?

Second, I began to realize that even the Dobson approach to spanking children has moved far away from the Bible and its clear teachings[17] about the subject of child discipline

---

16. My father continues to edit almost everything I write in its prepublication form. Thanks, Dad.

17. Again, I speak of what "the Bible teaches" at a concrete-specific level of the text and without any due consideration for redemptive-movement meaning.

through beatings with the rod. Along these lines, this CP example of going beyond the Bible biblically, as developed below, will highlight six ways in which contemporary Christian pro-spankers have themselves inadvertently departed from biblical moorings (in one sense) and taken their own journey—a journey that no longer "obeys" the concrete instructions of Scripture.

Third, I have come to realize that faithfulness to Scripture has a whole lot more to do with carrying further its redemptive spirit than attempting to replicate its frozen-in-time ethic. Christian scholars often do what I like to call "museum-piece" ethics. It is an attempt by Christians, and biblical scholars in particular, to live out the Bible as if we were doing an archaeological dig. You get a toothbrush and painstakingly dust any sand and soil off the words of Scripture (through textual, lexical, and grammatical studies) and then set these fossilized forms gently into place as a painstaking reconstruction project. The words of the text are displayed in all of their rugged specificity like ancient dinosaur bones mounted inside of a museum. At that point those Christians who can most closely replicate the museum piece in their contemporary lives get the prize for being "most faithful" to Scripture.

Please do not get me wrong. Textual, lexical, and grammatical studies are all good work. They provide a cornerstone component of biblical studies—I have devoted much of my life to teaching these sorts of things within a seminary context. But if we stop there and simply scan an electronic copy of the reconstructed museum piece onto our behavioral foreheads with naïve or automatic assumptions about ultimate ethic, we have surely chosen an impoverished way of applying Scripture to our lives. Working with the slavery texts and numerous other examples has pushed me—I have journeyed slowly and somewhat reluctantly—to appreciate the incremental nature of the ethic that we find within Scripture. What I have discovered in the CP/spanking texts is that this same feature of incremental ethics is very much a part of how Christians ought to (but often do not) understand these texts. Accordingly, I will highlight a sampling of the RM meaning that one encounters when reading Scripture's CP texts within the broader ANE environment.

Having sketched my own awakening on this subject, let me summarize some of my discoveries about the CP/ spanking texts through the following chart. It will highlight ways in which contemporary pro-spankers have themselves unknowingly "gone beyond" the Bible in their application of the spanking texts today:

	Concrete-specific teaching of the Bible	Pro-spanking ethic of Köstenberger, Mohler, Wegner, et al.
Age limitations	No age limits; CP used throughout teen years	Primarily preschool age, less so up to age 10–12; no spanking teens
Number of lashes	Graduated increase to forty max. strokes (reasonable inference within Scripture)	One or two smacks max.
Bodily location	Back	Buttocks
Resultant bruising, welts, and wounds	An acceptable practice; seen as a virtue	Unacceptable practice; viewed as abusive
Frequency and type of offences	Broadly/frequently used; defiant and nondefiant actions	Infrequently used; last resort among methods; only defiant actions
Emotive disposition	Rod expresses parental love and anger (reasonable inference within Scripture)	Spank only in love; no anger permitted

In sum, there are six significant ways that pro-spanking advocates such as Köstenberger,[18] Mohler,[19] and Wegner[20] today have "abandoned" what Scripture teaches, either

---

18. Andreas J. Köstenberger with David W. Jones, *God, Marriage and Family: Rebuilding the Biblical Foundation* (Wheaton, IL: Crossway, 2004), 157–62.

19. Albert Mohler, "Should Spanking Be Banned? Parental Authority under Assault," www.crosswalk.com/1269621 (accessed Jan. 18, 2008).

20. Paul D. Wegner, "Discipline in the Book of Proverbs: 'To Spank or Not to Spank,'" *Journal of the Evangelical Theological Society* 48:4 (2005): 715–32.

explicitly or implicitly, about corporal punishment. In *The Rod, the Whip and the Meat Cleaver* I devote an entire chapter to this point. Within this short essay, however, I simply provide the biblical evidence through a series of footnote citations that draw attention to some of the more important texts. I would encourage readers to take a look at these biblical passages in order to get a better understanding of what the Bible actually teaches about spanking/CP.

- For instance, unlike contemporary spankers who impose strict age restrictions on spanking (no spanking teenagers), the Bible explicitly teaches that corporal punishment is a beneficial form of discipline for all ages, including teens and adults.[21]
- Unlike Dobson-type pro-spankers who limit spankings to only one or two smacks, the Bible explicitly teaches a maximum of forty strokes for adults and thus by implication some sort of gradual/proportional movement toward the forty strokes maximum as children and youth approach adulthood.[22]
- Unlike evangelical scholars who advocate the buttocks (or hands) as the location for spankings, the Bible explicitly teaches that beatings are for the backs of fools.[23]
- Unlike Christian pro-spankers who are outspokenly opposed to leaving marks and bruises (they see them as "abusive"), the Bible views resultant welts and markings from beatings as a virtue.[24]
- Unlike today's spankers, who want to use corporal punishment as a last resort and only for willful and defiant misbehavior, the Bible seems to teach CP for

---

21. Ex. 21:20–21; Deut. 25:1–3; Prov. 10:13; 18:6; 19:29; 26:3.

22. Deut. 25:3.

23. Prov. 10:13; 19:29; 26:3; cf. Deut. 25:2; Isa. 50:6; Sir. 30:12.

24. Prov. 20:30; Sir. 23:10; 28:17 (cf. the similar functional objectives of Prov. 22:15). Moreover, Ex. 21:20–21 and Deut. 25:3 suggest the logical probability of wounds and markings in adult corporal punishment. For the same idea within the realm of theological analogy, see Isa. 1:5–6; 30:26.

a much broader range of infractions, including both willful and nonwillful ones.[25]

• Unlike pro-spanking scholars who repeatedly warn against spanking in anger (a parent must only spank in love, never in anger), at least by inference the Bible seems to bless the rod of parental anger.[26]

In their defense of spanking today, Köstenberger,[27] Mohler,[28] and Wegner[29] make rhetorically explosive claims about their own unwavering faithfulness to Scripture. With a seriousness like that accorded to prophetic pronouncements, they contend that only their pro-spanking position upholds the authority of Scripture. They chide those who embrace noncorporal methods for departing from what the Bible teaches. Of course, what they fail to share with their readers is exactly how they themselves have moved away

---

25. Deut. 25:2 ("proportionate to the offence"); cf. Luke 12:47–48.

26. Note the anger within God's disciplinary practices in general and within his use of the rod: Pss. 6:1; 38:1 (cf. Jer. 10:24); Isa. 10:5, 24–25; 30:30–31 (cf. 30:27, 32); Lam. 3:1.

27. Irony runs a mile deep in Köstenberger's statement: "Rather than relying unduly on the surrounding culture and conforming to cultural values, norms and expectations, Christian parents must take their cue from Scripture, and only from Scripture" (see Köstenberger, *God, Marriage and Family*, 162).

28. Mohler caricatures the nonspanking position as "parental authority under assault" and as influenced by "humanist psychology" that is diametrically opposed to the Bible and to a biblical worldview. Mohler communicates the biblical correctness of his pro-spanking position and the mandatory requirement of physical discipline for Christian parents to comply with what the Bible teaches: "Does the Bible instruct parents to spank their children? The answer to that must be an emphatic, *Yes*." From the rest of Mohler's address it would appear that a Christian parent who is not pro-spanking stands in direct disobedience to God. See Mohler, "Should Spanking Be Banned?" 1–2. Köstenberger cites Mohler's point with approval (*God, Marriage and Family*, 383, note 11). For further discussion of spanking as a required part of a Christian ethic, type "spanking" into the search entry of Mohler's website, www. crosswalk.com.

29. Thankfully, Wegner's biblical-authority stance is somewhat quieter. Nevertheless, an inference is obviously present when he concludes that spanking is clearly taught within Proverbs and that, like God who as a loving father practices perfect discipline, so also should we as Christians be obedient to these (perfect) God-endorsed spanking practices (see Wegner, "Discipline," 728, 732).

from what Scripture teaches on the subject of corporal punishment. They seemingly assume that what indeed honors biblical authority is only their own highly concretized and static approach to applying the biblical text. However, there appears to be a touch of irony in the fact that they themselves freely choose what they wish to ignore within the corporal punishment texts.

Now I would hardly want my banter colleagues to change their contemporary spanking practices. Despite what the Bible teaches at a concrete-specific level, I do not really want them to begin spanking their teenagers, let alone adopting some sort of graded scale moving upwards to forty strokes (making for a smooth transition between teenage years and adulthood) as the new parenting maximum. Nor would it be such a good idea to revert to beatings upon the back of foolish kids instead of their buttocks. Also, I certainly do not want them to start leaving marks and bruises on their children or to begin seeing these physical wounds as a virtue.[30] Nor would it be helpful to broaden the use of corporal punishment to include nonwillful infractions by children along with an introduction of parental anger into the equation.

Compared to the concrete specificity of Scripture, I genuinely like their kind-and-gentle "two smacks max" approach. I would argue that each of these six changes is not simply a swapping of equivalent alternatives between the ancient text and our contemporary third-millennium setting. It is far more than that. These changes evidence a significant ethical movement toward an improvement in the discipline of children.[31] Or, to put it a better way as illustrated above

---

30. In our Canadian context we would lose our children for beatings that left marks.

31. In this essay I cannot enter into a lengthy discussion of how each of the six departures from Scripture evidences ethical development. However, one obvious improvement is the simple switch from the classic location of beatings on the *back* to the *buttocks*. Pro-spankers readily admit that their choice of this present-day location (buttocks) is because of its greater protection of internal organs. In other words, it is the least likely location on the body where corporal punishment could result in permanent or serious physical damage. For further discussion on the other issues see *The Rod, the Whip and the Meat Cleaver.*

in the slavery texts, these changes take the ethical trajectory of Scripture itself to a new and better realization.

So how does the contemporary Christian pro-spanking scene with its marked departure from Scripture nonetheless reflect a positive sense of "going beyond the Bible *biblically*"? Why should their departure be celebrated as a good thing? I would like to provide my pro-spanking colleagues with a biblical basis for their movement beyond the concrete specificity of the text by appealing to three crucial areas of biblical meaning: (1) purpose meaning, (2) abstracted meaning, and (3) redemptive-movement meaning. Each of these aspects of meaning within the biblical text is fulfilled, and the third aspect to an even greater extent, within the contemporary Dobson-style spanking ethic.

PURPOSE MEANING

The first biblical basis for the pro-spankers' journey beyond the Bible's concrete-specific teaching is founded in the *purpose* meaning of the text. Within Proverbs the purpose for beating children with a rod is stated in two ways: (1) [negatively] to turn the child from folly,[32] and (2) [positively] to help them embrace wisdom.[33] Surely, these are good purposes. If alternative or modified approaches to discipline can still achieve the same twofold purpose, then at least at the level of purpose meaning the biblical text is still fulfilled. Even so, contemporary Dobson-type spanking methods, despite their departure from explicit biblical instructions at the concrete-specific level, ought not to be judged too harshly. They are faithful in fulfilling Scripture's purpose meaning.

ABSTRACTED MEANING

Within most concrete-specific instructions of everyday life there is often an embedded element of meaning at an abstract level. We might label this as *abstracted* meaning. For example, as a parent I might call my teenager to the garage, hand him a broom, and say, "Joel, please sweep out the

---

32. Prov. 22:15; cf. 10:13; 18:6; 19:29; 26:3.
33. Prov. 29:15; Sir. 30:12; cf. Prov. 19:25; 29:19.

garage for me. Thanks." Suppose I come back in an hour and I find my teen diligently vacuuming the garage with our shop vacuum, which he had to haul up from the basement. The shop vacuum actually did a much better job of my sweep-with-the-broom instructions, and it surely fulfilled my commands at an abstract level, namely, "Clean up the garage." What does it matter if he did not use a broom and did not sweep up the garage (my concrete-specific instructions)? Even so, a good father would not scold or quibble with his son or daughter over an alternative way of fulfilling the abstracted meaning within their instruction.

Similarly, the biblical text often gives instructions at a concrete level but with an understood or embedded element of abstracted meaning. The book of Proverbs repeatedly instructs parents about their responsibility to judicially "beat their children with the rod." There is no escaping the clear teaching of Scripture on this point. Nevertheless, it is rather obvious that these concrete instructions include within them an embedded element of abstracted meaning, namely, "Discipline your children." As with our example about cleaning the garage, I am inclined to think that God cares deeply about the discipline of children, but surely he would not scold us ("You have transgressed biblical authority!") if alternative methods were used to accomplish that discipline. Unless there is something sacrosanct about the methodology itself, one would be hard pressed to think any other way. Even so, we should applaud the contemporary pro-spankers in their movement away from the Bible's concrete instructions about corporal punishment, because they nonetheless fulfill its abstracted meaning about disciplining children.

REDEMPTIVE-MOVEMENT MEANING

There is yet a third aspect of textual meaning that supports the pro-spankers' journey of ethical development beyond the concrete-specific instructions of the Bible. Just as the light bulb in one's mind should go on as we listen to the slavery texts within their ANE social setting, so also with the CP texts of Scripture. When one ponders these texts within their ancient-world setting, it ought to cause a reader to appreciate an absolutely crucial element of *redemptive-movement* meaning. This in turn offers a sense of the redemptive spirit of the text; it keeps one from getting mired down with looking for letter-for-letter equivalents in doing ethics and, conversely, suggests that we truly honor biblical authority through ethical extrapolation and development that carries the biblical spirit further.

So where does one see movement meaning within the CP texts of the Bible? I will have to be content here with a summary snapshot and leave the extensive source data to other publications.[34] Even so, here is a Canon or Nikon flash version of the brutal and barbaric treatment of human beings through CP in the ancient world. For example, the Egyptian law codes prescribed as many as two hundred strokes with the rod and five open wounds for certain offenses. This background portrait is especially significant, given Israel's first-hand experience of beatings in Egypt during their time of enslavement there.

In Babylonian codes we find only a couple of examples where the number of strokes is specified; in those cases, the prescribed amount was sixty strokes. Assyria yields numerous instances of a specific number of lashes/strokes paired with various offences, and not infrequently the number is as many as a hundred strokes. It is important to note that no maximum limit is set by any of these foreign countries. Furthermore, while difficult for us to fathom today, beatings with the rod were actually the more gentle treatment within a much larger repertoire that included all kinds of grotesque forms of CP. Egyptian, Babylonian, and Assyrian laws often included bodily mutilations and torture as part of their CP packages: gouging out eyes, castration ("turn him into a eunuch"), lacerating the face, pouring hot tar over the head, tearing out hair, cutting off fingers, hands, noses, ears, and breasts, and numerous examples of trial by river ordeal, where fate could potentially bring life or death as well as various bodily injuries.

Only now is a contemporary reader in a position to hear the movement meaning within the biblical text.

---

34. In *The Rod, the Whip and the Meat Cleaver*, I provide a detailed development of the ANE source material and a more extensive discussion of movement meaning.

Compared to other ancient law codes—Egyptian, Babylonian, and Assyrian—the more grotesque forms of CP have been almost entirely removed.[35] Thank God for just this element of movement meaning alone. But there is more. When we read the biblical text of Deuteronomy 25:1–3 within this ancient framework, where "justice" in that world often included beatings with upwards to two hundred lashes/strokes, various horrendous bodily mutilations, and other torturous means of CP, then the biblical text speaks in fresh, new ways. Within this sort of brutal and harsh world, Deuteronomy 25:1–3 (1) limits corporal punishment of adults to a maximum of forty strokes, (2) requires that the number of lashes to be proportionate to the offence—indicating a lesser amount for lesser infractions, and (3) explicitly states concern for limiting the number of lashes because otherwise "your neighbor will be degraded in your sight."

When the CP text of Deuteronomy 25:1–3 is read within the larger ANE social context, the movement meaning is huge. Once again, the English word that best captures RM meaning is "*Wow!*" The biblical text moves the covenant people toward a *kinder and gentler* administration of justice and toward a *greater dignity* for the human being who is punished; that is the spirit of the Bible as it is read within its larger ancient social framework.

Now I grant that in this example I am illustrating movement meaning within *adult* CP texts to establish a basis for understanding and applying the *children* CP texts of Scripture today. Nevertheless, the move is a reasonable one. A number of factors support taking movement meaning from the one domain and applying it to other CP domains. I will develop one reason here. For instance, the sort of justice and punishments prescribed in the "published" ancient codes for the adult population would logically set parameters for what was acceptable within the home. Just as it is reasonable to argue that the allowable strokes with the

---

35. There is only a singular incident within the OT of prescribed bodily mutilation, namely, Deut. 25:11–12. I devote an entire chapter ("Finally, the Meat Cleaver") to this text in *The Rod, the Whip and the Meat Cleaver.*

rod in the biblical scene for children was an age-graduated movement up to forty strokes (drawing an inference from the adult CP text), so it is also reasonable to assume that the adult law codes in the broader ancient world would have an impact on what was acceptable or unacceptable within the home situation. Other pieces of data confirm this sort of crossover and correlation between the public/adult realm and the private/home setting for the CP of women and children.[36]

I return to my main point. Movement meaning within the biblical CP texts gives one a sense of Scripture's redemptive spirit: a *kinder and gentler* administration of justice that underscores the *dignity* of the human being who is punished. When that sort of biblical meaning is applied in the case of the CP of children today, the pro-spanking approach of Köstenberger, Mohler, and Wegner (noncorporal discipline for teenagers and only two smacks max on the bottom for preteens) makes good sense. While clearly departing from the concrete specificity of the biblical instructions at a number of points, their contemporary ethical application of the CP texts permits a far greater realization of the redemptive spirit within the text. Well done!

One might ponder, however, one last, lingering question. Could it not be possible for Christian parents to embrace exclusively noncorporal methods of discipline and yet honor God and biblical authority on the same threefold basis? Let me explain. If by noncorporal methods parents can achieve (1) the *purpose* meaning of the CP texts (turning their children away from folly and helping them pursue wisdom) and (2) the *abstracted* meaning embedded within the CP texts (disciplining their children), while (3) also embracing what might possibly be seen as a little further extension of the same *redemptive spirit* evidenced in the Dobson-style movement already, then what is the problem? Why should pro-spanking Christians get their proverbial knickers in a knot over this sort of thing? It is not my objective to answer that question here. I suspect my reader has a hunch about the direction that I am going. I

---

36. Again, see *The Rod, the Whip and the Meat Cleaver* for details.

must leave a fuller discussion of that question to another time and place.

CORRECTING MISCONCEPTIONS

A number of misunderstandings have arisen as evangelicals have interacted with a RM hermeneutic.[37] In the following section I will attempt to correct some of these misconceptions and misunderstandings about a RM hermeneutic with a brief response and generally a citation where further discussion can be found.

1. *A RM hermeneutic is a new concept.* Attempting to call the method into question, one evangelical scholar has declared that a RM hermeneutic is an "entirely new" approach.[38] Granted, the approach may be new to some individuals. However, the charge of novelty within conservative Christian hermeneutics simply betrays a misunderstanding of and/or insufficient interaction with our interpretive heritage. For instance, Carl Sanders has shown that over three-quarters of the criteria referencing the slavery texts in *Slaves, Women & Homosexuals* have clear historical precedent within the slavery debates of the past two centuries.[39] Based on this historic Christian usage, Sanders concludes that the charge of novelty is simply incorrect.[40] One can come to a similar

---

37. The following discussion on misconceptions represents a revision of one section in an earlier article: William J. Webb, "A Redemptive-Movement Hermeneutic: Encouraging Dialogue among Four Evangelical Views," *Journal of the Evangelical Theological Society* 48:2 (June 2005): 334–40.

38. Wayne Grudem, "Should We Move beyond the New Testament to a Better Ethic? An Analysis of William J. Webb, *Slaves, Women & Homosexuals: Exploring the Hermeneutics of Cultural Analysis*," *Journal of the Evangelical Theological Society* 47:2 (June 2004): 299.

39. Carl Sanders, "The 19th Century Slave Debate: An Example of Proto-Redemptive-Movement Hermeneutics?" (paper presented at the annual meeting of the Evangelical Theological Society, San Antonio, Texas, Nov. 8, 2004). Dr. Sanders has kindly agreed to make his paper available upon email request (csanders@bible.edu).

40. Sanders' historical research is particularly helpful since it is written from the vantage point of hierarchical complementarianism. While Sanders himself embraces a RM hermeneutic, he would not agree with me about "how far" to take the movement on the women's issue.

conclusion about the role of the spirit of the text (over the letter) by reading Mark Noll's excellent work on the Christian interpretive crisis surrounding the American civil war.[41]

2. *A RM hermeneutic seeks to replace a grammatical-historical hermeneutic.* Pastors and laypersons will often ask: Why do we need a RM hermeneutic? Was not our standard grammatical-historical hermeneutic good enough? The short answer here is that a RM hermeneutic is actually a subcomponent (not replacement) of a *good* grammatical-historical hermeneutic. Christians have often paid lip service to the "historical" within a grammatical-historical hermeneutic. But the reality is that most of our energies have been focused on discovering meaning through textual, grammatical, and lexical routes. The renewed emphasis on a RM hermeneutic is in part attributable to the greater availability of historical documents that provide us with a better understanding of the broader ancient social context within which to understand Scripture. In fact, the historical interests of a RM hermeneutic — reading an ancient document within its broader historical and ancient social setting to sense "movement meaning" and the underlying spirit of a text — reflects what ought to be standard practice in the grammatical-historical investigation of any historical document.[42]

3. *A RM hermeneutic replaces continuity-discontinuity approaches.* Another common misunderstanding is that a RM hermeneutic replaces classic evangelical continuity-discontinuity approaches (herein, CD approaches) for understanding the relationship between the OT and NT. In short, the answer is "no" to any notion of replacing or displacing traditional CD approaches. Unfortunately, this replacement perspective reflects a significant misunderstanding of a RM hermeneutic; it is what neither I nor any other RM hermeneutic advocate, to my knowledge, holds. Rather, a RM hermeneutic augments or complements one's existing CD hermeneutic.

---

41. Mark A. Noll, *The Civil War as a Theological Crisis* (Chapel Hill: Univ. of North Carolina Press, 2006), 1–199.

42. See Webb, "A Redemptive-Movement Hermeneutic: Encouraging Dialogue," 338–40.

Perhaps the best way to dispel this replacement notion is to look at those who endorse a RM hermeneutic and observe that they come from a wide spectrum of traditional CD approaches. From a select/illustrative sampling of seminary professors, based on feedback that I have received, a RM hermeneutic has significant support at dispensational, historic premillennial, and Reformed seminaries.[43] Such evidence aptly demonstrates that a person's particular CD perspective is not at all displaced by or replaced by a RM hermeneutic. Scholars at these three strikingly different types of seminaries either choose to add (or not to add) a RM hermeneutic to their existing hermeneutical approaches. Nevertheless, the choice is as an augment, not a replacement, of their existing CD hermeneutics.

More important, CD perspectives simply do not settle many ethical issues where there is a considerable continuity between the Testaments. From a historical perspective, neither dispensationalism nor Reformed theology helped Christians sort out their application of the slavery texts. The fact that the ethical problem lingered for eighteen hundred years should be a clue that standard CD approaches were relatively ineffective here. The same could be said about the spanking texts of the Bible. Where there is minimal discontinuity between the Testaments, as is the case in both subjects addressed in this essay, CD discussions simply do not answer our questions about contemporary application.[44]

---

43. See Webb, "A Redemptive-Movement Hermeneutic: Encouraging Dialogue," 345–49.

44. For instance, Christians cannot simply appeal to OT/NT discontinuity in order to handle the problem of the slave-beating texts found within the OT. If one ponders the question of first-century Christians beating their slaves as it might well have emerged within the early church, it is almost inconceivable within such a slave-holding context that the early Christians would not have given some weight to these OT texts. While canonical development exists between the Testaments on the slavery issue, the degree of discontinuity is not radical enough within the slavery texts (OT to NT) to unambiguously support even the abolition of slave beatings, let alone the abolition of slavery. Let me qualify. Such abolitionist perspectives could not be well argued unless a sufficient weighting was given to movement meaning (foreign and canonical) within the slavery texts.

4. *A RM hermeneutic seeks to establish a "better ethic" than that of the NT.* Some evangelical scholars have misunderstood and in turn misrepresented a trajectory or RM hermeneutic by suggesting that such an approach wants to establish a "better ethic" than the ethic of the NT.[45] This better ethic would amount to establishing an ethic that is not really the ethic of the NT at all, but one that is indeed foreign to the NT ethic. There is no question that the language I use about "going beyond" can be (wrongly) construed in such a direction. Thankfully, most readers of *Slaves, Women & Homosexuals* observe that I repeatedly qualify such language to talk about a going beyond an "isolated words"[46] *understanding* of the Bible. With this important qualification in place there is no dislocation between any reference to a "better ethic" and the true ethic of the NT. They are one and the same. In other words, the "better ethic" developed through a RM hermeneutic is in fact the ethic of the OT (and NT) rightly understood and rightly applied.

5. *A RM hermeneutic undermines the authority of the Bible/ NT.* Closely related to the last misconception is the charge that a RM hermeneutic undermines the moral authority of the Bible. The basis for this "biblical authority" charge is that supposedly a RM hermeneutic no longer ties moral authority to "what the Bible says" or "what the New Testament teaches."[47] If a RM hermeneutic actually did this (divorced moral authority from "what the Bible says/teaches"), I would be the first to agree with my critic that his charge has substance. However, the basis for the charge is built on a faulty understanding of a RM approach.[48]

---

45. Grudem, "Should We Move beyond the New Testament," 299–346.

46. By "isolated" I mean an understanding of the words on the page in their literary context (up and down the page) alone; it is thus isolated from the "movement meaning" derived from reading the text within its ancient social context.

47. Grudem, "Should We Move beyond the New Testament," 306, 346.

48. See William J. Webb, "A Redemptive-Movement Hermeneutic: Responding to Wayne Grudem's Concerns" (paper presented at the annual meeting of the Evangelical Theological Society, San Antonio, Texas, Nov. 18, 2004). To obtain an ecopy through Zondervan, check the *Wednesday afternoon (PM)* ETS schedule for Webb's paper (www.etsjets.org/meetings/2004/papers/2004-papers-idx.html) and send an email request for the paper.

Advocates of a RM hermeneutic are clear in affirming that "redemptive movement" is an element of meaning within the actual words of the biblical text. The redemptive spirit derived from reading texts within their social/historical context *is* an important part of what the Bible says and teaches (but what Christians unfortunately often miss). For that matter, one might ponder whether a movement-meaning hermeneutic actually strengthens biblical authority in our lives rather than diminishes it. Perhaps it permits greater life transformation and ethical fulfillment of Scripture. Fortunately, numerous Christian leaders in different venues have pointed out that the charge of diminished biblical authority is achieved only through an incorrect understanding and, in turn, a misrepresentation of the view.[49]

6. *A RM hermeneutic does not view the NT as final and definitive revelation.* Some evangelicals have voiced a

---

49. A story or two might provide some insight. I remember one occasion where my most vocal opponent, Wayne Grudem, spoke against a RM hermeneutic with this "undermining biblical authority" charge. In the question time following Dr. Grudem's paper, a rather delightful thing happened. William Heth (Taylor University) stood up and said to Wayne, "I have read Webb's book three times, and it seems to me that the book that I have read is not the book you [Dr. Grudem] critiqued." Dr. Heth then sat down. Following Grudem's ETS Conference paper (November, 2003), other evangelical leaders made similar comments about Grudem's misrepresenting the view. Despite these caution flags, Dr. Grudem still published his conference paper in the *Journal of the Evangelical Theological Society* (2004). Again, at a Grand Rapids, Michigan, conference on "going beyond" methods, Daniel Treier (Wheaton College) counteracted the misconception about biblical authority and affirmed the legitimate role of a RM hermeneutic within Christian ethics and theology. Dr. Treier's comments were part of a panel discussion that concluded the Midwestern Regional Meeting of the Evangelical Theological Society, "Going beyond the Bible Biblically: The Hermeneutical Issues of Moving from Scripture to Theology" (Grand Rapids, March 24–25, 2006). More recently, in eight lengthy blogs on the *Jesus Creed* website (www.jesuscreed.org), NT scholar Scot McKnight (North Park University) reviewed *Slaves, Women & Homosexuals* and showed the fallacy of Grudem's arguments. See Scot McKnight, "Women in Ministry: The Redemptive Trend" (part I–VII; December 18, 2006 to February 8, 2007 entries) and "Redemptive Trend: Response to Grudem" (February 15, 2007) [accessed Jan. 18, 2008]. For a further sampling of scholars who advocate a RM hermeneutic across both hierarchical and egalitarian camps, see Webb, "A Redemptive-Movement Hermeneutic: Encouraging Dialogue," 345–49.

concern that a RM hermeneutic fails to understand the NT as final and definitive revelation.[50] Ultimately this "final revelation" concern introduces yet another misconception about a RM hermeneutic. Proponents of a RM hermeneutic readily agree that the NT is unquestionably God's final and definitive revelation. This is not really at issue. Rather, the real issue is what inferences might be drawn, rightly or wrongly, from such an affirmation about the NT as final and definitive revelation. I would argue against equating final revelation with the final realization of social ethics as portrayed in every detailed and concrete component of NT texts.

One might capture the distinction this way: understanding the NT as final and definitive *revelation* does not automatically mean that the NT contains the final *realization* of social ethics in all of its concrete particulars. Since I have responded in a full-length *Evangelical Quarterly* article with three supporting arguments (OT as precedent, NT slavery texts, and NT women texts) to make this case, I will simply cite that argumentation here.[51]

7. A RM hermeneutic cannot provide a clear ethical "end point" for its trajectory of redemptive movement. After students, pastors, or other professors have seen the value of a RM hermeneutic, they often ask, "How do we know how far to take the trajectory or redemptive movement?" In short, my answer is twofold: Christians must work through (1) a *logical* and (2) a *theological* development of the redemptive spirit in the biblical text. In other words, once one grasps the redemptive spirit within the slavery texts, the task is to develop that spirit through a logical trajectory. Each year I have students write a paper detailing specific examples of how the slavery

---

50. See Thomas R. Schreiner, "William J. Webb's *Slaves, Women & Homosexuals:* A Review Article," *The Southern Baptist Journal of Theology* 6:1 (2002): 46–64; idem, "Review of *Slaves, Women & Homosexuals*," *Journal for Biblical Manhood and Womanhood* 7:1 (2002): 41–71. Schreiner makes this affirmation about the New Testament as the "final and definitive revelation" numerous times in his critique of my work.

51. William J. Webb, "The Limits of a Redemptive-Movement Hermeneutic: A Focused Response to T. R. Schreiner," *Evangelical Quarterly* 75:4 (2003): 327–42.

texts could logically be developed in terms of a better treatment of human beings without even doing away with the institution of slavery (i.e., within a pro-slavery perspective). This is a logical exercise in thinking through extrapolated movement meaning.

Of course, adding the theological component enlarges the question to bring into the discussion any other pertinent data, biblical or extrabiblical (God is the author of all knowledge), that might impact the ethical equation. In other words, one has to ponder the nature of the redemptive movement in Scripture and then do some solid reflective thinking. It is hard work—plain and simple. There are no easy shortcuts. It takes time, research, prayer, reflection, and the joy of wrestling though complex issues, much like the delightful struggle of a caterpillar whose metamorphosis eventually moves from the baby cocoon to a beautiful and fully-formed butterfly.[52]

I do not pretend that a RM hermeneutic is the only method for "going beyond" the Bible biblically. A number of methods can function in a complementary fashion to achieve this goal. In that respect I am thankful for this volume where a discussion about the pros and cons of various methods might help Christians to better live out a powerful biblical ethic in their own contemporary context.

---

52. Sometimes extrabiblical examples help. I often use the changes in Canadian smoking laws over the past fifty years to show how a logical trajectory of that movement meaning will eventually lead to banning smoking in cars where there are children. I have argued this case for over ten years in seminary classes. Much to my delight, around the time I began writing this essay, the first Canadian city (Wolfville, Nova Scotia) on December 20, 2007, enacted such legislation—a historic moment! Of course, the movement can and should go further. Eventually, an extension of the underlying spirit or incremental development in the current (and past) smoking laws needs to bring about smoke-free homes where children and/or other nonsmoking adults are present. One can also illustrate the idea of logical extension of movement meaning within changes to our legislation impacting gas and oil consumption and related tax incentives on new vehicles, alternative energies, etc. (simply compare the United States, Canada, and Europe in these areas). There is clear movement in all of these countries but obviously at different paces. Movement meaning in these contexts often says more about where people really think an ethic ought to go than its frozen-in-time particulars.

CONCLUSION

Like John Henry Hopkins, we could "stop where the Bible stopped" in our handling of the slavery texts. Appealing to the concrete specificity of the text and its isolated on-the-page meaning can easily lead one to accept the legitimacy of beating slaves and of the rightful subordination of slaves to their masters as depicted within the NT household codes. We could stop there. Such an approach to Scripture provides a certain kind of safety and security.

Similarly, Christian parents today could "stop where the Bible stopped" in their practices of corporal punishment. They could adopt a spanking ethic that closely follows the concrete-specific instructions of the biblical text, which might well include the CP of teens and adults, leaving bruises and wounds, scaling the number of strokes toward a maximum of forty, returning to beatings on the back, and dropping the notion of CP as a last resort and only for willful defiance. But then again, maybe we have read the text incorrectly. Maybe such an approach does not correctly understand what God is trying to say to us within these texts.

Shall we go beyond the concrete specificity of the biblical text? Yes, most assuredly. For simply to read the text and do what it says on the page often misreads and misapplies the text. Such static methods produce museum-piece approaches to Christian ethics and an impoverished way of applying the Bible. In this essay I have presented a *redemptive-movement model* within the slavery texts and the spanking texts of Scripture. Only by moving beyond the concrete specificity of these biblical texts and by engaging their incremental ethic do we honor the authorial heartbeat of the biblical text itself. In using a RM approach, Christians must journey far beyond any surface-level appropriation of Scripture to an application of the text that listens intently to its movement meaning as heard within its historical and canonical contexts. When the slavery and CP texts are read within such contexts, one indeed discovers a profound sense of RM meaning. Our task as Christians is not to stay with a static understanding of Scripture but to champion its redemptive spirit in new and fresh ways that logically and theologically extend its movement meaning into today's context.

A RESPONSE TO WILLIAM J. WEBB

Walter C. Kaiser Jr.

I AM SO GLAD THAT PROFESSOR WEBB feels "a certain amount of discomfort with that little word 'beyond.'" He agrees we should never move beyond the Bible "in one sense," but if we will allow qualifiers, he is willing and ready to go beyond the Bible. What guides him is something he calls the "redemptive spirit [or 'redemptive movement'] of the text." This is what takes him beyond the original application of the text in the ancient world.

More specifically, he defines this going "beyond," that is, going beyond where there is *"concrete specificity,"* or *"time-restricted elements* of the Bible," or where we must "progress beyond the *frozen-in-time* aspects of the ethical portrait found in the Bible." Over against the "classy and subtle terminology of Kevin Vanhoozer's 'Continuing Scripture,'" "or the rugged, bold wording of an I. Howard Marshall's 'Beyond the Bible,'" "or even the delightfully punned wording of Gary Meadors' 'Moving beyond the Bible Biblically,'" he demurely views his own wording as "cautious" and "qualified."

Nevertheless, he still recommends for all who go beyond Scripture to outfit themselves with a "well-padded flak jacket" rather than look, as many more static interpretations do, for "safety and certainty" in these matters, presumably by staying with the Bible's text. In Webb's view, the ethic that Scripture gives us "needs in some ways to be developed and worked out over time," since that scriptural ethic has a *"limited* or *incremental movement* toward an ultimate ethic." This incremental movement becomes his basic assumption, and this "movement meaning," surprisingly seen even "within the text" of Scripture, now "tug[s]" at his "heartstrings and beckons" him to "go further" — presumably beyond the Bible. As opposed to understanding the text in isolation of its cultural/historical and canonical context (though few, if any, would do so in our educated day), such literalism misses the underlying spirit and thereby restricts its contemporary application of its original setting.

CAPTIVE WAR BRIDES

Webb's major asset is also his largest liability, namely, that meaning can come from the lens of a text's ancient and canonical contexts (the Ancient Near Eastern, Greco-Roman, Second Temple Judaism, and New Testament worlds). He illustrates this from Deuteronomy 21:10–14, where "movement meaning" goes beyond "on the page" or "isolated type of meaning" that comes from reading the words of Scripture. It uses ancient historical and social contexts as well as canonical contexts to capture the underlying spirit of the biblical text, thereby allowing us "to radically shape the contours of our contemporary ethical portrait" of female POWs in Deuteronomy 21.

But his contrasting war texts from the ancient Near East are precisely what we mean by the grammatical-historical method of interpretation. Of course this helps us to see the divine wisdom for the treatment of war brides in Israel's case as opposed to those of their contemporary neighbors. But once we learn this contrast and apply its principles, why must we go beyond this text to make it say what other cultures, times, or the later Testament says? Isn't that what we call eisegesis—reading an interpretation back into the text? And if there is a "redemptive spirit" hidden in this text, then under which word, syntactical construction, or interlinear rubric is this concealed meaning to be found?

BEATING SLAVES

In Professor Webb's analysis of the slavery texts, he incorrectly combines debt slavery with foreign slaves, thereby confusing contexts, categories, and conclusions. Moreover, pejorative and sensational language is used of the actions of masters toward slaves that does not appear "on the page," such as "beating the 'living daylights' out of the slave," in "very bloody and brutal beatings," "within a hairbreadth of their life." Wow!

In my commentary on Exodus 21:20–21, I noted that this law is unprecedented and unmatched in the ancient world, where in the outside world a master could do as he pleased to his slave, but this law, along with verses 26–27, acted to control and severely discourage brutality in Israel, for the master would not only hurt his own pocketbook if he struck any debt-slave so as to injure any part of his body, but he would also instantly lose the whole loan given to the debt slave. That master would lose his whole investment to this debt slave, in either case. "The aim of this law is not to place the slave at the master's mercy, but to restrict the master's power over him (cf. Code of Hammurabi 196–97, 200)."[53]

To introduce "the idea of movement meaning as it relates to the larger canonical context" is to first confuse and then to impose the later progress of revelation over top of the earlier revelations, thereby flattening out the Bible so that it says the same thing on the same topics everywhere. This is not what "progressive revelation" was ever intended to mean.[54] The movement Webb sees is the movement from the ancient Near Eastern context; but that is what we would expect, for the biblical laws are not the musings of fellow mortals of that time period, but teachings of the immortal God.

SPANKING AS BIBLICAL "MUSEUM PIECE[S]"

Professor Webb suggests that we carry out the Bible's redemptive spirit rather than attempt "to replicate its frozen-in-time ethic." "The words of the text are displayed in all their rugged specificity like ancient dinosaur bones

---

53. Walter C. Kaiser Jr. "Exodus," in *The Expositor's Bible Commentary*, ed. Tremper Longman III and David E. Garland (rev. ed.; Grand Rapids: Zondervan, 2008), 492.

54. See Walter C. Kaiser Jr. "Progressive Revelation," in *Toward Old Testament Ethics* (Grand Rapids: Zondervan, 1983), 60–64; D. L. Baker, "Progressive Revelation," in *Two Testaments, One Bible* (Downers Grove, IL: InterVarsity Press, 1976), 76–87.

mounted inside of a museum." But Webb does not want us to get him wrong; this kind of archaeological digging into the text is "good work," but we must "appreciate the incremental nature of the ethic we find within Scripture." It is good, then, to acknowledge this kind of work on the text, but it needs to be updated or understood in another way.

Webb takes a handful of spanking texts from the book of Proverbs[55] but forgets the well-known hermeneutical instructions for interpreting proverbial types of literature. My best brief summary is that

> *Proverbs* are brief sayings that are memorable, embody the wisdom of many, possess a fullness of meaning despite economy of words, and have a bit of a kick or bite to them to ensure their saltiness and continued usefulness. They are found in practically all parts of the Bible. By nature and form, proverbs are generalized statements with a wide application, but in no case are they to be taken as a set of unbending rules that must be applied in every case without exceptions.[56]

If this were not true, it would be possible to pit one proverb against another: "Answer a fool according to his folly ... Do not answer a fool according to his folly" (Prov. 26:4–5). To take a proverb and demand that it is to be understood as a literal word with no exceptions, but universally applicable to all in all situations is to run counter to the literary genre and its own rules of interpretation.

That is why the church father Origen incorrectly took Matthew 5:29–30 literally and castrated himself, but that was not only to misunderstand the text; it also left him unnecessarily maimed for life while still facing the problem that cutting off part of his body was supposed to heal! Others have foolishly followed in his train.

The point of the so-called "spanking texts" in Proverbs was to be "careful to discipline" your son or daughter and to train them up "in the way they should go" (Prov. 22:5;

---

55. Prov. 13:24; 19:18; 22:15; 23:13–14; 29:15, 17.
56. Walter C. Kaiser Jr. and Moises Silva. *Introduction to Biblical Hermeneutics: The Search for Meaning* (rev. and expanded; Grand Rapids: Zondervan, 2007), 151.

cf. 13:24; 19:18; 29:15). However, once again Webb searches the Bible topically (not staying with chair-teaching passages in context) and gathers teachings on all sorts of corporeal punishment, from Exodus 21:20–21 (slave passage) to punishments meted out by judges in the courts (Deut. 25:1–3), and lumps them (not to mention apocryphal material from Sirach) all together with proverbial material on raising and disciplining children. This is no way to do Bible study! Of course, as Webb says, the purpose meaning of the text of Proverbs is (1) negatively "to turn the child away from folly," and (2) positively "to help them embrace wisdom," which Webb admits was the purpose of these proverbs!

ABSTRACTED MEANING

For Webb, "often an embedded element of meaning at the abstract level" is found right there in the text. This is precisely what we mean when we talk about "principlization." But Webb sees a meaning that is "beyond the concrete-specific instructions of the Bible." He wants to keep from "getting mired down with looking for letter-for-letter equivalents in doing ethics." But what on earth is this? Is it *notarikon* (each letter of a word is taken as an initial or abbreviation of a word), *gematria* (where the numerical equivalents of the Hebrew letters form a hidden meaning), or *kabbalah* (some type of mystical philosophy which is hidden except to those who have been properly prepared to receive it)? If Webb is thinking of Romans 2:29, forget it, for "letterism" there is *gramma*. However, the Spirit in that text is never put into juxtaposition with *graphe* (what is "written"). God's words will never get us "mired down" if we approach them with the "obedience of faith." So, let's not confuse corporeal punishment of the state or its judges with any punishments used in raising children.

WHAT DOES THE REDEMPTIVE-MOVEMENT HERMENEUTIC REPLACE?

What is correct about the redemptive-movement hermeneutic has been operative in the best practices of Protestant hermeneutics for centuries now. The redemptive-movement approach is not meant, however, to replace the grammatical-historical hermeneutic and all continuity-discontinuity approaches to Scripture; instead, it is a "subcomponent" and an augmentation, not a replacement, of these methods.

At times, it appears Webb wants to derive the meaning of any earlier biblical context from the whole context of the Bible at once. Words in their literary context alone bother him, for he wants movement. But movement to where? And authorized under what sort of criteria?

The major problem here is with the sufficiency of Scripture in each of its contexts as parts of the whole. Webb takes the whole ("final revelation") as being most authoritative, but it is not clear to what extent each of the parts contribute to that wholeness and to the authority meaning. It is the absolutizing of the "ethical end point" of this trajectory or redemptive movement that seems to steal from the contributions that each of the parts has made that is the difficulty that attends this bit of hard work by Professor Webb.

A RESPONSE TO WILLIAM J. WEBB

Daniel M. Doriani

THERE IS MUCH TO COMMEND in William Webb's essay on the redemptive-movement model for traveling beyond the sacred page. Given that Webb has been at the center of extensive discussions since his publication of *Slaves, Women & Homosexuals*, he sensibly clarifies his position in remarks that should hearten most evangelical readers. With the other essayists in this book, Webb declares that, in crucial ways, "we should never move beyond the Bible." He encourages Christians "to embrace the redemptive spirit of the text, which at times will mean that we must move beyond the concrete specificity of the Bible" and its "time-restricted elements."

Webb warns of the danger of staying in the "safety" of "the concrete specificity of the text" and urges interpreters to read Scripture with an awareness of its "incremental movement toward an ultimate ethic" rather than a "stationary appropriation of Scripture" that restricts "contemporary application" of the words of Scripture to "their original setting." His decision to call certain biblical teachings "somewhat redemptive" and his notion that contemporary secular ethics may be more advanced than parts of both the OT and NT will trouble some readers and raise questions about his model. Most pointedly, he urges readers to trace movement through three or four stages:

X The original ancient Near Eastern or Greco-Roman culture.

Y The Bible's "somewhat redemptive" words in the "frozen-in-time" text.

Z The Bible's "ultimate ethic" reflected in "the spirit" of the biblical text.

Z' We may find assistance in locating the ultimate ethic if our culture happens to reflect "a better ethic" than the Bible's "somewhat redemptive" ethic.

Still, it is difficult to disagree with Webb's fundamental observations about interpreting Scripture. He puts his program to good use in a study of Deuteronomy 21:10–14. This difficult text specifies the proper treatment of attractive foreign women that successful Israelite warriors take in combat. Webb candidly appraises the way Christians avoid, and secularists object to, a text that seems to sanction a war ethic in which victorious soldiers "grab hot-looking women." First, Webb locates the law in its cultural context, showing that it vastly improves on the laws and customs of the time. Just as significantly, he observes that we read Deuteronomy through the lens of the Geneva or Hague war conventions for treatment of war captives. Webb's paradigm implies that recent war conventions "happen to reflect a better ethic" than Deuteronomy. Therefore we should go beyond them, following their "movement" or "trajectory" and finally reject all forms of slavery.

Webb's approach does more than ask that interpreters assess biblical and contemporary cultures. He insists that we recognize that our culture's common convictions inevitably taint our reading, limiting our capacity to recognize the way Moses' law does justice to prisoners and progresses beyond penal codes of the day. More radically, he urges Christians to consider the possibility that contemporary, uninspired codes may be "better" than the "frozen-in-time" words of Scripture that may be more closely related to their times than to the Bible's ultimate ethic. The thought is provocative and may fail fully to safeguard the authority of Scripture, but it seems to label the way we treat biblical texts on slavery. Further, Jesus himself gave us warrant to consider such steps when he declared that Deuteronomy 24 is not the Bible's ultimate position on adultery, but rather a concession to Israel's hardness of heart (Matt. 19:3–12).

The question for Webb's proposed paradigm is not, therefore, "Is it [ever] true?" but "Is it the best tool for interpretation?" The next portion of his essay proposes that it offers the best approach to texts on slavery and corporal punishment.

As Webb listens to OT slavery texts in context (including movement toward the NT), he shows how Moses' slave code protects and dignifies slaves. At point after point, the Pentateuch surpasses its age and "incrementally moves people toward an ultimate ethic" that is, "an abolitionist ethic." If space permitted, I would question the accuracy of his summary of certain "not so pretty" slavery texts, but otherwise this section is persuasive.

My appraisal of Webb's analysis of redemptive movement in corporal punishment (CP) texts is similar. He reiterates that we read from our context, including our personal experience of corporal punishment, first as a child, then as a parent. Further, Christians read CP texts both in light of our culture's well-founded concerns about child abuse and in light of popular teachers such as James Dobson.

While Webb's tone in this section can be irenic, he occasionally seems to court conflict by taunting his theological foils, the unnamed interpreters who have "minimal or no" interest in the "underlying spirit" of the text. These theologians create a "museum-piece" ethic, constructed with "naïve assumptions." They "freely chose what [texts] they wish to ignore."

Webb appears to score points against CP advocates, such as Andreas Köstenberger, who promote yet modify biblical teaching about CP. Webb is glad of their move toward moderation and tenderness, although it rankles him that they claim the high ground of fidelity to Scripture while softening its rule for discipline. But Webb's charge of inconsistency seems unjustified. As I read Köstenberger's *God, Marriage and Family*, he seems interested in the holistic, sensitive-to-the-spirit-of-Scripture approach that Webb promotes. Specifically, he places the biblical teaching on CP in the context of biblical teaching about the nature and goals of parent-child relationships in Scripture.

Meanwhile, Webb opposes CP, even though he well knows the passages that commend it. These remarks are a *condensation* of a full monograph on CP; perhaps that lies behind some disappointing omissions in his treatment of CP texts. He appears simply to dismiss the option of physical discipline for adults. Why? Because it seems unthinkable in Webb's culture? Illegal in his native Canada? I wish he had considered the merits of discipline by the rod. Are Western prison systems working so well? Are inmates chastened or rehabilitated by their experiences? If so, why do some experts believe prisons accelerate criminal behavior? Might the rod be an appropriate punishment for criminal battery? Leviticus 24:19–20 says so.

Given a choice, how many people would prefer five sharp whacks on the back with a rod to two years in jail, even if the rod might raise welts that leave a permanent mark? In polls I recently conducted, every man chose painful blows over lost years, and some women did too. My intent here is to raise questions, not advocate a position. Most pointedly, has Webb sufficiently examined the texts as they stand and the wisdom or principles behind them, or is he too quick to look for movement?

Lest the reader misunderstand, I note that I, like Webb, had a spanking-related epiphany, even if I construe my methods and goals differently. I trace my awakening to a comment from my wife when one daughter, then eleven, descended into a fortnight of rebellion. My wife said, "I don't know what to do. She's too old to spank. Take away her privileges? She hardly notices television or radio, and her piano and soccer are so worthwhile. And if I ground her I'll punish myself as much as I punish her." I knew she was right and also knew I had nothing helpful to propose. A month later, with the question still smoldering in my back pocket, I happened to read Exodus 21:22–25:

> If men who are fighting hit a pregnant woman and she gives birth prematurely but there is no serious injury, the offender must be fined whatever the woman's husband demands.... But if there is serious injury, you are to take life for life, eye for eye, tooth for tooth, hand for hand, foot for foot, burn for burn, wound for wound, bruise for bruise.

I read the passage in cultural context and recognized that it originally functioned to restrain (not promote) vengefulness. The law forbids the spiral of violence: not "if you knock out my tooth, I'll knock out all of yours," but "one tooth for one tooth, nothing more."

But like Kaiser, I detected a principle, the "principle of proportional punishment." That principle, which governs a fair segment of Mosaic penal code, says a punishment must suit the crime (or "fit" the crime, per Vanhoozer) and be proportional to it. The principle is perhaps clearest for perjury, where the convicted perjurer suffers precisely the punishment that his lie would have inflicted on his victim (Deut. 19:16–21). It is also visible in laws governing property violations, where a thief loses precisely what she would have gained by theft (Ex. 22:4–6), and also in cases of murder, manslaughter, and personal injury (Lev. 24:17–21!). These laws may have been abused, and they may "feel" rough to us. But let's not be wiser than God. At a minimum, we must consider them, as they stand, long and hard, before looking for movement toward what, in Webb's view, is a more mature ethic.

Returning to my family, I still had to adjust the biblical data, for I was reading Israel's civil or penal code and the family operates on different principles. Further, in terms of what my main essay called "questions the Bible approves," I had to ask another question: "What is a parent's goal?" The goal is loving, respectful relationships and the maturation of the child more than justice or compliance. Thus, in the home, it is better to think of the "principle of proportional *discipline*." Proportional discipline is relevant to the misdeed and measured to suit it. If tooth crimes merit tooth punishment, then clothing crimes, such as leaving clothes all over the floor, deserve clothing discipline, such as the loss of the offending clothes for some days. Similarly, "food crimes" (such as saying terrible things about supper) deserve "food discipline" (such as cooking one's own supper for two days). And sins of rebellion merit discipline that fits that rebellion — does spanking fit?

To say it differently, while I appreciated Webb's remarks about the progress of the OT compared to its culture, about the purpose of discipline, and about the "abstracted meaning" of the texts (reminiscent of Kaiser's principlizing), I had two questions: Had Webb sufficiently accounted for the fact that many of his CP texts are civil/penal code, not family law? And is "redemptive movement" most suited to serve as the dominant paradigm for analyzing CP?

Webb helped answer the latter question when he declared that his redemptive-movement approach seeks not to "replace the grammatical-historical hermeneutic" but to serve as a "subcomponent" bent on improving it. The redemptive-historical reader who also promotes the grammatical-historical method cannot possibly object to Webb's call for more attention to contexts and to progress in the Bible. Where, then, do we differ?

Perhaps the main question is how much movement we expect. Perhaps more crucially, does movement deserve to be the dominant paradigm? As we know, paradigms help us see some things but obscure others. If a method tells us to look for movement, then movement we will see. But how much of the biblical ethic shows substantial movement? The Decalogue surely deserves a privileged position in biblical ethics. How much movement is there in the Decalogue? One thinks of the fourth and seventh commands, but even there the changes are minor/tangential (the time of worship, the effects of the end of polygamy). There is scant change elsewhere. On the question "How much movement?" we may differ. We agree that there is movement in the teaching on slavery and that there is not movement on homosexuality; we disagree about gender roles.

A few questions remain. Does Webb's interest in redemptive movement so focus on ethical issues that he neglects the redemptive-historical character of the Bible and the capacity of Scripture to lead us to Christ? Does his focus on movement in Scripture shorten his attention to the text as it stands? Finally, given Webb's commitment to read Scripture in light of its contrast with the surrounding culture, the right understanding of ancient culture may become not desirable but *essential* to the task of interpretation. But can we have enough certainty about other cultures for this purpose? (For example, we can read the Code of Hammurabi, but do we know how people practiced or ignored that law?) Can a commitment to read Scripture against culture erode our commitment to read Scripture in itself?

Looking forward, I am thankful for Webb's affirmation that the NT is "God's final and definitive revelation." He did *not* say, "Who knows what Paul would say today?" With that in hand and with his affirmation of the grammatical-historical method, there is surely a basis for constructive dialogue.

A RESPONSE TO WILLIAM J. WEBB

Kevin J. Vanhoozer

WILLIAM WEBB'S *SLAVES, WOMEN & HOMOSEXUALS*[57] is one of the most significant evangelical attempts in recent years to wrestle with the "thither" end of hermeneutics, namely, the vexed question of how to move from the sacred page and its original context to social practice in contemporary context. An especially welcome feature of the book is its careful presentation and defense of the criteria Webb uses to decide what in Scripture is limited in its application to its original cultural context and what has ongoing applicational significance. His is the most important voice at present representing the trajectory view, and our book would be seriously lacking without it.[58]

And we will apparently be hearing much more from him, if his footnotes are any indication, for he there signals two forthcoming books on the subject. One will deal with the brutal war texts of the Bible, the other with brutal corporal punishment texts. The subtitles mention "Texts That Trouble the Soul." This leads me to wonder about his ultimate aim. When the church fathers found certain biblical texts embarrassing, they allegorized them. Is Webb's redemptive-movement approach similarly an apologetic, a "bibliodicy" that defends the Bible from the charge of brutality, comparable to a theodicy that defends God from the charge of doing evil?[59]

---

57. Downers Grove, IL: InterVarsity Press, 2001.

58. Other representatives of this view include F. F. Bruce, Richard Longenecker, I. Howard Marshall, and, most recently, Kenton Sparks.

59. Webb may have theodicy in his sights as well. At one point, he notes that God "accommodates" himself to meeting people where they are and gently moves them to something better. But should we be thinking of God "accommodating" himself to human brutality? Does this really explain God's command to destroy Canaanite cities?

My guess is that apologetic concerns loom large in Webb's thinking.

Webb wants his approach to help Christians deal with apparent difficulties in applying the Word of God to the issues of daily life, a laudable aim. Everything depends on just what these difficulties are, however, and what Webb proposes that we do about them. The chief difficulty, if I'm reading Webb aright, is that many texts are frozen-in-time and thus either irrelevant or unacceptable if followed literally. The ethic in the Bible, like the famous figures in Michelangelo's statues the "Unfinished Slaves," gives hints of its final form but calls for further work before it can fully emerge from the textual marble.

Webb's proposals have garnered him praise and censure in equal measure—not for nothing his pained reference to needing a well-padded flak jacket. It's a war zone out there; the jihadist you will always have with you, and the most painful wounds are those inflicted by friendly fire. I think that some of those taking shots are under the misimpression that having a definitive revelation is the same thing as having a definitive understanding of that revelation. It is not; the Spirit continues to guide the church as it strives toward a fuller understanding of and lived response to Scripture's truth. If it's any consolation, Bill, I'm with you on the battlefield, though we may be squatting in different hermeneutical foxholes.

My critical interrogation of Webb's position is in proportion to its importance and influence in the evangelical marketplace. I begin with an examination of his hermeneutics, and with a confession: I still don't have a good grasp of his basic concepts (e.g., "redemptive spirit of the text"; "movement is meaning"). Perhaps I am being overly pedantic. Nevertheless, everything in hermeneutics follows from one's understanding of what texts are, what meaning is, and where the latter is located. Webb states that redemptive movement is "an element of meaning within the actual words of the biblical text." Interestingly, Webb almost never refers to authors or to what authors are doing in using just these words in just this order in just this literary form. With authors out of the picture, he can then deal with the Bible's war ethic (including the "grabbing hot-looking women" part) by dismissing it as "a disturbing feature within the text" instead of ascribing something blameworthy to particular prophets, Jesus, or God, whose word it ultimately is.

The sidestepping strategy won't work. What we have in the Bible is *discourse*: something *someone* says about something to someone. Biblical interpreters read for the authorial discourse; it only confuses matters to speak of "the sense of the text."[60] Texts don't mean; authors do. Texts are the means by which authors perform communicative actions and do things with words.[61] What we ultimately have in Scripture is God discoursing by means of human discourse. This casts Webb's thesis that "movement is meaning" in new light. Is redemptive-movement meaning located in an individual author's thinking on a subject, or is it discerned only when we compare one author to another, or is it a matter of discovering the divine author's intention as it comes to light in canonical discourse? The most charitable interpretation is that Webb assumes divine authorship throughout and construes redemptive movement in terms of God's coaxing and cajoling his people to see things increasingly his way (I shall return to this theme of divine "accommodation" below).

What Webb identifies as "movement" may, I think, be better viewed in terms of "contrast." Consider the two ways in which he discerns "movement": first, he determines how what the biblical authors say contrasts with what others were saying in the ancient Near Eastern world at about the same time (call it "synchronic contrast"); second, he determines how what one author says on a particular subject contrasts with what an earlier author said (call it "diachronic contrast"). Speaking of these two forms of cultural-content

---

60. See Nicholas Wolterstorff, *Divine Discourse: Philosophical Reflections on the Claim That God Speaks* (Cambridge: Cambridge Univ. Press, 1995), esp. 171–73.

61. Another way of putting it would be to say that semantics without pragmatics is empty, while pragmatics without semantics is blind. The point is that words take on particular meaning not simply by virtue of their place in a system of signs but when a speaker or writer uses them on a particular occasion in a particular context for a particular purpose. Meaning is a matter not only of *langue* (i.e., position in a sign system) but *parole* (i.e., speech, use).

contrast is conceptually cleaner, I think, than "movement." What he really wants to establish in speaking of redemptive movement, of course, is that if we read Scripture in historical and canonical context, we will see that there is a "change for the better." Synchronic contrast highlights how viewing things biblically is a change for the better vis-à-vis the ancient Near East; diachronic contrast highlights change for the better within the Bible itself.

By "redemptive spirit" Webb means something like "underlying value" or "implicit ideal" or "the force behind change for the better." Here too, as with meaning, I wonder to what this spirit is attached: text or author? I also wonder whether Webb intends his redemptive-spirit approach to function as a general or a special hermeneutic. There are lively discussions going on right now, for example, about the "redemptive spirit" of the Constitution of the United States! There is nothing to suggest, however, that Webb himself thinks his approach applies anywhere else but the Bible.

It is nevertheless surprising that he never explicitly equates "spirit" with the Holy Spirit (or "redemptive" with the redemption won by Christ). My search for references to the Holy Spirit turned up not a single one, a discovery that troubles my soul given the plethora of references to the "underlying spirit" of the Bible. Whose text is it anyway? The most charitable reading would be that "redemptive spirit" does indeed refer to the Holy Spirit, specifically, to the Spirit's work in guiding the biblical authors into all truth (i.e., inspiration and progressive revelation). But this is not spelled out.

Webb's most significant claim is that readers should attend to the "trajectory or logical extension of the Bible's redemptive spirit that carries Christians to an ultimate ethic." He is clearly on to something important. It's "eschatology": the awareness throughout the New Testament that the first coming of Jesus has inaugurated, but not entirely realized, the new age of the kingdom of God. The Bible also depicts that final end, the day of the Lord, but the apostle Paul in particular reminds his readers that we are not there yet. The telos that completes redemptive history is thus "already" and "not yet."

As I say in my chapter, canon sense is the ability to connect the earlier parts of the theodrama to the larger whole in which they live and move and have their being. One purpose of the canon, after all, is to remind us that the meaning of the parts is ultimately a function of their relation to the whole. The ancient Rule of Faith mandated a practice of reading that related Old and New Testament together, centered on Jesus Christ. The result of that reading practice was not "redemptive spirit" but "plain sense" meaning: "the publicly accessible verbal sense of a passage interpreted according to the rules of faith and charity."[62]

Webb's whole project gets off the ground, however, by looking at what for him are the disturbing parts of the Bible as if they can be isolated from the canonical whole (I couldn't help seeing a certain parallel between Alan Jacobs' experiment to "live biblically" that I discuss in my own chapter and Webb's attempt to "apply" corporal punishment texts to today). In doing so, Webb accords a certain legitimacy to a subevangelical form of biblical interpretation that fails to take into account Scripture's unifying principle: that all things biblical ultimately cohere in, and are to be interpreted in light of, Jesus Christ. The Christian approach to all those awkward Old Testament stipulations is to remember that "we relate to God's law *in Christ, through Christ.*"[63]

The church has indeed been aware since the beginning of at least some aspects of what Webb calls redemptive movement. The question, therefore, is whether Webb's particular explanation of this phenomenon raises more problems than it solves. I concede that discerning what I have called the "synchronic contrast" between biblical and other ancient Near Eastern authors is, while difficult, often helpful. My main concern pertains to what I have called diachronic contrast: the notion that there is an upward trajectory that begins in, yet continues beyond the specific discourse of the

---

62. Katherine Greene-McCreight, "The Logic of the Interpretation of Scripture and the Church's Debate over Sexual Ethics," in *Homosexuality, Science, and the "Plain Sense" of Scripture*, ed. David L. Balch (Grand Rapids: Eerdmans, 2000), 248.

63. Christopher Seitz, "Sexuality and Scripture's Plain Sense," in ibid., 183.

Bible, such that no specific statement in the Bible articulates its end point.

Webb's fundamental insight is that being biblical is less a matter of replicating bits and pieces of the Bible than it is of following where these bits and pieces lead: an ultimate ethic. Clearly, there is movement in Scripture, for what else is history than movement? Evangelicals know that both revelation and redemption are progressive. The ancient Rule of Faith and the more recent redemptive-history approach agree, moreover, that the development reaches its definitive stage in Jesus Christ. Jesus Christ is the Christian's ultimate ethic. Because redemption has been accomplished in Christ's death and resurrection, the definitive word has been spoken, though the church continues to work out its implications. Strictly speaking, however, this continued working out is not a redemptive trajectory so much as a trajectory of "faith seeking understanding."

Those who lack the requisite hermeneutical scruples and spiritual virtues can abuse every interpretive method; hence it would be unfair to charge Webb for misapplications of his approach. The issues I raise are simply those that anyone espousing something like a trajectory hermeneutic will have to face. Yet some methods have more built-in safeguards than others.

How, for example, does the trajectory approach guard against the temptation to mistake the *Heilige* (Holy) Spirit for a Hegelian (Enlightenment) impostor? Hegel goes further than Webb in conceiving the whole of history in terms of "redemptive movement."[64] Hegel believes that certain seminal ideas (e.g., freedom), once conceived, will inevitably progress until they reach a fully actualized form. Some proponents of democratic capitalism believe that a similar dynamic ensures the success of their "ultimate ethic," as do some proponents of the gay and lesbian agenda. Webb discerns a "radical concept of equality" in the Bible. Others find in Scripture radical concepts of "love," "mutuality," and "inclusivity." Again, Webb is not responsible for everything

---

64. In Hegel's case, redemptive movement—*Geist* (Spirit) coming to self-knowledge—becomes a virtual metaphysics.

people discover while searching the Bible's redemptive spirit. However, he does provide them with examples of how to "trump" the specific things the Bible says by identifying redemptive movement and then plotting its logical trajectory.[65] In short, it's not clear to me how the redemptive genie—the trajectory of social values such as equality and inclusivity—once let out of the bottle, is canonically contained or regulated.

Webb anticipates this very concern toward the end of his article (see his correcting of misconception 7). He there speaks of the necessity of working through the redemptive trajectory not only logically but *theologically*, though he nowhere explains what the latter means or how to do it. He does give one hint: adding the theological component brings other data into the discussion because God is the author of all knowledge. Yet it is difficult to see this as distinctly Christian theology, given the absence of appeal to Jesus Christ as the definitive revelation of God (the one exception is a fleeting reference to Gal. 3:28, an "equality" text). It is less a question of divine name-dropping than of right hermeneutics: Christians should read the Bible in light of the person and work of Jesus Christ and the person and work of Jesus Christ in light of (i.e., as fulfillment and true meaning of) the Bible.

Webb does at one point speak of God rather than ethics. He asks whether God too changes for the better. No, he replies, redemptive movement does not mean that God changes his mind, only his strategy. God "in a pastoral sense accommodates himself" to where people at any given time are in their social ethic. The language of "accommodation" comes from Calvin, who uses it to explain how God adjusts his relation to human cognitive capacity—by "lisping," for example. The question, however, is whether in the moral realm a "lisp" becomes a "lapse." Is Webb suggesting that God "accommodated" himself to a certain degree of human brutality in allowing parents in ancient Israel to beat their

65. The idea of "trumping" Scripture comes from Kenton L. Sparks, *God's Word in Human Words: An Evangelical Appropriation of Critical Biblical Scholarship* (Grand Rapids: Baker, 2008), 295.

children's backs instead of their buttocks? Would it really have been beyond the bounds of Israel's social ethical plausibility structure had God set the limit at thirty rather than forty strokes? Some disturbing theological implications attend Webb's version of divine Realpolitik.

My final point is aimed not at Webb only (he will be glad to hear) but at all four of us. It strikes me as odd that a volume devoted to going beyond the sacred page lacks the perspective of the missiologist. After all, the first people to take the Bible beyond its original context were the early missionaries, and generations of missionaries have been going beyond ever since. Surely biblical scholars and theologians can learn something from those who have written on contextualization from the standpoint of Christian missions.[66]

The late missiologist David Bosch suggested that the very idea of having to apply ideas or principles in order to bridge the ugly ditch between the Bible and us comes from the Enlightenment separation of theoretical and practical reason and from Lessing's idea that the rational truths of religion sit uneasily with the accidental truths of history.[67] To some extent, both Webb and Kaiser are hung up on just this point, stuck on the flypaper of modern epistemology.

Bosch also identifies the weakness in thinking that we today are in a better position to plot a social ethic than were the authors of Scripture: "Christians tend to sacralize 'the sociological forces of history that are dominant at any particular time, regarding them as inexorable works of providence *and even of redemption.*'"[68] In this regard, I wonder how "Western" are the trajectories Webb identifies with the Bible's redemptive spirit. It would be interesting to learn what Christian readers in the non-Western world would say about the Bible's "redemptive movement."

None of us is ultimately in a position to throw stones. The challenge of living as faithful disciples to an old, old story

---

66. I find upon rereading my own chapter that I do speak of mission and cite missiologists—phew! [Editor's note: The reflection by Christopher Wright is also designed to bring the missiologist's voice to the discussion.]

67. David J. Bosch, *Transforming Mission: Paradigm Shifts in Theology of Mission* (Maryknoll, NY: Orbis, 1991), 421–23.

68. Ibid., 429, emphasis mine.

in a brave new world proves more than any one individual, or disciplinary approach, can handle. All the more reason, therefore, to combine our theological forces and encourage biblical scholars, theologians, ethicists, pastors, and missiologists to work together.

In the final analysis, it is the triune God who goes "beyond" Scripture each time the Father and the Son send the Spirit to minister the Word in new situations. Questions about how best to apply the text are best handled only in light of this triune mission; going beyond the sacred page is ultimately a matter of missional hermeneutics. May the church's reading of Scripture enable it to fulfill her mission—to go beyond hearing the Word to understanding and doing it for the glory of God.

CHAPTER FIVE

REFLECTIONS ON MOVING BEYOND THE BIBLE TO THEOLOGY

A REFLECTION BY MARK L. STRAUSS

ANYONE WHO HAS EVER SERVED in a pastoral ministry knows the benefits of open and constructive dialogue. I remember on one occasion, while serving in an interim pastorate, I received an angry note from one of my parishioners over something that had happened at church—something for which I was at least partially responsible. I invited this man to my office, where we had the opportunity to look each other in the eye, listen to the other's perspective, and—most important—take some time to pray together. (It's hard to stay angry with someone while praying for them.) Although we did not reach identical viewpoints, our relationship grew stronger through that encounter (we are still close friends). Equally important, we both matured as people by seeing the situation through the eyes of the other—by expanding our vision of the world.

The ongoing debate among evangelicals on hermeneutical method has the potential for great conflict and division or for great personal, intellectual, and spiritual growth. The manner in which we conduct this dialogue will make all the difference. In reading through the essays and responses, I was encouraged to see both constructive dialogue and even a measure of growth (redemptive movement?) among the authors.

Going "beyond the Bible" can be understood in a variety of ways, two of which are most important for our discussion. (1) In one sense, all of us go beyond the Bible whenever we encounter ethical and theological issues not directly addressed in the text. The doctrine of the Trinity—three persons, one God—goes beyond the Bible in explicating what is implicit in the biblical text. Developing a Christian ethic on abortion, euthanasia, or genetic research goes beyond the Bible to answer questions that did not arise in biblical cultural contexts.

(2) More controversially, going "beyond the Bible" can mean seeking an ultimate or better ethic than that explicitly set forth in Scripture. This ultimate ethic certainly clarifies, but may even "correct," the ethical standards found in the biblical text. The justification for this, it is said, is that the inculturated nature of the text somehow limited what the authors of Scripture could say. We must therefore go beyond the Bible to determine how the Spirit who was speaking then is speaking to us now in new and different circumstances. Both of these ways of going "beyond the Bible" are discussed at length in this volume. Yet while the former is accepted as an essential part of any hermeneutic, the latter is viewed by some as compromising the authority of Scripture. Whether this threat is real or merely perceived will be at the heart of hermeneutical discussion for years to come.

TWO QUESTIONS

Two questions are foundational for any hermeneutical discussion of this kind. The first is: What is the Bible? And the second: How does God communicate to us through it? The evangelical answer to the first is that the Bible is God's "word"—his message to humanity. All of the contributors in this volume unequivocally affirm the divine inspiration and authority of the Bible.

Yet if it were that simple, we would not be having this discussion. God would just tell us what to do, and we would do it. But the Bible is not only God's word; it is also human words (the "diversity" side of the unity/diversity of the Bible). And this dimension greatly complicates the second question. As divine-human communication, the Bible is both historically positioned and culturally conditioned. The former means that every part (whether narrative, psalm, letter, law, proverb, etc.) was written by historical persons at particular places and times to meet certain needs and concerns of that time. The Bible is not made up primarily of abstract or propositional statements of truth, but of historically situated "speech acts" or "utterances" — communicative acts from one person to another person or community.[1]

This latter element—the fact that the text is culturally conditioned—means that these authors and communities are embedded in particular cultures and therefore speak from within that culture rather than from above it. There is no such thing as an "objective" biblical author—that is, one who speaks outside the limitations of human language and culture. All biblical truth is perspectival and contextual. Even if we speak of the divine Author, God still speaks through the limitations of language and culture. The great evangelical challenge (and the topic of this book) is to move from the first question to the second: to discern how God speaks to us through the historically and culturally embedded voices of the past.

My task in this dialogue is to provide (New Testament) reflections on the views and responses presented by the four dialogue partners as well as on the hermeneutical issues in general. I like the word "reflections," since it means I can pretty much say whatever I want. Yet because I demand organization and clarity from my students, I will try not to offer random thoughts, but will provide a measure of systematic

---

1. This is not to say that the biblical writers had no awareness that they were writing inspired Scripture or that they intended their message to be *only* for their original readers. The gospel writers may have had a larger Christian audience in mind, even if they were writing especially to a particular community or communities (see R. Bauckham, ed., *The Gospel for All Christians: Rethinking the Gospel Audiences* [Grand Rapids: Eerdmans, 1998]). Similarly, Paul writes with apostolic authority and, at least in some contexts, expects his writings to be passed on to other churches (Col. 4:16). Yet this does not negate the historical particularity of his letters or the evidence that they were written primarily for their original readers.

analysis. (1) I will first summarize my understanding of the four authors' views and what I consider to be their greatest strengths and weaknesses. (2) I will then offer some suggestions related to models and methods that will hopefully clarify and supplement those offered by the contributors.

ASSESSING THE FOUR VIEWS
WALTER KAISER'S PRINCIPLIZING HERMENEUTIC

Walter Kaiser promotes a principlizing hermeneutic, which means to "[re]state the author's propositions, arguments, narrations, and illustrations in timeless abiding truths with special focus on the application of those truths to the current needs of the Church."[2] Kaiser identifies three steps in the process: (1) identify the "big idea" of the passage; (2) determine the emphasis; (3) state the passage in propositional principles. One important tool in the principlizing method is the "Ladder of Abstraction," where statements may be categorized as to their level of specificity or generalization. The lower on the ladder, the more specific and culturally bound the command. The higher, the more abstract and universal the principle. An ancient and specific command not to muzzle the ox (Deut. 25:4) leads upward on the ladder to the institutional or personal norm that animals are God's gift to humanity and should be treated kindly, to the top of the ladder with the general principle of the grace and generosity that takes place in the hearts of those who express kindness to those who serve well, whether animals or people (Paul's principle in 1 Cor. 9:10–12). Determining at what level of the ladder the principle crosses over from the biblical world to our own is a crucial step in this method.

After providing helpful illustrations of how principlizing works with contemporary ethical issues (euthanasia, women's roles, homosexuality, slavery, abortion, and embryonic stem cell research), Kaiser turns to the larger question of whether the interpreter must ever move beyond the Bible in the application process. His simple answer is "no." While

---

2. Cited in his essay from Walter C. Kaiser Jr., *Toward an Exegetical Theology: Biblical Exegesis for Preaching and Teaching* (Grand Rapids: Baker, 1981), 152.

acknowledging the fact of progressive revelation, he states that "there is also perfection of revealed truth at all stages along the process, even though that perfection was merely a perfection in seminal form with an incipient potentiality for increasing growth, clearness, and fullness." "Revelation in Scripture can be true, eternal in its source, and organically or seminally perfect without its being complete in its statements, its history, fully developed in its supporting doctrines, or fully apprehended by all its readers or listeners." In short, Scripture is always perfect, if sometimes incomplete in its affirmations, ethics, and commands.

The great strength of Kaiser's approach is its simplicity and pragmatism. Tried and tested tools of exegesis determine the meaning and intention of the passage in its original context. Underlying principles are then gleaned from what the story teaches about God and his relationship with human beings. These principles are then used to address ethical issues and contemporary situations not directly addressed in Scripture. This method has served the church well through the centuries and continues to be used in one form or another by almost everyone today. Indeed, most other theories and methods adopt some form of principlizing when moving from theory to praxis.

Yet, as many contemporary critics have noted, principlizing has problems and limitations. I share the concerns expressed by others both in this volume and elsewhere. Should establishing "principles" really be the goal of interpretation? The Christian life is not about asserting rules or principles, but about enacting God's Word in real life. As Vanhoozer rhetorically asks, "Are principles really more timeless than practices?" Which is more important when reading the parable of the prodigal son, identifying the principle of unqualified forgiveness or living out the story as the loving father by offering God's forgiveness to others? Here Vanhoozer's idea of "performing the drama" seems more apropos than Kaiser's principlizing.

Closely related to this is Doriani's criticism of Kaiser that principlizing inappropriately privileges one form of divine communication over others. The diverse literary forms of Scripture—commands, questions, parables, prayers, promises, curses, vows, and so on—are an asset rather than a liability for the communication of truth. Jesus' eight rhetorical questions in Mark 8:14–27 are a *more effective* means of communicating truth than if he had simply stated the principle, "I can provide all that you need." Flattening everything into propositional statements reduces the efficacy and potency of God's Word.

Third, principlizing tends to downplay the significance of the interpreter's own context by assuming that a propositional truth is somehow above culture. As David Clark observes, "principlizing obscures the fact that any articulation of the allegedly transcultural principles still reflects the culture of the translators."[3] There is no such thing as propositions free from cultural bias or worldview. Moreover, an interpreter's perspective will inevitably influence *which principle* is drawn from a particular passage. Paul's command for women to cover their heads in worship in 1 Corinthians 11 will likely be principlized by a complementarian as a call for female subordination, but by an egalitarian with reference to propriety in worship. Propositional truths are inevitably influenced by the interpreter's background, culture, and worldview.

Finally, the method of principlizing sometimes trivializes or glosses over deeper ethical questions. This is evident, for example, when Kaiser discusses Exodus 21:2–11, which allows a debt-slave, set free on the seventh year, to take with him only what he had brought into slavery. If the slave had a wife already, she could leave with him. But if he acquired a wife and had children while a slave, the wife and children had to stay with the master or could be purchased with savings acquired during his time of slavery. Kaiser suggests the principle here is one of personal responsibility. If the Hebrew slave did not show himself responsible while serving the master (by accumulating savings?), then he would likely bring hardship on his wife and children by once again falling into debt-slavery.

But this principle seems to miss the point of the concession, which is about rights of ownership.[4] If the master

---

3. David K. Clark, *To Know and Love God: Method for Theology* (Wheaton, IL: Crossway, 2003), 112.

4. See John I. Duran, *Exodus* (Word Biblical Commentary 3; Waco, TX: Word, 1987), 321: "both the wife and any children … are obviously the owner's property."

purchased the wife, she must be paid for by the slave. If the slave brought his own wife into slavery, she is his and not the master's. If the real goal were to protect the wife from financial hardship, should not the master keep any wife—whether acquired before or after enslavement—in "protective custody" while the slave proves himself financially responsible? The unanswered ethical questions therefore remain: Why would God allow his people to buy and sell human beings as property? How could the potential financial loss sustained by the master be viewed as of greater ethical concern than keeping a Hebrew family—husband, wife, and children—together? We must not simply gloss over the deeper ethical question of the apparent legitimization of the institution of slavery.

A similar example can be seen in Kaiser's critique of Webb concerning women captured in war (Deut. 21:10–14). Against Webb's redemptive movement hermeneutic, Kaiser argues it is enough to use the grammatical-historical method to contrast the horrendous treatment of captured women in other ancient Near Eastern cultures with the more humane treatment of prisoners of war in Israel. This principle (of humane treatment) can then be applied to new situations. But such easy principlizing fails to address the deeper question of the apparent condoning of forced marriage and sexual relations (rape?) with a prisoner of war (as well as easy divorce if the man later becomes displeased with the woman). Simple principlizing here seems to trivialize a complex ethical dilemma.

DANIEL DORIANI'S REDEMPTIVE-HISTORICAL METHOD

Daniel Doriani's redemptive-historical method (RHM) has as its foundation the affirmation that interpretation is both a technical skill and a spiritual task. While utilizing technical knowledge of Scripture's language and background to exegete the text, the interpreter must also affirm Scripture's authority, sufficiency, and clarity. *Authority* means that "we expect to be corrected when we read the Bible" rather than seeking to correct or improve Scripture; *sufficiency*, that "we need no God-given revelation beyond the biblical canon"; and *clarity*, that "Scripture is clear enough that we can take it at face value." While acknowledging that biblical authors accommodated to their cultures and that God's self-revelation unfolds through centuries, "we also affirm that the revelation is sufficient, clear, and complete at the close of the canon." Doriani's RHM therefore traces a redemptive movement *within* the canon of Scripture, but not *beyond* it.

In light of this foundation, Doriani asserts four "steps" of interpretation. The first is a close, accurate interpretation of the text (exegesis). The second is a synthesis of biblical data into doctrinal and ethical statements, always paying close attention to its place in redemptive history. The third is to consider the application of Scripture to daily life. For the fourth (not really a "step"), Doriani argues that the narrative genre deserves a greater role than it has often been given in the formation of theology and ethics, since the character of God is revealed in narrative.

How, then, does one go beyond Scripture on issues not directly addressed in the text? Doriani discusses two key methods: (1) the use of casuistry, defined as "the art of resolving particular cases of conscience through appeal to higher general principles"; and (2) asking the right questions and then using biblical principles to answer them. Key questions to be asked are those of *duty* (What should I do? What do I owe others?), *character* (Who should I be?), *goals* (What goals are worthy of my life energy?), and *vision* (How can I see the world as God does?). Doriani applies these questions to two issues, gambling and architectural standards, and finally ends with a lengthy discussion of the role of women.

There is much to commend in Doriani's discussion. His strong affirmation of the authority of Scripture and the use of the historical-grammatical method to determine the original meaning of the text should be foundational to any evangelical hermeneutic. Scripture is sufficient "for every good work" and "provides guidance sufficient for faithful living." Doriani's affirmation of the importance of drawing ethics from the diverse literary forms of the Bible—not just propositional statements—is also a welcome corrective. Narrative, for example, is a powerful medium for communicating truth and should not be diminished by asserting the supremacy of propositional statements or ethical commands.

Doriani's chapter is also full of helpful insights that should guide any hermeneutical theory: every text of Scripture should be interpreted with "close attention to its place in redemptive history." When seeking ethical imperatives, "we seek master texts to guide our reading" and affirm the unity within the diversity of Scripture: "We believe that God's plan of redemption for the nations through the line of Abraham is the unifying theme of Scripture." Application, in the end, is not just about obeying ethical imperatives, but about reproducing the life of Christ.

Against a few members of his own school, Doriani writes, "I maintain that the imitation of God / imitation of Christ motif pervades Scripture and is a leading source of ethical guidance." His use of critical questions with reference to issues not directly addressed in the text is also helpful. I resonate with these points since they confirm that the application of Scripture is not just about looking for the "answer," but about "thinking God's thoughts after him," walking in the power of the Spirit, and living a transformed life where right actions flow naturally from righteous character.

Doriani's second step of interpretation—the synthesis of biblical data into doctrinal and ethical statements—seems little different from Kaiser's principlizing (as Kaiser himself asserts in his critique of Doriani). Indeed, Doriani's own definition of casuistry uses the language of principles. This is not really a criticism since, as noted above, most hermeneutical theories utilize this kind of language to one degree or another. But it makes it difficult to distinguish Doriani's method from Kaiser's. Both exegete; both principlize; both seek to read texts in their context within redemptive history.

While generally sensitive to cultural and contextual issues, at times Doriani leans toward a more naïve objectivism. He criticizes those who "try to guess what Scripture would have said next—about gender or hell or whatever—if there had been more revelation." He responds that the question, "What would Paul say if he were here today?" is moot. "No one knows what he *would* say. But we do know what he *did* say, and we know Scripture itself says its content equips believers for every good work." But this misses the more important question, which is *how* Scripture equips believers. We know, for example, how the Holy Spirit, through the apostle Paul, guided the Corinthians in specific first-century issues, but how do these commands guide us in new and different circumstances? Everyone must ask, based on the values, patterns, and principles in the text: How would Paul have addressed this new situation? Or, perhaps better, How is the Holy Spirit speaking to us today through speech-acts embedded in the language, culture, and circumstances of the past? Everyone must seek the redemptive spirit (Spirit) of the text to find contemporary application.

Doriani may also overstate his case for the clarity of Scripture when he repeatedly insists on a "face value" reading of the text. It is noteworthy that he and Kaiser utilize the same exegetical tools to reach diametrically opposed conclusions on gender roles. (It is not clear here whether it is Kaiser or Doriani who needs to say, "I stand corrected," in the face of clear biblical teaching.) Such exegetical stand-offs by evangelical scholars with equally high views of Scripture should caution us toward greater humility and a desire to better unpack our own cultural baggage. We must not forget that for centuries the church affirmed the institution of slavery based on just such a face value reading of the text.

The simple fact is that we are all products of our culture, background, and worldview. Nobody reads the Bible free of bias (as Doriani readily affirms). Here Vanhoozer's caution for more "catholic sensibility" by listening to other voices is especially appropriate. Paying attention both to voices from the past and to other voices within global Christianity can help us recognize our own blind spots.

We must also remember that Scripture itself comes to us in cultural clothing. Doriani chides those who imply "that the canonical writers were so constrained by their age and audience that we lack sufficient direction on vital matters" and those who deny "that the Lord had the capacity to say what he wished before the canon closed. He lacked the power to overcome local conditions." Later, he rejects the "feeble" argument of egalitarians that Jesus was responding to culture and convention when he chose twelve males as apostles. After all, "Jesus defied cultural conventions whenever he saw fit. He touched lepers, called tax collectors and prostitutes his friends, and violated sacrosanct Sabbath codes." While no one would deny that Jesus defied certain cultural conventions, this does not mean that scriptural commands are never culturally influenced or constrained. If we deny any condescension to culture in the biblical text, how do we explain the Old Testament allowance of polygamy, Paul's commands for female head coverings, or his failure to call for full emancipation of slaves? Does not Jesus himself identify the divorce regulations of Deuteronomy 24:1–4 as a condescension to human sinfulness rather than an ultimate ethic (Mark 10:1–12)?

It is easy to say that *"the Bible contains what God wants it to contain"* and that "God does not gaze ruefully at the church and long for what might have been." But we are still faced with enigmatic texts that seem—at face value (!)—to contradict the righteous, just, and loving character of God as expressed elsewhere in Scripture.[5] Why would God condone the genocide of apparently innocent women and children in the Canaanite conquest (Deut. 20:17; Josh. 10:40; 11:14, 15, 20)? Why would God provide guidelines related to a father's selling his daughter into slavery (Ex. 21:7) rather than condemning the practice outright? Do we simply let these texts "correct us" and accept them at face value, or do we critically engage them, seeking to what degree they may be culturally conditioned?

Webb (in my opinion) rightly criticizes Doriani for making Paul sound more like an abolitionist than the apostle's own words justify. The claim that "Paul flatly tells slaves, 'If you can gain your freedom, do so' (1 Cor. 7:21)" must be balanced by the fact that Paul also flatly tells slaves that they should "remain in the situation in which God called you" (1 Cor. 7:24). For Paul emancipation is a good option, but not an ethical imperative. It is going beyond the meaning of the text to say that "Paul's letter to Philemon (11–21) seeks to

---

5. I. H. Marshall, *Beyond the Bible: Moving from Scripture to Theology* (Grand Rapids: Baker, 2004), 47, makes a similar point: "if minds nurtured at least to some extent by the gospel come to conclusions that seem to clash with what is taken to be scriptural teaching, then this establishes a prima facie case for reconsideration of whether we have correctly identified the latter."

persuade him to free his slave Onesimus." Paul certainly tells Philemon to welcome back Onesimus as a Christian brother, but he only opaquely hints that this might entail emancipation (v. 22). Paul's commands to (Christian!) masters and slaves in Ephesians and Colossians confirm that he did not consider emancipation essential for authentic Christian brotherhood (Eph. 6:5–9; Col. 3:22–4:1). It seems beyond dispute that Paul's commands here are at least in part conditioned by cultural and historical constraints and so do not represent an "ultimate ethic" for human relationships.

Indeed, in his response to Webb's article, Doriani seems to acknowledge a scriptural movement toward a better ethic. After noting some positive points in Webb's approach, he writes that "the question for Webb's proposed paradigm is not, therefore, 'Is it [ever] true?' but 'Is it the best tool for interpretation?'" and later, "We agree there is movement in the teaching on slavery and that there is not movement on homosexuality; we disagree about gender roles." In short, Doriani seems to acknowledge a redemptive movement (toward a "better ethic"?) *within the canon.* Yet he insists this movement has reached its apex at the close of the canon: "The RHT seeks to trace movements *within* the canon. We do not deny that biblical authors accommodate to their culture.... But we also affirm that the revelation is sufficient, clear, and complete at the close of the canon."

Yet even Paul and the other New Testament writers were very much a part of their cultures. Do their commands ever contain accommodations to culture (e.g., with reference to slavery, head coverings, foot-washing, etc.)? And if so, might there be a "better ethic" in the redemptive spirit of the text than in its (culturally-conditioned) concrete specifics? I am not advocating Webb's position *in toto*; but I wonder whether, by acknowledging redemptive movement within the canon, Doriani may have let the RMH cat out of the bag.

KEVIN VANHOOZER'S DRAMA OF REDEMPTION

This volume in general confirms what is clear from hermeneutical discussions of recent years: *everybody likes Kevin.* And what's not to like? Vanhoozer writes in an engaging and whimsical style full of metaphors and wordplays. He reads widely and deeply, drawing insights from the best philosophical, theological, and linguistic thinkers of our day. He demonstrates awareness of global and contextual issues. His epistemology strikes a nice balance between extremes of postmodern relativism and naïve objectivism. He also advocates one of the most compelling models of hermeneutical method in recent years: the drama of redemption.

It is curious that, despite the strong differences between Doriani and Webb, both almost unanimously affirm Vanhoozer's contribution. Doriani's only real criticism is that he thinks Kevin needs to get to church more and get his hands dirtier in Christian service. Webb affirms Vanhoozer's global and comprehensive approach but thinks it could use more concrete hermeneutical tools for "slogging their way through tough textual trenches." Both apparently could integrate Vanhoozer's method into their own with little or no modification.

Walter Kaiser, however, is less than convinced. Like the little child in Hans Christian Andersen's *The Emperor's New Clothes*, he just doesn't get it—and is willing to say so: "After reading and rereading Kevin's chapter many times over, for the life of me I cannot explain to anyone else, much less myself, how the 'drama-of-redemption approach' works or really solves any of the crucial questions being put to the Bible in our day." There you have it. All words but no clothes.

At critical points, I think Kaiser is misreading Vanhoozer, especially when he suggests that the drama-of-redemption approach threatens the authority and sufficiency of Scripture and claims that "improvising" means deliberately turning away from the author's intentions. But I will return to Kaiser's general criticism a bit later. First, however, let us summarize the drama-of-redemption approach.

For Vanhoozer, the best model for understanding and applying Scripture is *theodrama*. "Going beyond the Bible biblically is ultimately a matter of participating in the great drama of redemption of which Scripture is the authoritative and holy script." In this theodramatic model the Bible is the church's holy script, which tells the church about the drama and solicits its participation as active performers. We achieve understanding not by processing the information of the text but by "inhabiting" the world it projects. Since doctrines do not always tell us exactly what to say and do, believers "improvise" the script by "grasping the relationship between what the Bible says about God and what we know about the contemporary situation, and then acting accordingly." In order to determine what is textually and contextually fitting, the church needs canon sense, catholic sensibility, and a sensitivity to circumstances.

Vanhoozer tests his approach with two case studies, one doctrinal (the place of Mary in Christian theology) and one ethical (the morality of transsexualism). Mary's greatness in the biblical text (which should not be diminished) comes *not* from her sinlessness or her role as mediator, but because she is a model disciple who directs all interest away from herself and to the Lord. Transsexuality (possibly the church's next big ethical issue) is a distortion of God's created order because one's personhood cannot be divorced from one's biological sex. In his conclusion, Vanhoozer summarizes his method with an acronym—AAA ("attend; appraise; advance"). We *attend* (see) to what is going on in Scripture, we *appraise* (judge) where we are in the theodrama, and we *advance* (act) into the world in front of the text to the glory of God.

Vanhoozer acknowledges the strengths of other approaches but asserts the superiority of this dramatic motif. While the redemptive-historical approach (of Geerhardus Vos and Doriani) rightly identifies revelation as a book of history that unfolds organically, it cannot go beyond the sacred page since "the church today shares the same redemptive-historical context with the authors of the New Testament."[6] A narrative-of-redemption approach correctly recognizes the overarching story of redemption, but does not adequately account for our active participation (or "performance") in that story. And a "logic of redemption" (= principlizing) approach falls short because it seeks abstract and elusive *principles* rather than revealing how to become a wiser *person* by considering particular instances of canonical wisdom.

6. This is similar to my criticism that Doriani's assumption of an ultimate ethic at the close of the canon does not adequately account for the inculturation of the NT writings themselves.

There are many strengths in this drama-of-redemption model. It recognizes the meta-narrative of Scripture and identifies believers as active participants in that drama. The goal is not to strictly replicate a prior blueprint or to apply a principle, but to "canonically cultivate the mind of Christ" by discovering "the kind of world we live in and the kind of thing God does in the world and the kind of people we are to be in response."

But what of its weaknesses? Perhaps the most obvious is that while metaphors or analogies enhance our understanding, they also inevitably break down. The comparison of Scripture to a dramatic script is inexact since a script explicitly tells an actor what to say or do. Vanhoozer responds to this objection by qualifying that *"strictly speaking, however, we do not perform the discourse per se but the theodrama it describes and enacts."* And later, "In speaking of 'performing' the script, then, I have in mind not reproducing the world behind the text or of re-creating the scenes depicted in the text but rather of living in a way that conforms to the world as it is being transformed 'in Christ.'" While helpful, these clarifications simply affirm the limitations of the analogy. "Performing the script" would perhaps be better stated simply as living out the worldview, values, and purposes of God that are implicit in the text. The metaphor of drama and its accompanying vocabulary sometimes obscure rather than illuminate.

Metaphors and analogies can also be ambiguous, trading aesthetic and rhetorical power for precision of expression. When reading Vanhoozer, I sometimes find myself saying, "That's an engaging and evocative image, but what exactly does it mean and how far can you take it?" Like great art, these word pictures are sometimes easier to experience than to critically analyze.

This leads to a third criticism, namely, that Vanhoozer's approach is more about identifying what Scripture *is* (an essential first step) than about *how* we actually live it out, that is, moving from text to *praxis*. The general imperative to "perform the script" does not provide much concrete help (hence Kaiser's criticism). It is significant that, when discussing the nuts and bolts of method, Vanhoozer introduces the vocabulary of *attending, appraising,* and *advancing* — terms not exclusive to a dramatic model, and terms that could probably be adopted by many different hermeneutical theories.

Finally, a more specific criticism related to one of Vanhoozer's case studies. Although I affirm his conclusion that transsexuality is a distortion of God's intention for human sexuality, I find some of his arguments less than convincing. When asserting that human beings are psychosomatic unities, Vanhoozer writes that one's personhood cannot be divorced from one's sex and that it is not possible to separate the question "Who you are?" from the question "What sex are you?" While this is generally true, the situation can be more complex. How do we deal theologically with hermaphrodites (also called androgynes), whose gender is ambiguous or who have both male and female genitalia? Are they any less persons because of their ambiguous sexuality?

We can certainly account for such abnormalities theologically by appealing to the fallen state of creation, and most theologians would likely agree that such confusion of biological sex would justify corrective surgery. But what about those whose sexual confusion is psychological, or part psychological and part physical, as in the case of an effeminate man who is convinced he is a woman? If plastic surgery is justified to correct the detrimental psychological effects of say, a cleft palate, what is the argument against surgery to "correct" the detrimental psychological effects of a confused sexuality?

Vanhoozer argues that the transgender liberation movement is "an overt rebellion against the binary divide between male and female bodies and behavior." But many biologists, psychologists, and medical doctors would deny that such a strict binary divide always exists — either in bodies or (especially) in behavior. Vanhoozer concludes that "in the final analysis, human creativity is unable to alter the created order." Yet theologians uniformly affirm the use of human creativity to correct the effects of a *fallen* creation. We protect against natural disasters and fight against the ravages of disease, famine, and war. Once again: I agree with Vanhoozer's conclusion here. But it seems to me a more robust theological engagement will be necessary to answer this challenge.

WILLIAM WEBB'S REDEMPTIVE-MOVEMENT HERMENEUTIC

If Kevin is the darling of today's hermeneutical drama, Bill is sometimes cast as its villain. Yet I find Webb's writings honest, intellectually stimulating, and personally stretching. He asks and answers hard questions that evangelical scholars sometimes gloss over or avoid.

Webb's RMH claims that many of the specific commands of Scripture represent a less-than-ultimate ethic because of cultural or historical limitations. Yet we need not despair of finding God's will, since the Bible reveals a clear redemptive movement that enables us to move beyond the concrete specificity of inculturated texts toward an ultimate ethic.

What is most controversial about Webb's theory is the claim that this ultimate ethic is not necessarily to be found within the limits of the canon. In some cases it must be surmised by a *trajectory* of the Spirit that begins in the canon, but which reaches its fullest expression beyond the first-century culture in which the New Testament arose.

Webb's most important defense for his model is the biblical teaching on slavery. The commands related to slavery in the Old Testament reveal a quantum leap ahead of the ruthless attitude toward slaves in the surrounding ancient Near Eastern cultures, but still seem cruel by today's standards. People are still treated as property to be bought and sold, and masters—though warned against excessive cruelty—are at liberty to beat their slaves with impunity (Ex. 21:20–21). The New Testament shows a clear advance, with affirmation that both slaves and free have the same Master and all believers are equal "in Christ" (Gal. 3:28; Eph. 6:9). But slavery is never condemned outright, and New Testament writers encourage their readers to live righteously within the system rather than to work to abolish it. There is surely room here for movement toward an ultimate ethic "beyond" the cultural specificity of these canonical texts.

Webb finds the same kind of redemptive movement in the Bible's teaching on corporal punishment. If this is true for slavery and corporal punishment, it is potentially true for other ethical issues where the canonical text may not represent an ultimate ethic (e.g., the role of women). This thesis is developed in detail in Webb's *Slaves, Women & Homosexuals* and other writings.[7]

So what is to prevent an anything-goes hermeneutic, where contemporary culture rather than the Bible dictates our theology and ethics? Webb's answer is that if the Bible reveals no redemptive movement or upward trajectory, then there is no justification for going beyond the biblical text. The consistent condemnation of homosexual practice throughout Scripture confirms the transcultural nature of these commands. There is no danger of ethical relativism since it is the Bible—not culture—that establishes the trajectory.

In response to the hits he has taken, Webb answers a number of "misconceptions" related to his theory. For example, he denies that a RMH replaces the grammatical-historical method, since the latter is essential for analyzing cultural dimensions in the text. Nor does a RMH seek a "better ethic" than that of the NT; rather, it seeks to identify the ethics of the NT (and OT) *rightly understood and applied*. Against critics, he affirms that a RMH views the NT as the final and definitive revelation. But being the final *revelation* "does not automatically mean that the NT contains the final *realization* of social ethic in all its concrete particulars." Webb helpfully clarifies his position:

> The idea of a RM hermeneneutic is not that God himself has somehow "moved" in his thinking or that Scripture is in any way less than God's Word. Rather, it means that God in a pastoral sense accommodates himself to meeting people and society where they are in their existing social ethic and (from there) he gently moves them with incremental steps toward something better.

There are many strengths of Webb's approach. He rightly recognizes that all Scripture comes to us in enculturated form and that we must first engage in rigorous exegesis to comprehend its original context and meaning. The message to them is not necessarily the application for us. Webb is

---

7. William J. Webb, *Slaves, Women & Homosexual: Exploring the Hermeneutics of Cultural Analysis* (Downers Grove, IL: InterVarsity Press, 2001).

also willing to face head-on the most troublesome and perplexing biblical texts. If *all* Scripture is God-breathed and is profitable for teaching, rebuking, correcting, and training in righteousness (2 Tim. 3:16), then why do we so shy away from the slave-beating and daughter-selling texts of the OT? Webb's method allows the preacher to say "Wow! Just look at how far the OT message has advanced on the pagan cultures around it, and look at where the Holy Spirit is taking it. God really is redeeming his world."

Yet Webb's approach is also fraught with dangers. Identifying trajectories is a tricky business. As products of our culture, we will always tend to view as a "better ethic" those things that our culture finds acceptable. In critiquing Webb, Doriani raises the intriguing question whether we in the West too quickly dismiss the benefits of corporal punishment of adults. In his informal survey, "every man chose painful blows over lost years." We must be cautious about assuming too quickly what is or is not a better ethic.

I also wonder whether an upward trajectory is sufficient to explain the diversity of ethical imperatives found in Scripture. Is it really the case that there is always an upward trajectory? Even the issue of women and men that is at the heart of Webb's thesis in *Slaves, Women & Homosexuals* receives mixed results. Paul's most egalitarian statement appears in what is likely his earliest letter (Gal. 3:28) and his most restrictive statement in one of his latest (1 Tim. 2:11–15). Assuming Paul is the author of the Pastorals, is he moving in the wrong direction? Might it be more accurate to speak of commands given to fit particular situations and contexts than a definitive trajectory of the Spirit?[8]

Finally, I share Vanhoozer's concerns about Webb's terminology. If I understand Webb correctly, "redemptive movement" means that God is gradually coaxing his people toward an ultimate ethic. But then what is "movement meaning"? Webb seems to define this as the ultimate ethic or the ethical

---

8. This raises the intriguing (and disturbing) question of whether there might be cultural situations today where Christians should provide ethical guidelines related to polygamy, slavery, and the inequality of women, but should not teach against them.

ideal to which the historical meaning of the text is implicitly pointing. This (I believe) would be synonymous with the "redemptive spirit" of the text. But to label this as "meaning" creates confusion, since meaning refers to the conceptions, intentions, and communicative acts of *persons*. Whose meaning is the "movement meaning"? It cannot be the human authors', since it clearly goes beyond the discourse or contextual meaning. So it must be God's purpose, goal, or intention as surmised through the broader testimony of Scripture (and the guidance of the Holy Spirit?). Perhaps I am still too Hirschian, but I am uncomfortable labeling something as "meaning" that is not a part of the human author's communicative intent as expressed through speech-acts.

OTHER MODELS FOR THE HERMENEUTICAL TASK

Analogies and metaphors are not reality but give us a particular angle, vantage point, or framework to comprehend truth. Even a powerful metaphor like the drama of redemption breaks down at certain points. I would like to review briefly two other models that are helpful for envisioning the hermeneutical task.

The first—a well-trodden one in hermeneutical circles—is a "bridge" stretching across a gorge or chasm.[9] The chasm represents the time, space, culture, and language that separate us from the original authors and settings of Scripture. Our first hermeneutical task is to cross the bridge from our world to theirs, determining the author's meaning in its original context (*exegesis*). Then we must bring that message back across the bridge, determining its significance for today (*contextualization*).

The strength of this analogy is that it reminds readers of the distance between the world of the Bible and our own and of the need for sound exegesis. There is always a danger we will misread the Bible because of our own cultural blinders.

---

9. See, e.g., J. Scott Duvall and J. Daniel Hays, *Grasping God's Word: A Hands-On Approach to Reading, Interpreting and Applying the Bible* (2nd ed.; Grand Rapids: Zondervan, 2005), 21–25.

One weakness of this model is its emphasis on discontinuity over unity. The world of the text is not in fact a different world, but another place in the same redemptive story as our own story. Those on the other side of the bridge are not strangers or foreigners but our spiritual ancestors.

A second model that may provide insight into the hermeneutical task is that of a *journey* or *walk with God*. This motif, of course, is an ancient one. The first century church found it so compelling they adopted it as their name: *hē hodos*—the "Way," "Path," or "Road" (Acts 9:2; 18:26; 19:9, 23; 22:4; 24:14, 22). The journey with Jesus meant following the one who himself is "the way and the truth and the life" (John 14:6). Of course the early Christians did not invent the image, but drew it from their biblical heritage. In the Old Testament Adam and Eve walked with God until fellowship was broken by sin (Gen. 3:8). Enoch "walked with God" so that God took him (5:24). Noah (6:9), Abraham (17:1; 24:40), and Isaac (48:15) all "walked" faithfully with God. The person blessed by God does not "walk in step with the wicked," but meditates day and night on God's law (Ps. 1:1–2). Jesus calls his disciples ("followers") to walk with him on the way of the cross. Walking with God is a rich and pervasive biblical image. In this great tradition Bunyan's *Pilgrim's Progress* allegorizes the Christian life as the journey of its protagonist "Christian" from the City of Destruction to the Celestial City.

Although Vanhoozer adopts drama as his controlling motif, he repeatedly drops into journey language. The subtitle of his introduction is "Of Pathways, Wrong Ways, and Other Ways of Going Beyond," and he begins with a discussion of "the way of the Way." He later asks "what a disciple on the Way" should do "when she comes to an unfamiliar crossroads," and affirms that Christians "perform" the kingdom of God "by continuing Christ's way."

Like redemptive history, a journey has a beginning and an end—from creation to the new creation. Those who came before walked the same road, but at an earlier time and place, in different surroundings and circumstances. The world beside the road changes, but our travel companion—the Creator God—does not. In new circumstances, he gives new commands. These may modify, but never contradict, his earlier instructions since they arise from his unchanging nature.

How, then, does the Bible fit into this journey motif? Scripture is our divinely inspired "Travelogue" (Travel-*logos*?), the authoritative record/story/drama of God's actions throughout history. From this record of earlier travelers and past journeys we learn who God is, who we are as his people, and how we ought to live in relationship with him and with others. The biblical covenants represent key landmarks along the road, places where God sets out standards, conditions, and blessings through which his people maintain their relationship/walk with him through a particular segment of the road. This salvation-historical journey may be divided into two parts, with the cross of Christ as the great climax and center point. Those walking with God before the cross trusted in his promise of future salvation. Those walking on this side of the cross experience its salvation blessings and the indwelling presence of the Spirit.

The diverse genres of the Bible fit comfortably into this model, as the divine Travelogue contains the stories of God's people as well as their divinely inspired laws, psalms, proverbs, prophecies, and correspondence between pilgrims on the road. Reading the Bible is both a grammatical-historical and a devotional task. We study the lessons of the past in order to live/walk in fellowship with God in the present. The Bible speaks to us today because God through his Spirit is present on the journey, illuminating the message of the text and its significance in new and changing circumstances.

How do we go "beyond the Bible" in this model? Like travelers crossing from rural farmland to an urban metropolis, we in the modern world encounter new opportunities, challenges, and threats. We face these by learning the ways of God in the past and by experiencing his guidance in the present. Immersing ourselves in Scripture, we come to know who God is (his character), who we are as his people, and what his purposes are in the world. This awareness, together with daily dependence on ("keep[ing] in step with"; Gal. 5:25) God's Spirit and journeying together in a community/caravan of faith, allows us to choose the right path at each crossroads—making good and godly decisions. Doing theology is not just about obeying the commands of the text, since many were never intended for us, but about walking so close to and such a distance with God that we can identify the mind of Christ in each new situation (1 Cor. 2:13–16).

These models are, of course, not mutually exclusive. Each provides insights into the hermeneutical task and each leaves gaps in our understanding. Together they help to conceptualize the task.

CRITERIA FOR CONTEXTUALIZATION

The strength of models like bridges, journeys, and dramas is that they provide a comprehensive vision of the Christian life and the place of Scripture in it. We are actors performing a drama or travelers along life's road. The weakness is that such models do not provide specific steps or criteria for evaluating and applying biblical texts. In this final section, I would like to (briefly) discuss such evaluative techniques.

There is general agreement on three basic steps for contextualization: (1) establishing the meaning of the text in its original historical and literary context; (2) identifying the divine ethic, ethical ideal, or mind of Christ behind the specific teaching or commands of Scripture (often the term "principles" is used here); and (3) determining ways in which this ethical ideal can be lived out in contemporary contexts.[10] These steps are not necessarily linear, and each informs the others. It is impossible to exegete a text, for example, apart from a broader perspective on Christian ethics.

Informing such steps are rules, guidelines, or criteria that aid in cultural analysis. Almost all hermeneutical theorists set out criteria of one sort or another. Kaiser identifies five

---

10. Most practitioners utilize these steps in one form or another (cf. Vanhoozer's "attend, appraise, advance"). Duvall and Hays (*Grasping God's Word*, 22–25) introduce four, distinguishing one for determining the differences between the biblical context and our own. A similar four-step method appears in William W. Klein, Craig L. Blomberg, and Robert L. Hubbard Jr., *Introduction to Biblical Interpretation* (rev. and expanded; Nashville: Nelson, 2004) 485.

guidelines for cultural interpretation.[11] Cosgrove provides five hermeneutical rules for appealing to Scripture in moral debate.[12] Webb develops eighteen (!) criteria for cultural analysis.[13] Similar lists are provided by Fee and Stuart,[14] Osborne,[15] and Klein, Blomberg, and Hubbard,[16] and others. Below we briefly survey six such criteria.

It should be noted that the goal is not, strictly speaking, to identify which commands in the Bible are cultural and which are supracultural. All commands in the Bible are cultural in that they are given within the context of human culture. Nor are we distinguishing between commands intended for an original audience (say, Timothy, or the churches in Asia Minor) and those intended for all believers. Virtually all commands in Scripture were intended for a specific audience, whether a nation (Israel), a particular church or churches, or an individual. What we are seeking is the divine ethic behind the text, God's will for human behavior, the standards of right and wrong that God demands of his human subjects. The following criteria are among those most often cited to delimit this divine ethic from within the culturally and historically embedded commands of Scripture.

1. CRITERION OF PURPOSE

One of the most widely acknowledged criteria is the identification of the purpose or intention behind the specific commands of Scripture. This purpose will go far in determining

---

11. Walter C. Kaiser Jr. and Moisés Silva, *Introduction to Biblical Hermeneutics* (rev. and expanded; Grand Rapids: Zondervan, 2007), 234–37.

12. Charles Cosgrove, *Appealing to Scripture in Moral Debate: Five Hermeneutical Rules* (Grand Rapids: Eerdmans, 2002).

13. Webb, *Slaves, Women & Homosexuals*, 73–235.

14. Gordon D. Fee and Douglas Stuart, *How to Read the Bible for All Its Worth* (3rd ed.; Grand Rapids: Zondervan, 2003), 74–87.

15. Grant Osborne, *The Hermeneutical Spiral: A Comprehensive Introduction to Biblical Interpretation* (Downers Grove, IL: InterVarsity Press, 2006), 422–26. Osborne discusses eight "principles" or criteria "for determining supracultural content."

16. Klein, Blomberg, Hubbard, *Introduction to Biblical Interpretation*, 485–98: Ten questions for evaluating the level of specificity of the original application.

the manner in which the passage can be applied today. Cosgrove puts it this way: "The purpose (or justification) behind a biblical moral rule carries greater weight than the rule itself."[17] Peter's rationale for commanding believers to greet one another with a kiss of love (1 Peter 5:14) is no doubt that believers are family and so should show familial affection toward one another.[18] This purpose may be fulfilled in different ways in other cultural contexts. The purpose supersedes the rule. Similarly, Paul's command for women to cover their heads in worship (1 Cor. 11:1–16) is secondary to the purpose or intention behind that command. The challenge, in cases like this, is exegeting the text accurately to discern the cultural significance and purpose behind the command. Exegetical uncertainty results in applicational ambiguity.

2. CRITERION OF CULTURAL CORRESPONDENCE (COHERENCE; ANALOGY)

This criterion asserts that the closer the cultural or historical context to our own, the more likely the command (directly) reflects a universal value. Fee and Stuart speak of "comparable particulars": "Whenever we share comparable particulars (i.e., similar specific life situations) with the first-century hearers, God's Word to us is the same as his Word to them."[19] Osborne similarly writes that "we must determine the degree to which the commands are tied to cultural practices current in the first century but not present today."[20]

Paul's command not to get drunk with wine provides a good illustration. Drunkenness in the ancient Near East and the Greco-Roman world resulted in the same kinds of social and societal damage as alcoholism today: loss of control, poor judgment, and a tendency toward physical or verbal abuse. Contrast this with head covering for women, which does not have the same cultural connotations in most Western cultures as it did (and does) in most Middle Eastern

---

17. Cosgrove, *Appealing to Scripture*, 12; cf. Webb, *Slaves, Women & Homosexuals*, 105–10.

18. Cf. Rom. 16:16; 1 Cor. 16:20; 2 Cor. 13:12; 1 Thess. 5:26.

19. Fee and Stuart, *How to Read the Bible*, 75.

20. Osborne, *Hermeneutical Spiral*, 423.

cultures. Cosgrove calls this the criterion of analogy, citing a definition by James M. Gustafson: "Those actions of persons or groups are to be judged morally wrong which are similar to actions that are judged to be wrong or against God's will under similar circumstances in Scripture."[21]

3. CRITERION OF CANONICAL CONSISTENCY

This criterion asserts that ethical imperatives that remain unchanged throughout the Bible — in diverse cultural, social, and historical situations — are more likely to reflect God's will for today than those that differ in times and places.[22] The classic example is homosexual behavior, which receives universal condemnation throughout Scripture. Contrast this with the role of women in leadership, which, while broadly consistent, exhibits notable exceptions (Miriam, Deborah, Priscilla, Phoebe, etc.).

4. CRITERION OF COUNTERCULTURAL WITNESS

This criterion claims that when "teaching transcends the cultural biases of the author and readers, it is more likely to be normative."[23] Jesus' command to love one's enemies (Matt. 5:44) runs contrary to the conventional wisdom of his day and so must be judged as reflecting the heart of God. Paul's instruction to husbands to model Christ's self-sacrificial love toward their wives (Eph. 5:25) was given in a culture where wives were generally viewed as the possession of their husbands. Such commands run counter to contemporary cultural standards and so may be viewed as divine "correctives" to the failures of human culture.

---

21. Cosgrove, *Appealing to Scripture*, 51, citing James M. Gustafson, "The Place of Scripture in Christian Ethics: A Methodological Study," in *Theology and Ethics* (Philadelphia: United Church Press, 1974), 121–45 (citation from p. 133). Jeannine Brown, *Scripture as Communication: Introducing Biblical Hermeneutics* (Grand Rapids: Baker, 2007), while reluctant to develop lists of guidelines, identifies *purpose* and *coherence* as two key questions to ask when (re-) contextualizing passages. These parallel our first and second criteria.

22. Fee and Stuart, *How to Read the Bible*, 82–83.

23. Osborne, *Hermeneutical Spiral*, 424. Cf. Cosgrove, *Appealing to Scripture*, 90–115; Klein, Blomberg, and Hubbard, *Introduction to Biblical Interpretation*, 494–95.

5. CRITERION OF CULTURAL LIMITATIONS

The flip side of the previous criterion is that caution must be exercised when an author is operating within strong cultural or societal constraints.[24] The classic example is slavery. Paul's failure to call for the full emancipation of slaves must be judged within a cultural context where to do so would have resulted in immediate arrest and execution. While Paul repeatedly hints at the discrepancy between the redemption provided by Christ and the institution of slavery (1 Cor. 7:22; Gal. 3:28; Eph. 6:9; Col. 3:24; Philem. 16–17), he is unwilling or unable to openly oppose it. Just as countercultural statements in Scripture are likely to transcend specific situations, so imperatives that appear to be concessions to culture are *less likely* to have universal application.

6. CRITERION OF CREATION PRINCIPLE

This criterion asserts that "a component of a text may be transcultural if its basis is rooted in the original-creation material."[25] The rationale here is that all of God's created order prior to the fall was "very good" (Gen. 1:31), so patterns established in Eden transcend cultural norms. One example is heterosexual monogamy, which is clearly the pre-fall standard for human sexuality (2:24). Both Jesus (Matt. 19:5) and Paul (Eph. 5:31) appeal to this text when discussing sexual ethics.[26] All other sexual behaviors (polygamy, homosexuality, adultery, etc.) fall outside of God's will. Although divorce (Matt. 19:8) and polygamy (Gen. 29:15–30) are tolerated in certain cultural contexts, neither represents God's intention for human relationships.[27]

These criteria represent a sampling of guidelines for cultural analysis. Others could be added, such as a criterion of the *character of God* or a criterion of *redemptive priority*. The

---

24. Fee and Stuart, *How to Read the Bible*, 83–84.

25. Webb, *Slaves, Women & Homosexuals*, 123–45. Cf. Klein, Blomberg, and Hubbard, *Introduction to Biblical Interpretation*, 493. Webb has separate discussions of creation patterns and the principle of primogeniture.

26. Klein, Blomberg, and Hubbard, *Introduction to Biblical Interpretation*, 493.

27. This criterion also relates to Paul's appeal to the created order when asserting male leadership in the church (1 Tim. 2:13). For cautions and a contrary view, see Webb, *Slaves, Women & Homosexuals*, 134–45.

former suggests that fundamental attributes of God, such as love and justice, provide adjudication in disputed areas or when cultural background is obscure. The latter is similar, claiming that commands directly related to God's historical-redemptive purpose take priority over (lesser) issues of church order and function. A command that implies a particular mode of baptism (if this could be established exegetically) would be assigned lower priority than the fundamental command to make and baptize disciples. Or, to propose a more controversial example, a disputed injunction against women teaching men (1 Tim. 2:12) might be viewed as of secondary importance to the pressing need for gospel proclamation in a particular arena.

CONCLUSION

The essays in this volume provide a helpful introduction to how the church can go "beyond the Bible" in addressing the pressing theological and ethical issues of our day. With a myriad of old and new questions facing the church—abortion, euthanasia, gender roles, homosexuality, transsexuality, gambling, genetic and stem cell research, environmental concerns, and many of which we have not yet dreamed—this is surely the beginning, not the end, of this discussion.

With the misuse and abuse of Scripture rampant both within and outside Christendom, it is essential to continue to explore how the biblical text provides normative guidance for God's people today. As this discussion continues, it is hoped that all participants will exhibit true Christian unity, charity, and humility and will apply the—certainly universal—injunction to "make every effort to do what leads to peace and to mutual edification" (Rom. 14:19).

A REFLECTION BY AL WOLTERS

I AM HONORED to be included among those who offer their reflections on the significant hermeneutical discussion in this volume. It has been a challenging but rewarding exercise to read the presentations and responses of the four principal contributors and to formulate my own reflections in reaction to theirs. I have learned a great deal.

In the interest of full disclosure, let me begin by saying a little bit about my own professional and confessional background. I was raised and trained in the Dutch Reformed tradition, sometimes called Neocalvinism, which is associated with such names as Abraham Kuyper and Herman Bavinck in theology and Herman Dooyeweerd in philosophy. I did my graduate work in philosophy at the Christian university that Kuyper founded, the Free University of Amsterdam. I subsequently taught philosophy for ten years at the Institute for Christian Studies in Toronto, a small graduate school standing in the Neocalvinist tradition. In 1984 I switched my disciplinary focus to biblical studies and joined the faculty of another institution in that tradition, Redeemer University College in Ancaster, Ontario. My work since then has been mainly in Old Testament and cognate fields. It is this background, also reflected in my little book *Creation Regained: Biblical Basis for a Reformational Worldview*, which in large measure shapes the reflections that follow.[28]

As I read the contributions and interactions of Kaiser, Doriani, Vanhoozer, and Webb, I am first of all struck by the fact that they are not all talking about the same thing. They

---

28. Grand Rapids: Eerdmans, 1985; 2nd ed., 2005 (the 2nd ed. has a postscript coauthored with Michael W. Goheen).

deal with going "beyond the sacred page" in overlapping but distinct ways. As I see it, they understand the topic in at least the following four senses:

1. bringing the authority of Scripture to bear on issues that Scripture itself does not directly address (e.g., in contemporary bioethics)
2. dealing with ethically troubling biblical injunctions or assumptions (e.g., gender hierarchy or harsh punishments)
3. forging theological categories that, though not themselves explicitly taught in Scripture, systematize and develop explicit biblical teaching (e.g., in understanding Mary as *theotokos*)
4. focusing on the reception history and exegesis of a biblical theme (e.g., gender hierarchy)

Sense number 4 is peculiar to Doriani, who uses it in connection with his discussion of gender roles in Scripture. However, most of Doriani's discussion falls under senses 1 and 2, as does Kaiser's, although Kaiser does not think of his approach as going "beyond" Scripture at all. Vanhoozer deals mainly with senses 1 and 3, while Webb focuses on 2. Needless to say, this diversity of focus does not always make for fruitful interaction between the four authors. Not infrequently, they do not address each other's concerns and thus largely talk past each other.

Since only Doriani addresses sense 4, and only Vanhoozer deals at any length with sense 3, I will leave aside these two senses of going "beyond" Scripture in my further reflections. This can be done the more readily because both are relatively uncontroversial. No one denies that dogmatic theology can legitimately go beyond the explicit formulations of Scripture or that exegesis properly involves historical or linguistic matters that are strictly speaking extrabiblical.

Of the remaining two senses, it is number 2 that is most controversial. What are we to make of passages in Scripture that we find ethically troubling, such as those that require harsh corporal punishment, appear to condone slavery, or sanction gender inequality? Here our authors diverge sharply. Vanhoozer is largely silent on texts of this kind, preferring to lay out his overall hermeneutical approach in general terms. But the other three are prepared to tackle these ethically contentious texts, and their differences are clear. It is especially on the point of gender inequality, as it comes to a head in the interpretation of 1 Timothy 2:11–14, that we see the differences come into sharp focus. Doriani accepts both the traditional face value meaning of the apostle's instruction and its contemporary normativity. Webb also accepts the traditional face value meaning of the passage, but by applying his redemptive-movement hermeneutic denies its contemporary normativity. Kaiser, finally, by engaging in some very fancy exegetical footwork, challenges the traditional understanding of the apostle's words and accepts the contemporary normativity of the passage as reinterpreted by him. Similar strategies are involved in dealing with other kinds of ethically challenging texts. It is clear that it is especially with respect to these texts that the hermeneutical shoe pinches.

It is less controversial to speak of going "beyond" Scripture in sense number 1. It may be difficult to bring to bear the authority of Scripture—that is to say, to *apply* Scripture—on matters that it does not expressly address, but most would consider it a legitimate—in fact, necessary—undertaking. May Christians gamble? How should they celebrate their weddings? Is sex-change surgery acceptable? How about euthanasia? Here our principal authors again adopt different hermeneutical strategies, but now their diverging approaches are more complementary than mutually exclusive.

Kaiser speaks of abstracting general principles from Scripture, which may then be applied to other situations about which Scripture is silent. Doriani emphasizes the importance of Christian character formation geared to the imitation of biblical examples and thus defends the ethical value of biblical narrative. His approach involves both emulating exemplary biblical characters—divine as well as human—and following patterns of behavior that emerge from a careful study of biblical topics. In addition to this, he seeks to retrieve the value of "casuistry" in its original sense. Vanhoozer explores the implications of reading Scripture as the unfinished script of a drama, in which believers are the actors who must creatively improvise in a way that is faithful to the script. As for Webb, he is more interested in dealing with topics that the Bible does address, albeit in a troubling way, than with topics on which it is silent. Nevertheless, his redemptive-movement hermeneutic, which abstracts a "redemptive spirit" from the specificities of the biblical text, has clear implications for going "beyond the sacred page" also in sense number 1.

As I mentioned, these approaches are not all mutually exclusive. In fact, it is striking how our authors tend to agree with each other on this level. Both Webb and Vanhoozer state that their own approach is really a kind of special case of Kaiser's "principlizing" method, while Doriani's rehabilitation of "casuistry" also readily fits here. Surprisingly, both Doriani and Webb, although they strongly disagree with each other when it comes to dealing with the "troubling" texts (sense number 2), both declare themselves to be in basic sympathy with Vanhoozer's theodramatic proposal, while Vanhoozer in turn largely endorses Doriani's overall approach. It is also noteworthy that all but Kaiser emphasize the nonpropositional dimensions of biblical meaning, whether that be symbol, narrative, "spirit," or plot.

I turn now to my own reflections, in critical dialogue with the four principal authors, on the hermeneutical move "beyond the sacred page" in these two senses. I begin with the most contentious one, which deals with passages in Scripture that we find morally offensive. When I say "we," it is important to note that this is not a universal "we." It is probably true to say that most Christians over the last two thousand years, and perhaps even most Christians worldwide today, do not find it particularly offensive that the Bible — to mention only three representative examples — sanctions disciplining children with a rod, raises no moral objections to slavery, and in many ways assigns women a subordinate position in human society. The "we" I am talking about refers largely to educated Christians in the West over the last century or two. In fact, the "we" who are offended by the Bible's instructions and assumptions about corporal punishment and gender roles were a small minority even among educated Western Christians, male and female, only a generation ago.

It is useful to remember that the Bible has been offensive to different people in different ways throughout church history. The church fathers took offense at the unabashedly material depiction of God's blessing in the Old Testament, at the Bible's frank description of God's passions, and its failure to live up to the linguistic and literary standards of the Greek classics. Modern Christians have taken offense at the Bible's miracles, or its "blood theology," or its apparent theological or historical inconsistencies. Contemporary Christians take offense at its depiction of God in masculine terms or its teaching concerning eternal punishment. In every age there have been attempts to find hermeneutical ways to reduce or remove the offense, perhaps by allegory, perhaps by demythologization, perhaps through an appeal to God's "accommodation" to our understanding.

In our day, what is especially troubling about Scripture, both in our culture at large and among "us" educated Western Christians who are a significant part of that culture, is the way Scripture appears to accept as a matter of course what we instinctively find morally unacceptable: wars of extermination, harsh punishment, slavery, gender inequality, and racial favoritism. In a civilization in which individual "human rights" represent something like the ethical *summum bonum* and the list of cardinal sins begins with racism and sexism, followed closely by violence and authoritarianism, the Bible cannot fail to be a highly offensive book.

I take it to be one of the chief virtues of Webb's contribution to this volume (as well as his other recent publications) that he has brought this reality to the attention of North American evangelicals. I believe he is right when he argues, against Kaiser and Doriani, that the Bible accepts the institution of slavery. Likewise, I believe he is also right (against Kaiser and with Doriani) that Paul in 1 Timothy 2:12 forbids women to teach and have authority over a man. Furthermore, I believe he is right that contemporary evangelical leaders need to acknowledge that their pro-spanking advice represents a considerable softening of the Bible's explicit teaching on the matter of corporal punishment. In general, there is a considerable gap between what the Bible recommends with respect to disciplining children with the rod and what "we" (including conservative evangelical leaders) find acceptable in contemporary North American families.

However, although I believe Webb is right in diagnosing the problem, I believe he is wrong in the solution he proposes. Let me briefly explain why I take issue with his "redemptive-movement hermeneutic," taking my cue from the diagram he offers. There are two primary phases in the overall trajectory of his "redemptive movement." The first is the movement from the original culture (designated as X: ancient Near Eastern culture in the case of the Old Testament, Greco-Roman culture in the case of the New) to the concrete words in the biblical text (Y), and the second is from the latter to an "ultimate ethic" (Z). The biblical text must be read in the light of this double movement; in fact, a crucial part of the *meaning* of Y (its "movement meaning" or "redemptive spirit") is the way it is situated between X and Z.

In the case of Old Testament texts there is the further complication that there is canonical movement from Old Testament to New, but this is not included in Webb's diagram. In fact, the canonical component of his "movement meaning" plays only a marginal role in his discussion in this volume, because he sees little discontinuity between Old and New Testaments on the topics of slavery and corporal punishment. Here I would ask the question: Is there not significant discontinuity in the way the Mosaic law functions in the New Testament?

My first problem with this model is that it treats "ancient Near Eastern" culture as an ethically monolithic entity. Chronologically, the model does not distinguish between centuries, or even millennia, of ancient history. Nor does it distinguish geographically between such diverse cultures as those of Egypt, Canaan, Assyria, Babylonia, Sumer, and Persia. The same goes for "Greco-Roman" culture, which includes at least the different cultures of the Greeks and Romans, not to mention that of Second Temple Judaism. Furthermore, it assumes without argument that the "movement" from X to Y (I would prefer, with Vanhoozer, to speak of "synchronic contrast") is always one of ethical *improvement*—improvement measured against an "ultimate ethic," which is left undefined but seems to be allied to a Western ideal of individual human rights.

But is the movement always an improvement? Is it not possible that the legal position of women in the Persian Empire, for example, might be better than the legal position of women in Israel? I suspect it was. Is it not possible that Roman law, at least measured by modern Western standards, was in many ways an *advance* over Israelite law—for example, in giving a wife the right to divorce her husband? I suspect it was. Furthermore, if we look at the question of female cultic leadership from the standpoint of an "ultimate ethic," the Bible does not seem to offer any improvement over its surrounding cultures, since it excludes women from the priesthood throughout the Old Testament and restricts their ecclesiastical role in the New. By contrast, in the cultures of both the ancient Near East and the Roman Empire, priestesses were common.

It is clear that there were other areas, too, where the cultural practices of pagan cultures were more "advanced" than those presupposed or prescribed in the canonical writings of the Jews and Christians. I think, for example of their art, philosophy, and literature. If it is objected that these matters are cultural, not ethical, then a case will have to be made for making that distinction. After all, we are talking about bringing the authority of Scripture to bear on *all* areas of human life.

Another objection against this part of Webb's proposal, especially since it is a crucial component of what he calls the "redemptive spirit" of the biblical text, is that it depends on historical information that the biblical exegete, let alone the ordinary Bible reader, may not have. Before the nineteenth century our knowledge of ancient Near Eastern culture was extremely limited. The languages and cultures of the ancient Egyptians, Sumerians, Babylonians, Assyrians, and Canaanites were largely lost until that century, and Persia was imperfectly known, mainly from Herodotus's *Histories*. And even now, after all the decipherments and excavations, there are huge lacunae in our knowledge of these cultures. Is our ability to understand properly the "redemptive spirit" of the ethical injunctions of the Bible dependent on that kind of historical knowledge? I venture to doubt it. It certainly does not square well with the Reformers' notion of the *perspicuitas* of Scripture.

I hasten to add that I believe it is legitimate and useful to note, wherever we can, the ethical "synchronic contrast" between the moral teaching of the Bible and that of its surrounding pagan cultures. In the same way I believe it is crucial to be alert to the progressive revelation of Scripture, notably the "diachronic contrast" between Old Testament and New. My objection is to seeing these two contrasts as part of the same "redemptive" trajectory that leads from ancient pagan culture to a postcanonical ultimate ethic that bears a close resemblance to contemporary Western values.

This leads me to the difficulty I have with the second phase of the overall movement Webb sketches, that from Y to Z. My problem here is that there appears to be no standard by which to measure what an "ultimate ethic" might be. A clue to what is in fact the implicit and unacknowledged standard for Webb is provided by the proximity in the diagram of "Ultimate Ethic" to "Our Culture." To be sure, the latter is qualified by the words in parentheses: "where it happens to reflect a better ethic than Y," but no criterion is provided by which we can judge that "our culture" on this or that point reflects a better ethic than Y. This is a remarkable statement when we recall that Y represents "the concrete words of the text," that is, the biblical text. For all practical purposes it seems that Webb's "Ultimate Ethic" is pretty well equated with "Our Culture," at least insofar as the latter is the bearer of humane and liberal values. It looks for all the world as though the values "we" hold trump the explicit ethical instruction of Scripture.

Webb is aware that he is theologically vulnerable at this point, and therefore he argues that the "movement meaning" (or "redemptive spirit") that leads to, and thus gives biblical warrant for, the better ethic found in our culture is actually found *within* the biblical text. He does this by distinguishing two kinds of meaning in the ethical instruction of Scripture: (1) the meaning derived from reading the text in its immediate literary context, which can be characterized as "on the page" or "isolated" meaning, and (2) "movement meaning," captured from reading the text in its historical and canonical context, which yields the "underlying spirit" of the text. It is in this *spirit* of the text that an ultimate ethic is reflected (see his diagram). Both kinds can be described as the "meaning of words." The second kind of meaning is often missed, but it is "absolutely crucial" for contemporary Christian ethics. In fact, it constitutes the "integral heartbeat of the text," "the authorial heartbeat of the biblical text itself."

It is by means of this theory of two kinds of meaning that Webb is enabled to defend himself against the charge that his method seeks to establish a "better ethic" than the ethic of the New Testament. After all, the better ethic is already contained in the "movement meaning" of the New Testament, properly understood. Yet he can also say, as we have seen, that our culture does in some significant ways reflect "a better ethic than Y," where Y represents the concrete words of the biblical text—that is, the "on the page" meaning. In this way he can have his cake (hold to contemporary values) and eat it too (claim faithfulness to Scripture). In fact, according to his scheme, the same text can have contradictory meanings. Thus, the "on the page" meaning of Paul's prohibition in 1 Timothy 2:12 is that he forbids women to teach or have authority over a man, but the "movement meaning" or "redemptive spirit" is that women are free to do just that.

I conclude, therefore, that Webb's solution to the problem of the ethically troubling biblical texts is to be rejected. Although I take seriously his assurances that he does not mean to undermine the divine authority of these ethically troubling biblical texts or the finality of the New Testament, and although I do not doubt his sincerity in affirming his allegiance to a classical evangelical doctrine of Scripture, I do not find his protestations theologically credible.

Nevertheless, Webb has identified a serious problem, and he is to be commended for insisting that it not be swept under the rug. Much of the ethical teaching of Scripture really is offensive to many in our culture, Christians included. In briefly throwing out some suggestions for an alternative approach, I want to begin by acknowledging that these suggestions do not offer a definitive solution either. I want to take to heart the words of Wendell Berry quoted at the head of Vanhoozer's chapter: "It may be that when we no longer know what to do, we have come to our real work; and that when we no longer know which way to go, we have come to our real journey." Perhaps the best way forward is to acknowledge our own bafflement and to proceed with an attitude of epistemological humility and willingness to learn from each other and church history.

Undoubtedly a good place to begin is Doriani's maxim: "If Scripture says something I do not prefer, then so much the worse for my preferences." When we are offended by something in the ethical teaching of Scripture, the fault is probably our own. We may very well be taking offence at something that is in fact good and true. As already noted, Christians in the past have taken offence at — or been embarrassed by — all kinds of things in Scripture, from its unabashed earthliness and frank eroticism to its flawed heroes and passionate God. Yet it is these very "offensive" features of Scripture that later Christians have come to treasure, to regard as something to glory in, not be ashamed of. Each age has devised its hermeneutical strategies to diminish or eliminate these scandalous aspects of Scripture, from patristic allegorizing to the "lisping" metaphor of Calvin's accommodation theory, to the *Geschichte/Historie* distinction devised by Bultmann. Yet in hindsight these hermeneutical strategies seem questionable. Perhaps their devisers should have been more critical of the assumptions and sensibilities that they adopted from their own milieu, and we should do the same.

At the same time, I believe that there is an important sense in which many distinctively Western values are the product of Christian influence. The many centuries of Christian cultural dominance in Europe and its colonies, despite its undeniable shadow sides, is also largely responsible, I believe, for the rise of such key notions as human rights, the dignity of human beings (male and female), equality before the law, and a concern for the disadvantaged. To be sure, especially through the Enlightenment and its revolutions, this Christian heritage has been largely secularized, but it remains significant that these ideals have only arisen in the erstwhile Christian nations of the West. To that degree I believe that there is some validity to Webb's thesis that there is a connection between contemporary Western values and the ethical teachings of Scripture. But I differ from him in his uncritical acceptance of these values, in his attempt to read them back into Scripture, and his use of them (paradoxically) to judge the ethical adequacy of Scripture.

It is my belief that an appropriate attitude to Scripture is one that affirms everything Scripture affirms, however unpalatable that may be to us today. In the case of the ethically offensive texts we are talking about, that means that we should affirm that it was right and just for Moses to regulate slavery rather than call for its abolition, for Solomon to recommend that children be disciplined with the rod, and for Paul to bid women to be silent in the churches. That would be true even if by contemporary standards the surrounding cultures in biblical times were ethically further advanced than Moses, Solomon, and Paul—although usually that is not the case. Any set of values that serves to undermine such an attitude of Scripture affirmation, or to suggest that Scripture in some of its teaching is inadequate or deficient, should be viewed with suspicion.

This does not mean, however, that there cannot be a process of refinement or enrichment of the ethical teaching of Scripture. Especially with regard to slavery and corporal punishment, both of which are strictly speaking *juridical* matters, we can simultaneously affirm the legitimacy of what Scripture says about them and recognize that a normative unfolding of culture calls for a richer and more nuanced understanding of what justice requires. In the language of the Dutch Christian philosopher Herman Dooyeweerd, whose disciplinary specialty was the philosophy of law, the normative principle of justice, which is given in creation, allows for a deepening of its meaning as society differentiates and unfolds. Thus a strict "eye-for-an-eye" legal system, though genuinely *just* in an undifferentiated sense (not least because it recognizes the principle of proportionality), is nevertheless relatively undeveloped compared to more advanced conceptions of the legal order, which take into account (for example) mitigating circumstances in determining appropriate punishment, or which recognize individual human rights. In Dooyeweerd's view this is all part of a much larger—indeed cosmic—"opening-up process" that is implicit in creation and that legitimates many features of modern society, even in the midst of secularization.

This is not the place to explain Dooyeweerd's philosophy more fully, but it should be noted that in developing this view he was giving philosophical expression to the basic Neocalvinist worldview articulated by Kuyper and Bavinck, which among other things is characterized by the following seminal ideas: a broad and differentiated view of *creation*, the normative *unfolding* of that creation in culture and society, and *general revelation* as the epistemological basis for human knowledge about creation and its unfolding. In addition, this tradition stresses that creation (with its general revelation) can only be read aright in the light of Scripture (with its special revelation). As Calvin put it, Scripture functions like the spectacles (the corrective lenses) through which we must learn to read the world. My own little work, *Creation Regained*, was conceived as a popular introduction to the Neocalvinist understanding of the biblical worldview and its elaboration in the philosophy of Dooyeweerd and others.

I turn now to a discussion of what I have called sense number 1 of the notion of going "beyond the sacred page." Here we are dealing with questions of Christian discipleship that Scripture does not address directly, so that the problem is not that explicit biblical teaching is troubling, but rather that it is lacking. Since Webb has little to say about this way of understanding our topic, my remaining reflections will interact mainly with the other three.

Although Kaiser prefers not to speak of going "beyond" Scripture at all, he does apply Scripture to a wide array of contemporary issues. His method is to abstract principles from Scripture and to apply these principles to the issues in question. In one sense, this is uncontroversial. As we have seen, both Vanhoozer and Webb see their own approaches as a version of "principlizing" as well, and Doriani's casuistry also deals with the application of principles to cases. My problem with Kaiser's chapter is that three of the five issues he deals with (women in church leadership, homosexuality, and slavery) are questions that *are* addressed in Scripture, and his discussion is largely devoted to exegesis of the relevant passages, not with abstracting more general principles from them. Furthermore, when he does lay down a number of principles, such as the six he lists for dealing with the question of euthanasia, it is unclear how they are derived from Scripture, or indeed whether they are valid principles at all.

With respect to his first principle, does Scripture really teach that life is sacred? Even if this is qualified to say that all *human* life is sacred, and "sacred" is here understood to mean *inviolate*, it is doubtful whether this common maxim is biblically valid. Clearly not all taking of human life is forbidden. Kaiser mentions self-defense and just war as exceptions, but there are also other kinds of homicide that the Bible appears to sanction, such as the slaughter of the priests of Baal in 1 Kings 18:40. It also seems perilous to derive Kaiser's second principle—really a further specification of the first, namely, that life is sacred even in desperate circumstances—from the story in 2 Samuel 1, where David executes the Amalekite for allegedly killing Saul in his extremity. It is not at all clear that the inspired narrator is here condoning this summary execution, which was in any case based on false information. Besides, what made the Amalekite guilty in David's eyes was not that he took a human life, but that the life he took was that of "the LORD's anointed" (2 Sam. 1:14). It may be that ethical principles can be derived from Scripture, but this is not the way to derive them.

At the same time I want to express my appreciation for Kaiser's critical discussion of I. Howard Marshall's book *Beyond the Bible: Moving from Scripture to Theology*. In my opinion he is exactly right when he writes: "We cannot agree that we, who are the subsequent readers of this text [i.e., Scripture], can in some similar way 'go beyond' the text based on an alleged apostolic example. Our interpretive contributions are not in the same stream as the revelatory words of God." In my judgment this is the crucial issue with all forms of "trajectory" hermeneutics.

There is much in Doriani's chapter with which I resonate strongly. I appreciate his insistence that we must be suspicious of our own sensibilities when something the Bible teaches offends us, his emphasis on the value of nonpropositional modes of communication (especially narrative) in Scripture, and his resolute refusal to make the Bible say things it doesn't say about gender roles. Nevertheless, I was in some ways disappointed by his chapter. I am myself an advocate of a redemptive-historical approach to Scripture and an admirer of Geerhardus Vos, so I expected to agree with most of what Doriani had to say. However, his chapter spends much less time in explaining and defending the classical redemptive-historical approach (in the tradition of Vos, Ridderbos, and Gaffin) than in trying to compensate for what he takes to be its weaknesses.

Essentially, I take Doriani to be saying that this approach, for all its strengths in other areas, is not helpful for giving biblical answers to questions not addressed in Scripture. Consequently, for the subject of this volume it needs to be supplemented by other approaches, especially the *imitatio Christi* (and *Dei*), the ethical formation of character through nondoctrinal literary genres, and ethical reasoning in the tradition of classical casuistry. Ironically, therefore, we find Doriani becoming a defender, among other things, of the very "exemplarism" that so many advocates of the redemptive-historical approach, at least in the Dutch tradition, so vigorously opposed.[29]

There is a sense in which I think Doriani is right in his assessment of the redemptive-historical approach to Scripture; its strength is not that it helps us plan God-pleasing weddings, or discern a faithful way to do architecture, but rather that it helps us see the progressive revelation-in-history, the organic unity, and the christocentric focus of the

---

29. See Sidney Greidanus, *Sola Scriptura: Problems and Principles in Preaching Historical Texts* (Kampen: Kok, 1970).

Scriptures as a whole. In addition, by reading everything in
Scripture in the light of what God is doing in Christ over the
centuries to salvage this wretched, sin-cursed world, it also
has a bias against the tendency of many Christians to read
the Bible primarily for the sake of moral lessons or clues to
other kinds of right and wrong behavior. From the point of
view of redemptive history, this misses the central religious
point (i.e., Christ) and wrongheadedly focuses on matters
that are at best secondary and at worst irrelevant. In the
Neocalvinist tradition in which I was raised and educated,
we speak here of moralism or more broadly of biblicism.

I see something of this tendency in Doriani when he
searches the Scriptures for clues as to how Christians should
celebrate weddings, or when he points out in his response to
Vanhoozer that there are actually more texts that could have
been cited to give biblical support to the category of "fittingness" in the latter's hermeneutical theory. I see the same tendency in his reply to the Christian architects who came to
him for biblical advice on how to properly balance the competing claims of aesthetics, safety, and cost-effectiveness.
Is the answer really to be found in the eminently sensible
Mosaic rule about having a railing on a flat roof? To my
mind this is to read the Bible against the grain, to ask it
questions that it was not meant to answer.

I do not for a moment wish to deny that reading biblical
narratives shapes a Christian's moral character, or that there
is a significant sense in which we should emulate the saints
of Scripture (flawed though they be) and should imitate the
character of Christ and God. But in most cases that is not the
point of the biblical narratives, and in any case it is often difficult to decide whether the behavior of a biblical character
is something to be followed or avoided. Was David right or
wrong to have the Amalekite killed—or is that beside the
point? Was Rahab justified in lying about the whereabouts
of the spies in Jericho, or is this question an unwarranted
distraction from the message of the narrative? All these
questions become even more acute when we interrogate the
Scriptures on matters that are far removed from the biblical world, such as reproductive technology, Christian day
schools, or industrial relations.

It is not that Doriani is unaware of this. In an excellent passage he writes the following: "Of course, Scripture is not sufficient in the sense that it tells us everything we need to know. Farmers and engineers must study the physical and technological world, athletes must know the rules and techniques of their game, fathers must know their children, and theologians need their lexicons, grammars, and histories." To this I can only say "Amen." But then he adds the following telling sentence at the conclusion of this paragraph: "But we need no God-given revelation beyond the biblical canon." Here I would demur. It seems that Doriani is forgetting about another kind of God-given revelation, which in fact comes through, however imperfectly, in the very things that farmers and engineers and athletes need to know and enable them to be good at their jobs. What I have in mind is the revelation we briefly alluded to above, namely, general revelation.

It is no accident that the same tradition that did so much to promote a redemptive-historical approach to Scripture and therefore warned against moralism and biblicism is also the tradition that has an especially robust doctrine of general revelation, tied to an equally robust doctrine of creation. It is perhaps not surprising that Neocalvinists like Dooyeweerd, following in the footsteps of Kuyper and Bavinck, prefer to speak in this connection of "creation revelation." I shall return to this theme in a moment.

It is perhaps fair to say that Vanhoozer is like Doriani in both affirming a redemptive-historical approach and seeking to elaborate on it. In Vanhoozer's case, this involves working out the implications of conceiving of redemptive history as a drama, with Scripture as the script and contemporary believers as the actors who improvise the penultimate act of the drama. In adopting this metaphor for biblical hermeneutics, Vanhoozer is picking up (with modifications) a suggestion put forward by N. T. Wright, who has been followed on this point by a number of other evangelical writers, notably Brian Walsh and Richard Middleton[30]

---

30. Brian Walsh and Richard Middleton, *Transforming Vision: Shaping a Christian Worldview* (Downers Grove, IL: InterVarsity Press, 1984).

and Craig Bartholomew and Mike Goheen.[31] I myself have adopted the model in the new chapter which Goheen and I wrote for the second edition of *Creation Regained* (2005).

As I see it, the chief advantages of this way of looking at Scripture are that it highlights the grand narrative that ties together the diverse biblical materials, that it places the reader of Scripture in the position of a *participant* in that biblical grand narrative (rather than spectator), and that it underscores the element of *improvisation* involved in the church's calling to be faithful to that grand narrative. It is, of course, especially the third element that comes into play when we reflect on bringing the authority of Scripture to bear on matters that it does not itself directly address. There is a significant measure of discretionary judgment, with little or no explicit guidance from the playwright's words, in an actor's improvisation. I take Vanhoozer's chapter to be in large part a defense of the legitimacy of improvisation—creative and faithful improvisation—in the life of Christian discipleship.

It is true that Vanhoozer's entire project, hinging as it does on the metaphor of a drama, is itself a bold example of going beyond the sacred page. Drama as we know it did not exist in ancient Israel (it is in fact a product of pagan Greece), and the metaphor of acting has a decidedly negative ring in the New Testament. Jesus was not being complimentary when he called the scribes and Pharisees "actors" (*hypokritai*). Nevertheless, we need not dismiss the image of Scripture as "script" on that account, any more than we should rule out other unbiblical metaphors to describe Scripture, such as musical score, love letter, library—or indeed "book." However, we do need to be cautious in not pressing the dramatic analogy too far. With that proviso, I am basically sympathetic to Vanhoozer's proposal.

Central to that proposal is the distinction between three "worlds": the world *behind* the text (the original historical situation of the biblical author), the world *of* the text (redemptive history—the theodrama—as projected or implied by

---

31. Craig Bartholomew and Mike Goheen, *The Drama of Scripture: Finding Our Place in the Biblical Story* (Grand Rapids: Baker, 2004).

the text), and the world *in front of* the text (the historical situation of the believing reader). Improvisation occurs when the believer (or the church) performs the second world in the third. That improvisation must be creative, but it must also be *faithful* to the theodrama of the second world, the one projected by the script.

The key question, therefore, becomes: How can we know when the improvisation is faithful? What criteria apply? On this question Vanhoozer is remarkably vague. One "criterion" or "norm" he proposes is the "implied canonical reader," who is someone "who knows how to follow the direction not only of specific texts, but of the larger story of Scripture of which they are a part." I find this singularly unhelpful. It is saying in effect: "If you want to know how to be faithful, take as your norm the person who would hypothetically be faithful." It does not provide us with standards for discrimination. What we need, as Vanhoozer himself puts it, is "a set of criteria with which to distinguish script-ural from unscriptural improvisations, faithful from unfaithful performances." He then proceeds to speak of the category of "fittingness," but to my mind that is just another way of saying "faithfulness" and does not bring us any further.

Vanhoozer does provide us with what he calls "six tests for discerning right theodramatic correspondence," but these tend not to deal at all with the correspondence (or faithfulness, or fittingness) between the second and third worlds, which is the crucial point at issue. Thus, while I resonate with the overall way in which Vanhoozer frames the question, I am frustrated by the lack of conceptual tools that can help in actually deciding cases. In general, then, Vanhoozer's theodramatic model does more to give an overall theological justification for the exercise of discretionary judgment (improvisation) than to provide guidelines for doing so.

This conclusion is borne out by the examples he discusses. Although his discussion of doctrinal issues (Mary as *theotokos* and her immaculate conception) properly belongs to sense number 3 of our topic, it can also serve to illustrate the point that his approach makes little difference in the way we assess these matters. At least I have not been able to discover this difference. I am quite prepared to grant that Mary plays a key redemptive-historical role in Scripture, but is it really significant that she may be the only biblical character (apart from Jesus himself) who appears in Acts Two, Three, and Four of the biblical drama? Were there no other Jews, later to become Christians, who were contemporaries of Mary and lived through those same Acts, though perhaps they happen not to be mentioned in Scripture?

As for the application of Vanhoozer's method to ethical questions, I note that he restricts himself to a single example (transsexuality), and here too it is not clear to me how his theodramatic approach makes a difference to either his mode of argumentation or his conclusion. He simply argues from creation, as most orthodox Christians would, but the fact that creation is Act One in the theodrama makes no appreciable difference, as far as I can tell.

I return finally to the point about general revelation. It is telling that none of the four authors refer to it, even though it is part of standard Protestant theology. Instead, their discussions are all about special revelation as contained in the Bible. The only kind of normativity that they want to acknowledge is that which comes from the Bible. In my judgment, this is a misconception of the Reformation doctrine of *sola Scriptura*. Special and general revelation need to be read in the light of each other. To be sure, biblical revelation has epistemological priority over God's revelation in creation, but both come with divine authority. God speaks to us through the very structure of creation—creation conceived in a broad biblical sense to include the God-ordained fabric of human culture and society.

The structure of the family, the dynamics of our emotional life, the principles of art and jurisprudence, are all part of God's creational design, and he speaks to us through them. That is how the sages of Israel acquired their wisdom and how they themselves talk about others gaining practical know-how in everyday experience. I like the picture of the farmers in Isaiah 28, of whose farming methods the prophet declares: "Their God instructs them and teaches them the right way" (Isa. 28:26). God instructs the farmer, not through inspired prophecy, but through familiarity—in the light of such prophecy—with the creational realities of his daily work. As I put in *Creation Regained*:

> God's revelation in creation is not *verbal*; its message does not come to us in human language. "They have no speech, there are no words," writes David of the heavens telling the glory of God (Ps. 19:3). Mankind has in large measure lost the capacity to interpret what the heavens are saying in their wordless message. The Scriptures, on the other hand, are couched in the words of ordinary human discourse. In traditional terminology, they are *revelatio verbalis*, "word revelation," as opposed to *revelatio naturalis*, "revelation of nature" (i.e. of creation). They are plain in a way that general revelation never is, have a "perspicuity" that is not found in the book of nature. In a way, therefore, the Scriptures are like a verbal commentary on the dimly perceived sign language of creation. Or, to change the image slightly, the revelation of God's will in Scripture is like a verbal explanation that an architect gives to an incompetent builder who has forgotten how to read the blueprint. Without the explanation the builder is at a loss, able to puzzle out in general terms what the blueprint indicates perhaps—how many rooms and stories the building is to have and the like—but in the dark about some of the most basic features of its style and design, or even whether it is to be a house or a factory or a barn. With the explanations everything becomes much clearer, and the builder can proceed with confidence.
>
> Perhaps the blueprint image can also make another point clearer. Let us suppose that the architect has tape-recorded the explanation. Unable to consult the architect directly on every small point, the builder would have to depend on both the recording and the blueprint for sufficient information to put up the house—the recording for general information, and the blueprint for all the specific measurements and sizes and many other details that would likely become clear only on careful study and through experience as the building progresses. It is in this same way that we must continue to discern, through empirical study and historical experience, what God's specific norms are for

areas of human life that the Scriptures do not explicitly express—industrial relations, for example, or the mass media, or literary criticism.[32]

In my opinion it is such an understanding of creation and creational revelation, coupled with a redemptive-historical/theodramatic understanding of Scripture, that offers the greatest promise for going "beyond the sacred page" in these kinds of matters.

---

32. Wolters, *Creation Regained* (2nd. ed.), 18–19.

A REFLECTION BY CHRISTOPHER J. H. WRIGHT

WHEN I FIRST READ THE TITLE of this book and was invited to be among the respondents, my inner response was, "I do that every time I preach—and so do all preachers who seek to do biblical exposition." One could, of course, simply read aloud the Bible passage and thereby not go "beyond the Bible" (at least not any more than every translation necessarily goes beyond the original texts in some sense). But the moment one opens one's mouth to *preach* the text, one is "going beyond" it—in at least this crucial sense: the text was not *written to* the people in front of me, but my sermon is *preached to* them. And the implicit claim of the preacher is: "Here is what the writer of this text said to the people he was writing to or for, and here is what I believe God wants to say through it to you today."

My second early thought was that although I like the original title of the book ("Beyond the Sacred Page"), which reflects a hymn familiar to those of us of a certain age at least, the book's present title uses a similar phrase in a somewhat different way from the original hymn (moving beyond it, one might say). The hymn "Break Thou the Bread of Life" says,

> Beyond the sacred page
> I seek Thee, Lord;
> My spirit longs for Thee,
> Thou Living Word.

Our book is about moving beyond the sacred page in the sense of using and applying the Scriptures in contexts that are chronologically "beyond" (i.e., after) the Bible—a hermeneutical task. The hymn was about gazing "beyond" (i.e., through) the Scriptures to the living person of Jesus

Christ and encountering him in the reading of them—a devotional or relational task. For the devout reader of Scripture, however, the two merge into one, since one seeks the clearest hermeneutical understanding of the text in today's world, not to claim academic credits, but to enable faithful discipleship of the living Christ. I believe all four authors who present views in the book would argue that this is indeed what they are seeking, explicitly or implicitly.

As I then read all four views carefully, there seems much to appreciate in each one, and it seemed increasingly unlikely that I might choose one and reject the rest. Each view takes the Bible seriously in different ways.

- *The principlizing approach* of Walter Kaiser treats the Bible (rightly) as containing objective revealed truth that can be grasped and expressed by human minds in indicative and imperative moods. There are things that can be known and stated to be true, and there are moral implications that call for our response.

- *The redemptive-historical approach* of Dan Doriani sees the Bible (rightly) as fundamentally bearing witness to what God has done in Christ for the salvation of the world, such that Christ is the central point of all biblical hermeneutics.

- *The drama-of-redemption approach* of Kevin Vanhoozer sees the Bible (rightly) not merely as a narrative that we read "from the outside," as one might enjoy a novel, but as the script of the great divine drama in which we are actually participants. The act of faithful biblical hermeneutics is necessarily self-involving and performative.

- *The redemptive-movement approach* of William Webb perceives the historically embedded nature of the biblical text (rightly) and urges us to take note that God has given us his Word within the flow of human history and culture, such that it is necessary for us to take account of that flow within the Bible itself, and to discern the direction and destination of that flow as we seek to be faithful and obedient to the Lord in our own historical context.

So I concluded that the four views are not only complementary in various ways, but actually *need each other*, in order to avoid obsessive imbalance at key points. The redemptive-movement approach, for example, has to arrive at some formulation of what obedience to the text will mean in today's world, and thus it cannot avoid some degree of "principlizing" from the text—even if the principle arrived at will take into account more than may be contained in a single text itself. And the most dedicated "principlizer," working within some understanding of the canonical wholeness of Scripture, cannot isolate the principles he or she draws from any particular text without the contribution and modification that comes from knowing the rest of the Bible story with its fundamental witness to Christ, discerning the guiding hand of God in the drama (then and now), and perceiving where the text itself is pointing—both within the Bible itself and (dare I say it) beyond. Thus, although all four authors have helpfully critiqued each other's views, none has completely rejected another but has sought to show the inadequacies of any single approach taken on its own.

MOVING "BEYOND THE BIBLE" IN THE BIBLE ITSELF?

Does the Bible help us in the task of moving beyond it when responding to it in our own day, by giving us examples of people moving beyond the sacred page within the Bible itself? That is, do we find cases where someone comes to an ethical stance or decision in new circumstances on the basis of a text from whatever Scriptures existed at the time? And if so, does the Bible provide cases of people doing so in any or all of the four ways explored in the views? As I scanned the Bible with this question in mind, it did indeed appear that all four views could claim some biblical precedents. I am sure that further thought could multiply the examples suggested below.

APPLIED PRINCIPLES

When Amaziah came to the throne of Judah, he executed those who had assassinated his father, Joash. He did not, however, slay their sons along with them, on the basis of the law found in Deuteronomy 24:16: "Parents are not to be put to death for their children, nor children put to death for their parents; each of you will die for your own sin" (2 Kings 14:5-6). The law embodies a principle of individual account-ability before the law (in normal human judicial affairs), and Amaziah understands the principle and applies it (even though it might have been more politically expedient not to leave the sons of the assassins alive).

Paul perceives a principle in a rather more obscure Old Testament law and does not hesitate to apply it in a com-pletely different situation: "Do not muzzle an ox while it is treading out the grain" (Deut. 25:4). One might see a gen-eral level principle here: "Be kind to animals." But the law is more specific and so must our principle be, for the ox is a *working* animal, whose labor is for our benefit. At least one should let it eat while it works, since it is providing food for its owner. So the principle might be refined, "A working animal should be allowed to enjoy the product of its own effort."

Paul, however, is talking about working missionaries like himself and asks the fundamental question, "Don't we have the right to food and drink?" (1 Cor. 9:4). In answer, he quotes (among other things), the law from Deuteronomy, on the assumption that if God is concerned about working animals, he must be concerned for working humans. So he articulates the principle in human form: "When farmers plow and thresh, they should be able to do so in the hope of sharing in the harvest" (v. 10). It seems unquestionable that Paul is going "beyond the Bible" here in his use of this text and applying it in a situation that the text itself knew nothing about. But he makes his hermeneutical move (with its ethical and pastoral implications) by discerning the prin-ciple within the text and extending it by fairly self-evident analogy.

REDEMPTIVE HISTORY

The Council of Jerusalem (Acts 15) was convened in order to tackle the theological and ethical challenge presented by the successful Gentile mission (would that all church councils had such origins). Undoubtedly the critics of

Paul's missionary work (not just the unbelieving Jews, but also Jewish believers in Jesus as Messiah who had not yet grasped the full implications of their faith, it seemed) were convinced that Paul had gone "beyond the sacred page" altogether. Surely his practice of telling Gentiles that they were now part of the covenant community of God's people without circumcision or strict obedience to the law of Moses was dangerously unscriptural. Paul's own writings and the record of James's conclusion to the Jerusalem debate show that, on the contrary, the "new thing" of Gentile inclusion was entirely in accord with the flow of redemptive history, now reaching its fulfillment in the events of Jesus' death and resurrection. So their hermeneutic of key texts was governed by this central understanding of what the texts led up to.

THEODRAMA

The narrative of the exodus provides the theodrama that was to govern Israel's behavior. This is seen positively in the way many laws include reference to the exodus in motivational clauses that link what is required of Israel (e.g., in treatment of foreigners) to what God did for them in Egypt. They were to play out that same script in new circumstances in their own land.[33] And it is seen negatively when the prophets reminded Israel of the script and condemned them for failing to perform consistently with it.[34]

The New Testament drama of the cross not only accomplished our salvation, but it provides the script for Christian behavior, even in oppressive circumstances, as Peter pointed out to Christian slaves suffering unjustly (1 Peter 2:18–23).

MOVEMENT MEANING

The case quoted above of Amaziah's refusal to kill the sons of his father's assassins could also be seen within this category. The law itself in Deuteronomy needs to be seen as a movement beyond the accepted legal practice in some ancient Near Eastern laws of vicarious punishment. A law

---

33. E.g., Ex. 23:9; Lev. 25:38, 42, 55; Deut. 15:12–15.
34. E.g., Hos. 13:4ff.; Amos 2:10ff.

in the Code of Hammurabi[35] prescribes that if a builder builds a house that then collapses and kills the son of the house-owner, the son of the builder is to be put to death. The Deuteronomic law rules out such vicarious punishment (executing a son *instead of* the father). Amaziah extends the principle of the law to exclude also collective punishment (executing sons *along with* their fathers).

The laws in Leviticus about the effects of touching certain things or people have to be understood within the worldview of ritual cleanness and uncleanness that ranged, in Old Testament Israel, from the ultimate holiness of God (whose holy mountain, or ark, could not be touched), to the ultimate uncleanness of dead bodies. But the way these laws are given meaning in fresh circumstances is fascinating. Haggai, for example, uses a case study based on them to condemn Israel's moral and social behavior as defiling (Hag. 2:10–14). Isaiah uses them as a call for separation from the unclean land of Babylon in the new exodus that would be the return from exile (Isa. 52:11). Paul then uses that text to urge moral and spiritual distinctiveness that Christians must exercise toward unbelievers and idolatry (2 Cor. 6:14–17). Yet elsewhere he can declare that any further *literal* imposition of the laws of touching is to fall back from the freedom we have in Christ into elemental worldliness (Col. 2:16–23). One could look similarly at the way Paul "moves" in his handling of the Sabbath laws and slavery.

A BIBLICAL CASE STUDY

Having observed that all four approaches to applying the ancient text to new situations can find biblical precedents, it seems appropriate to take a single case where early Christians faced a difficult and divisive issue, on which there was no simple solution provided on the surface of their Scriptures (i.e., the Old Testament), but on which they needed to come to some *modus vivendi* that could be biblically defended. That issue was whether Christians should eat "unclean" meat. As we watch Paul helping believers in Corinth and Rome to

---

35. Code of Hammurabi 230.

wrestle with this problem and think through it biblically, it is fascinating that all four of our views find some place in his methodology.

There is no doubt that here was a matter that went "beyond the sacred page," since there was no straightforward text that could be applied to the new situation of Jewish and Gentile believers in Jesus. There were laws about clean and unclean food, but how and to whom did they now apply? There were narratives about Jews living in Gentile lands, where food would be problematic, but the lesson to be learned was somewhat ambiguous,[36] and in any case, Gentile believers were not Jews like Daniel. There were prophetic texts that condemned eating unclean meat in the same breath as the most provocative idolatry (Isa. 65:3–4). Surely, then, it would seem, meat that had actually been sacrificed to idols could not be chewed by Christian teeth.

So how did Paul do the hermeneutical, ethical, and pastoral task?

PRINCIPLES

Paul does not hesitate to draw some fundamental principles from quoting Scripture. For example, he quotes Psalm 24:1 in 1 Corinthians 10:25–26 as the foundation for the principle that all and any food is fundamentally a gift of God, to be received and eaten without problems of conscience — unless other principles (such as love for a brother in Christ) supervene (cf. Rom. 14:14a, a clear statement of principle, followed by qualifying principles).

The Shema (Deut. 6:4) is virtually quoted (though in an expanded christocentric formulation to which we will return, 1 Cor. 8:6) as foundation for the principle that "an idol is nothing at all in the world and that there is no God but one," so meat is not ontologically affected by idolatrous sacrifice.

Deuteronomy 32:17, however, is quoted (1 Cor. 10:20) in order to establish the balancing principle that, while meat from a sacrificed animal can be freely eaten when bought

---

36. Daniel and his friends refused meat and wine from the king's table (in Dan. 1), but Dan. 10:2–3 implies that this had been a temporary symbolic stance, not a commitment to lifelong vegetarianism.

at the butcher's shop, the Christian must not participate in the idolatrous sacrifice itself—not because the idol is "something" but because of the reality of the demonic realm and the danger of participating in it.

Isaiah 45:23 is quoted (Rom. 14:11–13) to establish the principle that since we must all give account to *God*, we should not stand in judgment on one another in such matters.

REDEMPTIVE HISTORY

The christocentric narrative of redemption that has reached its climax in the events of Christ's life, death, resurrection, ascended role, and future return is prominent in the way Paul uses the Scriptures on this issue, relegating some (the clean/unclean distinction), while emphasizing others (the commandment to "love your neighbor as yourself," Rom. 13:9–10, which forms the preface to the food discussion in Rom. 14–15).

The first and most astonishing way in which Paul does this is in his application of the Shema to the issue (in itself it is remarkable that Paul should throw the whole weight of such a massive creedal text at a *relatively* minor matter of disputed practice). This is where he launches his whole discussion (which continues for three chapters, 1 Cor. 8–10). The transformative truth of Old Testament monotheism has itself been transformed by the recognition of the full deity of Jesus of Nazareth. Thus, the classic Old Testament phraseology ("One God and one LORD [Yahweh]") is expanded to "One God, *the Father*... and one Lord, *Jesus Christ*." So the deity and lordship of Christ now governs the behavior of Christians in such matters, just as the sole deity and lordship of Yahweh had done for Old Testament Israelites.

But Christ is not only Lord. Christ died. And at several points Paul makes the example of Jesus the model for the kind of loving regard for others that is happy to sacrifice rights and freedoms for their sake (Rom. 14:9; 14:15; 1 Cor. 8:11–12). More particularly, the Christian chooses to adjust his or her exercise of such rights and freedoms according to the situational demands of the gospel—the fruit of Christ's death and resurrection. That is Paul's own practice in all things (1 Cor. 9:12, 19–23), including the very matter under discussion. For Paul, whether to eat meat or not was governed by gospel priority and opportunity, not merely by the biblical text of the law. Indeed, Paul's life could be lived either way—as if under the law, or as if not—depending on the context in which the gospel had to be communicated effectively (9:19–23; 10:33). That might be expressed as the principle that relativized other equally scriptural principles. But it was an option available to Paul *only as a man in Christ*. He could never have spoken that way as a Jew before accepting Jesus as Messiah, or on the basis of Old Testament texts alone, any more than he could possibly have given the advice of 1 Corinthians 10:27.

Likewise, it was only, but quite explicitly, "as one who is in the Lord Jesus" that Paul could affirm, "I am fully convinced that no food is unclean in itself" (Rom. 14:14). Such a statement stands in contradiction to Old Testament texts until they are drawn into the wider biblical context of God's redemptive purpose in Christ that would bring people of all nations into a multinational community of faith, in which the clean/unclean distinction would be abolished because that which it symbolized (the distinction between Israel and the nations) had been dissolved in Christ. And that is a missiological perspective to which we will return shortly.

THEODRAMA

Twice Paul appeals to the great biblical drama—once negatively, once positively—with ethical implications for the way believers are to perform it in new circumstances.

Negatively, he recounts the drama of the exodus and its sequel (1 Cor. 10:1–13), pointing out how the Israelites of the exodus generation had in fact *not* performed in a way that reflected and responded to the events they had participated in. Twice Paul then says, "these things occurred as examples" and were written down for our benefit (10:6, 11). The point is that we should avoid behaving as they did, in this or any other matter. Our performance of the Scriptures can take the form of knowing how *not* to behave. The theodrama includes scenes that are there as warnings to avoid.

Positively, he summarizes the whole thrust of Old Testament soteriology in a single sentence (Rom. 15:8–9) that encompasses the promise to Abraham and its fulfillment in the ingathering of the Gentiles via the servanthood of Jesus Christ. This in itself binds together the drama that stretches from Genesis 12 to Isaiah 53, but Paul flows on to quote four more texts from the Law, the Prophets, and the Writings,[37] just to show how the drama comprehensively flows throughout the whole canon. After all, has he not just said, "everything that was written in the past was written to teach us" (Rom. 15:4)?

However, the reason why Paul flashes the whole drama of redemption (in promise, achievement, and effects) before his readers' eyes is precisely to invite them to perform in relation to one another the same accepting love that led Christ to accept us, as the one who became the Servant for the sake of others so that they would come to praise God: "Accept one another, then, just as Christ accepted you, in order to bring praise to God" (Rom. 15:7). The theodrama provides the script by which those who could easily be divided in mutual contempt and condemnation over sincerely held convictions of conscience were to accept and bear with one another (14:1–3).

The issues that were dividing Jewish and Gentile believers in Rome and Corinth were not ones for which any Old Testament text, taken at surface meaning, could provide a simple, unambiguous answer. But the whole drama of salvation, from Abraham, to Christ, to the ingathering of the nations, provided ample resources for a distinctively Christian ethic and pastoral practice.

MOVEMENT MEANING

This is a more subtle perspective, as is the presentation of this view in our symposium. But if we consider that the whole issue revolved around food — what you may or may not eat and with whom you may or may not eat — one can

---

37. In Rom. 15:9–12, quoting from Ps. 18:49; Deut. 32:43; Ps. 117:1; Isa. 11:10.

see a significant shift in emphasis. The food laws of the Old Testament had their primary rationale in the way they symbolized the holiness of Israel — that is, their separation and distinctiveness from the Gentile nations. Every Israelite kitchen and table silently affirmed that the Israelites were different and were called to maintain that difference in their religious, social, and ethical life. Food declared separation.

Now in the New Testament, the call for holiness, the demand that God's people should be distinctive from unbelievers, is reiterated, but through other metaphors (e.g., salt and light). Food, which had been primarily governed by concerns for *purity* (as we see in Jesus' conflicts in the Gospels), becomes instead governed by two primary commands of Christ, namely, that we should be one and that we should love one another. The unity of believers (Jews and Gentiles) is of the essence of the gospel, according to Paul (e.g., in Ephesians), and it must manifest itself in a willingness to eat with any other believer. The old table laws are abolished. In Christ there is neither clean nor unclean, Paul might have added, at least as far as food is concerned. And the love commandment sets boundaries to the exercise of our freedom in Christ, even in matters of food where our own conscience is at ease. So, in a sense, food is still governed by biblical law — not by the food laws of the Old Testament, but rather by the second great commandment of the law, to love your neighbor as yourself.[38]

---

38. Of course, the Council of Jerusalem in Acts 15 did not entirely part company with Torah teaching on this point. The instructions in their letter to the Gentile churches, with their limitations on what seems an otherwise complete freedom from obligations to Mosaic law, have been variously interpreted. The variety can be explored in the commentaries, but one possible view is that Gentile Christians who had substantial Jewish communities in their midst, some of whom would have been believers in Jesus and others not, were being urged to exercise cultural restraint — in the way that Paul himself says he did. The basic principle of the decision of the Council seems broadly unaffected: the whole weight of OT law was not to be imposed on new Gentile believers in Christ, and this was in order "that we should not make it difficult for the Gentiles who are turning to God" (Acts 15:19).

BIBLICAL ETHICS AND THE BIBLICAL STORY LINE

Having reflected first on how all four of the views seem to have biblical precedent, and then on how they all seem to play some role in the complex and subtle way in which Paul handled a single issue in his own missionary work, by applying the Scriptures in a variety of ways that go "beyond the Bible," I turn to the way in which I myself have encouraged people to make use of the Scriptures when addressing some moral issue that is not directly encountered in the Bible — at least in the contemporary form that challenges us in our context. It has most in common with the redemptive-historical and theodramatic views here, but it does also involve the recognition and articulation of principles and the observation of movement-meaning in its process.[39]

Whenever Christians start to thrash out some moral issue — personal or social — sooner or later they bring the Bible into the argument. But the trouble is, this is frequently haphazard: a verse here or there, overemphasizing some texts and ignoring others. Such deficient practice does not take the Bible seriously for what it is — structurally, namely, a story. Or rather, *the* story, by which the whole Christian worldview is shaped.

I find it helpful to visualize the biblical story as an actual line on which one can plot key points. We can then draw whatever issue we are considering along the line and ask what each point on the line contributes to our understanding of it as a whole. The four major sections of the biblical story line are the familiar: Creation, Fall, Redemption in history, and New Creation.[40] Within the Redemption in history

---

39. I first articulated this approach in a little booklet, *The Use of the Bible in Social Ethics* (Nottingham, UK: Grove Books, 1983), but its fuller expression came in several other works that were combined into the expanded and updated *Old Testament Ethics for the People of God* (Leicester and Downers Grove, IL: InterVarsity Press, 2004).

40. I am aware that it is possible to divide the line differently, as some have done in this book, but these four seem the broadest possible sections compatible with the sweep of the Bible.

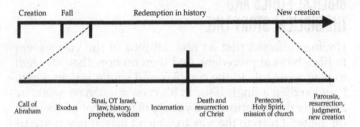

Creation | Fall | Redemption in history | New creation

Call of Abraham | Exodus | Sinai, OT Israel, law, history, prophets, wisdom | Incarnation | Death and resurrection of Christ | Pentecost, Holy Spirit, mission of church | Parousia, resurrection, judgment, new creation

section, of course, falls by far the largest portion of the biblical story, and it needs further subdivision.

The simple method, then, is to pause at each point on the line and ask what light is shed on the issue under consideration by the biblical revelation at that point. What affirmations may be made? What questions should be asked?

CREATION

This is the foundational platform for all biblical faith and ethics. So whatever issue is before us, it must be brought here first of all. We must ask what light is shed on it by our understanding of the great creational truths: one personal, living God, the Maker of heaven and earth; the goodness of creation; human beings made in his image; the triangle of interlocking relationships between God and humans, God and the earth, and humanity and the earth; the creational patterns of human life on earth—care for creation, work, sexual complementarity, marriage, relationship with God.

FALL

Human disobedience and rebellion against the Creator God bring disastrous results. Evil and sin weave their way into every aspect of God's creation and every dimension of human personhood and life on earth. Physically, we are subject to decay and death, living within a physical environment that is itself under the curse of God. Intellectually, we use our incredible powers of rationality to explain, excuse, and "normalize" our own evil. Socially, every human relationship is fractured and disrupted—sexual, parental, familial, societal, ethnic, international; the effect is consolidated horizontally through the permeation of all human cultures, and vertically by accumulation through the generations of history. Spiritually, we are alienated from God, rejecting his goodness and authority. Romans 1:18–32 outlines all of these dimensions in its analysis of the fruit of Genesis 3.

Whatever our issue, we must not bring to it any shallow or sentimental optimism, but analyze to their fullest extent the radical dimensions of human fallenness that will be evident within it. Biblical ethics begins with the orientating ideals of the creation narrative, but it cannot overlook the disorientating realities of our fallen condition.

REDEMPTION

God chose not to abandon or destroy his creation, but to redeem it. And he chose to do so within history through persons and events that run from Abraham to the return of Christ. While every part of this great story has its particular contribution to the whole, we do need to see this whole section of the line as a fundamental unity—the great saving act of God. So while asking distinct questions at each point along this section, we will not isolate any point from its meaning-in-relation to the whole. What follows is the barest outline of key points in the story of redemption, selected because they do seem to offer distinctive resources for biblical reflection on any issue.

Abraham. The covenant with Abraham, in the context of the climax of the primal history at Babel in Genesis 11, indicates God's commitment to bless all nations on the earth (a vision that in itself moves "beyond the Bible" as the awareness of nations expands), to do so by means of a historical nation (later called Israel) in a historical place (the land). That people was to be taught to live by ethical standards that contrasted with the world around them (Gen. 18:19). Thus, we are alerted that any ethical issue we wrestle with must be set in the context of God's mission to bless the nations, in the context of the realities of social, ecclesial, and economic life (the triangle of God, people, and land/earth), and take account of the ethical and missional demands of our election.

Exodus. The Old Testament story line moves from election to redemption, and the exodus functions not only as the prototype of biblical redemption, but also as the paradigm of the kind of ethics that such an understanding of redemption generates. For in that one event, God achieved a fourfold liberation for the Israelites: politically from tyrannical oppression as an immigrant minority; socially from genocidal invasion of their family life; economically from the exploitation of their labor for the benefit of the host nation; spiritually from the realm of imperial gods to the worship of the living God. The exodus releases a liberating and transformative dynamic into biblical ethics that cannot fail to inject comparable agendas into the multiple complexities of human oppression all through history, far beyond its own historical specifics.

Sinai and beyond. Election and redemption are followed by covenant. Thus we face the challenge of asking what light is shed on any issue through considering it in relation to Old Testament law. We have noted one instance already where Paul finds a principle at work in a particular law (about working oxen) that he can apply to a very different situation (working missionaries). The hermeneutical steps that allow (indeed encourage) such handling of the law include asking a similar set of questions to those suggested by Doriani, but with greater specificity to the legal nature of the text at this point. They include:

What is the objective of this law?
What kind of situation did it intend to promote, or prevent, or mitigate?
For whose benefit or protection would this law operate?
Whose power would be restricted by this law?
What are the principles, priorities, and values that are instantiated in this law?

Such an approach may sound identical to Kaiser's principlizing, but my own approach takes it a step further by suggesting that we need to look not only at the principles that may be discerned in specific individual laws, but also at how the whole fabric of Israel's law and the socio-economic and political structures embodied in it constitute an overall paradigm of the kind of society God calls his people to be. Paradigms by their very nature imply moving beyond the specifics of a particular case to discerning how the pattern adapts to different circumstances.[41]

Incarnation. The line of biblical history moves on until "when the set time had fully come, God sent his Son, born of a woman" (Gal. 4:4). The incarnation of God in Christ brings two new factors to be considered in relation to whatever issue lies before us: the inaugurated presence of the kingdom of God and the incarnational model and principle itself.

In Jesus, the reign of God entered human history in a way not previously experienced, though the expectation of it and the ethical implications of it are thoroughly rooted in the Old Testament. The dynamic action of the kingdom of God in the words and deeds of Jesus and the mission of his disciples changed lives, values, and priorities and presented a radical challenge to the fallen structures of power in society. Whatever our issue, we must ask what it looks like when confronted with the reality of the kingdom of God.

But, as the parables of Jesus emphasized, God inaugurated his reign in hidden, humble ways, choosing to enter the world himself and coping with all its limitations and frustrations. It is a pattern that Jesus then laid on his followers for their costly incarnational engagement with the world and all its issues: "As you sent me into the world, I have sent them into the world" (John 17:18).

Cross and resurrection. The cross and resurrection of Jesus bring us to the central point of the whole line of redemption in history. Here is God's answer to every dimension of sin and evil in the cosmos and all their destructive effects. The gospel presents us not with an eternal striving but an accomplished victory that will ultimately be universally visible and vindicated. If we have been as radical as we ought in

---

41. I have explored this paradigmatic methodology in Old Testament ethics in great detail in *Old Testament Ethics for the People of God*. In the UK, the work of the Jubilee Centre (see www.jubilee-centre.org) has made this approach the foundation for applying biblical ethics to contemporary public issues in the social, economic, and political realms, where it is necessary to think and act "beyond the Bible" but is explicitly governed by it.

our analysis of the effects of the fall on our issue, we must be equally radical and comprehensive here in our understanding of all the ways in which the cross and resurrection reverse and ultimately destroy whatever aspects of our fallenness that the particular issue embodies. The cross must be as central to our social ethics as to our personal evangelism.

Church. Just as the exodus redemption led to the creation of the covenant people of Old Testament Israel, so the Easter redemption led to the eschatological gift of the Holy Spirit at Pentecost and the birth of the church as the multinational fulfillment of the hope of Israel, that all nations would be blessed through the people of Abraham. The expansion of Israel to include the Gentiles (note: not the abandonment of Israel in favor of the Gentiles), in and through Christ, fulfilled the promise to Abraham and thus leads to the final great act of the biblical story.

Two realities from this part of the line must have their bearing on whatever issue we are considering: first, the presence of the Holy Spirit making available to the people of God the same transforming power that energized the life and ministry of Jesus and raised him from the dead; and second, the existence of the church itself as the missional community of those who have responded to, and entered, the kingdom of God by repentance and faith in Christ, and who now seek to live as a transformed and transforming community of reconciliation and blessing in the world.

New creation. The return of Christ will not only bring to its grand finale that section of the Bible story line that we have called redemption in history; it will also inaugurate the ultimate fulfillment of the whole point of the story, namely, the redemption and renewal of God's whole creation. Beyond the purging fire of judgment and the destruction of all that is evil and opposed to God's good purpose, there lies the new heavens and new earth, in which righteousness and peace are eternal realities because God himself will dwell there with his redeemed people from every nation.

When we bring our issue into the light of this final part of the line, it generates biblical faith and hope—that incurable optimism that should characterize all Christian action in the world.

This then is the grid of the Bible's own story line to which we should bring our specific ethical issue. Each point or section of the line sheds its light, informs our thinking, questions our assumptions, and challenges us to fresh obedience in relation to that issue. Sometimes in public contexts or classrooms, I am asked the question, "What do you think is the biblical position on this or that current issue?" In other words, I am being asked to take the sacred pages of Scripture but move beyond them to address a contemporary question. I find myself saying, "Well now, let's go back to the beginning ..." I then draw the issue steadily along the line above, encouraging the questioner or class to think about it successively in the light of all the Bible can contribute, sequentially, and not resting content until the matter is finally viewed from the perspective of our glorious future hope. This takes some time and is not the kind of sound-bite answer that such questions usually hope for.

- Creation provides our foundational values and principles.
- The fall brings us down to the realities of the cursed earth and the pervasive tentacles of human and satanic wickedness.
- The Old Testament shows us the scope of God's redeeming purpose, worked out in a specific historical and cultural context, and models for us in amazing detail (from the law, the narratives, prophets, wisdom, and worship of Israel) the kind of practical responses that please God (and those that don't).
- The incarnation brings God right alongside us in our struggle and calls us to embody and be agents of the reign of God through Christ. This creates the familiar tension, of course, of living between the already and the not yet (so that on many issues, we have to live with a degree of ambiguity and tension).
- The cross and resurrection enable us to experience and share the power of true reconciliation, love, hope, and peace, and to seek the atoning, redemptive work of God even in the most apparently irredeemable human situations.

- The Holy Spirit in the church provides the guidance and the power to expect real change in lives and societies, while keeping our eyes on the corporate, not merely individual, dimensions of Christian ethical living.
- Our great future hope of new creation gives value and worth to all that we do in the present, for our labor is not in vain in the Lord, and it shapes our response to the present by the revealed shape of the future.

So then, as we necessarily have to move "beyond the Bible" to the contemporary issue that faces us, we do so with our minds filled with and shaped by the content of *all* the sacred pages of the biblical narrative.

Such a disciplined method of approach seems to me to have four main benefits:

1. It is *canonical*. That is, it respects the form, order, and structure of the Bible itself (as Jesus did on the road to Emmaus).
2. It is *comprehensive*. It makes use of the whole range of the Scriptures and so is more likely to arrive at a balanced biblical view of the matter in hand. And let's face it, some of the issues we face in contemporary life are horrendously complex and unlikely to be satisfied with a single proof text. Take politics, for example. Christians often tend to take up simplistic, black-and-white positions, largely through having only one "sacred page" in their heads. The state? Romans 13. End of discussion. But the moment you embark on taking any political issue along the grid of the Bible's story line as above, the first thing you see is the wonderful richness and complexity of resources that God has deposited in the Bible on the topic of how believers relate to the state.[42]

---

42. Thinking biblically about the state, one has to start by asking "Which state? When?" The people of Israel related to many different kinds of external states, and Israel itself went through many transformations of political reality in its long history (pilgrim family, tribal confederation, monarchy, exiled minority, imperial province). I have explored this historical dimension of the Bible's teaching on the state in chap. 7 of *Old Testament Ethics for the People of God* ("Politics and the Nations").

3. It is *community oriented*. Moving "beyond the Bible" is not something we should do alone, for God created a people for his mission in the world. The social dimension of the biblical story should save us from rampant individualism, without destroying the vital role of personal faith and action. "It seemed good to the Holy Spirit and to us" is the revealing phrase by which the early church moved beyond their sacred page in addressing a novel issue thrown up by successful mission (Acts 15:28).

4. It is *contemporary*. As Vanhoozer observed, on the basis of N. T. Wright's "five-act drama" metaphor, when we move "beyond the Bible" there is a sense in which we stay within it. For the Bible itself includes the last great act of its own story—the act in which we ourselves participate. We are not detached observers striving to make sense of some ancient and alien ethos. We stand in organic spiritual continuity with the biblical people of God in both Old and New Testaments. Our story is part of theirs, and their story part of ours. That is certainly how the earliest Christians saw themselves in relation to the Old Testament, well before the sacred pages of the New Testament had even been written.

BEYOND THE BIBLE—IN MISSIONAL PERSPECTIVE

Kevin Vanhoozer, in his response to William Webb's paper, comments on the lack of a missiological perspective among the views discussed in the book, and he expects that we would have something to learn in the hermeneutical task from those engaged in, and reflecting on, cross-cultural mission. Indeed so, for missionaries, like preachers whom I mentioned at the start, have been going "beyond the Bible" every time they have taken the gospel to a new culture and watched it take root and bloom in different cultural soil—and they have been doing so since New Testament times. Now at one level, this process of continuously fresh enculturation of the gospel has been serendipitous and unpredictable. It is always a matter of surprise and sometimes disturbing when fresh expressions of the gospel arise as the gospel works its transforming power within the kaleidoscope of human cultures.

Again, this is nothing new. The background music of the book of Acts and the life and writings of Paul was the challenge of coming to terms with the way a faith that was born in Galilee and Judea, with its roots in the Hebrew Scriptures for many centuries, was now being lived out in the different clothes of Ephesus, Galatia, and Rome. The first council of the church, in Jerusalem (Acts 15), was summoned precisely to seek hermeneutical clarity and faithfulness in moving beyond the Old Testament into the new realities that *God* had engineered through the successful mission of Paul and his companions.

Unpredictable? Not in principle, for the Old Testament had made it abundantly clear that people of all nations on earth would one day be drawn into the light of Abrahamic blessing and saving relationship with the God of Israel.[43] But unpredictable certainly in what that would then look like when they actually came. The Old Testament could not predict in detail what Christianity would look like in Corinth, any more than Paul could have predicted what it would look like in Ireland, or Ethiopia, or among the Inuit, or in the islands of the Pacific Ocean.

Serendipitous? Only in the sense that it may not have been planned by the human agents of missionary endeavor, but not merely serendipitous in the missional purpose of God. There it fits entirely with the constantly expanding, constantly translatable nature of the gospel itself. As Andrew Walls has reminded us so passionately, the gospel only shows its true reality when it is crossing cultural barriers, for to dissolve such barriers is of the essence of the gospel itself.[44]

---

43. I have explored in extensive detail the missiological dimensions of the Old Testament's eschatology in relation to the nations in *The Mission of God: Unlocking the Bible's Grand Narrative* (Downers Grove, IL and Leicester: InterVarsity Press, 2006).

44. See, e.g., among his extensive writing, Andrew F. Walls, *The Missionary Movement in Christian History: Studies in the Transmission of Faith* (Edinburgh: T&T Clark; New York: Orbis, 1997).

Furthermore, every new culture in which the gospel takes root reveals some new facet of the fullness of the gospel—not in the sense of adding to the core events that constitute what the good news is in itself, but in filling out the ways in which that good news addresses and transforms people in multiple historical and cultural contexts. When the body of Christ is complete in its inclusion of people from every nation, tribe, and language, then the gospel will be seen in all its infinite glory, shining with all the richness of multiple redeemed cultures bringing their splendor into the city of God. Even the task of Bible translation, with all its earthy, slow, deeply incarnational challenges, is an integral part of this missional vision.[45]

In other words, a missional perspective is necessarily eschatological and, in that respect, demands that the church continuously move "beyond the Bible," because its sacred pages, originating in a distinct set of historical cultures, point beyond themselves to the ends of the earth and the whole of history. Thus every new generation and every new cultural embodiment of the gospel both enrich what went before and are enriched by it, so that it is "better" for all concerned.

That is how the writer to the Hebrews, somewhat surprisingly, finishes his great historical trajectory of the heroes of faith when he moves beyond his Old Testament Scriptures and addresses his contemporary readers. "None of them received what had been promised," he writes, and we might have expected him to say, "because God had planned something better for *them*." But rather he says, "God had planned something better for *us* so that

---

45. It is clear that God *wants* his Word to be translated into every language. The point is made early when Ezra arranged for Levites to translate and explain the sacred text of the law of Moses into the ordinary language of a generation of returned exiles who were probably already speaking some form of Aramaic rather than classical biblical Hebrew. They had to move "beyond the sacred page" as they did that task (Neh. 8:7–8). Then came the Septuagint, allowing some centuries for the Scriptures to exist in Greek before the New Testament gospel overflowed into Greco-Roman culture. And every translation of the Bible is a cultural challenge, not just a linguistic one, for the hermeneutical process starts right there.

only together with us would they be made perfect" (Heb. 11:39–40, my emphasis). That is, every present generation of believers is all the better for being "together with" those of the past, and the perfection of all past generations of believers is only possible eschatologically when all are gathered in. If you add the multiplicity of cultures to that historical flow through the generations, you have a truly missiological perspective on the great river of faith, with its source in the Abrahamic covenant and its ocean destiny in the blessing of all the nations on earth. The "sacred page" takes the flow from its source to the first generation of the post-Pentecost mission of the church, but the hermeneutical task continues beyond that in every historical-cultural context.

Recently, the search for a missional hermeneutic of Scripture has gathered pace and critical mass in the form of a group of engaged practitioners and a growing volume of published works exploring what it means to read the Bible from a missional perspective. A group has convened in the context of the Society of Biblical Literature for several years now to share and reflect on work being done in this field. At the 2008 SBL Convention in Boston, George R. Hunsberger offered an analysis and synthesis of the product of this group so far in an unpublished paper entitled "Starting Points, Trajectories, and Outcomes in Proposals for a Missional Hermeneutic: Mapping the Conversation." He perceived four complementary emphases in the distinct approaches of different scholars, and I close by summarizing his helpful "map," since at several points it seems to resonate well with certain emphases already expressed in the four views in this book, and to remind us of the fundamental purpose of all Bible reading and hermeneutics—a purpose that is integral to our own raison d'être as the church. Or, in the words of Kevin Vanhoozer, we need to ask ourselves: *"Why are we, the church, here? The answer to that question takes the form of a mission statement: we are here to participate rightly in God's triune mission to the world"* (emphasis his).

Hunsberger identifies the following approaches, and in each case offers some summary and critique.

THE MISSIONAL DIRECTION OF THE STORY

The *framework* for biblical interpretation is the story it tells of the mission of God and the formation of a community sent to participate in it.[46] The Bible, taken as a canonical whole, tells the story of God's mission in and for the whole world, and with it the story of the people of God whom God has called and sent to participate in that mission. Interpreting any specific biblical material thus requires attending to this pervading story of which it is a part. Every part must be read in the light of this whole purpose. The mission of God provides the framework, the clue, and the hermeneutical key for biblical interpretation.

THE MISSIONAL PURPOSE OF THE WRITINGS

The *aim* of biblical interpretation is to fulfill the equipping purpose of the biblical writings.[47] The purpose and canonical authority of the biblical writings flows from their formative effect. "Jesus personally formed the first generation of Christians for his mission. After that, their testimony became the tool for continuing formation."[48] Thus, the New Testament writings have as their purpose to equip the churches for witness.

Though this purpose is easier to identify in the New Testament writings, it is not difficult to argue that the Old Testament Scriptures also came into existence in the process of God's shaping Israel for their role as the people of God in the midst of the nations, in terms of their faith, their worship,

---

46. In each of his four mapping points, Hunsberger cites representative authors taking that particular approach. In this case it is my own work (Christopher J. H. Wright, *The Mission of God*), in which I attempt to argue that the mission of God is an overarching framework for the whole biblical narrative.

47. Darrell Guder, "The Missional Authority of Scripture: Interpreting Scripture as Missional Formation," and "The Missional Vocation of the Congregation: The Congregational Calling and How Scripture Shapes that Calling," in *Mission Focus Annual Review* (forthcoming). Also, *Unlikely Ambassadors: Clay Jar Christians in God's Service* (Office of the General Assembly, Presbyterian Church USA, 2002); "Biblical Formation and Discipleship," in *Treasure in Clay Jars: Patterns of Missional Faithfulness*, ed. Lois Y. Barrett et al. (Grand Rapids: Eerdmans, 2004), 59–73.

48. Guder, "Biblical Formation and Discipleship," 62.

and the witness of the kind of society they were called to be. Thus, the basic question that guides interpretation needs to include this one: "How did this text equip and shape God's people for their missional witness then, and how does it shape us today?"[49]

Such an approach to biblical hermeneutics, of course, generates and requires a comparable approach to the task of theology as a whole. That is to say, if the Bible itself is fundamentally missional in its equipping and formative purpose, how much more should that also be true of all theological reflection and construction that is based upon it?

THE MISSIONAL LOCATEDNESS OF THE READERS

The *approach* required for a faithful reading of the Bible is from the missional location of the Christian community.[50] This shifts the hermeneutical focus from the perspective of the text to that of the reader (without sliding over into a totally reader-centered approach that ignores authorial intention and normal exegetical disciplines). A missional hermeneutic of this kind is an approach to Scripture that intentionally and persistently brings to the biblical text a range of focused, critical, and located questions arising from the life of the Christian community engaged in mission in its own community.

This task is not one for scholars or pastors alone, providing the community with top-down answers to predecided questions on what the Bible means. Rather, the community is itself the active subject of biblical interpretation in the midst of its own missional life. The social location of the people of God is at the heart of a missional hermeneutic. There are connections here, of course, with the hermeneutical dimensions of liberation theologies that stress the importance of contextually engaged missional praxis as the proper place for biblical interpretation to take place.

---

49. Guder, *Unlikely Ambassadors*, 5.

50. Michael Barram, "The Bible, Mission, and Social Location: Toward a Missional Hermeneutic," *Interpretation* 61 (January 2007): 42–58; also, idem, *Mission and Moral Reflection in Paul* (New York: Peter Lang, 2006).

One thing that this would add to the perspectives of our four views would be that, whatever helpful questions are proposed as heuristic tools for getting at an understanding of the Old and New Testaments that is both biblically faithful and contextually relevant, two further questions would have to be added: "Who is asking the questions?" and "Where are the questions being asked?" In other words, the social, cultural, and historical locatedness of the interpreter and the nature of their missional engagement in the world are also important factors.[51]

THE MISSIONAL ENGAGEMENT WITH CULTURES

The gospel functions as the interpretive *matrix* within which the received biblical tradition is brought into critical conversation with a particular human context.[52] As we read the New Testament, we can see how its authors made use of Old Testament texts in a way that was shaped by how they understood the nature of the gospel itself and the way in which the gospel engaged with the new cultures in which they carried forward their mission. Their use and application of Scripture was not random but focused and determined by the gospel—in its claim and summons (repentance and allegiance to Christ), in its universal scope (addressing all cultures), and in its central and paradigmatic content (the death and resurrection of Jesus). Thus, the church must use the Bible in order to live out the gospel and make it visible and plausible in every cultural context. And that gospel engagement in turn guides and shapes the way we read Scripture.

---

51. The book of Jeremiah might provide an interesting biblical example here. The book records the preaching of Jeremiah in the four decades or so prior to the exile. Yet the editorial introduction and conclusion of the book make it clear that it was read by those on whom the exile had already come. So we need to read it not only through the ears, as it were, of those who first heard Jeremiah preach in Jerusalem (and who so dismally failed to respond), but also through the eyes of those who read his words in the "social locatedness" of Babylonian exile. What now was their missional role, assuming they still even had one?

52. James Brownson, *Speaking the Truth in Love: New Testament Resources for a Missional Hermeneutic* (Valley Forge, PA: Trinity Press International, 1998).

This perspective ensures that the social locatedness of the previous point does not degenerate into irresponsible relativism (we read the Bible in any way we like from our own context) but is governed and controlled by the objective shape and content of the gospel itself.

Hunsberger closes his summary by suggesting, then, that a missional hermeneutic will ask at least four questions in the way it seeks to move "beyond the sacred page":

1. What is the story of the biblical grand narrative, and how does it involve us? (the mission of God)
2. What is the purpose of the biblical writings in the life of the readers? (equipping them for witness)
3. How shall the church read the Bible faithfully today in its own context? (socially located questions)
4. What guides our use of the received tradition in that contemporary context? (gospel matrix)

The hope of the Missional Hermeneutics group is that this interaction will continue and refine these approaches further or add to them, so that moving "beyond the Bible" will be done in the good company of those who cross cultural boundaries in missional engagement as they do so.

CONCLUSION

THE COUNTERPOINTS SERIES typically presents debated issues that have become relatively settled in their theological viewpoints. This volume is a bit of an exception. How authoritative Scripture is relevant is a current center stage discussion in both the academy and the church. There are more variations than this book can include, and a number of writers are searching and probing for the best way to relate Scripture to the modern world.

Over the last decade a number of publications have tested the waters in regard to how an ancient text applies to contemporary issues (see the bibliography). This can be a "testy" discussion since our base text is the Bible. How can "all Scripture" (2 Tim. 3:16–17) be profitable when parts of it seem to be so different than the sensitivities of modern culture? What about those parts of the Bible that seem to be silent in regard to cultural issues we believe it should address (e.g., slavery, abortion), or in regard to its treatment of subjects that give us pause in our modern world (e.g., sexuality, gender), or regarding the fact that certain areas were not advanced enough within ancient culture for Scripture to provide a direct statement (e.g., medical issues)?

The authors in this volume have probed numerous issues and illustrated how they believe Scripture has ongoing authority and relevance in the modern world. The three subsequent reflection articles have provided summaries, critiques, and further questions so that this conclusion need not rehearse their fine work.

The purpose of this volume has been to bring to a broader reading audience the issues and challenges that are part of this debate in order to advance awareness of the discussion. The fact of "going beyond" is ever with us, as C. Wright has illustrated; the remaining task is for each reader to determine when and how such extension of the Bible is appropriate.

SELECT BIBLIOGRAPHY
FOR HERMENEUTICAL ISSUES IN THE "BEYOND THE BIBLE" DISCUSSION IN THEOLOGY AND ETHICS

Adam, A. K. M., Stephen E. Fowl, Kevin J. Vanhoozer, and Francis Watson. *Reading Scripture with the Church: Toward a Hermeneutic for Theological Interpretation.* Grand Rapids: Baker Academic, 2006.

Beal, Lissa Wray. "Evaluating Jehu: Narrative Control of Approval and Disapproval in 2 Kings 9 and 10." In *From Babel to Babylon: Essays on the Primary History in Honour of Brian Peckham.* Ed. John E. Harvey et al. Sheffield: Sheffield Academic Press, 2007.

Cosgrove, Charles H. *Appealing to Scripture in Moral Debate: Five Hermeneutical Rules.* Grand Rapids: Eerdmans, 2002.

_____, ed. *The Meanings We Choose: Hermeneutical Ethics, Indeterminacy and the Conflict of Interpretations.* Journal for the Study of the Old Testament Supplement Series 411. London: T&T Clark, 2004.

Doriani, Daniel M. *Putting the Truth to Work: The Theory and Practice of Biblical Application.* Phillipsburg, NJ: Presbyterian & Reformed Publishing, 2001.

Grudem, Wayne. "Should We Move beyond the New Testament to a Better Ethic?" *Journal of the Evangelical Theological Society* 47:2 (2004): 299–346.

Harrill, J. Albert. *Slaves in the New Testament: Literary, Social, and Moral Dimensions.* Minneapolis: Fortress, 2006.

Hays, Richard B. *The Moral Vision of the New Testament.* New York: HarperCollins, 1996.

Hollinger, Dennis P. *Choosing the Good: Christian Ethics in a Complex World.* Grand Rapids: Baker Academic, 2002.

Johnston, Robert K., ed. *The Use of the Bible in Theology: Evangelical Options.* Atlanta: John Knox, 1985.

Longenecker, Richard N. "Four Ways of Using the New Testament." Pages 185–91 in *Readings in Christian Ethics*; vol. 1: *Theory and Method*. Ed. D. K. Clark and R. V. Rakestraw. Grand Rapids: Baker, 1994.

_____. "Is There Development in Paul's Resurrection Thought?" Pages 171–202 in *Life in the Face of Death: The Resurrection Message of the New Testament.* McMaster New Testament Studies 3. Grand Rapids: Eerdmans, 1998.

_____. "Major Tasks of an Evangelical Hermeneutic: Some Observations on Commonalities, Interrelations, and Differences." *Bulletin for Biblical Research* 14:1 (2004): 45–58.

_____. *New Testament Social Ethics for Today*. Grand Rapids: Eerdmans, 1984.

_____. *New Wine into Fresh Wineskins: Contextualizing the Early Christian Confessions*. Peabody, MA: Hendrickson, 1999.

_____. "On the Concept of Development in Pauline Thought." Pages 195–207 in *Perspectives on Evangelical Theology*. Ed. K. S. Kantzer and S. N. Gundry. Grand Rapids: Baker, 1979.

Marshall, I. Howard, with K. Vanhoozer and S. Porter. *Beyond the Bible: Moving from Scripture to Theology*. Grand Rapids: Baker Academic, 2004.

Martens, Elmer A. "Moving from Scripture to Doctrine." *Bulletin for Biblical Research* 15:1 (2005): 77–103.

Packer, J. I. *The Collected Shorter Writings of J. I. Packer. Honouring the Written Word of God*; vol. 3: Carlisle UK: Paternoster, 1999. [See Chapter 10]

Scalise, C. J. *From Scripture to Theology: A Canonical Journey into Hermeneutics*. Downers Grove, IL: InterVarsity Press, 1996.

Schreiner, Thomas R. "William J. Webb's *Slaves, Women & Homosexuals*: A Review Article." *Southern Baptist Journal of Theology* 6:1 (2002): 46–64.

Scorgie, Glen G. *The Journey Back to Eden: Restoring the Creator's Design for Women and Men*. Grand Rapids: Zondervan, 2008.

Swartley, Willard M. *Slavery, Sabbath, War, and Women: Case Issues in Biblical Interpretation*. Scottdale, PA: Herald, 1983.

Thompson, Mark D. *A Clear and Present Word: The Clarity of Scripture*. New Studies in Biblical Theology. Downers Grove, IL: InterVarsity Press, 2006.

Treier, Daniel J. "Canonical Unity and Commensurable Language: On Divine Action and Doctrine." Pages 211–28 in *Evangelicals and Scripture: Tradition, Authority and Hermeneutics*. Ed. Dennis L. Okholm et al. Downers Grove, IL: InterVarsity Press, 2004.

_____. "The Superiority of Pre-Critical Exegesis: *Sic et Non*." *Trinity Journal* 24., n.s. 1 (Spring 2003): 77–103.

_____. *Virtue and the Voice of God: Toward Theology as Wisdom*. Grand Rapids: Eerdmans, 2006.

Vanhoozer, Kevin. *The Drama of Doctrine: A Canonical Linguistic Approach to Christian Theology*. Louisville: Westminster John Knox, 2005.

_____. "Lost in Interpretation? Truth, Scripture, and Hermeneutics." *Journal of the Evangelical Theological Society* 48:1 (2005): 89–114. Reprinted in *Whatever Happened to Truth*. Ed. Andreas Köstenberger. Wheaton, IL: Crossway, 2005.

Watson, Francis. *Text, Church and World: Biblical Interpretation in Theological Perspective*. Grand Rapids: Eerdmans, 1994.

Webb, William J. "Balancing Paul's Original-Creation and Pro-Creation Arguments: 1 Corinthians 11:11–12 in Light of Modern Embryology." *Westminster Theological Journal* 66 (2004): 275–90.

_____. "The Limits of a Redemptive-Movement Hermeneutic: A Focused Response to T. R. Schreiner." *Evangelical Quarterly* 75:4 (2003): 327–42.

_____ "A Redemptive-Movement Hermeneutic: Responding to Grudem's Concerns." Paper delivered at the Evangelical Theological Society, San Antonio, Texas (November 2004).

_____. "A Redemptive-Movement Hermeneutic: Encouraging Dialogue among Four Evangelical Views." *Journal of the Evangelical Theological Society* 48:2 (2005): 331–49.

_____. *Slaves, Women & Homosexuals: Exploring the Hermeneutics of Cultural Analysis.* Downers Grove, IL: InterVarsity Press, 2001.

Wittmer, Michael. *Don't Stop Believing: Why Living Like Jesus Is Not Enough.* Grand Rapids: Zondervan, 2008.

Wright, Christopher J. H. *Old Testament Ethics for the People of God.* Downers Grove, IL: InterVarsity Press, 2004.

_____. *Walking in the Ways of the Lord: The Ethical Authority of the Old Testament.* Downers Grove, IL: InterVarsity Press, 1995.

Wright, N. T. "How Can the Bible Be Authoritative?" *Vox Evangelica* 21 (1991): 7–32.

_____. *The Last Word: Beyond the Bible Wars to a New Understanding of the Authority of Scripture.* San Francisco: HarperSanFrancisco, 2005.

SCRIPTURE INDEX

SUBJECT INDEX

meaning, redemptive-move-
   ment, 237
men, bear responsibility, 112
menoun, 116
Messiah, accepting Jesus as, 328
meta-narrative, of Scripture, 285
metaphor, 285, 290, 315
mind of Christ, cultivating the,
   170–72, 285
mission, in the world, 269, 339,
   342
missional perspective, 339–46
Mohler, Albert, 232, 234
monotheism, 97
moralism, 313–14; leads to, 61;
   viewed as, 86
Moses, 78, 85
movement: is meaning, 220–21,
   226; in Scripture, 267;
   in teaching on slavery,
   282; toward an improvement, 235. See also, movement meaning, trajectory
   method
movement meaning, 140, 143;
   seen as, 324; what is, 289–90.
   See also, movement, trajectory method
murder, injunction against, 29

narratives, 57; imitation of,
   87–88; have a paradigmatic,
   122, 127, 129
nature, 318
Neocalvinism, 299, 313
new creation, 336, 338
Nicene Creed, 172
Noll, Mark, 71, 242

O'Donavan, Oliver, 98–99,
   176–77, 195
obedience, born of, 206
Old Testament: Jesus interprets,
   152; use of, 46
Onesimus, 42, 66–68, 83, 282

original context, 288. See also,
   ancient-world context, context, contextualization
original culture, 83. See also,
   culture
original sin, 190, 332
Osborne, Grant R., 141
oude, 111

Packer, J. I., 46, 101, 161
pagan slavery, 64
paradigm narratives, 122, 127,
   129. See also, narratives
Paul: commanded women, 81;
   perceives a principle, 323,
   326; recounts the drama, 328;
   says women, 109–10; teaching of, 46; writes with, 273
performance: and interpretation, 165; notion of, 163–64;
   some kind of, 160
perspicuitas, of Scripture, 306
Peterson, Eugene, 152
Pharisee, yeast of, 54–55
Philemon, 42, 65–68, 73, 135, 282
Pilgrim's Progress, 291
plain sense, 266
Plato, 167
polygamy, 119–20
power, 30–31, 125. See also,
   authority
predicated arguments, 145–46
premarital sex, prohibition of,
   97
principle: extracted, 54; behind
   this, 24; determining the, 19;
   given priority, 21; meaning
   is called a, 144; of proportional punishment, 259;
   stating the, 23
principles: appeal to, 130; as
   better than, 158; for discerning the Word, 200; one must
   use, 204; are purer, 60; quest
   for, 55; the term, 293

AUTHOR PAGE
IN ORDER OF APPEARANCE

Gary T. Meadors, ThD
Professor of Greek and New Testament
Grand Rapids Theological Seminary, Grand Rapids, Michigan

Walter C. Kaiser Jr., PhD
Colman M. Mockler Emeritus Distinguished Professor of Old Testament
    and Ethics and President Emeritus of Gordon-Conwell Theological
    Seminary, South Hamilton, Massachusetts

Daniel M. Doriani, PhD
Senior Pastor of Central Presbyterian Church; Adjunct Professor of New
    Testament at Covenant Seminary
St. Louis, Missouri

Kevin J. Vanhoozer, PhD
Blanchard Professor of Theology
Wheaton College and Graduate School, Wheaton, Illinois

William J. Webb, PhD
Professor of New Testament
Heritage Seminary
Waterloo, Ontario, Canada

Mark L. Strauss, PhD
Professor of New Testatment
Bethel Seminary San Diego, San Diego, California

Al Wolters, PhD
Professor Emeritus of Religion and Theology, and Classical Studies
Redeemer University College
Adjunct Professor at the Paideia Centre for Public Theology
Ancaster, Ontario, Canada

Christopher J. H. Wright, PhD
International Director
Langham Partnership International
United Kingdom